Plastic Glasses and Church Fathers

OXFORD STUDIES IN ANTHROPOLOGICAL LINGUISTICS
William Bright, General Editor

Classificatory Particles in Kilivila
Gunter Senft

Sounds Like Life
Sound-symbolic Grammar, Performance, and Cognition in Pasta Quechua
Janis B. Nuckolls

Plastic Glasses and Church Fathers
Semantic Extension from the Ethnoscience Tradition
David B. Kronenfeld

Plastic Glasses and Church Fathers

Semantic Extension from the Ethnoscience Tradition

David B. Kronenfeld

New York   Oxford
OXFORD UNIVERSITY PRESS
1996

Oxford University Press

Oxford   New York
Athens   Auckland   Bangkok
Calcutta   Cape Town   Dar es Salaam   Delhi
Florence   Hong Kong   Istanbul   Karachi
Kuala Lumpur   Madras   Madrid   Melbourne
Mexico City   Nairobi   Paris   Singapore
Taipei   Tokyo   Toronto

and associated companies in
Berlin   Ibadan

Copyright © 1996 by David B. Kronenfeld

Published by Oxford University Press, Inc.
198 Madison Avenue, New York, New York 10016

Oxford is a registered trademark of Oxford University Press, Inc.

Library of Congress Cataloging-in-Publication Data
Kronenfeld, David B., 1941–
Plastic glasses and church fathers : semantic extension from the
ethnoscience tradition / David B. Kronenfeld.
p. cm.—(Oxford studies in anthropological linguistics)
Includes bibliographical references (p.) and index.
ISBN 0-19-509407-7; ISBN 0-19-509408-5 (pbk.)
1. Semantics. 2. Anthropological linguistics. 3. Reference
(Linguistics) 4. Componential analysis in anthropology. I. Title.
II. Series.
P325.K72   1996
401'.41—dc20   95-10092

1   3   5   7   9   8   6   4   2

Printed in the United States of America
on acid-free paper

To the memory of my father,
John Kronenfeld,
who taught me the beauty and rigor of the life of the mind
and
to my mother,
Elsie Weinkle Kronenfeld,
who first introduced me to anthropology

Acknowledgments

I want first to thank James D. Armstrong, Henry Decker, and Stan Wilmoth who have been my coauthors on various of the papers that have fed into the present volume, and who have allowed me to make use of the products of our joint labor. I owe a similar debt to those whose work provided the sources for central parts of the current discussion: Stan Wilmoth, J. Z. Kronenfeld, and Carol C. Mukhopadhyay.

I want to thank Jack Goody for first urging me to write this book, and Eugene N. Anderson, B. N. Colby, Stephen A. Tyler, and Jack Goody for their continuing encouragement with it.

I am greatly indebted to E. N. Anderson, Alan R. Beals, J. Z. Kronenfeld, Robert L. Moore, Martin Orans, and Stephen A. Tyler for the careful readings that they have given various avatars of this manuscript. I am grateful to two anonymous readers from Oxford University Press for their many helpful suggestions. I am thankful to Lynn L. Thomas, Victor DeMunck, Halvard Vike, Susan Gal, and Sharon Klein for fruitful discussions of some of the matters covered here, and for their readings of parts of the argument.

Parts of this volume draw on previously published articles of mine, including Kronenfeld 1973, 1976, 1979, 1980a, 1989. In chapter 5, extensive use has been made of text and figures from Kronenfeld 1974, and in chapters 9 and 10 similar use has been made of materials from Kronenfeld, Armstrong, and Wilmoth 1985. Additionally, significant parts of chapters 9 and 10 are drawn from the paper "Full Bloods and Protestants: Semantic Extension in Complex Domains," which I presented at the Conference on Complex Cultural Categories and the Contribution of Cognitive Anthropology at Kings College (Cambridge), March 22–24, 1989. The discussion of ethnicity in chapter 10 is based in part on a talk entitled "Ethnicity and Society," which I delivered on May 19, 1994, at the University of Oslo.

I am grateful to the Academic Senate of the University of California for the Intramural Research Grants that supported much of the work reported here. Writing and research for this volume have been supported over the years by two sabbatical leaves provided by the University of California, Riverside. The most recent sabbatical was spent in France as an affiliate of l'École des Hautes Études en Sciences Sociales; I am grateful to Maurice Godelier, Helena Meininger, and Serge Tcherkézoff of EHESS for their generosity, support, and stimulating interaction. Parts of the writing were carried out while I was a Fellow at the Center for Ideas and Society of the University of California; I am thankful for that support and for the calm, warm, and intellectually stimulating collegial environment provided by the center and its fellows.

Pieces of research reported here were conducted while I was supported by a National Science Foundation Cooperative Predoctoral Fellowship; other parts were supported by Public Health Service Fellowship No. F1-MH-34, 116 and attached Grant No. R04-MH13769 from the National Institutes of Mental Health while I was a research associate at the University of Ghana, Legon. I owe thanks to the chiefs, elders, and citizens of Egyaa No. 1, Ghana, for their generous cooperation with my kinship research, and to Hiroshi Fukura for his great help with the drinking vessel research.

Finally, I want to acknowledge my great intellectual debt to my teachers and intellectual sources: Brent Berlin, Roy G. D'Andrade, Charles O. Frake, Joseph H. Greenberg, Paul Kay, Floyd G. Lounsbury, and A. Kimball Romney.

Riverside, CA   D.B.K.
September 1995

Contents

I

INTRODUCTION AND LINGUISTIC BACKGROUND

1

Overview

The Theory, Its Aims, and Background

How we use words in speech to refer to things in the world around us presents a major problem. What makes an understanding of our use of words difficult and necessitates a complex theoretical treatment is the great and well-attested polysemy of natural language. In ordinary language usage, there is no one-to-one relationship between words and things. Opposed or contrasting words are used in different contexts to refer to the same thing, while very different things—different in their form, use, or in any other attribute that we choose to note—are referred to by the same term. This variability of reference made Bertrand Russell want to redesign language so that there would be a one-to-one relationship between a word and the conjunctively defined set of things it referred to. It is the problem that led Wittgenstein to claim that the best we could do was merely to describe the chained linkage of "family resemblances" among the various referents of any term.

Wittgenstein's claim precludes the possibility of any real theory of the semantics of natural language—that is, of any theory that would formally and systematically account for meaning and reference. Contra Wittgenstein, my goal is just such a theory—one that describes the structured regularity that underlies the variability of reference and shows how structure and variability are used in communication. That theory should explicate the usefulness to natural language of such variability and should explain how we manage to communicate as well as we do—as well as we are willing to spend the time and effort to do—with a tool as inexact as natural language. Such a theory necessarily involves an understanding of the paradigmatic sense relations among words (that is, of the ways in which related words contrast with one another and of the structures formed by putting together sets of related contrasts), of the implicit referents that the words themselves (apart from any particular context-of-use) evoke in our minds, and of the ways in which the structures formed by the contrast relations are in particular contexts first joined to implicit referents and then applied to the external world of things. To take an example, how does an American English speaker know that when I say "Grab a chair," an ottoman or an orange crate will serve, but that these objects will *not* serve when I say "Let's *buy* a chair"?

The semantic theory I am presenting in this volume separates word meaning into sense relations[1] of contrast and inclusion[2] (e.g., "Red is the color I mean, not orange") among words (that is, Saussurean signs); and referential relations, whereby terms are related

3

to things in the world. Referential relations are split, in turn. First, there are those internal to the sign whereby concepts represented by signifieds (the concepts that represent what the words refer to and that participate in the cognitive structures associated with the words/signs—e.g., "I mean the 'red' that I see in my mind's eye.") are defined. Second, there are those external to the sign whereby signifieds are related to referents outside the sign (and outside language—e.g., "I mean by 'red' that color there"). Sets of mutually opposed signs that share their inclusion relations make up "contrast sets," The signifieds of contrast sets, besides being associated with one another by their defining semantic relations of contrast and inclusion, are also associated with one another (and with relevant terms from related contrast sets) via the cognitive structures that represent their functional relations to one another and that reflect the reasons it is useful or important to distinguish them from one another.

Simple contrast sets can be expanded into larger semantic structures first by enlarging the number of included items from two (opposites, on a single dimension of contrast) to some larger number (still on a single dimension of contrast), but that number typically cannot be larger than 7 ± 2. Further expansion comes either by adding more dimensions of contrast (producing a multidimensional paradigm of contrast, a structure of the sort examined in "componential analysis") or by concatenating inclusion relations (producing a hierarchical or taxonomic type of structure). The choice depends partially on the intrinsic structure of the conceptual domain being represented and partially on the frequency with which terms from the domain, and cover terms for subsets of the terms, are used in conversation.

The theory has its roots in the ethnoscience school of anthropology, where the technique known as componential analysis was elaborated. Componential analysis evolved in anthropology from its linguistic roots as a way of inferring contrast relations from a set of reference relations; at the time of its inception the two kinds of meaning relations were considered to be two alternative ways of looking at the same categorizations. Later work showed that the features of contrast extracted from componential analysis only consistently applied to relations among prototypic (that is, best or ideal) referents, and that other referents within the wider range of things a term referred to could fall well outside the componential range. That is, componential analysis did not help, at least in any direct sense, with contrasts such as

real "red" (color)	vs.	the "Red" Army
my (genealogical) "uncle"	vs.	"Uncle" Tom
my "father"	vs.	"Father" O'Malley
my "cup" of tea	vs.	the "cup" my Coke is in

The theoretical insight that emerged from the problems of componential analysis, and which lies at the heart of my theory, is that reference relations are of two sorts: (a) Actual, real reference relations are those in which the particular class of referents is tied to (bound by) the term's definition. These referents are directly related to the term by its definition, and are the referents that are represented in the cognitive structure that represents functional relations among the terms of the given set or domain. These are "core" (or kernel or prototypic) referents. I sometimes speak of the connection between terms and their core referents as the "referential lock". (b) Ad hoc reference relations are those in which the referents are tied to the term only indirectly, via their connection (normally similarity, equivalence, or conceptual nearness) to the "real" referents. These are referents that have not generated their own signs, and so are labeled in conversation by whatever sign, in context, seems best able to pick them out. These are "extended" referents. (I want to draw attention to the fact that "extension," as used in this book, refers to "semantic" extension, as sketched in the paragraphs following and as defined in chapter 11, and I want to point out that this meaning of "extension" differs considerably from the meaning the term has in logic and philosophy.)[3]

The semantic theory is based on distinguishing core referents of a term (or Saussurean "sign") from extended referents. In this theory "core" referents do *not* represent some sort of average or typical referent but rather a *prototypic* referent. By "prototypic" referent I mean a referent that unites all the features that are in some sense definitional; by way of contrast, "typical" or "average" referents can and often do leave out many such features. For the Fanti *egya* or "father" category, prototypicality depends on the person's being understood as one's biological genitor, even though the most common usage is for other kinds of "father"; for the "cup" category in American English, prototypicality depends on being made of china, on being concave and hemispherical in shape, on having a handle, and on having a capacity of about eight ounces, even though exemplars are commonly cylindrical and made of plastic. For conceptions of specific ethnic groups, attributes of prototypicality often include biological ancestry, appearance, language and accent, style of dress, behavioral and gestural mannerisms, occupational specialization, and so forth. The totality of such features represents what we conjure up in our mind's eye when we think of the category in question, even though the actual exemplars we encounter often lack various of these features. In natural language, the typical application of a label is often not to a prototypic referent.

The constitution of language enables us to use the limited number of words in our lexicon flexibly, to speak of the infinite variety of things that we deal with in the world and to express the infinite shadings of meaning that we require in discussing these dealings.[4] One device by which we achieve this flexibility is to extend labels from their core referents to other referents that lack separate labels. The contrast set from which a particular label comes is either that which is functionally directed to the issue involved in the act of labeling or referencing (e.g., the set of color terms when we are referring to a nonkernel hue), or the set which in the context of the extension will highlight that issue (e.g. the set of kinterms when we are referring to a nonrelative with whom we have close solidary relations). The label chosen from the contrast set is that whose kernel is, in the relevant context, conceptually closer to (or more similar to) the thing being referred to (or to relevant aspects of it) than are kernels labeled by contrasting terms.

There are three kinds of extension:

1. "Denotative" extension is based on form, or on the appearance of the particular thing or action that is typically used for the purpose entailed by the term; "appearance" refers to shape, color, structure, or whatever else allows us to recognize an instance when we encounter one. A term can be extended to other items whose form is similar to that of the core referent.

2. "Connotative" extension is based on function, or the use of the thing or action referred to that makes it important enough to rate its own category; "important enough"

refers to a combination of the usefulness of the category for thought and the frequency with which the category is used in conversation (that is, usage must be sufficient for the category's label to be maintained in the language). A term can be extended to other items whose function is similar to that of the core referent. ("Denotative" and "connotative" refer in this theory to folk-definitional usage and not to lexicographers' evaluations.)

Extension that simultaneously fits both denotative/form and connotative/function definitions produces applications of a term that are simply "correct," even though not the "best" applications. Extension on the basis of denotative/form that does *not* fit the connotative/function definition can be identified by hedges such as "Well, yes, *technically*, he/it is a . . . but . . . ." Extension on connotative/function bases that does *not* accord with the denotative/form definition can be identified through hedges such as "He/it is not *really* a . . . but I just call him/it a . . . ."

Thus, the Fanti "father" category contains, as denotatively "correct" referents, the brothers and parallel cousins of one's father; the extension is made on the basis of the terminological equation of any father's "brother" with "father." The American English "cup" category includes as proper or genuine members cylindrical cup-like containers (which are also called "mugs") and "cups" made of a variety of other materials (such as plastic, paper, or tin); the extension is based on the greater similarity of the items (in terms of shape and material) to core "cups" than to the cores of contrasting terms. As examples of connotative extension, we can take the common application in English of "uncle" by children to close family friends of their parents' generation; such a person is, by the users' accounts, not *really* an "uncle," but a person who treats one the way an uncle should treat one and toward whom one feels as one should toward an uncle. That is, such "uncles" are empathetic, concerned senior males. Connotative extension of the American English "cup" category might be exemplified by referring to an empty tin can as a "cup" in some context (such as a camping trip, perhaps) when one needs a cup (functionally, for a hot drink) and it is the most cup-like thing around.

3. "Metaphoric" extension is extension that is based on attributes of a term within the context of its paradigmatic sense relations and/or within the cognitive structure that defines its conceptual relations to other terms in the domain, but that fits neither the denotative/form nor the connotative/function definition. Normally, metaphoric extension refers a term to referents in domains outside the domain the term (that is, its core referent) belongs to. The contextual proviso ("within the context of . . .") in metaphoric extension means that in actuality it is primarily the contrast set or paradigm of oppositions that is extended, and only secondarily is the best-fitting term out of that set (e.g., "father" vs. "uncle" from the kin paradigm, or "red" vs. "blue" from the color paradigm) then specifically applied to the referent.

The selection of a paradigm to be used metaphorically for an extended referent depends on how well relations among items in the source paradigm can be related to the relevant relations of the target item, and on what one wants to use the metaphor to do—for example, simply to identify the item, to impute certain qualities to the item, or to evoke certain psychological connections. The basis for selecting a particular term from within the set (that is, what makes a particular term "best fitting") can be almost anything that in context is sufficiently salient—similarity of form or function between the item and the core referent of the term, complementarity of the item's functioning to the functioning of the core referent, assistance by the item to the functioning of the core referent, similarity of the item's location to that of the core, typical contextual association of the item with the core referent, a part-whole relation between the two, and so forth. Reference to "the thought" as "father to the deed" or discussions of the "mother of wars" are examples of metaphoric extensions in which the functional focus of kinterms (on interpersonal behavior) has not been carried over, and thus in which the reader/hearer has to look to the conceptual situation being discussed to see what particular contrasts between father (or mother) and other kinterms might be relevant to it.

This multiplicity of kinds and bases of extension is crucial to the flexibility of natural language, which permits a finite vocabulary to be used to talk about an infinite variety of things and actions (and also permits an infinite variety of shadings of emphasis and attention relative to these).

The definitions native speakers consider to be "technically correct" refer to form (denotation), not function (connotation). The definitional primacy of form perhaps seems strange when, according to the theory, it is the importance of the function of the class of things or actions that generates the linguistic category in the first place. Reasons for the primacy of form seem to involve (a) the fact that forms yield clear, crisp *Gestalten*, while functions (because of the range of alternative fillers of any given function) present a muddier basis for communication; (b) the fact that communication is more typically about things/actions that can fulfill the function than about the function itself; and (c) the fact that folk definitions seem more likely to be used to tell how to recognize a member of a category than to tell why the category achieved linguistic recognition. Function-based definitions would be circular. Compare the functional definition. "A cup (that is, a hot-drink container) is whatever you drink hot drinks from," with the form definition "A cup is a roughly hemispherical, six- to eight-ounce ceramic container with a handle." If the function were unclear, one might append a functional observation such as "which is used for sipping hot drinks" to the form definition. A question about the function of a known form takes the form "What is X used for?" rather than "What is an X?" (or, for verbs, "Why does one Y?" rather than "What is Ying?").

Over time, with changing technology, environment, taste, and so forth, typical instantiations of terminological categories change, and so, too, denotative definitions also change. "Pen" has moved from being defined as a quill to a stick pen with a metal nib to a fountain pen to a ballpoint pen—and perhaps now to a felt-tipped pen.

This volume and the theory it offers are strongly rooted in the Saussurean paradigm and in the ethnoscience work that implemented that paradigm in anthropology. The excesses of structuralism in the 1960s[5] did produce a reaction against Saussure, but the time has come for a synthesis that restores him to his proper place. Saussure's work—key theoretical insights of which have not been independently re-produced by anyone else—has important implications for the shape of a modern semantic theory that have not heretofore been recognized. Ethnoscience was correctly seen to be too narrow and too limited in its objectives. However, the narrowly denotative semantics of ethnoscience, although leaving untouched the major part of our everyday use of language, did deal (and deal well) with the crucial paradigmatic[6] relations that underlie the rest of the complexity of everyday usage and which must be understood before one can, in any rigorous way, make sense of that wider complexity.

For convenience and simplicity I often speak simply of "words" and the "things" they refer to. But I want to make clear that when I say "words" I am really speaking of Saussurean signs, that is, unions of signifiers (sound images) and signifieds (concepts), and when I say "things," I refer to the pragmatic phenomena in the external or nonlinguistic world to which signs (via their "signified" faces) refer. Such "things" may be things (or actions or attributes) that are visible or tangible, or things we only imagine to be there, or things as abstract as platonic triangles. In this Saussurean context, language itself is totally mental or conceptual, and thus signs can best be seen as participating in schemas of the sort described in Piagetian psychology (see Flavell 1963:52–58). Language imposes a discrete carving-up on the world of natural phenomena, which in themselves are sometimes continuous and sometimes discrete but even when discrete not necessarily segmented by nature the same way as they are by language. Language itself creates neither the phenomena nor the structural relations among them; however, the phenomena that are structured and labeled in language can include hypothetical or imagined entities (such as unicorns or hobgoblins) and abstractions (such as love or intelligence). Following Saussure (1959:6, 9, 11–14, 77–78) and Durkheim (see, for example, 1938:2–8), I see language as a collective representation par excellence, and thus as the passively given set of shared (and largely subconscious) understandings from which we construct our particular communicative acts of speech—even if this collective representation may be actively modeled by each individual in constructing her or his own internal representation from the regularities she or he encounters in social interaction.

Since we are not explicitly taught natural language as a formal code, but induce it from our various individual speech experiences, an understanding of the role of core referents in language entails a consideration of factors that shape our specific inductions. The question of how each new generation of speakers induces its own version of the language's rules of contrast and reference leads in turn to the question of how language changes, of how new categories with new exemplars emerge and thus of how changes in our material, social, religious (or whatever) existence are tracked by our language.

According to the present extensionist theory, when categories of things (or actions) become sufficiently important in a given speech community, they get their own words, that is, Saussurean signs. As these words come into existence they are defined, in part, in contradistinction to words already coding opposed or contrasting concepts. The most salient exemplars of any category (in the broad sense of salience that combines frequency, effectiveness, noticeability, etc.) become the core exemplars of that category—the instances that are conjured up in the mind's eyes of speakers when they have to answer questions about the category in the absence of any further information than what is carried by the word itself about what is meant. The form attributes (that is, the descriptive attributes that enable the core instantiation or exemplar of the category to accomplish the function[7] at issue for the category) by which these cores differ from the cores of contrasting or opposed words provide the bases for denotative extension of the word to other exemplars. The functional attributes of the category in question (that is, the reasons for distinguishing it from contrasting categories) provide the bases for connotative extension. The remaining attributes of these core exemplars become potential bases for metaphoric extension.

Core referents are tied to their words (by what I sometimes speak of as the "referential lock"), while extended referents/things are free to be represented by whatever words do the job best in the context at hand. The referential lock of cores provides us with the structure we need to avoid the infinite regress of overlapping similarities implied by Wittgenstein's "family resemblances," while the variability we have in the application of words to other referents gives language the flexibility it needs to be used in reference to an ever-changing world by speakers whose induced representations of the world are themselves ever changing.

The contrast between core and extended referents becomes important, as do the various mechanisms of extension, when we attempt to explicate usages such as that in the chair example presented earlier. What is a "chair," if orange crates and ottomans can both be and not be instances of it? When do we "buy" a chair and when do we "hire" one? How do we know when "the anthropology chair" refers to a newly endowed professorship, to the departmental chief executive, or simply to the chair that the anthropology representative sits in?

Things that do not have their own words (that is, that are not themselves core referents of words) are referred to by words belonging to other things (that is, by words that have other things as their core referents). In a general sense, in nonmetaphoric extension, a noncore thing (within the relevant domain) is labeled by the word whose core is nearest to it or most similar to it, either in form or function, depending on the context of use. (Metaphoric extension is similar, but with, as we shall see shortly, important differences.) But this closeness or similarity is calculated differently in different domains. For example, for color hues, "form" similarity is calculated arithmetically on continuous dimensions of hue, saturation, and brightness; for cups and glasses, on a mixture of continuous dimensions of height and breadth, categorical dimensions of shape, and an oppositional dimension of handle possession; and, for kinterms, often by a relative product calculus. Furthermore, since the goal of the use of the word is to communicate about some particular thing or things, the similarity calculation is affected (or biased) by local context—such as the nature of the objects from which the given one is to be distinguished, the functional reason for the distinction, the way the information is to be taken (canonically, loosely, ironically), and so forth.

Beyond the simpler case of extension within a domain is that of metaphoric extension across domains. Metaphoric extension is treated in the theory in a way that does not artificially separate or overly distance it from other kinds of extension. In my theory, "metaphor" refers broadly (cf. Halliday 1985; cf. also Keller and Lehman 1991:276 n. 5) to extension of a term out from its source domain to another domain where the root feature of the source domain (that is, the feature the items in the given contrast set all share but which differentiates that set from other, related contrast sets) is lacking, or, less commonly, to extension within the source domain where some normally essential feature is ignored. Within this theoretical framework, metaphor has its more traditional, narrow sense of implicit comparison ("in which a word or phrase is applied to a person, idea, or object to which it is not literally applicable. A metaphor is an implied analogy which imaginatively identifies one thing with another," Shaw 1976:171). This is not usefully to be distinguished from metonymy (in which "the name of one object or idea is used for another to which it is related or of which it is a part," Shaw 1976:174) or synecdoche ("in which a part is used for the whole or the whole for a part, the special for the general or the general for the special . . . , a kind of metaphor" Shaw 1976:267). The understanding process is not tuned to or shaped by any specific kind of presumed relationship, but instead relies on whatever kind of relationship happens to be foregrounded by the combination of linguistic paradigm (that is, contrast set and associated schemas) and pragmatic context.[8] For example, in a parking lot (perhaps in Texas), "Get me my hoss!" will produce pretty much the same results[9] as "Get me my wheels!": that is, the car will appear and the garage attendant will notice the slightly lame cuteness of the request.

The theory described in this volume involves a treatment of semantic extension that differs from other treatments in fundamental ways. The theory is not about extension per se, though it certainly includes the extension mechanism; rather, it relates the particular forms of extension to the functions of language, and particularly to language's functioning for communication.[10] It treats semantic relations (here, specifically, of words) as mechanisms selected and honed as tools for furthering the human ends served by natural language. Communication is presumed to be one major such end; information storage and social coordination might be others. Communication includes not only the transmission of information but also the use of such transmission to manipulate the thoughts and actions of others.

In the present volume, words—including their relations of contrast, their presumed referents, and some aspects of how they are learned—are the units of language we are exploring. A consideration of the units of language raises the question of how those units function—what purposes they appear to be serving and how they act to serve these purposes. Functionalism, as an anthropological explanatory theory, has for good reasons largely been abandoned, but functionalism's demise does not lessen the importance of the task of trying to understand the functions served by the forms of culture (or biology).[11] How are our normal everyday communicative aims served by the semantic structure being described in this book? Why do they seem never to be served by the pure distinctive feature design that Bertrand Russell, among others, thought so superior ?

A way of thinking about the success of a theory is to consider the degree to which it contains the information that would enable a computer program to use the everyday words of everyday language as they are ordinarily used, or to "understand" everyday words in the sense of being able to apply them to explicate situations or to paraphrase, expand on, or comment on usage. Since this theory relates word meaning and usage to conditions in the phenomenal world of our experience, an actual version of the test would also entail some effective representation of the relevant part of that world. Work in cognitive sciences such as that of Schank and Abelson (1977) suggests that such representations, at least for specific domains, are within reach.

For some particular domains, such as those of kinship terminologies and common household objects, the specific local versions of the theory are beginning to approach the explicitness and rigor needed for the semantic side of some version of the test. In other domains, even ones discussed in this book, the specific details of the theory are much less well developed. The semantic theory is not yet sufficiently developed even to approach such a test for the general case; there are not yet a sufficient number and variety of specific particular applications to make possible the comparative treatment from which any rigorous and testable statement of the general theory would have to come.

The standard discussed is important at this stage as a device for defining goals and success in their attainment. Our use of language is regular enough and shared enough to suggest that it should be possible to represent this use in a computer program. Such representation will be important, eventually, as a way of separating metaphors about language from actual theories, and as a way of separating what a proposed theory actually can do from what its creator claims for it. Such evaluation of the present theory is still premature, but programs already exist that show the plausibility of various small pieces of the project and that bode well for future developments; my own contributions are to be seen in Kronenfeld 1976 and in Kronenfeld and Kaus 1984.

The chapters leading up to the actual exposition of the theory in Chapter 11 serve the purposes of presenting and explaining the major findings and problems which led to the present theory, of providing definitions and illustrations of key concepts, and of rooting the present theory in its intellectual antecedents.

At the end of part I, chapter 3 describes and analyzes the Saussurean sources and presents the Saussurean perspective and framework of my theory.

Part II, the ethnoscience tradition, explains the ethnoscience work on which the theory is based. Chapter 4 relates the Saussurean roots to the early ethnoscience work of Lounsbury and Goodenough on componential analysis, and of Frake and Conklin on folk taxonomies. The kinds of structures that can be built up out of elaborated and combined contrast sets, paradigms, and taxonomies are introduced and compared. Chapter 5 examines in detail the classic componential analyses of English kinterms produced successively by Wallace and Atkins and by Romney and D'Andrade; after presenting the analyses and the claims explicitly made in each, it analyzes the analyses and the differences between them.

Part III, explanatory principles, uses selected cognitive and linguistic findings to explain some of the major structural features of semantic structures in language. Chapter 6, based on Bruner, Goodnow, and Austin's work (1956) on concept formation, explores what is meant by conjunctivity, the empirical evidence for its importance, and the specific implications of that evidence for category definitions in natural language.

The idea of marking, as explicated and extended by Greenberg, is introduced in chapter 7, which discusses the relationship of marking to hierarchical structures of contrast (taxonomic or tree structures) and to Berlin's work on the development of folk taxonomies (including the ways in which new categories emerge). Finally, in that chapter, the ways in which marking relations within taxonomic structures act to extend word meanings are explored. Chapter 8 summarizes George Miller's cognitive psychological work (1956) on the limits of our information processing capabilities, shows how his discussion of ways to get around such limits accounts for paradigmatic and taxonomic semantic structures, and relates to reasons for semantic extension.

Part IV, semantic extension, examines prior extensionist work and then presents the current theory. Chapter 9 treats semantic extension within the ethnoscience tradition prior to the current theory. It first introduces extensionist models via the classic analyses by Lounsbury of Crow- and Omaha-type terminologies and by Berlin and Kay of basic color terms. These analyses made clear the limitations of componentially analyzing whole categories, and showed the strong advantages of an approach that limited componential relations to core exemplars of categories while using other mechanisms to extend the categories out to other referents. Chapter 9 subsequently treats three more recent examples (from my work on Fanti kinship, Kempton's work with *ollas*, and Basso's work on Western Apache use of horse partinomy terms for pickup trucks) that illustrate specific points concerning data collection, variability (both within an individual's usage and among the individuals of a community), and the logic of extension. Chapter 10 presents the current theory.

Part V (that is, chapter 11) applies the theory first to the prosaic but decidedly cultural, domain of cups and glasses, and then to the more politically contested cultural domains of Blackfeet political factions, Renaissance English religious controversy, and modern American struggles with the sexual division of household labor. Chapter 12 offers a brief concluding overview of the theory and applications.

Notes

1. The word "meaning" is sometimes used—more narrowly than in my usage—to refer only to sense or contrast relations.

2. Trubetzkoy (1969:68), writing in a Saussurean framework, noted that "opposition" (our "contrast") presupposed the properties that both members had in common, properties that in "bilateral" oppositions were shared with no other members of the wider system. These shared properties, then, defined an entity equivalent to what we are speaking of as the superordinate term that includes the contrasting terms—our "inclusion" relation.

3. In logic and philosophy an extensional definition is one that defines the reference of a concept by listing its denotata and is contrasted with an intensional definition that defines the reference of a concept by its properties. Thus, in the logical sense, componential analysis in anthropology can be seen as the process of moving from extensive definitions of the reference of terminological categories of a domain such as kinship (via lists of kintypes) to intensive definitions of those categories (via distinctive features). We will see that the reference of terminological categories in extensionist semantic theory is still defined by intensive definitions, but in this case definitions of the reference of extended kinterm categories are built out of a combination of distinctive feature definitions of core referents and separate procedures for linking other referents to the core ones (such as, for kinterms, the iterated application of equivalence rules).

4. The expression of an infinity of "different concrete concepts and ideas" through the use of a "limited . . . number of lexical meanings in the system of language" was already noted by Trubetzkoy in 1939 (1969:3).

5. To my mind, the problem was really more one of naiveté and misinterpretation—concerning both Saussure's theoretical assertions and the role played by culture and language in human behavior—than of simple excesses. See Kronenfeld and Decker 1979.

6. "Paradigmatic," taken here in its Saussurean sense, refers to the relations existing among alternative occupants of some structural position, and thus contrasts with "syntagmatic," which refers to relations of co-occurrence. Paradigmatic relations in this Saussurean sense include both componential (also called "paradigmatic") structures and taxonomic structures.

7. My use of the term "function" relates to the communicative function of some sign/word—the reason it is distinguished and spoken of enough to get its own label/sign. I am

not (cf. Atran 1990:57) talking necessarily or particularly about its cultural or utilitarian function—unless, of course, the communicative focus is on such functioning. In my theory, "function" thus characterized contrasts with "form"—the description/definition of kernel or core exemplars, that is, the indication of how you can recognize an exemplar when you encounter it.

8. My aim here is not a taxonomy or classification of "types" of figures of speech or tropes such as that which Lakoff offers (1987) and Quinn and Holland elaborate (1987:31). Instead my aim is to explicate the *process* by which we use words to communicate.

9. Of course, unlike Basso's Western Apache informants (1967), our Texan garage attendant will find the "horse" label for a car less familiar (and, perhaps, more lame) than the "wheels" one.

10. My concern with language's functioning is not unrelated to Trubetzkoy's similar concern (see, for example, Trubetzkoy 1969:11).

11. My concern with how language functions does not mean that my theory falls into the trap that proved fatal for functionalism in anthropology; that is, it does not make the presumption that some functional need guarantees the presence either of some particular filler of the need (versus some variety of alternatives), or that some functional need guarantees any successful filler at all (versus our limping along with the kind of inefficient solution represented, in our physiology, by the lower back), or even that the given functional need must necessarily be met (versus the system's moving into different adaptive niche entailing some other functional needs). The point is simply that our biological and cultural capacities are both shaped by selection (even if via different mechanisms), and thus what we do (especially where what we do is in some sense expensive—in terms of mortality, learning investment, etc.) is likely to be done for some reason; in this case, our understanding of the doing is likely to be aided by some insight into the reasons.

2

Intellectual Context of the Theory

One common kind of book is an eclectic summary of a field, discusing the major theoretical developments and focusing on some common themes or issues among them. Another, contrasting kind is a careful and more or less self-contained explication of a particular theoretical argument. My aim is the latter; the works I cite and analyze in the text are used to explore the presuppositions that underlie my work, to lay out the base of previous findings on which I am building, and to credit the sources of my thinking. It may be useful to the reader, however, if I briefly sketch how the present work relates to some other relevant work in contemporary anthropology, cognition, and semantics.

Cognitive Anthropology

This book is about language, about words in particular. It concerns how things (potential referents) come to be linked to words (Saussurean signs). It does *not* deal with which aspects of objects or events in the world or which aspects of our perceptual or conceptual apparatus cause objects or events to be recognized as "things" in the first place—what gets them seen as bounded instances and causes different exemplars to be seen or recognized as instances of the same thing. It is about the meaningful use of language, particularly of words, rather than about the forms of thought or perception that are expressed or might be expressed in language—whether such forms are universal (like those proposed by Atran 1990) or culturally specific (like those proposed by a number of people working in the area of "cultural models"; see, for example, articles by Quinn 1982, by Quinn and Holland, Holland and Skinner, D'Andrade, and Quinn in Holland & Quinn 1987, and by Strauss, D'Andrade, Holland, Quinn, and Strauss in D'Andrade and Strauss 1992). In its emphasis on the properties of words that allow their flexible use, my semantic theory contrasts with semantic theories such as that of Wierzbicka that aim at finding or defining a universal set of semantic primitives in terms of which words and phrases of different languages may be defined and then translated from one language to another. In its emphasis on the functional process by which we understand words and use them to communicate, my theory contrasts with descriptive approaches to extension (such as that of Rosch).

Much of the work just cited on categories of thought takes language as providing some sort of privileged access to thought[1] or cultural knowledge[2] (see, for instance, Atran 1990:chap. 3, especially pp. 52–64, also p. 6; Holland and Skinner 1987:79–

80,103; Lakoff and Kövecses 1987:220; Lutz 1987:292,300–301; 1992:182; Quinn 1982:777,797n. 4; 1987:173,174–180; 1992:94; Quinn and Holland 1987:24). Because they are present in individual minds as entities, linguistic categories are indeed categories of thought, and it is reasonable to take them as such. But, as will be shown in a variety of places in this volume, there is a real risk in taking the categories of language in some domain to simply and directly represent the thoughts of speakers of the language regarding things in that domain (cf. Keesing 1987:387). For example, there are people who hold diametrically opposed positions on substantive issues who nevertheless clothe those positions with identical language (see the discussion of Renaissance religious positions in this volume, and Keesing 1987:378,380), and we have examples from different languages of widely differing linguistic expression of similar cultural attitudes (such expression varies in accordance with the grammatical resources and usage patterns already available in the language; see Kronenfeld 1991:24–25[3]). The flexibility of language use, which will be illustrated throughout this volume, means that any inferences from language to thought or values entail substantial risk of error, and thus such inferences should be subject to independent psychological corroboration before being accepted.

The equation of language with thought exhibits a more general underlying problem. Thought, belief, and understanding are all individual matters, while language is a collective representation. The collective tool is shaped so as to allow us to communicate about our various different individual knowledge and attitudes, and even is a device by which we shape the knowledge and attitudes of our children. But the looseness and flexibility of language, which allows us to use its finite resources to communicate an infinity of shadings and alternative meanings, also means that it is never terribly precise in communicating any particular individual's understanding. Thus language is more a device for saying things about our beliefs and knowledge than it is for directly expressing these beliefs and this knowledge.[4] As such, language can be used to frame propositions about values or beliefs that most members of a culture might assent to, but such assent might still obscure a great range of interpretative or instantiative variation among members of the cultural community on the matters at issue.

Natural Kinds

Atran's concern (1990) is with our recognition and understanding of "natural kinds," and with the history of scientific views of such kinds. Natural kinds, in his view, are categories of living things, such as animals and plants, that we have an innate biological predisposition to recognize and to see as having some particular properties. He is really speaking of categories of perception and cognition, and not of anything restricted to language or related to linguistic functioning. He only uses language, or, more properly, such categorizations in natural language, as evidence regarding the universality of natural-kind categories and of the attributes of such categories. Since the semantic theory being proposed in this volume concerns linguistic functioning (that is, how some cognitive categories come to be coded in language and how language is used to communicate about a wide range of cognitive categories), and since it makes no particular claims about the origins or natures of the *underlying* cognitive categories that happen to be linguistically coded (examples discussed will include domains ranging from the domain of color that is tightly biologically structured by the physiological make-up of the retina, to domains of cultural artifacts, such as that of pens and pencils, that seem highly unlikely to be structured in any direct way by any biological basis.

Innatism does, however, raise the important issue of how our biological predispositions are to be understood, and of when they become relevant to some theory regarding our behavior—especially a theory regarding possible universals of human behavior. The issue is broader than Atran's work; it was raised prominently in linguistics by Chomsky (see 1968, 1975, and Kronenfeld 1979), on whose work Atran models his own (Atran 1990:51); the problem of innate propensities is also raised by any discussion of how language in general or thought in general works. The question is, What do we mean by "innate," and with what form of noninnate are we contrasting it?[5] It is common in thinking about language to infer from the universal occurrence of some kind of linguistic category some sort of innate predisposition to think or act in some manner. But one should be aware that nature can have its effect in very different ways. The universalities of color nomenclature seem to be rooted in the very neurology of our perception (Berlin and Kay 1969, Kay and McDaniel 1978; see also Kay, Berlin, and Merrifield 1991 for modifications and MacLaury 1992 for a contrasting view), while those of kinship nomenclature seem to have much more to do with commonalities in the way members of our species care for their young, and thus in the experiences we generally have of family roles. Even much of our physical nature seems not to be as directly or simply wired-in as is our perception of colors; Washburn has pointed out (see Kronenfeld 1979:215) that the very shape of our bones depends as much on the pull of muscles against the growing bone as it does on the genetic program for the bone. The point is that biological evolution, the mechanism that produces whatever innate properties we have, is not a mechanism for constructing ideal genetic plans, but only a *satisficing* mechanism, which creates just enough coding to get whichever job we are talking of done in the context of whatever else is happening at the time.

It is obvious (and tautological) that we have the genetic capacity to do whatever it is that we do. It also seems plausible that there should be some genetic element involved in anything that all humans do but that no other species, especially those closest to us, can do, or, at least, "can do easily and fully," such as talk, (depending on how one reads the attempts to teach human languages to chimpanzees and gorillas). But there is nothing in such universality itself that tells us what kind of genetic mechanism might be involved—that is, how general (versus specific to the problem), or how detailed in its specifications (versus leaving the specification to some other mechanism). Innate and universal foundations can range from almost undifferentiated all the way to well articulated and inherently differentiated. My own sense (see Kronenfeld 1979) is that Chomsky implied much more detailed and language-specific mechanisms for his posited genetic mechanism for language than are either logically necessary or biologically reasonable; I say "implied" because he never spelled out any details about the actual logical or physical form of the mechanism, and so we have no way of knowing what he actually was claiming and no way of evaluating alternative approaches. Finally, then, I am not now making any claim regarding the genetic underpinnings of the theory or mechanisms discussed in this volume. Insofar as the theory seems accurate and insightful, the question of genetic underpinnings becomes an interesting one for later speculation and research.

Cultural Models and Schemas

The "cultural models" approach reflects the interest of a number of contemporary cognitive anthropologists in finding appropriate means for representing culturally structured differences in perception, cognition, motivation, and action.[6] Many of these theorists come out of the same intellectual tradition I do; the difference is that they are trying to look *through* language at the cultural understandings it codes, while in the present volume I am concentrating on (one part of) the language medium itself. In one sense the interest in "cultural models" represents a continuation of American anthropology's concern with values, but with a strong interest in the structures or mechanisms by which values are tied to goals and motivation and thus to action. Initially, "schemas" were taken from psychology as candidates for such structural mechanisms. Various authors within the school have derived culturally standardized or shared forms of schemas, often spoken of as "cultural models," in different ways from different types of psychological schemas (Quinn and Holland 87:25). In general, in the cultural models literature, the "cultural models" label seems to be used for the general, culturally shared device while the "schema" label is reserved for a form or an application that is in some way more individualized.[7]

From my point of view, this splitting of "cultural models" from "schemas" is desirable because, from the perspective of the present volume, schemas are structures that develop in the mind of each individual and that cannot be directly shared. However, insofar as people in a culture share significant shaping experiences, their schemas will be similar. Insofar as people publicly deal with their schemas or with the values, goals, and actions entailed within them, these schemas can become collective representations of the same sort language is. In this event, each individual acquires his or her own internal representation of the pattern of schematic relations that *seem* to him or her to be shared by members of the relevant community, and this representation can define a set of expectations the individual has about the motives and actions of others—expectations that the individual takes account of in his or her own actions. From the perspective of the conceptual structure of the present volume, "the pattern[s] of schematic relations which seem [to community members] to be shared by members of the relevant community" form the collective representations that can be equivalent to "cultural models," and it is via individuals' internal representations of those collective representations that the cultural model is embodied in individual action.[8]

When I use the word "schema" in this volume, I am using it as it is used in the Piagetian tradition and not as it is used by many others, particularly those working with cultural models. The difference is not simply a matter of different tastes or preferences in naming, but relates to the important issue of the relationship between individual cognition (and action) and culturally shared cognitive structures, including those described in the relevant literature as "cultural models."

Piagetian schemas are structures of knowledge linked to action and goals that are constantly in the process of being adapted within individual minds. Such schemas are never shared in the sense that several different individuals actively participate in the same structure; on the other hand, they can be shared in the sense that different individuals can develop similar schemas in areas of behavior (including cultural domains) in which their experiences are similar. But even these "shared" schemas are never static or fixed, never totally shared—and never abstracted from their behavioral context or schematized into some generic form. Shared schemas of this Piagetian sort can never constitute "cultural models," since cultural models are understood as abstracted and idealized paradigms (or pictures) of knowledge and behavior. Appendix 1 outlines my understanding of Piagetian schemas and indicates more fully my reasons for preferring the Piagetian version to others.

My Piagetian schemas are *individual* and exist only in individuals (cf. Keesing 1987:377). On the other hand, by my conceptualization, cultural models, with their posited or presumed linkages between ideas, feelings, actions, motivation, and so forth exist as collective representations in the same way/sense in which *langue* exists (as explicated in chapter 3's discussion of Saussure). That is, each individual experiences socially shared models (and takes account of them in her or his action) as if they were the actual schemas of some kind of collective individual—some "other" in opposition to her or his own self, and so not (for this collective purpose) including her or his self. Such a collectivity can be carved out of the wider society by any slicing needed to produce the desired collective "individual" (that is, "Americans," "Southerners," "my family," "anthropologists," "academic whites," "undergraduate males," and so forth). These slices are often ad hoc but *can* be more or less included in the shared culture as stable, named concepts, in the same way any other collective representation emerges, via frequency of use, from some combination of usefulness, salience, and delimitability. Individuals experiencing such putatively shared schemas include in the presumed content of these schemas the elements that the individuals have typically or saliently come to associate with members of the collectivity in question.

Insofar as such cultural models or their components are recognized by native speakers of a language and labeled within the language, the words thus formed become as any other words in the language. That is, I would expect the semantic theory of the present volume to apply as much to the emergence of such words (for cultural roles and values and culturally appropriate behavior) and the use of these words as to any other words. The cultural models theorists use linguistic expressions as a means of determining and explicating cultural values (see Quinn and Holland 1987:24) and the implications of such values for action. My concern in this volume is with the processes by which words acquire meaning and by which those meanings are used in communication, and not with the cultural values the words may represent. Thus, as was the case with Atran's universals, there is no incompatibility between the theory advanced in this volume and the kinds of proposals advanced by cultural models theorists. But as was the case with Atran's work, I would suggest that the flexible linguistic mechanisms detailed here should make cultural models theorists wary of resting any claims about values too directly on linguistic data alone or on interpretations of the meanings of words or phrases. Anthropologists run risks when they rely too directly on native speakers' characterizations of psychological phenomena in natural language. One example of such risk is the problem D'Andrade, in a late 1960s comment on D'Andrade 1965, described small-group psychologists as having gotten into when they developed their theories about people's behavior in small groups using what they presumed (from the way people expressed them) were folk theories of individual motivation, but which turned out to be more on the order of folk *warnings* about what to look out for in interaction.

One kind of problem often encountered in trying to understand and describe culturally patterned systems of motivation concerns how to describe the individual actor's relationship to the proposed cultural motivations without either reducing the actor to a sort of automaton mindlessly carrying out a cultural plan or causing the specificity of the proposed cultural regularities to evaporate (see, especially, Strauss 1992a: 9–11, Shweder 1992:46–47, Holland 1992:62, Lutz 1992:186–7, D'Andrade 1992b:228). Too often, anthropologists especially seem to fall into the former trap—which I sometimes characterize as the Dead Hand of Culture fallacy—by treating traditional cultural rules (or beliefs or presuppositions) as automatically being held by members of the culture being described, even though they know full well that the patterns of their own culture are not held by its members in such a manner. This problem seems to pertain not simply to "exotic" or "distant" but to all "other" cultures, even those represented by variant subcultures of the ethnographer's own culture. I do not think the ethnographers in question actually believe the actors they are describing to be different in this way from themselves; I think the problem instead comes from our not having any good model for thinking about or describing cultural patterns or other collective representations in a way that both captures the patterning involved and still keeps distinct the individual actor's autonomous process of using, manipulating, and playing against the pattern.[9] I offer the present volume's approach to language—collective representation—as one way of dealing with this problem.

Since any approach to culturally shared or collectively held cognitive systems, including both the "natural kinds" and the "cultural models" approaches, has to work largely through the medium of natural language and to make use of the evidence for cultural presuppositions, values, beliefs, explanations, and so forth provided by expressions that have proved salient enough and shared enough to become included in the language spoken by members of the culture in question, pursuers of such approaches will be best served by relying on as sophisticated and insightful a theory of language functioning as they can find. Consequently, developers of such theories stand to benefit from having as clear an understanding as possible of which aspects of language usage derive from the nature of language and its use by humans. Such an understanding would serve to throw into clearer relief the facts concerning language usage that are not explained by recourse to language itself (and thus invite some other explanation) and to provide a clearer idea of the manner and form by which cultural or biological presuppositions may be coded within language. The theory being developed here represents an approach to one aspect of the linguistic problem—and, it is hoped, will prove useful, both in the problems it raises and in the solutions it offers to those who are trying to use language data to explore cultural and cognitive problems.

Linguistics

Universal Semantic Primitives

Wierzbicka aims at developing "a framework for cross-cultural comparison of . . . concepts" (1992:177), a list of universal semantic primitives in terms of which the full lexicons of all languages can be defined (1992:10). Her goal of defining and comparing concepts coded in language places different constraints on her work than does my concern with understanding how we use the limited conceptual apparatus of language to communicate (with ourselves and others) about the infinite variety of objects and shadings of meaning that we do, and my concern with understanding how our languages come to acquire the resources we need for such communication. Her comparisons can be more usefully stated in terms of features,[10] while my concern with the flexible application of linguistic categories to the phenomenal world places more emphasis on processes of analogy and inference than she needs to be concerned with, given her goal.

I want to point out that my approach is compatible with one such as Wierzbicka's that focuses on semantic primitives. I have, though in materials not dealt with in this volume (see Kronenfeld 1980b and Buchowski et al. 1994), found it useful to distinguish (within a set of signifieds and their associated kernel referents) between relatively primary and relatively derivative linguistic concepts, but without having elaborated any worked-out theoretical treatment of the distinction. I thus see Wierzbicka's work on semantic primitives as speaking to a clear need. I would at the same time suggest that her approach would benefit from separating out, in the manner of the present volume, the conditions that cause a potential referent to get its own sign from the ways in which the reference of existing signs is extended to new referents. I think that such clarification would simplify her search for semantic primitives and, in particular, would give her a more consistent basis for dealing with questions involving polysemy than she presently has. An approach to semantic functioning like that of the present volume would also save her from the emptiness of her definition of extended "father" (that is, "I can think of him like I think of my FATHER," 1992:334) by getting in the relevant specific ("connotative," in my system) functional relations and by relating those to the relevant ("denotative") genealogical constraints (see Kronenfeld 1973, 1980a, 1980b). Employing an approach to semantics such as that of the present volume would also enable her to distinguish in a systematic and motivated way the difference between the kind of "father" a father's brother is in a classificatory terminological system and the kind of "mother" a "mother superior" represents in languages such as English. Such a theory would enable her to make systematic use of the "father as opposed to what" information entailed by paradigmatic contrast, and thereby to address in a systematic fashion the question of which "father-like" people are "fathers" and which are "uncles" in languages such as Fanti versus languages such as English.

Roschian Prototype Theory

The work of Rosch and related scholars, mostly in psychology (see, for example, Rosch 1973, 1978; Rosch and Mervis 1975; and Rosch et al. 1976), which has commonly been labeled "prototype theory" (Atran 1990:53, 1993:55; Quinn and Holland 1987:22–23; Wierzbicka 1992:175) shares with my semantic theory its distinguishing of core from extended referents and its development from the pioneering work of Berlin and Kay. It shares little else. Rosch's work involves a circularity in that she defines prototypes as the most typical or average referents (out of the set of referents labeled by the term in question) while at the same time she defines extended referents relative to the prototype. In the present theory, by contrast, core (kernel or prototypic) referents of a sign are defined without reference to the extended ranges of that sign or the extended set of referents, and without reference to other aspects of that sign; the core referents are defined by reference to events, actions, or experiences outside the language game, or by combinations of, or operations on, other signs. In my theory, prototypicality, which differs substantially from Rosch's "typicality," will be fully explained as the concepts needed for its definition are fully explicated. For now I want only to note that it relates either to the commonness with which the prototypic referents of the sign/term are involved in the *functional relations* that give rise to the sign/term or to the conceptual appropriateness of these things to those functional relations.

Rosch offers no functional motivation for distinguishing core from extended referents, and no systematic explanation for the variability and inconsistency of extension from one situation to another. The mechanisms of the present theory—including the distinction of signifieds from referents; the focus of semantic relations of contrast and inclusion on signifieds; the special identification of signifieds with core (that is, prototypic) referents; the distinction of form versus functional definitions; the distinction of denotative, connotative, and metaphoric extensions from one another; the role of full-contrast sets in the semantic extension of terms from the set; the role in semantic extension of functional relations among core referents of terms in a contrast set; and so forth—are not shared with Rosch's prototype theory and are not matched there by any comparable conceptual apparatus.

As my presentation unfolds, my theory will, where appropriate, be contrasted in more specific ways with Rosch's approach. For the moment I want only to strongly emphasize the difference between the present theory and Rosch's as a way of alerting readers to the fact that analyses or criticisms of Roschian prototype theory (such as Wierzbicka 1992:23 or Atran 1990:55) or of Lakoff's (1987) development of it (such as Keller and Lehman 1991:286) do not necessarily or automatically apply to the present extensionist semantic theory.

I should also note that my semantic theory does not place prototypes in any "simplified world" of the sort Quinn and Holland (1987:23–24,30) have taken from Fillmore (1975, 1982), though the idea that knowledge about the world, including the cultural world, is included in semantic schemas in a relatively clean form is one I would agree with.

In a similar vein, I want to make clear that the extensionist semantic theory I am presenting does not appeal to any Wittgensteinian "family resemblances" view, and is not vulnerable to criticisms of such a view (such as Atran 1990:54). In contrast to Wittgenstein's view, it does distinguish between what information is essential to our understanding of a term and what is not, but it does so in a different and more complex way than theories that have proved vulnerable to the kinds of objections that Wittgenstein raised. It accounts for the referential variability that led Wittgenstein to speak of "family resemblances" (Wittgenstein 1953:32e[11]) while still providing the order and structure needed to account for the effectiveness with which we use words in normal communication; it avoids the more ad hoc any-word-can-mean-anything implication of Wittgenstein's "family resemblances" notion.

Lakoff and Langacker on Metaphor

Understanding why we rely so much on metaphor in natural language and how metaphor works is one of my major analytic goals in this volume. Metaphor is an important part of what linguists and anthropologists study, but any account that aims at science (a goal of mine, if not one universally shared in the field) cannot itself simply be framed and analyzed metaphorically. Lakoff (1987), drawing on Rosch's work, importantly advances the study of metaphor by contributing specific descriptions of a range of distinct patterns of metaphoric extension. But Lakoff's work still leaves undescribed the cognitive machinery that enables us to use metaphor in actual communication, the reasoning process we go through in constructing and decoding metaphors, and the communicative ends our extensive use of metaphor in communication serves. If metaphors are actively constructed and understood via some kind of reasoning capability, then a taxonomic classification of kinds of metaphors (such as that produced by Lakoff) is interesting and useful as a data compendium, but does not represent a theory. Only if one wanted (as Lakoff does not) to assert that we have these particular metaphoric templates innately present in our minds would Lakoff's classification have direct theoretical import; in that situation, accounting for the evolution of such templates via natural selection would pose a very challenging biological problem.

Langacker (1987) provides an elaborate and extensively thought-out machinery for describing metaphoric extension (among other things), but he provides no account of why such extension exists or of which pieces of his machinery represent learned cultural knowledge and which reasoned applications of that knowledge. Langacker's machinery—although modern and in many ways interesting—ultimately represents an extreme example of the kind of taxonomic approach to grammar that Chomsky so effectively attacked thirty years ago; it provides a framework in which any conceivable regularity can be described and located without offering processes that constrain possibilities and that might account for which conceivable possibilities actually occur and which do not. I say "interesting" and "extreme," though, because, unlike both Chomsky and the subjects of Chomsky's critique, Langacker (correctly, to my mind) includes cultural knowledge, reasoning, and semantics in his system along with what has more traditionally passed for grammar.

Unlike both Lakoff and Langacker, I analyze the reasoning process by which words are chosen and understood, including the roles played *in semantics* by paradigmatic contrast; by core referents; by denotative, connotative, and metaphoric extension; by our knowledge of the world; and by our suppositions about other people's knowledge. I examine how speakers construct metaphors and how hearers recognize metaphors and infer what the speaker must have meant. I look at our use of language to see what communicative aims and needs are served by this semantic system and to understand why human language so insistently takes a semantic form that seemed so unreasonable to Bertrand Russell. Thus, although I certainly deal with the issue of motivations for disjunction, I still strongly assert that the pressures toward conjunction remain operative, and thus that there are special costs (in terms of cognitive effort) involved in maintaining active disjunctions; in a sense, the problem for evolution was to find a framework or system that enabled natural language to maintain maximal conjunctivity while still being flexible.

Other Issues in Contemporary Semantic Discourse

The present work is explicitly limited to the semantics of words, and so by design it does not treat complex verbal forms or sentences. However, I do point out some of the relevance of my discussion to more complex linguistic (and cognitive) entities. The contrast between grammatical particles and open class terms is not relevant to the present theory, though it obviously exists and is relevant to syntactic theorizing and to the semantic load carried by syntax. The same comment applies to collections versus functionals. Some instances of hedges are extensively discussed in the present work, though not as "hedges" per se; Kay's work on hedges is not treated since I am looking at different issues. Because my concern is with the semantics of words, I do not explicitly go into the issue of pragmatic function, even though, of course, my treatment of communicative use of words deals with many pragmatic issues. The issue of the presuppositions that underlie any discourse event and that underlie the sense in which any words are to be taken in any particular context is basic to the present work, but not treated in any separate theoretical framework.

Psychological Sources

My thinking has been influenced in general ways by a range of recent work in cognitive sciences. In this connection I have in mind, inter alia, work on schema theory (summarized by Schallert 1982; see also Casson 1983); PDP, or parallel distributed processing (see Rumelhart et al. 1986); scripts, plans, and goals (Schank and Abelson 1977); and natural reasoning processes (especially Hutchins 1980, but also the bodies of work by Kahneman and Tversky [see, for example, Kahneman, Slovic, and Tversky 1982] and by Simon, Newell, and others on the General Problem Solver program and related issues [see, for example, Newell and Simon 1972]). My use of this recent cognitive work is, however, only metaphorical, allusive, and suggestive, as is the use made of such material by almost all other anthropologists except Hutchins (1980), and hence unlike the very tight deductive use I make of Miller's work and of Bruner, Goodnow, and Austin's.

There are a couple of reasons for my more rigorous use of the somewhat older psychological work. First, my discussion is not intended as a general overview of new developments or exciting ideas. I am trying to develop a specific theory. If the theory is pertinent to issues of current concern and if it is not superseded by other, perhaps newer work, then my neglect of whatever is momentarily "hot off the press" might perhaps be accepted. The psychological and linguistic work I cite is what is relevant to the argument that I am making—and, if sometimes considered a little passé, has still decidedly not been overturned.

Second, there does exist more recent work that is potentially relevant, but is not yet in an assimilable form. Work on parallel distributed processing will eventually become highly relevant to the issue of socially distributed cognition I am raising (and faulting others for not sufficiently attending to), but work on PDP has not yet been developed to the point that rigorous deductions about cultural systems, of the sort I make from the work of Miller and Bruner et al., can be made. Similarly, formal work with scripts and plans (such as Schank and Abelson 1977) will eventually greatly enrich our understanding of cultural forms (see, for example, Randall 1985), but only when the basic theoretical insight has been sifted from the epiphenomenal effects of current computer hardware and software limitations, and when, furthermore, some problems of scale have been resolved. For example, in a limited universe of discourse (such as that of Schank and Abelson's work) most of the issues that drive research on syntax can be successfully finessed using a combination of keywords and simplifying assumptions; these finesses, however, cannot be generalized to language use in general. Work on reasoning processes such as that already effectively applied in anthropology by Hutchins (1980) promises to greatly advance our understanding of the ways in which cultural knowledge and rules are brought to bear on specific events. But such work requires a much more sophisticated ethnography than we are used to producing or seeing.

I might also point out that, for excellent psychological reasons, it takes much longer for the operational control of new developments in one discipline to filter into related disciplines than it does for the language or jargon in which such developments are expressed to so filter. It takes even longer for arguments and theories developed within one disciplinary conceptual paradigm (or community of discourse) to be sufficiently decoupled from the specifics of that paradigm to be usefully and insightfully applied within another disciplinary paradigm. In particular, it takes some time and effort to understand psychological findings well enough to filter out the artifacts of laboratory situations and theoretical presuppositions from robust empirical findings, and then to figure out the proper application of such findings for natural systems. This problem is particularly acute for gaining useful anthropological inferences from the controlled experimental approach in artificial laboratory situations that characterizes much American psychology, though it is somewhat less so for the more descriptive approach in manipulated natural situations used in the Piagetian paradigm and other American work. The problem, obviously, applies to some degree in any borrowing across disciplinary paradigm lines.

Anthropology is, I think, too often content with only loose and metaphorical use of material from psychology; we in anthropology continually work the latest jargon into our rhetoric without ever actually working through the implications of anything it stands for. In contrast, I have used the psychological findings of Bruner and Miller to construct logically tight inferences about relevant cultural systems. The Miller/Bruner work has important implications for culturally shared knowledge systems, and these implications have not heretofore been worked out (outside of the one specific Nerlove and Romney example, which is part of the argument I refer to in chapter 6). I think it better to draw real (and new) conclusions from somewhat older psychology than to recast, merely rhetorically, old conclusions in the latest psychological phrasing.

Some Thoughts on the Current Moment

While well aware of the limitations and narrowness of the old ethnoscience/cognitive anthropology paradigm, I do value its advances and see those advances as well worth building upon. I also share with my ethnoscience teachers of the 1960s the goal of producing descriptions, analyses, and theories that meet the canons of ordinary science—that is, that are explicit, formal, and logically susceptible to disconfirmation. The elite view in anthropology today is based much more on the kind of concern with indeterminacy and subjectivity that characterizes the current universe of literary criticism. While valuable insights have been contributed to anthropology by those with such interests, and while I welcome the presence in anthropology of such a position, it is not mine. As Eco (1990:666) suggests, even in the humanistic world of criticism, the impossibility of reaching conclusions now seems to have been overstated. I feel that the future development of anthropology lies not just on the side of traditional scholarly concerns with fidelity of representation and understanding, but even more on the kind of precision and generalization embodied in science—even if the specific topics and techniques that fall under the science label have changed and will change. Tomorrow's cognitive anthropology will be effectively integrated with the other cognitive sciences, will contribute in a leading way to the understanding of socially distributed cognition, and will be clearly within the scientific mainstream—and will solve many of the theoretical problems that have long vexed anthropology. I see the present volume as building toward that future.

Notes

1. In ordinary human behavior we usually treat language as if it were a transparent medium. Thus, we normally do not distinguish in our long-term memory and understanding between what we see ourselves and what we have been told—unless we make some special effort either as an individual or as a culture/language to mark the difference. Language itself is part of our "natural" world. Hence, for us as native speakers of a language, "dog" (or "chien" or "perro") is as intrinsic a part of a dog as its legs, snout, and so forth. The fact that "they" call the dog "perro" (or "dog" or "chien") is acceptable, because that is their equivalent (their word for the nominal property)—the animal is still, for us, a "dog." On the other hand, to call it "cat," another word in our own language that labels another kind of animal, is not merely confusing for us, but almost inconceivable.

As for the situation presented in Buchowski et al. (1994:570–571), possibly some of this "intrinsic-ness" is a function of when, in our language-learning process, we learn the terms in question. Labels learned later, after we have formed our individual internal representation of *langue*, may be felt as less intrinsic and more a matter of convention than those learned before forming that representation (and which thus contribute to the forming of that representation). In that article, we do talk of a situation (regarding "freedom" vs. "democracy") where the time and manner of learning seem to make a difference.

The fact that the mechanics of our use of language are usually subconscious and automatic—subconscious as they must be if we are to be able to focus our conscious attention on *what* we are trying to say, and automatic if we are to be able to construct the message in any reasonable time frame—contribute to this feeling of transparency.

The transparency issue was what was involved in Saussure's insight that language is not a nomenclature (that is, a simple labeling of already existent things, whether the things be in the world or in the mind). Our normal use of language as a tool for communication is facilitated by the fact that its use is automatic and outside our focus of conscious attention—we want to be able to focus on the content of what we are saying, and not on the medium. But on occasion this apparent transparency can mislead us into confounding our actual thought with the medium we use to convey that thought. Atran, for instance, sometimes writes as if categories of language were to be taken automatically as categories of thought (for example, 1990:5–6, 33) . Such an assumption of isomorphism misses the complex, though subconscious, situational and contextual reasoning that goes into our actual communicative use of words.

Kronenfeld 1975 demonstrated a clear *lack* of isomorphism between kinterm categories (linguistic categorizations of thought) and the categories of thought implicit in behavior among kinsmen. That demonstration is enough to rule out any automatic, Whorfian equation of thought with language. Linguistic categories are categories of thought, but they are not the only such categories, and they are not necessarily the ones we use in reasoning about the world we live in.

2. I agree with what Keller and Lehman (1991:281n. 10) say regarding "problems connected . . . with collapsing the distinction between encyclopedic knowledge and lexico-semantic representations. . . . We need a finite version of lexico-semantic meaning as an account of the linguistic/lexical coding of understanding. This is consistent with the program of embedding linguistic knowledge within a broader theory of cognition and is important for that part of the program intended to overcome the not uncommon tendency for extension of linguistic semantics to cover all of cognition."

3. The example in Kronenfeld 1991 (pp. 24–25) involves alternative ways of distinguishing siblings by sex. The difference is between English, where separate "brother" and "sister" terms are used; Spanish, where a single "herman-" term is used with obligatory grammatical gender-inflectional endings; and Fanti, where a single "nua" term is used with optional general-purpose male or female adjective modifiers as needed. In the article I discuss the cultural and communicative rationale for treating these alternative approaches as comparable, and I show how they are comparable in usage.

4. We can see this looseness of the language-thought fit in the way we—including authors who take language as directly representing thought—fish for paraphrases and modifiers to convey some concept that our basic phrasing does not quite capture. This common experience implies that we have some thoughts we are unable to directly capture in our language, and thus that our store of concepts is not limited to those in our language. It also implies that while our language may bias our thought it does not imprison it.

5. Atran writes as if he does not expect general cognitive processes to produce any kinds of structures or events that are not immediately built into them, and thus that there must exist in our human cognitive base (or in our repertoire of cultural processes) some special, bounded and specific piece designed to accomplish the specific processes those structures describe. He does not appear to give much attention to the kind of view most elaborately worked out by Piaget but also clearly present in Bateson's work within anthropology: that relatively simple cognitive structures can, through recursion, metalearning, feedback loops with the environment, and feedback loops with other individuals produce fairly rapidly stable and cross-culturally consistent cognitive structures that are in no direct sense built into the cognitive machinery.

Approaches like Atran's appear to ascribe to our species a number (potentially, a large number) of detailed, species-specific cognitive and perceptual "mental organs," to borrow Chomsky's old phrase (1975:23). The approach solves the problem of how people learn all the complicated material and actions the author in question is discussing by saying people do *not* learn it, that they just are born knowing it. It solves the learning problem, though, at the cost of creating an even worse phylogenetic problem: the objection Piaget raised regarding Chomsky's innatism claims (Piaget 1970:12), that is, that there is simply not enough phylogenetic time/distance between us and our nearest phylogenetic relatives for us to have developed such complexity totally since our split from these relatives. Thus, the genetic (or biologically given) component of the relevant differences between us and those phylogenetic neighbors must be much smaller than asserted, and the remainder of the differences attributable either to general cognitive functioning or to biological structures that are phylogenetically broader and deeper in time than implied by a purely hominid limitation. If relevant structures (or significant components of relevant structures) are pre-hominid, then they must be preverbal (or nonverbal)—which would require that they be drastically recast from the very linguistic form they are given by the indicated scholars.

My own sense (cf. Kronenfeld 1979:219–227) is that both conditions are likely to obtain; that is, that significant parts of the structures cognitive anthropologists and linguists find are likely to derive from general cognitive functioning, and that significant elements are also likely to represent wider primate or mammalian activities to which the only distinctly human addition has been to bring them into language (that is, to allow them to receive names and to be reasoned about within the linguistic sign system).

But I also want to point out that no one has seriously examined within this cultural/semantic context the potentialities of feedback models of the sort proposed by Piaget and Bateson for structuring the human cognitive base; we don't know how many of the various kinds of problems we are talking about can be handled by such models and how many cannot. I know of no way to make such an evaluation by direct reasoning, but instead would suggest that simulations (normally by computer) provide the most fruitful currently available approach to assessing the potentialities and plausibilities of such models.

6. Current research in the cultural models area seems concentrated on describing specific structures and people's use of them in reasoning about behavior. The latter goal concerning reasoning seems to be well addressed; the former goal of describing structure seems still, by and large, at the rough-sketch level. My guess is that good descriptions of such structures will require an improved set of conceptual tools such as the concepts and variables of Hutchins (1980) or the very different ones of Schank and Abelson (1977). Such improvement will also involve, as we can see in the Hutchins and Schank and Abelson examples, the breaking apart of the research problem into on the one hand the understanding of the general processes involved, and on the other hand the discovery of what it is in particular that elicits the particular cultural structures under discussion and maintains their uniformity.

Relevant work in cognitive sciences, such as that of Schank and Abelson (1977) and Rumelhart et al. (1986), although read, cited, and used by cognitive anthropologists as a source of ideas, seems to have been dismissed too quickly as a serious source of specific insights into the structure of knowledge systems or the specific theoretical concepts needed for the description or modeling of such systems.

In other words, for example, when the limitations of Schank and Abelson's specific set of concepts and associated programs were perceived, the response was often to compare Schank and Abelson's model with a hypothetical model created so as not to have those problems, to then find Schank and Abelson's model wanting, and to move on to a discussion of the hypothetical model as if it had won the day (cf. Quinn and Holland 1987:22). No attempt was made to construct improved implementations of Schank and Abelson's concepts or to improve on their set of concepts. The problem with the hypothetical alternative model was that it had been neither constructed nor tried out; one had no assurance such a model could be built or that, if constructed, it would do what was claimed for it. The problem with this approach was that it gave up on what Schank and Abelson's impressive simulation had gained rather than attempting to use new insights concerning areas in which Schank and Abelson had failed to suggest improvements in their work or their technical apparatus.

The Schank and Abelson example is of special interest regarding the kind of "reaches" that anthropologists will have to make if we are to make effective use of work from cognitive sciences. The tasks Schank and Abelson set their programs regarding restaurant visits and storytelling are important, but limited. Nonetheless, I am most impressed with what their programs have accomplished. Their concrete procedures do the jobs at hand quite well. The kinds of units that they have had to introduce into their programs, the kinds of ways they have had to organize the use of these units in operations, and the kind of operations they have needed are all interesting and revelatory, offering important insights not just into how to write such a program, but also into the problems with which our human capabilities must deal. On the other hand, as with any model, they take many shortcuts (compared with what we humans do), they dichotomize what seem likely to be (in our human usage) continua (such as the central contrast between script and plan), and they use much more carefully selected and restricted situations than we normally encounter in real life. What these reservations mean is that we cannot simply take their procedures as any kind of direct representation of human thought or of the procedures involved in our thought; we have instead to factor their findings in with other things we know about our processes—even if many of these other things are ones which no one has yet managed to computationally model. Such a caveat would seem obvious, except that in chapter 9 Schank makes the very attempt I am warning against in interpreting a conversation with his daughter as if all she knew or thought was what was in his program, and thus well illustrates the problems that inhere in such a simple and direct extension from the computer program to people.

Schank's error is a shame, because it skews attention (in anthropology, at least) away from what he and Abelson have accomplished, and away from what they have found out about human information processing—and directs such attention to the ways in which their model of human thought is still inadequate.

Nevertheless, finding failures and limitations is easy; no such model has yet come remotely close to general human capabilities. What one wants to do is to try to understand the elements of the model that account for its successes and those that account for its failures, and then move on to build on the one while eliminating the other. When it comes to this process of analysis and improvement, I might add, the creator has no privileged position; Schank is just another commentator when he starts discussing the application of his model's insights to human behavior (as in chapter 9's analysis of his daughter's conversation). The model is not responsible for whatever flights of fancy its author may embark on, or for any failure he may show in his understanding of what humans actually do.

Ideally, improvements should be cast in the form of improved simulations, but that takes a combination of skills, time, and resources most of us lack. Hutchins's example (1980) eloquently illustrates the analytic benefits that can come from actually carrying out such an effort for an anthropological problem. A less satisfactory but still worthwhile response is to make a serious attempt to deal analytically with the elements of the model discussed. An example of what I mean by such a process of building on concrete analytic devices rather than simply taking them or leaving them (though the example does not involve any simulation) can be seen in the present volume in the use I have made of George Miller's and Jerome Bruner's work on human information processing limitations.

7. Holland and Skinner (1987:85), following Neisser (1976), define cultural models as "mental representations or schemas" that "actively guide attention to components of the world and provide inferences about these components and their various states and form a framework for remembering, reconstructing, and describing experiences." Thus, they do not distinguish

cultural models from schemas, and do not deal with the problem of relating collective representations to individual knowledge. Holland (1992:86n. 4) speaks of "cultural models" as "shared, conventional ideas about how the world works. . . . Defined cognitively, cultural models consist of 'schemas' that guide attention to, draw[] inferences about, and evaluat[e] . . . experience."

D'Andrade for example, takes schemas as simple but hierarchically structured scenarios (meeting the Miller 1956 constraints) involving roles and actions, each of which can itself be decomposable into a further schema (following Rumelhart 1980 and Fillmore 1977). He takes sharing and known sharing (where everybody knows [something], and everybody knows that everybody knows [something] 1987:113) of some schema as the criterion for a cultural model (1987:112). He uses known sharing to explain why much information in people's references to their culture's folk models can be left implicit; this is his version of what I sometimes will refer to as relying on context. And he uses that sharing to explain why interpretations made on the basis of the model are treated as obvious facts about the world. However, he does not offer any view of how these shared schemas are created, learned, and kept linked from one person to the other, and he offers no mechanism by which individual versions might evolve with experience or changed circumstances or by which the shared version might change over time. His structures are rich and complex, but also fixed and static.

Elsewhere (1992a:29) he offers a variant definition: "A schema is an interpretation which is frequent, well organized, memorable, which can be made from minimal cues, contains one or more prototypic instantiations, is resistant to change, etc. While it would be more accurate to speak always of *interpretations with such and such a degree of schematicity*, the convention of calling highly schematic interpretations schemas remains in effect in the cognitive literature." He speaks in this essay of "cultural models" as equivalent to "cultural schemas," which make up "a very important subset" of the schemas an individual learns (p. 34). He talks of how individuals internalize cultural norms, but does not deal with how these collective representations arise or are shaped by the situations people in a culture encounter.

Strauss (1992b:197) cites Casson's (1983:430) characterization of schemas as "conceptual abstractions that mediate between stimuli received by the sense organs and behavioral responses," and Rumelhart's (1980:34) characterization of a schema as "a data structure for representing the generic concepts stored in memory" where "all knowledge is packaged into units," or the schemas, and where the units contain not just knowledge itself but "information about how this knowledge is to be used." Strauss herself speaks of "cultural models" as "culturally formed cognitive schemas" (1992a:3) and "schemas [as] learned, internalized patterns of thought-feeling that mediate both the interpretation of on-going experience and the reconstruction of memories."

8. I think that the distinction in the cultural models literature between schemas of words and schemas of images (as in Lakoff's 1984 distinction between "propositional models and image-schematic models" and in Quinn and Holland's 1987:25 development of Lakoff's distinction) is sometimes overdrawn. While we do indeed have some explicitly verbal machinery (such as aphorisms and a few explicit propositions), my sense is that in our internal coding of individual knowledge (including cultural knowledge) we do mostly not keep track of whether any particular bit of knowledge came in via an account (words) we heard, scenes we actually saw, or actions we participated in—unless we make use of some explicit individual or cultural/grammatical device for marking verbal reports. Instead, I suggest, we normally treat language as if it were a transparent medium and code verbal reports of something as if they were the thing itself.

My sense is that schemas in general (leaving out specifically linguistic ones, but see the further argument below)—those schemas by which we know and act on the world (whether the relevant "world" be material or social, natural or created)—are not particularly (or especially) verbal. We do seem able to use both nonverbal generalizations (gestalts) and verbal generalizations (from word combinations) in our creation of functional schemas for sets of signifieds.

Elsewhere I accept the Piagetian understanding that our actual knowledge is always rooted in action, and can never be simply passively acquired either by observing others do "it" or by having others explain "it" to us. Two conclusions follow from the combination of this Piagetian understanding of knowledge with the preceding comments about verbally learned information. First, much of what we feel we know turns out not to be knowledge (in the action sense) when we are placed in the situation of having to concretely implement that knowledge. Second, the actual knowledge we gain through much of our linguistically mediated cultural interaction is not knowledge of how to do something but rather knowledge of how to talk about that something as if we could do it. That is, we learn the behavior we participate in—talking—and we lose any direct sense of the relationship between what we can talk about and what we can actually do (or see or experience in some other way). One might note, of course, that much of what is interesting in culture seems to develop in this gap between talking and experiencing.

Even those schemas that include signifieds and the referents of words seem often to be more a gestalt or some nonverbal sense or picture than any kind of word game. That is, as children we learn a specific use for a word, then try to generalize it—by leaping to some salient feature along which to extend it, and then by using (negative) feedback either to make minor adjustments or as a sign that we need to make a different leap. When the feedback is cleanly positive, then the representation we have in place is the one we use—in that context or at that level. There are two points that follow from this. (1) Relatively rarely used schemas may not get enough feedback to lead us totally to match them to forms already present in the community; in such areas of thought (or language or culture), and where there exists no other device to produce uniformity, one would expect a far less clear cultural or linguistic consensus about the concept (or the term or cultural entity to which the concept links) in question than one would expect for more frequently used ones. (2) The agreement-producing mechanism only affects the aspects of concepts that do participate in such feedback; we get more agreement on how to talk about angels or unicorns than we do on how to picture their digestive tracts.

9. Related to the problem of relationship of the individual to the cultural model is the question of the nature of the model itself. Sometimes one gets the impression that some of the cultural models theorists (cf. Quinn and Holland 1987:25–26, Strauss 1992b:199,217) are asserting that each different kind of learning or motivational problem requires its own (and, hence, new) kind of cognitive structure. These special-purpose structures are at the same time presumed to be uniformly shared within a culture. Thus, people do not have to learn how to handle situations or evolve their cognitive structures for doing so; the culture provides them with this information in a prepackaged form. The problem is not with the idea of culturally standardized or packaged knowledge, but with the apparently posited level of detail and specificity. To the degree that the models are felt to be innate, then we are back to the biological problem of phylogenetic time discussed relative to Atran's work. Insofar as the models are learned, then we have to consider how. If they are learned as complete, concrete packages, then we have the ontogenic problem that led to Chomsky's innatism claims: How are such complex structures so uniformly learned in such a short time with so little actual teaching? The answer has to be some recourse to general purpose learning and knowledge in culturally repeated, shared contexts either of action or communication that are uniform enough to produce the cultural regularities and the native sense that these are culturally shared structures.

10. Wierzbicka's sets of defining statements for concepts are, logically, equivalent to feature definitions, even if she puts some special (and reasonable) constraints on the nature of those features.

11. In discussing what various "games" might have or not have in common, Wittgenstein (1953:31e–32e) winds up with the following:

67. I can think of no better expression to characterize these similarities than "family resemblances"; for the various resemblances between members of a family: build, features, colour of eyes, gait, temperament, etc. etc. overlap and criss-cross in the same way.—And I shall say: 'games' form a family.

3

Saussurean Roots, Structural Linguistics, and Basic Concepts

This volume takes a Saussurean approach to language and meaning in language. Our first task will be briefly to examine Saussure's work in order to see what we mean by a Saussurean approach and why such an approach is useful and desirable. Next we will, again briefly, examine the two schools of structural linguistics, Praguean and Bloomfieldian, on which the ethnoscience tradition in anthropology directly drew.

Saussure

Langue and Parole

We begin our consideration of this volume's Saussurean underpinnings with Saussure's original conception of the opposition between *langue* and *parole*—or, language and speech. *Langue* refers to the common system of expectations that we all share, and that we each induce from the practice of our speech community when we learn to speak. Langue is analogous to a code as opposed to a message (though it differs in significant ways from "artificial" codes such as computer languages or Morse Code[1]). In the Saussurean system, native speakers' knowledge of langue is similar to what Chomsky later called "competence" (with the reservation that Chomsky defines as intrinsic to this system certain syntactic operations (1965: 4, 1964: 59–60), that Saussure did not know existed). *Parole* (cf. Chomsky's "performance") refers to actual messages that we individually and uniquely construct on the basis of the regularities (or code) provided by langue, joined with various other code-like systems (which Saussure did not name, but which presumably include social class markers, situation markers, and so forth), various communicative intents,[2] and chance factors.

The contrast between langue and parole, then, is not a symmetric one between one system and another, but is an asymmetric one between a system in isolation and the concrete situation in that system is instantiated and interacts with other systems. The asymmetry explains why various calls for a theory of parole, or speech, comparable to a theory of langue (e.g. Bourdieu 1977) are misguided; the rules of langue are the axioms that generate a system, while the "rules" of parole are the devices by which

31

the products of different systems are combined with each other and adapted to whatever situational constraints exist.

Saussure was at one with Durkheim[3] regarding the *collective* and *passive* nature of the sign. Language was, for Durkheim, the example par excellence of a collective representation (Durkheim 1938:2–8; cf. Meillet 1904–05:1–2). In Saussure's formulations it was a human creation that any single human was nonetheless powerless to change. Saussure's strong assertion of the collective, social nature of language[4] was basic to his conception of the science of linguistics (Ardener 1971:xxxiv)—though not to his more general postulated science of semiology, which, in dealing with motivated as well as unmotivated symbols, would necessarily have had to encompass individual as well as collective representations. Saussure made clear that langue is intrinsically social,[5] inhering not in individual users but in communities. This assertion does not entail any mystical claim about any group mind; it only means that the term langue (that is, "language") and the theoretical concept to which it refers are restricted to those parts of individuals' linguistic knowledge that are shared generally by other members of their speech communities. Langue is a collective phenomenon that only exists in the shared understandings that enable communication to take place. It follows that we, either as linguists studying language or as children learning our native language, have no direct access to language (langue), but can only induce representations of it from the samples of speech behavior (parole) to which we are exposed. Each individual also induces or creates additional, idiosyncratic linguistic knowledge that forms part of only that person's personal instantiation of language (his or her own individual *representation* of langue) and that enters into only that person's speech performances (parole); on the other hand, any particular piece of language (langue) may not necessarily be shared by *all members of the speech community in question.*

Saussure emphasized the passive nature of language (langue) as opposed to the active nature of speech (parole). What he meant is that we create speech acts. In them we produce novel combinations of shared elements and sometimes even include some novel elements. But in order for these freshly and actively created speech acts to communicate to others they must be understood. To be understood, they must be constructed out of known, and thus shared, elements—or provide enough redundancy and context for the meaning of novel elements to be inferred. The linguistic part of what enables this understanding is language: the regularities of pattern and reference that we have experienced in (and induced from) our speech community. Language is passive, in one sense, because we form it by taking the regularities we are given, rather than by seeking out the regularities we might want. But, more important, it is passive because it depends not on the regularities that any particular one of us, may experience, whether actively or passively, but on the regularities that happen to have been felt by enough of us to be shared by our speech community (as well as on the commonalities of the innate perceptive and cognitive apparatus we use to experience these regularities and to reason from them).

The passive and collective nature of langue has important consequences for language change. Langue is never experienced directly, but only indirectly through the vehicle of acts of parole. It therefore is not taught directly to new generations of speakers, but rather is induced anew from parole by each new generation. It is thus a distillation of (and abstraction from) regularities experienced across the wide range of speech that the learner encounters. Individuals are powerless to change langue (its subconscious nature makes it largely immune to effective political manipulation), but the cumulative (statistical) effect of a large number of parallel individual creations is to change the sample of events that one generation experiences from that experienced by the preceding generation, and thus to change the langue that generation induces from the langue of the previous generation. If enough new members of a community are exposed to the same new speech situation, and if enough of them make similar inferences from it, then the new regularities they infer from that new situation will be shared widely enough to become part of their language. Similarly, old regularities of speech, which had been incorporated into the language but subsequently drop out of use, cease to be experienced by new members, and thus cease to form part of the representation of the language that these new members induce; when enough members lacking the features in question have entered the community, the features then cease being part of the language. It is this (what we might call) "sampling shift" that accounts for *linguistic drift*, and thus for the changes over time that give us language shifts and the family trees of diachronic (or historical) linguistics.

Our experiences now, unlike many people's experiences over much of the past, include written as well as verbal stimuli and products of mass media as well as of conversations within our local communities. These changes expand the range of sources from which we can induce regularities, and tend to retard the loss of some old regularities as well as to speed the spread of some innovations. However, they do not affect the nature of our induction of our individual representation of language, nor do they change the definition of language as that which is shared among our individual representations.[6]

We each participate in various alternative speech communities, and thus in groups in which slightly variant forms of language inhere. A "speech community" is accidental and incidental in the same way language is; it is a set of people who share enough speech experience to induce common regularities, whether or not they see themselves as a community, meet all together at one time, like one another, and so forth.

Signs: Signifiers and Signifieds

The key unit of langue is the sign, or the union of a "signifier" and a "signified." Related concepts from various vocabularies include word, morpheme, lexeme, and segregate. The signifier is the "sound image"—that is, the sequence of phonemes— that represents the phonic substance of the sign, and the signified is the concept referred to by the sign. Because sound itself is a continuum that we segment and make into discrete units as we hear it, we understand that the signifier is not the physical sound itself, but instead is our mental image of that sound (e.g., of the phoneme sequence /tri/). Similarly, the signified is not some entity (e.g., some tree) that exists outside of us, but is instead the mental concept by which we represent that entity. The sign is, thus, a totally mental or conceptual entity.[7]

Neither a signifier nor a signified (linguistic concept) has any linguistic significance without the other; they only become part of language when a signifier (sound image) is differentiated from other signifiers in the system of the language (see the next section of this chapter) by its isolating a signified that is then, and thereby, differentiated from other signifieds. A signifier is only a signifier if it signifies something (without signification, a phoneme sequence is only a nonsense syllable or syllables), and a concept (or a potential signified) is only a part of language if it is signified by something. By their linkage to each other, each signifier-and-signified pairing is given an existence in the system, and contrasted with the other linked signifiers and signifieds of the system. Sound images, in turn, point out of language to actual phonic substance, and concepts point, at least most often, to the external, pragmatic world of experience.

In terms of the system, neither signs nor their signifiers and signifieds exist in isolation from other signs. Signifiers exist only in opposition (contrast) to other signifiers; that is, /p/ does not signify by itself, but only by contrast with /b/, /m/, and so forth (for instance, as English speakers hearing the Polynesian l/r, we do not determine what actual sound was made, but instead decide only to which member of the relevant English opposition, l vs. r, it is to be assigned). Similarly, signifieds only exist in opposition (or contrast) to other signifieds; *tree* contrasts with *bush* and so, again as speakers and hearers, we decide, not what the ambiguous object in front of us is on its own, but rather only to which of the pre-existing opposed categories it is to be assigned. In this sense one might think of the content of linguistic categories as relative rather than absolute, though Saussure knew (and we shall see) that they have absolute aspects as well.

Individual signs thus participate in a variety of relationships. Regarding the elements of the individual sign,

> There are three relationships that can be more or less independently investigated: (1) the relationship of sound to sound-image (signifier); (2) the relationship of signifier to signified; and (3) the relationship of concept (signified) to external referent. At one step further removed we have the relations of signs to one another: (4) the syntagmatic relations by which signs are combined with one another to make larger linguistic units; and (5) the paradigmatic relations of contrast that exist among alternative signs (and sets of signs). We have (6) the relationship between the representation of signs (or other linguistic phenomena) in one head and in another head; this relationship is by definition constrained for true signs in langue, but is more fully investigable in parole and among other semiological phenomena such as symbols. Finally, if at more remove, a Saussurean view of the function of sign systems would entail a consideration of the syntagmatic relations existing between the concepts entailed in a given sign system and other, pragmatic, concepts and a similar consideration of paradigmatic relations among alternative sign systems and among alternative pragmatic possibilities. (Kronenfeld and Decker 1979:511)

One of the senses in which the theory I am presenting is Saussurean is in its reliance on this analytic framework.[8] In the present volume we will be concerned primarily with relationships 2 (signifier to signified), 3 (signified to external referent), and 5 (paradigmatic relations among signs). Throughout the volume will be periodic discussion of relationship 6 (the relation of representations in one head to those in another). In chapter 8 we will briefly consider some of the ways in which our cognitive insights might apply to relationship 4 (syntagmatic relations by which signs are combined into larger linguistic units).

Langue as a System

For Saussure, langue is not a happenstantial collection of isolated signs but is instead a *system* of signs. Because it is a system, changes in one area have ramifications throughout the rest of langue (even if each separate element doesn't *directly* affect every other element). Signs relate to each other in two general kinds of ways: *syntagmatically* and *paradigmatically*. Syntagmatic relations are ones of co-occurrence—of what goes with what, and how. Rules of syntax provide one example of a kind of syntagmatic relationship. Since spoken language (and its written representation) is linear, syntagmatic relationships in language tend to be sequential; but in other kinds of language, such as the sign languages of the deaf, that are not linear, syntagmatic relations can be spatial.

Since we are concentrating on word meanings, and since we are not attending to any particular syntactic theory by which words might be concatenated into sentences, we are not in a position to look much at syntagmatic relations among words or at syntagmatic semantic structures. Our concentration, thus, will be on paradigmatic structures, though we will in chapter 8 point a little to how some of the same cognitive processes involved in certain paradigmatic structures may also explain some aspects of syntactic structures.

> Paradigmatic relations . . . are [those] . . . which obtain among alternative possible fillers of some position in a syntagmatic chain (or fabric) and among the alternative forms that some particular filler might take in alternative positions (Saussure 1959, pp. 125–126, 128–131). Such relations in language can be phonological (spot vs. spit), morphological (run vs. ran), syntactic (brought vs. had brought), semantic (hit the ball vs. catch the ball). or other (e.g. sociolinguistic; yes ma'am vs. yeah). For semiological systems in general, paradigmatic relations are those which we isolate when we ask "X as opposed to what?" . . . these relations are important because they represent all the non-present associations (or planes of contrast) which the use of some particular form raises or potentially can raise; it is through this aspect of the systematicity (cf. Saussure 1959, pp. 113-117) of language that a change in one place (e.g. the addition of "pork" to English along side of "pig") affects the whole system of a language (the meaning of "pig" in opposition to "pork" is notably different from the meaning of "pig" in opposition to "cow," "sheep," etc.; the meaning of syntagmatic units that include "pig" is also thereby affected). (Kronenfeld and Decker 1979:509)

Paradigmatic relations, thus, are ones of contrast or opposition—the relationship among entities in a set (or paradigm) from which one makes a selection at some particular point in a speech production (or a syntagm). We will consider examples of phonological and morphological paradigms shortly, in our consideration of Praguean componential analyses. Elm, oak, beech, birch, and so forth represent a paradigm of tree species; love, hate, respect, detestation, and so forth a paradigm of emotional responses.

Before progressing we should remind ourselves of the different senses in which we are using the term "paradigmatic." First, at the most general *linguistic* level (the level we have just been using), it is the term Saussure used to label relations among the alternative items within the set from which a given item was selected at a given point in a given act of *parole*. Paradigmatic relations thus taken include phonological, morphological, syntactic, and semantic contrast and similarity (including inclusion, superclasses, and subclasses). Second and more specifically, in linguistics, the term has been used to refer to structures of contrasting items formed by the intersection of two or more defining features. This usage developed out of the inflectional paradigms used in teaching the grammar of classical languages, where noun endings, for instance, could differ according to case and number. Phonological, morphological, and syntactic examples of such structures in which items contrast on a set of intersecting features are presented elsewhere in this chapter. It is in regard to this second sense that we have spoken of componential paradigms, and will continue to do so. Third, a more general usage than Saussure's made popular some years back by Thomas Kuhn (1962) uses "paradigm" and "paradigmatic" to refer to the shared rules of the game and shared presumptions (theoretical framework, important questions, needed data, relevant data, and so forth) that underlie the everyday practice of science—and that are overturned in a scientific revolution. In this usage, "paradigm" carries the sense of a canonical framework, and one may speak of the Bloomfieldian paradigm in American linguistics having been supplanted by the Chomskyian.

Arbitrariness

Saussure's name is often associated with the idea of the arbitrariness of linguistic relations. He clearly considered that all of langue was socially constrained or motivated. But he did assert that there was, in general, *nothing* about the *substance* of any particular signifier that caused it to be linked its particular signified; the linkage of /tri/ to *tree* was, in that sense, arbitrary. The kinds of sound symbolism investigated by Jakobson[9] vitiate this claim a little, but only for a very few vocabulary items and only in minor ways that have no general relevance to the system of language. Saussure also treated the relationship of signifiers to actual sounds as arbitrary, but in a less radical way: our languages do not group sounds into phonemes arbitrarily or randomly (in terms of their physical substance), but our languages do arbitrarily decide where to segment natural continua—for example, whether $[t^{alveolar}]$ and $[t^{palatal}]$ are to be in the same category or in contrasting categories. Similarly, the boundaries of our signifieds/concepts are arbitrary, as are aspects of their paradigmatic and syntagmatic relationships; the line between *tree* and *bush* in English is a little different from the comparable line in French, and our English associations with *father* are a little different from Fanti associations with their translation equivalent, *egya*.[10] The issue here is one we will return to later, in our discussion of "natural conventions."

Words in Semiology

Because it is focused on the sign, Saussure's linguistics is therefore one that deals directly and firmly with meaning, as opposed to a linguistics concerned primarily with the structure of signifiers, and thus focused on phonology, syntax, or some other aspect of the formation of simple or complex signifiers.[11] For Saussure the central topic of linguistics was the sign, a word-like unit that was from one perspective a sound image and from the other perspective a concept. Linguistics dealt first of all with the relationship between signifier and signified—with semantics. The study of the paradigmatic relations by which signs contrasted with one another and the syntagmatic patterns by which they were concatenated came only secondarily, within the context of that primary concern with the sign; in the *Course* . . . (Saussure 1959:122–131, esp. 126,130) it is clear that syntagmatic and paradigmatic relations refer as much to conceptual relations as to grammatical relations.

It is for these Saussurean reasons, among others, that I feel a theory of word meaning represents a basic and important contribution to linguistics (as much as to anthropology) and that such a theory is best stated independently of any particular theoretical work on signifiers or their structure. Saussure's insistence that both signifiers (sound images) and signifieds (concepts) were mental constructs, and his reasons for that insistence, explain why I am treating word meanings as a special instance of cognitive structures; there exists at least a sense in which the emerging field of cognitive sciences represents something closer to Saussure's projected science of semiology than do any of the more particular studies offered lately under the name of semiology.

Referents and Signifieds: My Usage

In the remainder of this volume I shall, unless I clearly indicate otherwise, refer to signifieds[12] (Saussurean conceptual referents internal to signs) as "signifieds," and to the substantive objects or actions outside of signs to which the signifieds "point" (or, in the case of nonexistent things such as unicorns, purport to point) as the "referents" of those signs. I adopt this usage for the sake of consistency with the sources I will be discussing and to avoid overly ponderous locutions, but I do want to warn readers against the danger it poses—of allowing one to slide too easily back into confounding the relationship between signifiers and signifieds with that between words (signs) and things (nonlinguistic phenomena) or with that between (external) sounds and (external) things.

Prague Componential Analysis versus American Descriptive Models

American Descriptive Linguistics

In Bloomfieldian or American descriptive linguistics, phone types were grouped (as allophones) into phonemes via free variation and conditioned alternation. Phone types were assigned to contrasting phonemes via minimal pairs. An example of conditioned alternation is provided by the patterning of aspiration of stops such as /t/ in English:

$\{[t],[t']\}$ = /t/, where [t] follows /s/ and [t'] occurs in other environments.

Free variation can be seen in the point of articulation of /t/ in English:

$\{[t^{dent}],[t^{alv}],[t^{pal}]\}$ = /t/

Phonemic contrast is illustrated by the role of voicing in English in distinguishing /t/ from /d/:

$\{[t],\ldots\}$ = /t/; $\{[d],\ldots\}$ = /d/

The same idea was applied to morphs and morphemes. Morphs were constructed out of sequences of phonemes, and grouped (as allomorphs) into morphemes. For example, the /s/ of "cats," the /z/ of "dogs," and the /ez/ of "bitches" are grouped together as allomorphs of the plural morpheme in English. In this example, we have phonologically conditioned allomorphs. With "is" and "was," we have free alternatives (even after we parcel out whatever we want to label as the tense marker). Debates about the nature of descriptions of syntagmatic constructions arose in connection with issues such as the phonological instantiation of the tense marker in such irregular verbs.

Words were constructed of one or more morphemes. Bloomfieldian descriptions typically were concerned heavily with phonology and with major inflectional classes (morphology). They contained only minimal syntactic information.

The major thrust of Bloomfieldian linguistics was descriptive; that is, linguists were primarily concerned with developing a metalanguage and a methodology that would enable them to easily and consistently describe previously unknown languages in ways that facilitated later comparison. This approach stemmed, at least in part, from the language situation in America, in which there existed a great number of American Indian languages that seemed on the verge of extinction. The immediate, primary enterprise was seen as a kind of salvage linguistics.

In their methodology, Bloomfieldians looked for *minimal pairs*, which were used to identify phonemes; then they found *frames* within which *substitution classes* could appear. So /b_t/ is a frame in English which isolates /i/, /a/, /ai/, /u/, /"uh"/, and so forth. Similarly, for morphology, in English /walk_ / isolates /0/, /s/, /d/, /ing/, and so forth. Thus, in English syntax, "The man hit the ball" yields a variety of frames:

The man hit the _____.
The man hit _____.
The _____ hit the ball.
_____ hit the ball.
The man _____ the ball.
(Etc.)

The man hit the _____
ball, puck, bag . . .
man, bull, dog . . .
big ball, big bad ball, ball that the pitcher threw.

From these kinds of patterns were induced word classes (noun, verb, etc.), types of members of classes (animate, inanimate, and human *nouns*, etc.), types of phrases (noun phrase, etc.), clauses, and the like.

Chomsky has since shown the impossibility of a completely automatic discovery procedure (that is, an algorithm that would automatically and mechanically make the indicated inductions), but the descriptive procedures worked out by the Bloomfieldians were quite good as heuristics, and provide the basis for all modern work on the description of unknown languages, especially where sensitive translation is a goal (for example, for Bible translators). These descriptive procedures have also provided the model for the frame elicitation techniques of ethnoscience (see Black and Metzger 1965 and Frake 1964).

Prague Componential Analysis

European structural linguistics was much more analytically (as opposed to descriptively) oriented compared to the American descriptive linguistics discussed in the previous section. The languages it dealt with were mostly known ones, for which basic description was not an issue. It was much more concerned with finding elegant analyses that revealed underlying regularities.

Before turning to Praguean componential analysis, let us summarize the ways in which Prague School structuralism differed from Saussurean.

First, the Prague theorists placed much less emphasis on the sign itself (the unit of signifier/signified) or on relations among signs, and instead concentrated on the contrastive and sequential (paradigmatic and syntagmatic) relations of signifier to signifier,[13] and on the basic elements—distinctive features that tend to be binary—out of which signifiers are built (cf. Jakobson 1971:718). . . .

Second, this focus on the relationship of Saussure's "sound image" to external sounds led them to think in terms of less arbitrary and more motivated linguistic phenomena than had Saussure (Jakobson 1971:717). Additionally, one gathers that the threat represented by archaic theories of the naturalness of linguistic signs was less significant by the time they were working than it had been when Saussure did his work, and that therefore they had less reason to make a point of stressing the arbitrary nature of linguistic phenomena. However, it is worth stressing that, even for Saussure, different aspects of the sign were arbitrary in different ways, and that it was only the relationship between signifier and signified that he called "radically arbitrary." (Kronenfeld and Decker 1979:509–510)

The major analytic contribution of Prague linguistics, originated by Trubetzkoy and elaborated by Jakobson, was componential analysis (sometimes called distinctive feature analysis). By way of illustration, let us assume articulator/point of articulation is one dimension that takes the values or features of bilabial (lips); apical/alveolar (tip of tongue, to place behind teeth); and labio/palatal (back of tongue touched to palate). Let us assume mode of articulation is another, with the alternative values being stop or continuent. Let us assume voicing is a third, with the alternative values or features being voiced or unvoiced. The values or features on these dimensions create a grid or paradigm (as in table 3-1), in which each slot represents a phoneme (or potential phoneme in the wider case of the full system).

In this system the question of allophones does not arise. One finds the proper set of components for the language at hand, and any strange sound is allocated to a category according to the values it takes on those components (that is, by the rules). Presumably, if the theory is correct, something similar occurs in our heads—as, for

TABLE 3-1. A Phonological Paradigm

		Articulation/Articulator		
		Bilabial	Apico-Alveolar	Labio-palatal
Stop	Unvoiced	/p/	/t/	/k/
	Voiced	/b/	/d/	/g/
Continuent		/m/	/n/	/n/

TABLE 3-2. A Morphological Paradigm

| | Number | |
Person	Singular	Plural
First Person	amo	amamus
Second Person	amas	amatis
Third Person	amat	amant

example, when English speakers hear the Polynesian sound that falls between the English [l] and [r] sounds clearly as either an /l/ or an /r/.

This phonological idea was in part an outgrowth of the European concern with morphological inflectional paradigms such as that (partially) shown in table 3-2, and in that sense was reflected the way in which they attacked morphological problems. However, they did nothing distinctive (from the point of view of our concerns in this volume) with syntax.

Notes

1. It is worth noting that natural human language and the genetic code (DNA), as what might be called "natural codes," share with each other certain characteristics that they do not share with codes that humans have created. Neither has any metalanguage in which messages *about* the code are expressed and thereby distinguished from messages *within* the code about content matter. As linguists, scholars, or scientists, we separate our use of language as speakers from our use of it as describers of language—and then use language *as if* it were a metalanguage to discuss and describe the processes by which it works. But *it* (natural language or the genetic code) has evolved and shaped itself without any such metalanguage. Messages about the code, messages that affect or change the code, are indistinguishable from ordinary messages within the code. The crucial shaping factor for such a code becomes the process of transmission, by which the code is passed on to new speakers, and the way in which each new speaker recreates the code.

As human beings, we learn natural human language quite easily. But that ease is not *simply* the product either of our logical powers or of our being genetically programmed for it. Language itself has been designed by natural selection (that is, through the selection process that has shaped it) to be *easy* for *us* to use. The "us" is human beings, creatures very similar to the other apes and a little less similar to mammals in general. It has been shaped by selection to fit our human needs, predispositions, and abilities. Its basic units (sound images and concepts) and forms of combination (concatenation and grammar) have been designed for our human ease and convenience. At the same time, as the tool of language has been shaped for us, we humans have also become better adapted to the use of the tool—better than we were, and better than our close primate cousins or other, more distant mammalian cousins. That is, my sense is that our biological adaptation has not been to the details of language but (a) to its basic features and (b) to the process of quickly inferring the details of the one we happen to be learning (particularly as children). Similarly, language is a tool whose shape has been adapted so as to make it easy for us to divine and represent internally.

2. Language is a tool that is used in communication, whether with others or internally with our own selves. Such use implies goals on the part of the speaker, and hence some sort of planning (cf. Vera and Simon 1993:40). Language is a symbolic system whose use does require

both planning and internal representations of some sort (cf. Vera and Simon 1993:12,38); and thus our present focus on language itself (as opposed to the knowledge of the world that it refers to) does put the present discussion (prototypically, perhaps) in the universe of "symbolic cognition," as opposed to "situated cognition" or "situated action"—regardless of how the debate between the two sides may fall out in cognitive science in general (Norman 1993:3; see also the rest of the special issue of *Cognitive Science*, vol. 17, no. 1 [1993] which is devoted to this debate).

3. See Kronenfeld and Decker (1979:505) for a discussion of Saussure's connections with Durkheim and for the sources of information on Saussure's thought.

4. The social nature of language is relevant to the debate in cognitive science (see *Cognitive Science*, vol. 17, no. 1 [1993]) between advocates of "symbolic cognition" and "situated cognition" or "situated action" (see Vera and Simon 1993:42; Greeno and More 1993:49). Natural language presents a kind of extreme case, since beyond taking place in a social environment and being socially shared, it is a *symbolic system* that is socially *constructed*.

5. Regarding the social nature of language, and why I go back to Saussure for it, it is interesting to see Keesing's observation (1987:387) that "early cognitive anthropology, taking its models from linguistics, grew up curiously innocent of social theory."

6. I do not mean to say that literacy and mass media are without cultural or cognitive effect. Goody (1986, 1987) has shown some of the impressive effects that literacy, of cultures and of individuals, does have on the shape and content of our culture and on the form of our thought. I am only pointing out that the basic definition of language, and of its collective and passive nature, is not affected by these modern phenomena.

7. See Kronenfeld and Decker (1979:511–512) for a fuller discussion of the particular psychological nature of the Saussurean sign and the associated views of language and semiology, and of its relationship to the philosopher C. S. Peirce's formulation of the sign and semiotics, including the view of language as an interpreted nomenclature. Psychologists (e.g., Vera and Simon 1993:9) sometimes seem unaware of the mental nature of the sign (in both its parts), even though such awareness would seem to accord well with the larger point regarding "symbols" and their use that they are trying to make.

8. Other Saussurean aspects of the theory will be noted as they come up.

9. Jakobson was very interested in "sound symbolism," that is, relationships between the phonological shape of a word and its meaning. [spl] words supposedly go "splat"; [spi] words such as "spit" do lanceolate, or stick in things; and so forth. These tendencies do, I gather, hold across many languages, but, contrary to what Jakobson thought, nowhere seem terribly important (in the sense of explaining very much of the semantics of language). This concern with sound symbolism is one expression of Jakobson's (and Prague linguistics') general concern with the substance versus the formal system of language. Other expressions of the Prague interest in linguistic substance include the idea of "marked" versus "unmarked" categories. Jakobson's theory of the sequence of the development of phonemes and of their loss in aphasia (which turned out not to be empirically valid) was based on marking relations among sound features.

10. For a full exploration of the various ways in which Saussure considered various aspects of linguistic phenomena to be arbitrary and of the additional assertions that have been erroneously imputed to Saussure by various writers on structuralism, see Kronenfeld and Decker (1979:506–507). Atran (1993:54) continues the tradition, after structuralism, by erroneously linking Saussure to the idea, associated with Whorf and Cassirer, that our perception of natural phenomena is structured by our language and culture, while being only arbitrarily related to the actual physical nature of the phenomena in question—that is, for example, that different cultures "each . . . apprehend the spectral continuum . . . in a wholly arbitrary manner."

11. Kronenfeld and Decker (1979:513) characterized the distinction between Saussure's concern with meaning and subsequent linguistic theorists' concern with forms as follows:

Saussure's science of signs was not intended as the mere study of the forms of signs and the combinatorial properties of these signs abstracted from their meanings and their communicative functions—as it has become in most modern linguistics. The Americans, after Bloomfield, explicitly eschewed meaning. Jakobson and other Prague linguists dealt only with the structure of form (that is, of signifiers) and ignored the structure of content (signifieds) even though they sometimes talked about meaning; their distinctive feature analysis dealt with the elements out of which signifiers were built, and had nothing to do with signifieds; other grammatical units, parallels, and the like were described and were asserted to carry meaning, but no theory of meaning was ever provided. Transformational linguists have presented themselves as mentalists, but their contributions have all dealt with the structure of signifiers—that is, with relations among forms. They have developed a new and powerful syntactic theory out of a Bloomfieldian base (their specific philosophic disagreements with the Bloomfieldians about the nature of the linguistic enterprise notwithstanding) (cf. [Jakobson 1959], p. 143) and have married it to a Praguean phonology. Semantic representations have been mentioned, but relegated to a background position (cf. [Lyons 1970], p. 34); the only attempt within the orthodox school to deal with semantics has been Katz and Fodor's ([1964]) unsubtle and inadequate stab; generative semanticists have given semantics a more crucial role, but have provided no explication of semantics itself (cf. Jakobson's characterization of Boas ([58], p. 142) in this connection.)

The exception to this neglect of the importance of meaning among early post-Saussurean linguists was Trubetzkoy (see, for example, 1969:2–3), even though he then went on to work on the signifier aspect of the sign.

Work in various schools of contemporary linguistics, such as functional grammar (see Halliday 1985) and cognitive grammar (see Langacker 1987) have more recently been improving the situation. We are now beginning to see the development of linguistic theory that is concerned with linguistic entities as meaningful units and with how language is used to communicate.

12. Signifieds are complex conceptual entities in the sense that they subsume all the conceptual relationships of the sign (that is, all the information about contrast, reference, social register, societal domain, speech level, and so forth that is carried by the sign). At the same time, since Saussure's langue has to do with the formal relationships of language itself and not with sociolinguistic or rhetorical relationships or regularities (each of which has its own langue-like system, and each of which feeds into the speech acts, or parole, via which they all are together instantiated), we tend to presume semantic relations (involving contrast and reference—as discussed in this book) as the normally meant (default or "unmarked") sense in which "signifieds" are to be taken. In this narrower sense, a number of signs can synonymously share their signifieds while being differentiated by their alternative signifiers. (In the fullest sense, however, different signs cannot, of course, have identical signifiers because, as Saussure said, it is only the difference among signifieds that gives any difference among signifiers significance within the system of langue, and vice versa.) Since in this volume I am concerned primarily with the narrow, formal sense of semantics (and not with the sociolinguistic and rhetorical questions with which others, including some of the authors whose work I am referring to, are concerned), I do not want to have to address such variations in usage.

For each of the kinds of concepts subsumed by signifieds (in the broadest sense of the term) there exist comparable relations (to those I am discussing in this paper) between signifieds and the external (to language) world we live in and interact with. For example, we can share the idea of a "black dialect of English" or "black English" while still having severe disagreements with one another (or just doubts within our individual minds) about whether or not we are hearing it in a given instance.

13. "Jakobson himself (Jakobson 1971:280–284) maintains that linguists must look at the whole sign (*'signum'*) including both its signifier (*'signans'*) and signified (*'signatum'*). However, the very discussion in which he makes the assertion illustrates the problem; he treats the signified (in the manner of C. S. Peirce) as if it were itself the (external to the mind) object being referred to and not a mental concept relating to that object. Such a view, besides being too simplistic, deprives the signified of any linguistic interest and thereby necessarily reduces the study of the sign to the study of its signifier (cf. Jakobson 1971:267–268)" (Kronenfeld and Decker 1979:510).

II

THE ETHNOSCIENCE
TRADITION

Generally speaking, over the course of this and successive parts, we will look first at sense relations among categories and then at reference. We will take up these topics in this order because this is the order in which the relevant associated theoretical developments arose in anthropology. Our discussion will proceed via an examination of the publications in which these issues were originally raised. This approach is useful because it places theoretical assertions in their proper (communicative) context. But this historical ordering will force some attention to reference before we otherwise would want, since some of the work concerning sense relations we will examine was developed in the context of a view of reference that has since been superseded.

Part II details the empirical context and conceptual apparatus on which later extensionist approaches, including mine, are based. Its two chapters provide an overview of the ethnoscience tradition, including an introduction to the major theoretical issues and the conceptual apparatus used to address these issues. Chapter 4 will provide the general overview and chapter 5 will offer an intensive consideration of the various approaches within the tradition to the componential analysis of English kinterms and of the empirical and theoretical insights that have come out of that work.

4

Defining Structures: Taxonomies and Componential Paradigms

Ethnoscience

The original aim of the linguistic anthropologists who developed ethnoscience in the late 1950s and early 1960s was to apply advanced linguistic methodology to the study of culture. Ethnoscientists began this application with semantics, because it was part of both language and culture. As the part of culture directly present in conversation, semantics provided a relatively easy linguistic entry point to the study of culture. In its linguistics aspect, ethnoscience was a natural extension of structural linguistics. Its descriptive methodology came from American structuralism, while its analytic methodology—componential analysis—came from Prague phonology (the only genuinely analytic device anyone in linguistics then had). But both schools of structuralist linguistics shared a focus on signifiers (as opposed to signifieds); members of both schools commonly conveyed a sense that semantics was too complex, too hard to study, and too enmeshed in psychology to be dealt with in any formal manner by contemporary linguistics, even if they held out hope for future advances. Since culture includes both the phenomenal entities—the "stuff"—speakers use language to refer to and the meanings speakers use language to convey, anthropology's focus on culture ensured that ethnoscience, as a part of anthropology, would have to deal squarely and primarily with meaning in language. It is interesting to note that, by virtue of this focus on meaning, ethnoscience came closer to implementing the Saussurean program than had any of the linguistics that preceded it.[1]

Once the need for analytic methodology was recognized, there was then a turn toward biological systematics (that is, the study of plant and animal taxonomies) as the source for another analytic approach (an alternative to componential analysis), especially, initially, on the part of Conklin and Frake. There was some early influence from lexicography as well.

Basic Units

Segregates

The basic units of study within ethnographic semantics were what Frake (1962:31–32) spoke of as "segregates." These were units that had a conventional meaning for speakers of the language—a meaning that went beyond what could be predicted from the meanings of the parts. Words such as "hot dog," with conventional meanings largely unrelated to the meanings of their constituent morphemes, eliminated morphemes as the units by which meaning and the cultural content of language were to be studied. Multiword categories such as "poison ivy," whose meaning could not be predicted from the meanings of their constituent words (*poison* and *ivy*), eliminated words as the basic units of study. The lexeme had developed as a semantic category whose meaning could not be predicted from its constituent parts (that is, as an exocentric category). But Frake pointed out that conventional phrases, such as "a ham 'n' cheese sandwich," while having basic meanings deducible from their constituents, functioned culturally as single items, had accretions of meaning beyond that entailed by their constituents, and had pronunciations indicative of their conventional status. Frake used the term "segregates" for such conventional categories (whether morphemes, words, lexemes, or phrases), and proposed segregates as the units via which the study of culture through linguistic categories was to be approached. Frake's term seems never to have caught on, but the problem of units he raised remains an important one for our understanding of the relationship between language and culture and for our attempts to use linguistic categories as vehicles for gaining an understanding of cultural content, including culturally standardized cognitive understandings. In this volume, when we speak of "words" (as an ordinary-language, nontechnical term), we will normally be referring to Frakean "segregates." Periodically, when the nature of the units under discussion is particularly at issue in my argument, I will explicitly refer back to Frake's conception of segregates.

Opposition and Inclusion

Saussure's concept of opposition was coded in American linguistics and subsequently in linguistic anthropology as "contrast." Pairs of opposite categories (such as black vs. white, male vs. female) or larger sets of opposite-like categories (such as red vs. orange vs. yellow vs. . . . , baby vs. child vs. teenager vs. . . .) were called "contrast sets," and were spoken of as "contrasting with one another" along various dimensions or features of contrast. The technique of componential analysis was taken by Lounsbury (1956) and Goodenough (1956) from Prague School phonology and used to identify the (minimal set of) distinctive features (such as male, female, adult, child) that defined each item in a contrast set (such as boy, girl, man, woman), and the (minimal set) of dimensions along which these features were opposed to one another (here, gender—male vs. female—and life stage—adult vs. child).

Implicit in the idea of opposition was the notion that the set of opposed categories shared all their defining features or attributes other than those by which they contrasted. This meant that, in effect, the contrasting categories within a given contrast set were all, together, members of, or "included in," a one step higher level category (whether that higher level category was implicit or explicit).

Structures of Opposition and Inclusion

Semantic Relations among Segregates

The meaning relations among segregates (words and phrases with conventional meanings) were defined in the ethnoscience paradigm by relations of contrast and inclusion. The minimal relationship structure, then, consists of two opposed terms that by virtue of their opposition are included in some (possibly implicit) superordinate category. Larger structures can be built up by elaborating either relation (contrast or inclusion), or by combining the two. Since a mixed (or combined) structure can be reduced to a joining of separate structures of one or the other type, let us put mixed structures aside for now. I will later suggest some reasons relating to considerations of cognitive ease and difficulty one might not expect to find many, if any, instances of actual mixed structures, as opposed to looser mixed congeries.[2]

The first possible elaboration of our minimal structure consists of increasing the number of opposed items, thus changing it from a binary opposition to a multinary contrast set. In this minimal elaboration, the contrasting items still differ along a single attribute dimension. By some interpretations,[3] color terms represent such an elaboration. A second kind of elaboration, the multiplication of contrast relations, produces a paradigmatic (or componential) structure by adding additional cross-cutting attribute dimensions. Kinship paradigms represent such a structure of elaborated contrast. A third kind of elaboration, the concatenation of inclusion relations, produces a taxonomic structure. In such elaboration, terms superordinate to contrast sets themselves contrast with other terms, which may also be superordinate to yet other contrast sets; the contrasts that make up an inclusion structure may be binary or multinary, but each particular contrast set only involves a single attribute dimension.[4]

For the present, we will leave multinary contrasts aside, and examine first taxonomic structures and then paradigmatic or componential ones.

The basic taxonomic notion is one of successive subdivision of categories by some criterion, and not necessarily one that directly translates into criterial attributes. The taxonomy is structured by the inclusion relations and *not* by feature/attribute contrasts (which are of only secondary, background importance). Examples of taxonomies include Linnaeus's structure of relations among species, based on a combination of general similarity and similarities in certain supposedly crucial organ systems; the modern, post-Darwinian version of relations among the species, based on shared ancestry with an overlay of adaptive similarity; and the structure Frake describes for Subanun diseases, which is based on recognition and treatment criteria. What is central to the idea of a taxonomy is the form of the arrangement, rather than any theory regarding how the entities being classified came to have such an arrangement, or any consideration of why the classification was created.

Field techniques derived from the use of eliciting frames in American linguistics for working down a taxonomic hierarchy were developed by Frake (1962, 1964), Conklin (1962, 1964), Metzger and Williams (1966), Black and Metzger (1965), and others as a kind of discovery heuristic. Thus, a set of explicit categories related hierarchically through inclusion relations represented a folk taxonomy in early ethnoscience.

Taxonomic structures have two dimensions: depth and breadth.[5] In folk taxonomies, a particularly salient aspect of breadth is the number of terminal taxa. Horizontal complexity—that is, the number of terminal taxa—seems to reflect the degree of cultural interest in the domain in question (or in parts of it).[6] The greater the interest, for whatever reasons, the more types are recognized and named. Vertical complexity—the number of levels of inclusion—seems to reflect social complexity, particularly the extent of the division of labor. The greater the number of different people doing different kinds of things, the greater the pressure toward separate vocabularies for different occupational groups (possibly with different levels of specificity), and toward a hierarchy of more abstract cover terms to enable people from groups with varying amounts of shared experience to communicate across their specialized vocabularies. As is generally the case with linguistic phenomena (see Greenberg 1966, 1968), too low a frequency of use is the pruning shears that keep the taxonomic tree trimmed; more complexity means more need, which means more usage, which means more branchings that survive the shears.

The basic paradigmatic (or componential) notion is multiple, multidimensional subdivision of a single level of inclusion. In this case, the attributes that structure the paradigm are foregrounded and criterial.

Paradigmatic structures require a universe whose raw phenomena[7] are plausibly seen as structured by cross-cutting attribute dimensions. In addition to the domain's showing such a paradigmatic potentiality, the individual terms of the paradigm each need to be used frequently enough to keep *each and all* of them alive, and the various subdivisions of the paradigm entailed by the features of the various cross-cutting attribute dimensions each have to be used frequently enough to keep the attributes that define the various subdivisions alive. For example, in our paradigm of English kinterms, we do enough things with males vs. females, children vs. parents, lineals vs. co-lineals vs. ablineals, and so forth to keep each of these attribute dimensions (sex, polarity, generation, lineality) alive and salient.

Componential Analysis

Conklin: Hanunóo Pronouns

The initial semantic examples of componential analysis were presented in Conklin's article on Hanunóo color categories (1955). Somewhat later (1962) Conklin provided a very nice analysis of Hanunóo pronouns that I would like to use to illustrate some of the essential features of componential analysis.

According to Conklin (1962: 13–136), the Hanunóo language has eight pronouns—*kuh, mih, tah, muh, yuh, yah, dah,* and *tam*—which may roughly be glossed, respectively, in English as "I," "we" (exclusive of "you"), "we" ("you" singular and "I"), "you" (singular), "you" (plural), "he"/"she," "they," and "we" (more than two of "us," including "you"). Conklin offers a presentation of this pronominal set in terms of a traditional pronominal paradigm derived from comparative Indo-European (shown in table 4-1) and shows that, on the one hand, the paradigm has many slots that lack distinct Hanunóo terms (if one applies each dimension of contrast—number, person, etc.—to the whole paradigm), while, on the other hand, Hanunóo has some categories that require special (we might say ad hoc) subdivision of other slots in the paradigm. In the sense illustrated by these problems, Conklin shows that the standard paradigm provides only an inefficient representation of the semantic relations involved in the Hanunóo pronominal set.

TABLE 4-1. Hanunóo Pronominal Set in Traditional Arrangement from Conklin 1962:134

Features					
	Person:	first	second	third	
	Number:	singular	dual	plural	
	Inclusion:	exclusive	inclusive		
Arrangement					
Number					
Person		*s*	*d*	*p*	*Inclusion*
1		*kuh*	*tah*	*mih*	e
		—	—	*tam*	i
2		*muh*	—	*yuh*	e
		—	—	—	i
3		*yah*	—	*dah*	e
		—	—	—	i

Conklin proposes by way of contrast another analytic paradigm, based on the relations he finds actually to exist among the terms (see table 4-2). This paradigm is defined by three binary dimensions: inclusion vs. exclusion of the speaker, inclusion vs. exclusion of the hearer, and minimal vs. nonminimal membership. He shows that this paradigm provides a more efficient representation of the Hanunóo semantic domain than does the traditional paradigm, in the sense that each slot in it has a Hanunóo term and no terms exist that require further subdivision of any of the paradigmatic slots.

Conklin has identified in a general sense the set of Saussure an oppositions that most efficiently distinguishes the Hanunóo pronouns from one another. If we assume that Conklin (or the ethnographer or analyst) is no smarter than are the speakers of the language being described or analyzed, and if we assume that the set of distinctive features (or paradigm) is not explicitly taught by one generation to the next but is each time inferred anew, then we can draw the inference that Conklin's analysis may well represent how some Hanunóo actually understand their pronominal domain. On the other hand, since the Indo-European–based standard paradigm does not grow out of the Hanunóo domain in any natural way, and since Hanunóo children have not

TABLE 4-2. Componential Paradigm of Hanunóo Pronominal Set from Conklin 1962:135

Features		
Minimality of Membership:	minimal,	non-minimal (m, $\overline{m}$)
Speaker Inclusion:	included,	excluded (s, $\overline{s}$)
Hearer Inclusion:	inlcuded,	excluded (h, $\overline{h}$)

Arrangement

dah	$\overline{M}\overline{S}\overline{H}$
yuh	$\overline{M}\overline{S}H$
mih	$\overline{M}S\overline{H}$
tam	$\overline{M}SH$
yah	$M\overline{S}\overline{H}$
muh	$M\overline{S}H$
kuh	$MS\overline{H}$
tah	MSH

normally studied comparative Indo-European at the time they learned their own language, we may also infer that the standard analysis is unlikely to represent their understanding in any direct sense.[8]

"Represent how they understand" is the way I have chosen to characterize what has been spoken of, in the literature, as the possible "psychological reality" of one or another proposed componential analysis. We will take up the issue of psychological reality in chapter 5.

We have already noted the criterion of efficiency by which the success of the two paradigms in representing the domain in question can be compared or judged. I would like, also, to mention two other criteria that are implicit in Conklin's example, and that we will shortly see as important for evaluating componential analyses. First, categories are defined by the joint presence of their set of defining features or attributes; that is, they are *conjunctively* defined by the *intersection* of their defining features, and never given the disjunctive definitions that would result from the union (that is, the "either feature x or feature y" type of presence) of such features. Second, all other things being equal, fewer dimensions of contrast are better than more, and fewer categories (values or features) per dimension are better than more. The latter two criteria in effect characterize the framework with in which efficiency is evaluated.

Conjunctivity of category definitions and the relative efficiency of representation of competing paradigms are criteria consistently used for evaluating componential analyses. Minimizing the number of dimensions and minimizing the number of categories per dimension are criteria that, taken separately, also are consistently used. However, at some point there comes to be a trade-off between minimizing dimensionality and minimizing the categories per dimension. There have existed various views concerning how to make this trade-off, both in work on componential analyses within anthropological semantics and in the Prague phonological work from which the anthropological work derives.

Conklin's analysis of Hanunóo pronouns nicely illustrates what a good componential analysis looks like, how it differs from a one less good, and what such an analysis accomplishes. It also shows that the analysis is not dependent on any kind of a priori universal cross-cultural ("etic") grid of analytically relevant features (contra some discussions in the literature regarding componential analyses of kinship terminologies), and, finally, it shows that componential analysis is not an algorithm (or even a heuristic) for arriving at some result, but rather an analytic form in which relations—however arrived at—can be expressed.

Lounsbury: Iroquois Kinship

Lounsbury, in his analyses of Morgan's (1871) Iroquois data, (1956; expanded and developed as 1964a) provided the clearest and most explicit treatment available (at least until recently) of the analytic and semantic assumptions involved in componential analysis. In addition, in his treatment of the Iroquois definition of cross versus parallel relatives (1964a: 197–204), he beautifully illustrated the use of the efficiency criterion to decide among alternative definitions of potentially defining features or attributes.

Lounsbury's analysis made explicit the importance of formally defined categories and relations to any explicit treatment of meaning, and the importance of conjunctively defined categories to any meaningful interpretation of the efficiency criterion. It also provided the clearest anthropological treatment yet seen of the distinction between referential and paradigmatic meaning. Referential meaning is the relationship of a term (say, "uncle" in English) to the things it refers to, that is, its Lounsburian *denotata* (which, in the case of a kinterm, would be its kintypes—in the English kin terminology, mother's brother, father's brother, and so forth), the set of which constitutes the Lounsburian *designatum* of the term. Paradigmatic, or sense, meaning refers to the relationship of a term to the other terms with which it contrasts (in English, for instance, "uncle" vs. "brother," vs. "aunt," vs. "father"), and to the features, that is, the Lounsburian *significata* (such as generation, gender, or lineality) by which the contrasting terms are distinguished from one another.

Lounsbury's terms, borrowed from the philosopher Charles Morris, have not been much used subsequently by semantic anthropologists; even so, his explanation of the distinction between referential and paradigmatic meaning is the clearest and most careful in anthropology. The distinction itself is crucial to Saussure's *Course . . .* and to everything in modern linguistics that follows from it. Componential analysis represents a way of reasoning from the denotata of a term to that term's significata. As such, its success depends on the clarity with which the denotata and their various (potentially defining) attributes can be dedfined. With data sets for which one has available active informants, such clarity initially can be achieved through successive approximations and interaction with the informants, provided that in the final result categories and attributes are explicitly defined. With data sets such as Lounsbury's, where one lacks informants and has only a listing of terms and their referents (perhaps with some additional information about usage), one can only apply componential analysis where one has some reasonably good a priori basis for inferring the full range of a term's referents from the sample given in an ethnography, and where one can reasonably impute some a priori set of potentially significant attributes to the set of terms. These a priori needs explain why the issue of a supposed "universal etic grid" arose in anthropological discussions in the 1960s. Kinship terminologies, for reasons relating both to the reasonably universal structure of the domain (deriving from the reasonably universal nature of the parent-child link and the need[9] for a parent of each gender) and to the long history of anthropological study of the terms' meanings, represented one of the few domains for which such a prioris seemed reasonably to exist. This need for a prioris (by homebound analysts, at least) provides one reason componential analysis in practice was largely restricted to kinship terminologies, even though many ethnoscientists spoke as though they expected the analytic technique to be as generally applicable as the descriptive field techniques elaborated by Frake (1964), Metzger and Williams (1963, 1966), and Black and Metzger (1965). Later, in our discussion of George Miller's work and Jerome Bruner's work, we shall see other reasons for the restricted range of application of componential analysis. Considerations relevant to this restricted range of application will also be raised in our discussion of semantic extension.

Notes

1. See Kronenfeld and Decker (1979:512–515) for a similar observation regarding Lévi-Straussian structuralism's relationship to its linguistic roots regarding meaning.

2. I do want to distinguish between actual structures, which define the *meaning* or *sense* relations among the constituent terms, and looser congeries of structures that do not have such defining force and are not so tightly structured. Though loose congeries do not have the defining force of actual structures, they do contribute to the network of presuppositions that underlies our understanding of natural speech. This contribution, I think, is what kept tempting ethnoscientists (and related linguistic psychologists) to try to come up with overarching structures of structures—"maps" of "semantic space." Certainly, most of what has been spoken of as "semantic space" seems made up of such congeries, and the logical looseness of such congeries would explain why convincing "maps" of semantic space have proven so hard to produce.

3. One such interpretation would be to take wavelength as the defining attribute. An alternative would be to treat the color circle as a one-dimensional figure in two-dimensional space.

4. Since—as we shall see later, especially in chapter 8—the role of defining attributes is considerably de-emphasized for taxonomic type structures, "single attribute dimension" should be interpreted as meaning that there is no internal structure to a given multinary contrast set.

5. My ideas concerning the reasons for taxonomic depth and breadth come from courses of Frake's that I took in graduate school. These ideas are implicit in various of Frake's publications (1961, 1962) and also of Berlin's (e.g. 1972).

6. This notion to some degree parallels Kroeber's idea of "cultural focus."

7. "Raw phenomena" here refers to conceptual elements prior to their linguistic coding but where such elements are understood in ways relevant to the purposes of their subsequent coding.

8. The question of more direct measures of the psychological status of analyses such as Conklin's is addressed in chapter 5's extended discussion of componential analyses of English kinterms and "psychological reality."

9. The need for male and female parents for biological reproduction is obvious and absolute. Less obvious, and of a more statistical than absolute nature, is the social need for two parents for feeding, protecting, and training children. By "statistical" I mean that single-parent families do exist in many socieities, but that in almost all socieities (that is, with no more than at most one or two known exceptions) social duties, norms, and expectations are constructed around the complementary roles of male and female parents. Normally, though certainly not in all cases, these social parents are also the biological parents, and in almost all socieities the null expectation is that the biological parents will be the social parents. Additionally, it seems likely that the move to two-parent child rearing played an important role in human evolution.

5

Componential Analysis: The English Kinterms Example

To illustrate the application of componential analysis to kinship terminological systems, and to explore some of the problems and issues that arose in that application, I would like now to turn to an extended discussion of two classic analyses of American English kinterms, those of Wallace and Atkins (1960) and Romney and D'Andrade (1964). I will first recapitulate the two analyses of the terminological paradigm as the respective authors presented them, and then follow with a summary of Romney and D'Andrade's comparison of the analyses and with their adducing of additional data to resolve the question of which analysis was more "psychologically real." I will conclude with my own comparison of the two analyses, my own discussion of the implications of Romney and D'Andrade's psychological data and of other data on this question published subsequently by Romney with various coauthors, and my own conclusions on the issue of psychological reality.

Before presenting the specific analyses of English consanguineal kinterms, I would like to present the list of terms that both analyses concern, the focal denotatum of each term,[1] and the range of denotata referred to by each (see column I of table 5-1). I have provided a characterization of the denotata of each term in the variant of Romney's notation scheme (see Romney 1965) developed to show category ranges. It is worth noting that each of these categories is also, in this table, shown to be susceptible to a conjunctive definition.

Wallace and Atkins

Wallace and Atkins's analysis of English kinterms is presented in column II of table 5-1 and the male subset is diagrammed in figure 5-1.

In the tables, in addition to providing the English terms and the standard names for each term's defining feature, I characterize the denotata of each *feature* in the Romney notational scheme referred to above. This representation allows us to examine the conjunctivity[2] of the category and feature definitions, and thereby to assess the efficiency of the analysis.

We can see that the major, overriding defining feature—relevant to every terminological category—of English kinterms in this analysis is lineality. The next feature, in terms of generality of relevance, is gender, which is relevant to all kinterms except

TABLE 5-1. English Kinterms: Referents and Componential Analyses

	I	II Wallace & Atkins			III Romney & D'Andrade			
Term	Referents							
Feature		Gen	Lin	Sex	Pol	Gen	D/C	Sex
GrFa	a+a+(a+)m	+2+	L	M	+	2+	D	M
GrMo	a+a+(a+)f	+2+	L	F	+	2+	D	F
Fa	a+m	+1	L	M	+	1	D	M
Mo	a+f	+1	L	F	+	1	D	F
Unc	a(+a)+aom	+1	CL	M	+	1	C	M
Aunt	a(+a)+aof	+1	CL	F	+	1	C	F
(self)	a	0	L	NR				
Br	aom	0	CL	M	NR	0	D	M
Si	aof	0	CL	F	NR	0	D	F
[Husb	f = m]							
[Wife	m = f]							
Cous	a(+a)+aoa–(a–)a	0	AL	NR	NR	0	C	NR
So	a–m	–1	L	M	–	1	D	M
Da	a–f	–1	L	F	–	1	D	F
Neph	aoa–(a–)m	–1	CL	M	–	1	C	M
Niece	aoa–(a–)f	–1	CL	F	–	1	C	F
GrSo	a(–a)–a–m	–2+	L	M	–	2+	D	M

cousin. The full set of distinctions among the third defining feature, generation, are only relevant within the lineal category; within the colineal category there are only three generational levels—greater than 0, 0, and less than 0—while within the ablineal category there is no generational subdivision.

In the preceding discussion we can see that the Wallace and Atkins analysis is capable of including the subdivisions English speakers optionally make of the terminological categories at the extremities of the three lineality features. The ≥2 and ≤–2

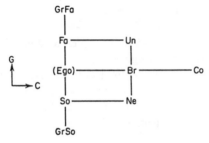

FIG. 5-1 Wallace and Atkins: Spatial Representation (from Romney and D'Andrade 1964:167)

TABLE 5-2. Wallace and Atkins: Distinctive Features

Features[1]	Value	Definition	Gloss
Generation (Gen):	+2+	.++(+)[(+)o(–).	
	+1	.+[(+)o(–)].	
	0	.[(+)o(–)].	
	–1	.[(+)o(–)]–.	
	–2+	.[(+)o(–)](–)– –	
		.	
Lineality (Lin):	L	/.+(+)+./	Lineal
	CL	/.(+)o./	Colineal
	AL	.+(+)o(–)–.	Ablineal
Gender (Sex):	M	m.	Male
	F	f.	Female
	NR	a.	Not relevant

1. Only links (i.e., +, -, o), and not persons (i.e., m, f, a, b) are shown for generation and lineality.

subcategories on the lineal feature can be further subdivided by the use of "great" modifiers (as in "great grandfather"), where the number of "greats" indicates the number of generations removed, up from +2 or down from -2, the kinsman is. The use of the modifiers is optional, but in the absence of their use the normal presumption is of generation +2 or -2. Unlike the case of the categories that follow, incidentally, a *grand*father is not a kind of father. Similarly, the first and last generational subcategories on the colineal feature can be further subdivided by use of the "great" or "grand" modifier—once for each generation of removal from 1. But these various "great uncles" (for example) remain kinds of uncles. The use of the modifier is optional,

TABLE 5-3. Romney and D'Andrade: Distinctive Features

Feature[1]	Value	Definition[2]	Gloss
Polarity (Pol)	–	(# of +) > (# of –)	Plus
	–	(# of +) < (# of –)	Minus
	NR	(# of +) = (# of –)	Not Relevant
Generation (Gen)	+2+	/.++(+)[(+)o(–)]./	
	+1	/.+[(+)o(–)]./	
	0	.[(+)o(–)].	
D/C	D	/.+(+)+./ *or* .o.	Direct
	C	/.+(+)(+)o(–)./ *or* .+(+)o(–)–.	Collateral
Gender (Sex)	M	m.	Male
	F	f.	Female
	NR	a.	Not relevant

1. Only links (i.e., +, –, o), and not persons (i.e., m, f, a, b) are shown for generation and D/C.
2. (# of +) and (# of –) refer respectively to the number of plusses and the number of minuses.

although in the absence of modification, generation +1 or −1, depending on the term, is presumed. Finally, the various systems of numbering cousins (i.e., first, second, third cousins) and the system of removal sometimes used with some of them (e.g., "second cousin, twice removed") represent ways of subdividing the single ablineal category. Some of these systems of cousin subdivision mark generation while others do not. As was the case with "great" and "grand," these further subdivisions are secondary and optional.

We can see that each distinctive feature within each dimension of contrast is conjunctively defined in this analysis. We can see that each terminological category is defined by the intersection (or set product) of one or more of these features, and so is thereby conjunctively defined within the analysis.

Romney and D'Andrade

Romney and D'Andrade's analysis is presented in parallel form in column 3 of table 5-1 and figure 5-2. Again, with each feature's label in the table is a definition, in the Romney notational scheme, of the set of denotata delimited by each.

The Romney and D'Andrade analysis differs in several respects from that of Wallace and Atkins. Regarding the dimensions of distinctive features, Romney and D'Andrade first divide the Wallace and Atkins feature of generation into (absolute) generation (with values 0, 1, and ≥2) and polarity (with values of + and −). Second, Romney and D'Andrade recast the Wallace and Atkins three-valued dimension of lineality as one of direct/collateral (with values of direct and collateral). Regarding the definitions of the features, we see that the Romney and D'Andrade direct/collateral dimension is made up of disjunctive features (though only minimally disjunctive); in table 5-3 there is an "or" in the definition of features D and C of the direct versus collateral contrast.

We can also see that, in the Romney and D'Andrade analysis, the optional internal subdivisions that we spoke of for the uncle, aunt, nephew, and niece categories (the Wallace and Atkins colineal extremity categories) are totally precluded, as are those that cross the generational line for the cousin category (Wallace and Atkins's one ablineal category).

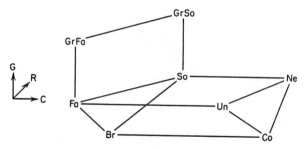

FIG. 5-2 Romney and D'Andrade: Spatial Representation (from Romney and D'Andrade 1964:167)

Comparison

Romney and D'Andrade's Comparison

In their article, after proposing their analysis as an alternative to that of Wallace and Atkins, Romney and D'Andrade went on to discuss the issue of psychological reality. They considered the two analyses to be equally acceptable on formal grounds, and so concluded that the question of which was preferable was to be settled on the psychological ground of which accorded better with native cognition. They chose three tasks as measures of cognitive structures: a sorting task, a semantic differential test, and a triads test. They compared the pictures implied by the two analyses (our figures 5-1 and 5-2) with the pictures implicit in the task data (figure 5-3) and found that the picture drawn from their analysis accorded significantly better with the psychological data than did the one drawn from the Wallace and Atkins analysis. They concluded that their componential analysis provided a more accurate picture of American-English psychological reality than did the Wallace and Atkins analysis, and hence was preferable. They proposed direct psychological testing as the way to deal with the problem of alternative analyses raised earlier by Burling (1964) and others.

Kronenfeld's Discussion of the Comparison

We have already noted that the two analyses were not, in fact, equivalent on formal grounds because Romney and D'Andrade's utilized disjunctively defined features while Wallace and Atkins's did not.[3] By the formal criterion, in fact, Wallace and Atkins had the superior analysis. However, this observation does not clear up our comparative difficulty, but rather poses a further problem: For reasons most clearly stated by Lounsbury (1964a:194), without this formal criterion we are lost at sea without a compass, yet we have substantial evidence that psychological criteria may actually contradict the formal one.

At the time of the Romney and D'Andrade analysis Romney had not yet carried out his work with Nerlove (Nerlove and Romney 1967; see also Kronenfeld 1974) based on Bruner, Goodnow, and Austin's findings (1956). This work was to make clear

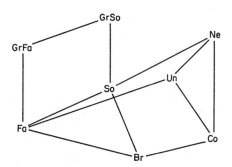

FIG.5-3 Spatial Representation from Romney and D'Andrade Triads Data (from Romney and D'Andrade 1964:166)

that the conjunctivity standard was not simply a requirement of mathematical elegance but also strongly constrained psychological reality—not only in the case of novel individual constructions but also in the case of culturally standardized collective representations of the sort represented by kinterms categories. Nerlove and Romney's findings save us from having to throw out the formal requirement of conjunctivity, but force us to look more closely at Romney and D'Andrade's data and at the particular disjunctivities involved in their direct versus collateral features.

Since Romney and D'Andrade's clearest and most interpretable results came from their triads test data, and since that task is the one that has attracted the most attention in subsequent anthropological work on denotative semantics, I will restrict my discussion of their psychological study to their triads data.

Romney and D'Andrade directly compared the total picture resulting from their triads data with the total pictures entailed by the two analyses. As we can see in table 5-4, such a comparison comes out unmistakably on the side of the Romney and D'Andrade analysis. However, we have noted that there are several differences between the two pictures. If we look at their triads' results in more detail to see which of these differences—which of these particular alternative forms for defining sets of distinctive features, or dimensions—are relevant to the cognitive decision entailed by the triads test and which are not, we find that the support rendered by the triads picture for the Romney and D'Andrade analysis over that of Wallace and Atkins is largely dependent on the difference in the way generation (or generation and polarity) was handled in the two analyses. The triads data were less sharp on the difference between Romney and D'Andrade's direct/collateral dimension and Wallace and Atkins' lineal/colineal/ablineal one. Thus, we see it is not so much the complete Romney and D'Andrade analysis (versus the Wallace and Atkins one) that is supported by the triads data, but more the way the analysis handles generation differences.

The differences between the ways the two analyses handle generation recall the issue we raised earlier concerning the relationship of the number of dimensions in an analysis and the number of features per dimension to the efficiency criterion for evaluating alternative componential analyses. The triads results for English kinterms might be taken as implying that reducing the number of features per dimension is more important, cognitively, than is reducing the number of dimensions. Such a finding

TABLE 5-4. Interpoint Distances between Male Relatives for 116 American-English Subjects (absolute distances estimated with c = 3.6): Romney and D'Andrade triads data compared with models (from Romney and D'Andrade 1964:163, 165)

	GrFa	GrSo	Fa	So	Br	Un	Ne	Co
GrFa	0	2.696	2.786	3.913	4.288	3.755	4.275	4.448
GrSo		0	3.793	2.881	3.782	4.215	3.572	3.861
Fa			0	2.544	3.248	3.422	4.334	4.344
So				0	2.943	4.205	4.807	3.620
Br					0	3.779	3.733	3.680
Un						0	2.980	3.099
Ne							0	2.801
Co								0

would at least loosely support the Jakobsonian/Lévi-Straussean position of restricting all contrasts (that is, dimensions) to binary oppositions. Later in this chapter we will examine further findings of Romney's that indicate a context in which the multi-valued dimension might occur; in chapter 8, we will examine data from cognitive psychology that is supportive of (and explanatory of) a probabilistic version of the binary claim (that is, as the number of dimensions of contrast increases, the number of distinctions per dimension rapidly approaches two).

Let us remember that it was a concern with the disjunctive nature of Romney and D'Andrade's direct/collateral dimension (and its included features) that brought us to the more detailed comparison. The relatively ambiguous result concerning this dimension that we saw above still leaves us with the apparent psychological reality of disjunctively defined analytic categories, and with the problem that such a finding entails for componential analysis.

We should now note that the triads test does not directly test for the dimensions of the paradigm by which the items in question are organized. Instead, it uses only judgments about relative similarities among pairs of items from the set. No explicit information is provided about the nature of the similarity to be considered, nor is any explicit context of judgment provided. The list of terms used in the text provides only an implicit context. Now we note that the issue in the lineality dimension comparison between our two componential analyses reduces to whether brother/sister are closer to father/mother and son/daughter or to uncle/aunt and nephew/niece, and whether cousin is closer to uncle/aunt and nephew/niece than is brother/sister or whether it is off by itself. There is nothing in the triads test that forces subjects (informants) to respond only to the semantic dimensions along which the terminological paradigm is defined; they are constrained only by the fact that they have available no information beyond that entailed by the individual terms or the context provided by the full list of terms in the test set. Any decision basis consistent with this terminological list could enter into subjects' similarity judgments.

The terms in question differ from one another not only on the criteria presumed in the two articles to have semantic importance, but also on at least one other important social criterion: some of the listed kinsmen are in one's nuclear family, while others are not. The ambiguous results found in the triads data regarding the comparison between Wallace and Atkins's lineality dimension and Romney and D'Andrade's direct/collateral one could be the epiphenomenal result of averaging some informants who responded to the triads in terms of conjunctive, Wallace and Atkins semantic features with other informants who responded at least in part in terms of the (also conjunctively defined) sociologically important feature contrast of nuclear family members versus non-nuclear.

Further Issues

We are now in a position to address a couple of questions that our discussion of the Romney and D'Andrade analysis raises about these native English-speaking analysts and the subsequent native English-speaking analysts who have examined their work. Why has the obvious disjunctivity embodied in their direct and collateral features not much disturbed anyone (even those who noticed it)? And why has their foregrounding of the generation dimension— which allowed it (in contradistinction to ethnographic reality) to override the actual cross-generational nature of the ranges of their "collateral" terms—felt reasonable enough to native critics not to occasion immediate dismissal of their analysis?

I want to suggest that the disjunctivity in Romney and D'Andrade's direct and collateral features was indeed, in a relevant psychological sense, a minimal one. It felt conjunctive to native speakers, I suspect, because they coded it as something like "the line of ancestors and descendants of ego and ego's nuclear family." The disjunctivity was buried in the fact that "ego's nuclear family" actually conflated two different nuclear families: the nuclear family of *orientation*, with members of which one shares one's ancestors, and the nuclear family of *procreation*, with members of which one shares one's descendants. The conflation was made less salient by the fact that one only lives in one of these at a time. The restriction of the terminological set to consanguineal terms, and the resulting omission of husband and wife terms, eliminated the 0 generation terms from the nuclear family of procreation that would have contrasted with the 0 generation nuclear family of orientation terms (brother and sister) and thereby forced the awareness that sons and daughters are shared with members of a different nuclear family than are fathers and mothers.[4] It is also possible that most of us, when we first encountered the Romney and D'Andrade article and developed our understanding of it, were young enough to be much more aware of the presence of our ancestral line (including with whom it was shared) than of our descendent line.[5]

I suggested above that the disjunctive direct and collateral features need not have been in the heads of even those subjects/informants who pulled brothers/sisters and cousins toward the father/mother–son/daughter line and the uncle/aunt–nephew/niece line, respectively. But, having now suggested that anthropologist native English speakers might have been lulled by the nature of the actual disjunction, of their experience of it, and of the data set into thinking of the features as if they were conjunctively defined, I should also raise that possibility for the nonanthropologists who provided Romney and D'Andrade's data. As college undergraduates, these informants were even more likely than the anthropologists to have had personal experience only with nuclear families of orientation, and to have combined an awareness of sharing of their ancestral line with members of that family with a lack of any particular awareness of a descendent line at all. If a disjunctively defined category feels conjunctive to native speakers, and if they can automatically fill in all its parts, then, for reasons we shall see later,[6] the psychological argument against disjunctivity loses much of its force. We shall also see, though, that such feeling and automaticity require unusually intense learning experiences.

I want to turn now to Romney and D'Andrade's apparently undue foregrounding of the generation dimension relative to the lineality (or direct/collateral) one. Again, I am concerned with why apparent problems with their analysis were accepted relatively unquestioned by the largely native English-speaking anthropologists who studied it, and with what such anthropological reactions may tell us about native speakers in general.

I want to suggest that generation, because of its close relationship to relative age, is felt as a direct perceptual category in a way that is impossible with lineality. Generation, in its relative-age guise, can have a recognition or identification function (relative to terminological category membership) that lineality cannot have. This perceptual aspect of generation, and its usefulness for category membership recognition, makes generation much more cognitively salient than lineality—even for anthropologists who sometimes seem unduly fascinated by various kinds of lineality. This is the same psychological tying of kinterms to generation (even where the terminological categories are not in fact generational) that I saw among the Fanti (Kronenfeld 1973, 1975). They had a skewed (Crow-type) terminological system in which relatives such as one's father's sister's daughter's daughter's son was technically one's "father," but they invariably answered questions about fathers in general as if they were speaking of people a generation older than one's own, and they extended the "father" term to nonkinsmen on a generational basis. We shall return to such cases of extended ranges of referents and treat the issue more fully when we get to extensionist semantic theories. However, the present discussion is relevant here, and to some degree stands independently of the extension issue; with or without semantic extension, one still wants to ask about the generational salience of English uncles and Fanti fathers.

The point about the potential usefulness of a perceptually functional feature such as generation for identifying denotata of a category—versus the lack of such usefulness for features such as lineality, which do not function perceptually—raises another question about componential analysis and the semantic paradigms of distinctive features one finds via componential analysis. Discussions have been written as if we used distinctive features of kinsmen to recognize instances of kinterm referents in the same way we use a flat surface at a certain height resting on legs to recognize a table—or the same way that, in componential analysis's phonological model, the features of stop, tongue articulator, and alveolar point of articulation are indeed the features by which we (native speakers and linguists) identify a /p/. As in the case of tables, we do seem sometimes to use perceptual features as the defining attributes of semantic categories, but the kinship case shows that such is not always true and cannot be considered intrinsically true of componential paradigms. A distinctive feature analysis in semantics cannot provide the same set of perceptually criterial attributes that it provides in phonology.

The componentially described paradigm of distinctive semantic features represents instead the pattern of contrast relations among terms in a contrast set that, as native speakers, we know, and that we use in our thinking about and reasoning about the terms of the paradigm. The set of significata (sets of distinctive features) produced by a componential analysis have much more to do with the linguistic significance of the terms than with the identification of denotata of the terms. The signification produced by a componential analysis relates to Saussure's signifieds, or mental representations of what we speak of as the semantic side of the sign (itself a *mental*—cognitive—category), rather than to any actual (non-mental) material objects that linguistic signs might refer to. As such, these sets of significata represent a basic part of the "system of values" that Saussure regarded as a crucial part of langue; the relationship of langue to the external world of our experience was (contra the apparent import of much structuralist writing of the 1970s) important to Saussure, but was not itself a part of the collective representation (that is, the shared cognitive structure) of langue itself. This match of our semantic findings from the realm of kinship with the framework proposed by Saussure constitutes one of my reasons for preferring a

Saussurean view of language to any more recent views (including modern forms of structuralism, or poststructuralism, promulgated—erroneously, see Kronenfeld and Decker 1979—in his name).

Later Romney Work

In follow-up studies with a series of other authors, Romney has significantly refined and developed some of the issues raised in the Romney and D'Andrade article. Wexler and Romney 1972 developed a "process model" for probabilistically deriving similarity judgments from componential models, and used the model to explore the Romney and D'Andrade data and additional similar data. The process models based on the two componential analyses produced clearer expected values for adherence to each of the two componential analyses than the rough-and-ready pictures used by Romney and D'Andrade. Wexler and Romney found that, while neither analysis fit the data precisely, the Romney and D'Andrade analysis provided a much more reasonable fit than that of Wallace and Atkins. Looking at individual variation among their subjects, Romney and D'Andrade found that many individuals who exhibited a basic Romney-and-D'Andrade type structure showed consistent Wallace-and-Atkins type structuring of whatever deviations they had from the basic Romney-and-D'Andrade type structure. These findings were based on the same set of terms (and, hence, implied cognitive context) as that used in the Romney and D'Andrade study— and thus did not contain the "ego" of the Wallace and Atkins' analysis.

Rose and Romney (1979) further explored the issue of individual variation. They use four data sets (the Wexler and Romney "ego"-less triads data, new with-"ego" triads data, new "ego"-less rating-scale data, and new with-"ego" rating-scale data) to explore the effects of different cognitive tasks (triads v. rating scale[7]) and "cognitive context" (here, presence or absence of a reference point[8]) on the results.

The "ego" or "reference point" issue embodies the difference between asking how similar (or conceptually related) "father" and "son" are in the abstract versus how similar (or conceptually related) some particular person's (my, Pat's, your, etc.) "father" is to that particular person's "son." What seems most clearly at issue here is the difference between the observation (on the one hand) that, for example, "grandfather" and "grandson" merely label the same relationship (or genealogical string) from opposite directions or perspectives, and the observation (on the other hand) that "*my* grandfather" has very little in common with "*my* grandson."

Rose and Romney's conclusions were "that varying the cognitive contexts can affect the similarity judgments made by subjects and, unexpectedly, that for the same cognitive context task difference could affect outcomes." They suggested a cognitive overload explanation for the latter finding. Regarding the effects of cognitive context, they found that under appropriate circumstances informants did use (and hence could use) the Wallace and Atkins componential features. Because of the fit between the kind of variant and the cognitive context, they attributed their informant differences to "cognitive pluralism" (wherein each individual has the full array of potential cognitive models available for use as circumstances dictate) rather than to absolute "individual differences" (wherein each individual would have his or her own specific cognitive model for use regardless of the context). I want also to note that they raised the possibility (p. 761) that some of the additional inter-individual variation might be correlated with age.

Rose and Romney did not give detailed analysis or discussion of the specific effects of the variations in cognitive context on the specific feature definition contrasts of absolute generation (1, 2, 3) and polarity (+, −) versus signed generation (+2, +1, 0, −1, −2) and of D/C (direct, collateral) versus lineality (lineal, colineal, ablineal). Their discussion referred to the two (entire) competing componential models. Their detailed data presentation in figures 5-2, 5-3, and table 5-4 did show the effect on both contrasts, though, to my eyes, considerably more sharply for the generation contrast than for the lineality one. This is perhaps relevant, since we have a clear basis for expecting the presence of a reference point to make a difference on the generation/polarity issue, while there seems no such obvious basis for expecting a reference point to have any particular effect on the lineality issue. As I have already indicated, my own feeling is that the lineality issue relates to the relative salience of shared nuclear family membership—which does not interact in any direct or immediate sense with the presence or absence of a reference point.

Psychological Reality

When ethnoscience borrowed componential analysis from linguistics, it received along with it the debate concerning the psychological status of the results of linguistic analysis in general and of componential analysis in particular. In phonological analysis, since what was at issue was the set of perceptual features by which one sound was distinguished from another, the debate had a clear focus.[9]

Initially, in work in anthropological semantics, it was presumed that the perceptual features that distinguished one semantic category from another were, similarly, the objects of analysis. Discussions were couched in terms of "defining features"; the issue of the (implicitly) perceptual nature of such features was not raised, but no other sense in which the semantic features under discussion could be "defining" was even hinted at. Early examples such as Conklin's work on Hanunóo color terms and pronouns, which did appear clearly to be dealing with perceptual attributes, contributed to this presumption.

In the early work on kinship the issue of what psychological status was to be imputed to componential features and, by extension, of what semantic model of language underlay componential analysis, was backgrounded by Lounsbury's emergence as the prime formal theoretician. He insisted that his analysis was a purely formal one aimed only at a most economical accounting for the assignment of kintypes to kinterms, and that it represented no assertions about psychological reality. While these assertions were accurate for Lounsbury's examples and appropriate for a situation[10] in which he had available no way of independently approaching the psychological question, his approach nevertheless served to deflect serious attention from the question of what kind of psychological structures or processes might properly be considered to be entailed by a "successful" componential analysis of a semantic domain.

Psychological reality became an empirical issue in cognitive anthropology through a two-stage process. Wallace and Atkins' analysis focused attention on how a componential analysis was to be understood relative to native-speaker semantic operations and thought (that is, on the analysis's "psychological reality"). It did so by applying the technique to a system that was well known (native) to the relevant anthropological community and by using the kinds of efficiency criteria that linguists had used for phonology to address the issue of psychological reality (1960:359, and cf. 375–379; see Goodenough 1956:195, who Wallace and Atkins cite). Romney and D'Andrade, in comparing their analysis with that of Wallace and Atkins, finally brought actual psychological data to bear on the psychological reality question. They thereby transformed the question of psychological reality (for the first time in anthropology, and for one of the first times, at least, in linguistics) into an empirical one rather than one of (purely) theoretically based logical inference.

By making the question of psychological reality an empirical one they also, perhaps inadvertently, forced anthropologists to consider what particular psychological actions were to be considered psychologically accurately represented. The implicit presumption had been that the anthropological analyst was attending to the distinctive features by which native speakers distinguished members of one category from another—to the features that were involved in implicit native-speaker definitions, where such native definitions formed the basis by which natives recognized an instance as belonging to one terminological category versus another (Wallace and Atkins 1960: 358–359). However, once anthropologists began thinking at all carefully about the issue, it immediately became clear that a feature contrast such as that between lineal and colineal (on a dimension of lineality) could not even be directly perceived, let alone form the perceptual basis for recognizing a given relative as a *father* versus an *uncle*. In fact, the inferences (for natives or anthropologists) have to go the other way around: one infers lineality from fatherhood. An uncle is known to be on a different "line," but a close one, since he is the brother of one of one's parents (or grandparents).

If terminological category membership is not calculated from distinctive features, how *is* it calculated (or known)? For kinterms, there seems to be a two-part answer. First, many of one's relatives are categorized according to their relationship to other of one's relatives. Thus, if I know a person is brother to my father, then I infer that that person is my uncle; my *uncle* category is defined by a set of such "relative products" (in my case, including *mother's brother*, *grandfather's brother*, *grandmother's brother*, and *aunt's husband*). Several of these relative products can be combined in summary form, as, for example, *parent's brother*.[11]

The need for a second part of our answer to the question of how natives decide or calculate to which kinterm category a given relative belongs—that is, to the question of native-speaker definitions—is apparent from an examination of the relative-products. Relative products all are of a form that only relates kinterm categories to other kinterm categories to other kinterm categories. A definitional system of relative products alone would be circular. To break the circle, one needs to have some categories defined from outside the relative product game. These categories should be basic ones in the sense that all the others can be defined by relative products constructed from them. In my usage, these basic categories are mother, father, child, and spouse (with gender); logically, what is at issue (however it is conceptualized) is the parent-child relationship, and the need for two parents of different genders. The definitions of these basics cannot be cast totally as perceptual feature definitions, for the same reasons we ruled out perceptual feature definitions for the full paradigm of terms.[12] These nonrelative product definitions, then, must be in terms of cognitive information—our knowledge of or about key defining actions or activities, here (in our English example) relating to sex and/or marriage and birth. For each kinship terminological system (English, Fanti, or whatever), the determination of which categories are to be defined outside the relative product systems and of the units in which such definitions are to be cast remains a separate empirical matter—even if some powerful ethnological generalizations about such systemic axioms (which enable significant predictions about individual systems) do seem to be emerging.

If we accept the primary claim in the above discussion—that the features produced by a componential analysis cannot be the (perceptual) features by which instances belonging to a terminological category are recognized—then we are left with the question of what the significance of componential analysis is. Romney and D'Andrade's demonstration of the psychological relevance ("reality") of their componential analysis (or, at least, of the features from which it is constructed) precludes us from simply dismissing such analyses as anthropological hocus-pocus. The answer, to my mind, is that folk definitions (or distinctive feature breakdowns) of terminological categories are not produced simply for the purpose of assigning the terms in question, but also for relating the terms to the various cultural uses that occasion the terms' existence. That is, "colineal" is not an important feature for recognizing an instance of an uncle, but the feature is very useful for dealing with the question of how uncles (and aunts) differ (in terms of rights, duties, feelings, interaction patterns, etc.) from fathers (and mothers) on the one hand and from cousins on the other hand. Romney and D'Andrade have given us a way of looking for (and recognizing) such categorizations in thought, apart from the question of whether or not (or in exactly what form) such categories are explicitly labeled in a given language.

In a general sense, we can say that the features turned up by componential analyses are important because, in Lévi-Strauss's phrase from a slightly different context, they are "good to think with." I should point out, incidentally, that while we have been talking explicitly only of sets (or paradigms) of distinctive features determined through a particular analytic technique—componential analysis—our discussion pertains more generally to the fuller set of relations that Saussure spoke of as paradigmatic relations among signs (taken as signifieds). We are here getting at one of the senses in which Saussure characterized language as a "system of values."

Our consideration of kinds of definitions and goals of definitions also allows us to understand the failure of those general semantic models of the sixties that, based on phonological models, tended to assume a kind of continuous, multidimensional semantic space in which all concepts and terms were located—as if all definitions were in terms of features, and as if perception, thought, use, and so forth were all of a single piece. I am suggesting instead that semantic relations among terminological categories are much more complicated and much more particularized (in terms of attributes of usage, the nature of the universe being referred to, what is conversationally at issue, and so forth) than such models allowed. The immediate task for those interested in constructing general semantic maps should be to begin sorting out what kinds of particular structures and/or relations can possibly occur, and under what conditions each does occur. We will later consider some similar structural complexities *within* terminological categories.

We see, in a general way, that what has been spoken of as psychological reality (of componential analyses) relates to a psychological model of the organization of a domain (Saussure's paradigmatic relations) rather than (simply) to definitions of terms within that domain.[13] It follows, then, that alternative psychological realities, based on alternative psychological models, become possible—*provided* the existence of each reality/model is still independently and effectively demonstrated and not merely presumed on the basis of some anthropological intuition. As a general hypothesis, one might consider the proposition that any model that looks to an anthropologist to reasonably fit the data of native usage (both direct and implied) may well also have occurred to native users and hence be psychologically real[14]—provided the domain is one that natives look at from enough different perspectives to pose the utility of each of the various alternatives, and is one that natives use in speech frequently enough for the alternatives to each became fixed as collective representations. Kinship seems the prime universal example of a domain that is overdetermined, in this sense of being representable by a number of very different formal definitional approaches.

In our domain of English kinship, such an example of yet another psychological model (beyond those proffered by Wallace and Atkins and Romney and D'Andrade) seems to be provided by the characterization of English kinterms as built up by children out of household modules that was proposed by Gerber and Chatfield (1971), and referred to by Gladwin (1974). In this model, each household has a "mommy," a "daddy," and "kids." In one's own unit, the kids are brothers and sisters. Another unit has an aunt and uncle in the "mommy" and "daddy" roles and cousins in the "kids" role; yet another unit has grandma and grandpa in the mommy and daddy roles and uncles and/or aunts in the kids role; and so forth. Eventually the child learns, for example, that her or his own mommy or daddy is in the kids role in the grandma/grandpa unit, and thus that the units overlap. Out of the set of overlapping nuclear units the child builds up a model of a genealogy and the framework for learning features such as lineality.

If such alternative "psychological realities" as represented by the componential model of English kinterms, the relative product model, and the household model are to work, each must be (largely) formally equivalent to the others—and thus all formally derivable from one another. On the other hand, since each model, by taking different aspects of the terminological system as axioms from which the rest of the system is derived, foregrounds different aspects of the terminological system, the differences among them are important. We will shortly come to the cognitive expense involved in such over- (or redundant) learning, and thus to the reasons why kinship is unusual in the degree to which it exhibits such overdetermination.

Having dealt with the nature of "psychological reality" and with the potential multiplicity of "psychologically real" models, we are in a position to raise the further question of whether only psychologically real models are of anthropological interest.

Lounsbury's work (1964b, 1965, and see Kronenfeld 1980b) shows the uses of formal models that are constructed in ways that preclude any detailed psychological reality. These uses include at least (a) the identification of the formal properties of a system, which properties then become candidates for ethnographic inspection and psychological investigation; and (b) comparison—with other systems, with posited social causes, with linguistic/grammatical structures, and so forth (see Kronenfeld 1980b and Kronenfeld and Gladwin n.d.).

Notes

1. The issue of focal versus nonfocal referents is not a direct concern at this point in our discussion, but will be our target of discussion later. I am providing the information now because it will aid our understanding of some otherwise inexplicable aspects of the analyses we are examining.

2. Conjunctive categories are those such as the set of red boxes, in which all defining attributes are relevant to each item (that is, each and all members of the set are boxes and are red). Conjunctive categories contrast with disjunctive ones. Disjunctive categories are those such as the set of containers that are either red or boxes, in which only one attribute need be relevant to any given member of the set (that is, every member either is red or is a box).

The difference is that, for a conjunctively defined set, a single (even if possibly complex) definition applies to all members of the set, while for a disjunctively defined set, there are at least two separate alternative definitions that apply to different members of the set.

3. This analysis benefits greatly from discussions of the Romney and D'Andrade article many years ago with Martin Orans.

4. I am, in effect, making the prediction that a similar test with a data set that included nuclear family affinal terms would show a nuclear family clustering that would pull relevant terms in from an otherwise clear consanguineal versus affinal split. I suspect that a fuller set of terms (including the affinals) would show a close-affinal line analogous to Wallace and Atkins's colineals, and that wives and husbands would be ambiguously located between that line and the line of lineal relatives in a way analogous to the ambiguous location of brother and sister between the lineal and colineal lines.

5. It occasionally strikes me as more relevant to anthropological theory concerning kinship than we might care to admit that most students of it not only come from a culture in which its importance is relatively minimal but also study it at a time of their lives when (being either unmarried or only newly married, with only very young children, if any) they only have themselves experienced half of kinship—and only the more passively received and less psychologically salient half (versus the created half, that is, producing offspring, in which one feels more of the stake that comes from procreation, training, and one's concern with one's own continuity) at that.

6. Those reasons will come in our discussion in chapter 8 of George Miller's paper on the magical number seven.

7. On the rating-scale task, informants were asked to rate the similarity of each pairing (for all possible pairings of terms from the kinterm set) on a one-to-ten scale.

8. The reference point they used was "Pat," as in "Pat's uncle." Among the relations examined were those between Pat and Pat's father, Pat and Pat's uncle, and so forth.

9. Subsequent work has, of course, complicated this picture, too, with distinctions having been found between criterial attributes and the perceptual cues that speakers actually use, and with the role of expectations (whether generated by semantic considerations or phonological patterns) looming larger than first expected. But, even so, the relationship of phonological

features to native perceptual features seems much more direct than has proven to be the case for semantic features.

10. Lounsbury was using Morgan's published data from almost a century before.

11. Relative products can be constructed in the analytic language of anthropologists as well as in a native language such as English. Lounsbury makes use of such analytic-language relative products in his later work, as we shall see in chapter 9. Issues concerning conjunctivity also arise both in terms of labeled native categories and in terms of metacategories that may be constructed out of native categories.

12. The basic definitions cannot be cast in terms of such perceptual features even though we often use perceptual features such as relative age as a basis for guessing category assignment when we see family-like groups. At the same time, nothing prevents perceptual features from entering into basic definitions; gender represents such a perceptual feature that is basic for my usage. I also am aware of the issue raised by Paul Kay, among others, concerning the difference between features (or attributes) of a person (such as gender) and features (or attributes) of a relationship (such as parenthood or lineality), but do not see this issue as relevant to the immediate discussion.

13. Wierzbicka (1992:329–331) offers another interpretation of "psychological reality." She appears to see it as inhering in "what native speakers mean by" the terms in question (p. 353), and she interprets these meanings as being best representable to us in terms of her universal semantic primitives (cf. p. 340). She implies at least that the definitions of kinterms she provides (pp. 329–370) are psychologically real by this standard. But she nowhere addresses the question of how she would directly evaluate the psychological status of her proposed primitives or of the definitions she casts in terms of them. Some of the particular instances in her discussion give one cause for unease—as, for example, her characterization (p. 356) of the Pitjantjatjara term *ngunytju* as having "two meanings. One meaning is the same, or roughly the same, as that of the English word *mother*, and the other can be stated, roughly, as follows: 'she is his $ngunytju_2$ = she is thought of as related to him like one's mother ($ngunytju_1$) is related to one.'" One problem concerns the notion that the primary reference of the Pitjantjatjara term is the same as the reference of the English term; denotatively, this might be true, but connotatively it cannot be true. A second problem concerns basing semantic extension on some general and unspecified similarity—a similarity, incidentally, that, as Wierzbicka states it, has to be of the connotative functional sort. Also worrisome is the considerable disjunctivity exhibited by many of her definitions (e.g., pp. 360–361).

Wierzbicka characterizes her definitions as "natural language definitions" (p. 338) since she is basing them on universal semantic primitives that, she asserts, underlie the semantic systems of all languages. A different approach to "natural language definitions" is that of Keen (1985). Keen systematically uses definitions cast in terms (and concepts) taken from the language from which the kinterms come. Keen's perspective represents a different, plausible interpretation of "psychological reality."

14. Lévi-Strauss's remarks (for example, 1963:103; 1969:13) to the effect that structures found by any human mind are in some sense there for all human minds (see Kronenfeld and Decker 1979:525) seem relevant here. Lévi-Strauss's idea implies that anything the analyst can reasonably think of (justify or explain) can also be produced by natives.

III

EXPLANATORY PRINCIPLES

In this part we will examine three principles drawn from cognitive psychology and linguistics that account for or explain major aspects of our findings concerning the shape of semantic structures and their usage. Chapter 6 will treat conjunctive versus disjunctive categories; chapter 7 will look at marked versus unmarked categories; and chapter 8 will consider limits on our information-processing capabilities and the cognitive devices we use to get around these limits.

6

Conjunctivity

We have already spoken of the importance for formal analytic practice of conjunctively defined definitions, whether definitions of analytic categories or features or of folk categories. In this chapter, I want first to summarize the formal reasons for this importance that have already been raised, and then to discuss work in psychology by Bruner, Goodnow, and Austin (1956) that illustrates the psychological importance of conjunctively defined categories for human thought and that somewhat narrows the psychologically relevant definition of conjunctivity from the more general mathematical definition. Next I will describe some classroom experiments of mine that closely relate Bruner, Goodnow, and Austin's psychological work to Nerlove and Romney's study (1967) of the role of conjunctivity in semantic categories. Our exploration of conjunctivity will conclude with a reconsideration of the problem that Nerlove and Romney' findings pose for Romney and D'Andrade's conclusions.

Lounsbury, Mathematics, and Elegance

Lounsbury's reasons for making conjunctivity a prime criterion for distinguishing acceptable from unacceptable features (see Lounsbury 1964a:194) corresponded to the basic reasons of mathematical formalism: without some criterion for the efficiency or effectiveness of an operation, two alternative versions of the operation could not be compared. The criterion was the general one of science known as Occam's Razor: all other things being equal, simpler (or more "elegant") explanations (definitions, mechanisms, or whatever) are preferable to more complex ones; and without explicitness, simplicity cannot be evaluated. The only way one could recognize an operation or category as a single unit was by the single definition by which one recognized these instances. Two definitions meant two units. If one tried to claim a disjunctively defined category or operation as a single unit, then one was left with the question, By what formal criterion could a single unit be distinguished from a set of units? The analyst's intuition did not count. The core of Lounsbury's Iroquois analysis was his search for a single definition by which all the relationships his anthropologically trained intuition told him should be alternative versions of a single cross/parallel distinction could indeed be shown to be such. There was no explicit psychological claim in Lounsbury's formal treatment, though there was, perhaps, the implicit presumption that the same criteria that make conjunctively defined units easier to deal with for mathematicians and formalists might as well make them more reasonable for native speakers.

Bruner, Goodnow, and Austin

In their classic *Study of Thinking* (1956), Bruner, Goodnow and Austin showed that, in experimental situations, individuals found conjunctively defined concepts much easier to learn than disjunctively defined ones.[1] They found, though, that only positively defined features counted toward the definition of a *conjunctively* defined concept; negations of features, which are allowed in mathematical definitions of conjunctivity, did not work psychologically. They further showed that individuals found concepts defined by relative features or attributes (that is, those such as *big* or *small*, that required a comparison) somewhat harder to learn than concepts defined only by absolute features or attributes (that is, those, such as *red*, that could be recognized from a single instance).

In their experiments, Bruner, Goodnow, and Austin used a specially constructed card deck. Each card had one, two, or three figures within a frame consisting of one, two, or three lines. Each card's figures were either red, black, or green, and were shaped either as squares, circles, or crosses. The deck consisted of the resulting 3^4 (or 81) cards. Concepts consisted of combinations of features, such as red circles, doubly outlined double figures, red squares or triply outlined cards, squares or crosses, and so forth. Conjunctively defined concepts were defined by the intersection of one or more features; disjunctively defined concepts had definitions that included unions of features. A positively defined feature was one, such as red, that could be stated directly. The union of black and green, in this limited universe, could be defined conjunctively as not-red according to the normal rules of mathematical formalism; but such negatively constructed definitions were treated by Bruner, Goodnow, and Austin's subjects as being disjunctive rather than conjunctive. Absolute features[2] were those, such as "red figures" or "three borders," that could be recognized directly without any comparison of one feature value with another; relative features were those, such as "the same number of figures as borders" or "more borders than figures," that could only be recognized by comparing one absolute feature value with another.

Kronenfeld Classroom Experiments

To make the link between Bruner, Goodnow, and Austin's research and Nerlove and Romney's project (which will be addressed next) more clear, and to give students an analog of the Nerlove and Romney research to hold onto as they studied that work, I constructed a classroom experiment that directly made clear the links between the two. My classroom experiment involved examining the ad hoc concepts found in individuals' responses to a task. My conceptual categories were like those of Bruner, Goodnow, and Austin in that they were defined by simple geometric features, were individually perceived and learned, and form part of no established cultural code. As such, my categories contrasted with those of Nerlove and Romney, which were nonperceptually defined and coded in language. On the other hand, my research design was quite closely modeled on that of Nerlove and Romney; it was based on the same number of items as was their research, and my items differed from one another in ways closely analogous to the ways theirs differed. My task, like Bruner, Goodnow, and

Austin's, involved subjects forming categories (that could be considered concepts), but it left subjects freer to form categories as they wished than did Bruner, Goodnow, and Austin's tasks and let them do so more passively. The manner of concept formation was intended to provide as close an individual analog as possible to the cognitive aspect of the collective process by which categories in a language are shaped. I am separating the cognitive aspect from the functional aspect, which has to do with the reasons speakers of a language find some categorization useful in their communication. My experimental idea, which looked ahead to Nerlove and Romney's study of word categories in natural language, was to see what kinds of categorizations individuals produced and how these categorizations related to those Nerlove and Romney found in natural language. My pedagogical goal was to familiarize my students with the Nerlove and Romney research design and, if the results came out as I hypothesized, to give them a direct sense of the relevance of Nerlove and Romney's issues to their own behavior.

In my experiments I drew the eight figures shown in figure 6-1 on the chalkboard in the arrangement shown in the figure. The figures were constructed along absolute feature contrasts of convex v. concave, and sharp-cornered v. rounded, and consisted of four shapes: squares, circles, check-like mashed squares, and mashed circles. Each figure was drawn in a large and a small form to provide one relative feature. Incidental information that the students had available for use (though it was not part of the planned design) included location of the figures (on the board and in relation to the group of figures) and attributes of the index numbers (odd vs. even, big vs. small, closed vs. open, angular vs. rounded, etc.).

I asked the students to pretend that each figure was on a card, and to sort the cards into piles, such that every card/figure was in one, but only one, pile, and then to write the numbers of the figures that went into each pile on a sheet of paper. Usually, I told them to give me three different "sorts" without telling them how many piles to form; sometimes I told them to give me three two-pile sorts and a three-pile sort. After the students made their sorts, I then surveyed the class to find out which arrangements had been produced and how many students had listed each. The experiments were fairly informally posed and scored, since their primary aim was pedagogical, but the results, clearly not forced by the design, are quite interesting. Before looking at the results, though, let us consider what we would predict on the basis of Bruner, Goodnow, and Austin's work.

Categorizations

First, let us define a "categorization" as a set of categories such that every item in the set of items to be categorized goes into one, but only one, category. To facilitate our comparison with Nerlove and Romney's study, we want to make our predictions about complete categorizations rather than about separate individual categories. Since Bruner, Goodnow, and Austin did not show disjunctively defined concepts to be impossible to learn, but only relatively difficult, our predictions are not of absolute presence or absence but only of relative frequencies of occurrence (assuming frequency to follow from ease). Because conjunctively defined concepts are much easier to form than are disjunctively defined ones, we predict that categorizations with

FIG. 6-1 Kronenfeld's Drawings and Summary Information for Two-Category
Categorizations

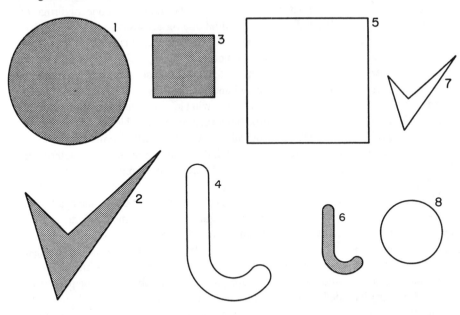

Summary Info for Two-category Categorizations

	1970		1972		1973		1979		1984		1987	
	A	S	A	S	A	S	A	S	A	S	A	S
Conj. on Figures	4	78	4	75	4	87	4	47	4	37	4	27
Conj. on Numbers	4	6	1	1	1	1	2	2	2	2		
Total Conj.	8	84	5	76	5	88	6	49	6	39	4	27
?	1	4	1	1	1	1						
C/-C	4	13	4	6	1	2					1	1
-C	2	2										
Total -C & ?	7	19	5	7	2	3					1	1
Disj.	2	2	5	6					5	5		
Total	17	105	15	89	7	91			11	44	5	28

The years at the top refer to the years in which the classroom data in the given column were collected. "A," number of
arrangements; "S," number of students (who produced that arrangement); "Conj. on Figures," conjunctive on the figures—that is, for arrangements that were conjuntively categorized in terms of attributes of the actual figures; "Conj. on
Numbers," conjunctive on the number—that is, for arrangements that were conjunctively categorized in terms of attributes of the identification numbers of the figures; "C/–C," part conjunctive, part not—that is, for arrangements in which
a conjunctively defined category was contrasted with a non-conjunctively defined one; "–C & ?," arrangements which
combined non-conjunctively defined categories with categories whose conjunctivity I was unsure of; "Disj," disjunctive
categorizations.

conjunctively defined categories will be more frequent than those without them, and we predict that categorizations with disjunctively defined categories will be less frequent that those without them. Finally, we predict mildly greater frequency for categorizations lacking relative features than for those having them.

The results from these experiments are detailed in table 6-1. They are overwhelmingly as one would predict from the Bruner, Goodnow, and Austin work, and, indeed, much more clearly so than I had initially expected. We find that there is very strong selection against systems of categorization that include any disjunctively defined category at all, and we find that categories defined conjunctively (in the mathematical sense) by the the negation of features are *not* treated by the students as conjunctive. Although it is less sharply defined, we can further see—beyond our Bruner, Goodnow, and Austin predictions—that simply defined categories and those based on salient or intrinsic features are preferred to more complexly defined categories or categories based on more incidental features. In presenting the stimulus set, I told the students nothing about what information to use or not to use, and so did not directly bias them either toward or away from what I spoke of above as "incidental information." It is interesting, therefore, to note (in connection with implicit cultural norms about what counts as part of a thing and what does not) that students did sometimes use this information—but not very often.

The relative features I built into this set did not involve a comparison of absolute features (as did the relative features of Bruner, Goodnow, and Austin), but involved only the lesser task of directly comparing two figures. Thus, recognition of my relative features (which consisted of picking out the figure to be compared with the one at issue, and then directly comparing the two) involves less work than recognition of Bruner, Goodnow, and Austin's relative features (which consisted of picking out and identifying two absolute features of a figure, and then comparing these), and, in fact, only involves a little more work than does recognition of my absolute features (directly examining only the single figure at issue). My choice of relative features was determined in part by the nature of the universe of figures I picked (in my effort to parallel the Nerlove and Romney study) and in part (and more directly) by my understanding of the nature of the relative features involved in Nerlove and Romney's domain of study (that is, kinship terminologies).

The relative versus absolute feature distinction did not loom large in my classroom experiment results. Possible reasons for this mild divergence from Bruner, Goodnow, and Austin include differences in the nature of the features involved, which were just discussed; constraints implied by the particular nature of the universe involved in my experiment; or something having to do with the relative salience of my relative features versus theirs.

I did not use in my scoring any information from the students about the features they thought themselves to be using in providing the categorizations. Instead, I did what Nerlove and Romney did when confronting their linguistic data—that is, I accepted any category as conjunctively defined for which I could find a plausible conjunctive definition. I have provided my definitions in table 6.1 in order to allow readers to draw their own conclusions about my decisions.

Our overall explanatory principle is something that might be called "cognitive ease"; we are assuming that, all else being equal, people are more likely to do easy

TABLE 6-1. Categorization Information for Kronenfeld's Drawings

Arrange-ment	Conj or Disj	Feature	No. of students choosing, and rank order (RO)											
			1970		1972		1973		1979		1984		1987	
			#	RO	#	RO	#	RO	#	RO	#	RO	#	RO
Two-category Categorizations														
1236 4578	C	Shaded vs. not	33	1	25	2	30	1	15	1	15	1	10	1
1245 3678	C	Big vs. small	9	4.5	9	4	15	3.5	4	4	11	2	6	3
1468 2357	C	Angle vs. rounded	22	2	28	1	27	2	14	2.5	7	3	8	2
1358 2467	C	Convex vs. concave	14	3	23	3	15	3.5	14	2.5	4	4	3	4
1357 2468	C	Odd vs. even	2		1				1					
1234 5678	C	≤4 , >4	2				1		1					
1278 2456	?	Edge vs. center	4	6	1		1							
1348 2567	D		1											
1458 2367	D		1											
1456 2378	D				2									
1257 3468	D				1									
1568 2347	D				1									
1346 2578	D										1			
1268 3457	D										1			
1457 2368	D										1			
678 12345	C	>5, ≤5	1								1			
123 45678	C	≤3 , >3	1								1			
124 35678	-C	Big, not-square vs. rest	1											
126 34578	-C	Shaded, not-square vs. rest	1											
145 23678	C/-C	Big, not-square vs. rest			2									
148 23567	D				1									
247 13568	D								1					
135 24678	D										1			
18 234567	C/-C	Circle vs. not-circle	9	4.5	1									
46 123578	C/-C	Curve vs. not-curve	1		2		2							
35 124678	C/-C	Square vs. not-square	2		1									
27 134568	C/-C	Check vs. not-check	1										1	
36 124578	D				1									
13 245678	D										1			
More Than Two Categories Per Categorization														
18 35 2467	C	(Circle vs. square) vs. concave	NA		NA		NA		NA		2	1	4	1
13 28 4567	D										1			
27 35 1468	C	(Check vs. square) vs. rounded corners									1			
23 145 678	D										1			
36 127 458	D										1			
16 234 578	D										1			
18 27 35 46	C	Circle vs. check vs. square vs. curve									14		5	
16 23 48 57	C	Shaded rounded/shaded sharp/clear rounded/clear sharp											1	

NA, not allowed in instructions given to classes

things than more difficult things. But cognitive ease, in this general sense, is undefined, and may be impossible to define. So we have taken conjunctivity as one particular attribute that makes for relative cognitive ease; we are also, in our discussion, assuming that simplicity (versus complexity) of definition, relative salience of a feature, and familiarity with the materials (on the part of the subject) are additional factors that make for cognitive ease.

Nerlove and Romney

Nerlove and Romney (1967)[3] investigated the applicability of Bruner, Goodnow, and Austin's results to the concepts entailed by the semantic categories of natural language. They saw linguistic categories as being the product of a kind of natural experiment in which successive generations each had to relearn the concept in question. Since the learning by each successive generation represented a new instance of concept formation, the presumption was that errors in transmission should be in the direction of greater cognitive ease, as predicted by Bruner, Goodnow, and Austin's work (as well as by marking theory, as developed by Greenberg, which we shall examine in Chapter 7). That is, we expect easy categories to be learned more often than hard, and to be more accurately learned than hard.

For their study of the effects of conjunctivity on natural language, Nerlove and Romney had to select a domain that was well described for a large number of languages. It had to be a domain for which the categories' defining attributes were well known, and for which those defining attributes were strictly comparable across the full universe of terminologies. Kinship terms provided one of the few domains for which the defining attributes were well known, but the full ranges of kinterms in different languages extended in various ways and embodied a wide range of alternative forms and meanings. To ensure comparability, Nerlove and Romney selected a subcategory of kinterms—sibling terms—that all languages possess. They dealt with the comparability problem by limiting their study to terms for "true siblings"—that is, to focal referents of terms in the sibling category (taking advantage of insights from Lounsbury [1964b, 1965] and Berlin and Kay [1969] that we shall shortly consider)—and not considering the full ranges of the various sibling terms, which can vary considerably from language to language.

Their units were terminologies, not particular terms. They were concerned with the full set of sibling terms in each terminology; that is, with the set of terms that partitioned the set of "true siblings" such that each member of that set was in one, but only one, terminological category. In the terms we defined above, Nerlove and Romney were looking for conjunctive categorizations (defined as a partition of the full set of "true siblings" such that each type falls into one and only one category, but wherein a single category includes one or more types) and not simply for conjunctive categories (wherein each separate category is treated as a stand-alone entity, each of which includes one or more types of "true sibling").

In order to get a measure of how likely or unlikely a chance conjunctive categorization was, Nerlove and Romney had to determine how many total categorizations were possible for the universe they were considering when conjunctivity was ignored.

To find this number, they first identified all the feature contrasts that seemed to be defining for any sibling terms in any formal treatment; they then maximally subdivided the universe of "true siblings" by these features, and took the resulting types as atomic units. Finally, they calculated the total number of categorizations that could be constructed out of these atomic units, which represented the total number of possible categorizations of focal siblings, against which they could examine the implications of Bruner, Goodnow, and Austin's (and of Greenberg's) findings.

All focal siblings consist of an alter (the relative), ego (the person whose relative the alter is), and a sibling relationship that links the two. There are no linking relatives, as there would be with English cousins or grandparents, or with extended siblings in many other languages. All defining features, then, must be attributes of ego, alter, or the relationship between them. Feature contrasts that were found to be relevant were sex of ego, sex of alter, relative sex of ego and alter (the same or different), and relative age of ego and alter. Other features on which siblings might differ, such as eye color or intelligence, were not found to be relevant to any terminological categories, and so were ignored. Absolute birth-order terms, either for the whole set or only within genders, are found in terminologies, but only as an overlay, and never as part of the basic partition of the set of sibling terms, and so were excluded. Allowing such empirically irrelevant features would have artificially inflated Nerlove and Romney's numbers and thereby have unfairly stacked the data in their favor.[4]

The set of atomic units defined by these features, consists of eight kintypes. In the Romney notation system, these are *mome, momy, mofe, mofy, fofe, fofy, fome,* and *fomy.* The sets of features used to derive these kintypes contain some redundancies or overlap (between sex of ego and sex of alter, on the one hand, and relative sex, on the other), and so each of these can be defined in alternative ways. For example, mom (whether -e or -y) can be defined as [male ego, male alter], [male ego, same-sex sibling], or [male alter, same-sex sibling].

Any unique allocation of these eight kintypes to hypothetical kinterm categories constitutes a categorization. Categorizations can range from those with a single kinterm (which contains all eight kintypes) through those with several kinterms (each of which contains several kintypes) to those with eight kinterms (each of which contains a single kintype). Conjunctive categorizations are those for which conjunctive definitions (in terms of combinations of features from the list of relevant contrasts) can be found for all the included terminological categories. Table 6-2 lists the total number of categorizations possible for this universe, broken down by number of kinterm categories per categorization and by number of kintypes per kinterm category. For each number-of-kintypes-per-kinterm entry the total logically possible number of such categorizations is indicated, and the number of those that are conjunctive is indicated in parentheses under the total number. The total number of categorizations (of all makeups) possible is 4,140, of which only 442 are conjunctive.

The remainder of the Nerlove and Romney deductive exercise is relevant to our general concern with the role of cognitive ease in shaping collectively held human cognitive systems (that is, collective representations).

Additional assumptions, based on aspects of Bruner, Goodnow, and Austin's findings other than conjunctivity, on Greenberg's work on marked versus unmarked categories (see chapter 7), and on other measures of cognitive ease, are used to further

TABLE 6-2. Number of Kintypes per Kinterm Logically Possible (from Kronenfeld 1974:502)

Number of Terms	Distribution of Kintypes per Term[a]				
1	8 (1)[1] 0:1 1:0:0:0				
2	1-7 (8)[0]	2-6 (28)[0]	3-5 (56)[0]	4-4 (35)[6] 2:4 0:4:0:0	
3	1-1-6 (28)[0]	1-2-5 (168)[0]	1-3-4 (280)[16] 16:0	2-2-4 (210)[27] 9:18 0:0:18:0	2-3-3 (280)
4	1-1-1-5 (56)[0]	1-1-2-4 (420)[50] 18:32 0:0:0:32	1-1-3-3 (28)[8] 8:0	1-2-2-3 (840)[32] 32:0	2-2-2-2 (105)[22] 6:16 0:4:12:0
5	1-1-1-1-4 (70)[12] 4:8 0:0:8:0	1-1-1-2-3 (560)[64] 64:0	1-1-2-2-2 (420)[88] 20:68 0:0:0:68		
6	1-1-1-1-1-3 (56)[8] 8:0	1-1-1-1-2-2 (210)[89] 17:72 0:0:16:56[b]			
7	1-1-1-1-1-1-2 (28)[18] 2:16 0:0:0:16				
8	1-1-1-1-1-1-1-1 (1)[1] 0:1 0:1:0:0				

[a]Taken from Nerlove and Romney's table 1 (1967:180). I have added the bracketed information and the ratios.

[b]The ratio of secondaries to tertiaries in this case is not automatically certain; it depends, in part, on the order in which one considers alternative arrangements of the eight kintypes in terms of features and, in part, on how some ambiguous cases are assigned.

Key: Numbers separated by dashes indicate the number of kintypes per term.
Numbers in parentheses indicate the number of unique combintations.
Numbers in brackets indicate the number of conjunctively defined categorizations.
First ratio compares the number of conjunctively defined categorizations using sex-of-elder or sex-of-younger as features with the number using only the other four features.
Second ratio divides the second number from the first ratio according to how many of the categorizations use no distinctions, only primary distinctions, only primary and secondary distinctions, and all three kinds, including tertiaries.

reduce the number categorizations (out of the remaining logically possible ones) that are predicted to be empirically possible. Let us number these additional assumptions (in order to maintain consistency with the original publications, especially Kronenfeld 1974, where the reasoning behind these assumptions is detailed). The first such assumption, Assumption 6, is that cognitively difficult features such as "sex of eldest (member of the sibling dyad)" or "sex of youngest" will not occur. Assumption 1, deriving from Bruner, Goodnow, and Austin's findings regarding absolute versus relative features, is that "two relative components will not occur as primary features." Primary features are ones that, in a given categorization, apply to the full set of eight sibling types; secondary features apply to half of the set (that is, to a subuniverse of four types), and tertiary features apply to a quarter of the set (that is, to a subuniverse of two types). In the sibling universe, Assumption 1 means that "relative age and same-sex/opposite-sex distinctions will not occur together as cross-cutting primary features." Assumption 2, deriving from Greenberg's work on marking, is that "relatively incompletely extended features will only occur on the unmarked side of relatively completely extended ones." For this purpose, male is assumed to be unmarked relative to female, and elder relative to junior; no marking relationship is presumed for the same-sex/opposite-sex distinction. There is no Assumption 3. Assumption 4, deriving from functional considerations, is that "if relative-age occurs as a secondary distinction where same-sex/opposite-sex as the primary distinction, it will be on the same-sex side." The final assumption, Assumption 5, deriving from considerations of cognitive economy, is that "sex-of-speaker will not be a feature of sibling terms."

Table 6-3 shows the deductive implications of Assumption 6, and breaks down the remaining, uneliminated categorizations according to their use of secondary or teritiary distinctions. Table 6-4 details the interaction of assumptions 1, 2, 4, and 5 with the minimal size of categories. Figure 6-2 shows Nerlove and Romney's twelve principal types (that is, types without tertiary distinctions that were not eliminated by the deductive exercise). Table 6-6 lists the subdivisions of these types that are possible through the use of noneliminated tertiary distinctions. Figure 6-3 shows other possible types.

Nerlove and Romney found empirical data on sibling terminologies for 245 languages. Their findings concerning the conjunctivity of the classifications embodied in these terminologies are summarized in table 6-5. The results show an overwhelming preference for conjunctive over disjunctive categorizations. Additionally, the results appear very similar to those of my classroom experiment, and therefore suggest that the experiments indeed provided a reasonable individual psychological model for the sibling study, and lend credence to Nerlove and Romney's view of their linguistic results as those of a kind of continuing natural experiment in concept formation.[5] The major difference regarding conjunctivity between my classroom exercise and Nerlove and Romney's sibling results is the even lower proportion of disjunctive concepts that arise in their interactively constrained, socially shared linguistic categories than arise by chance in the individual creations from my classroom experiment (where chance is strongly skewed by the cognitive ease gradient). The constraints of sharing appear to preclude passing on most of even those few difficult disjunctive categorizations that individuals do manage to create.

The difference in ease of concept formation found by Bruner, Goodnow, and Austin between relative and absolute features does not seem to have had much effect in Nerlove and Romney's kinship case. Possible reasons include the fact that kinterms

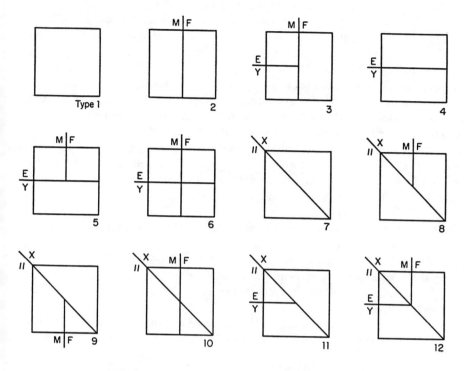

FIG. 6-2 Nerlove and Romney's Twelve Types Using Only Primary and Secondary Distinctions (from Kronenfeld 1974:493 [Figure 1])

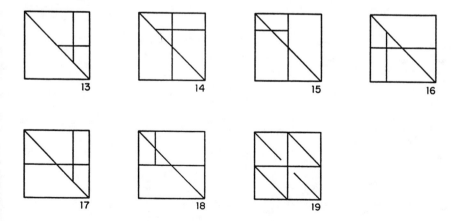

Fig. 6-3 Additional Uneliminated Types (from Kronenfeld 1974:504 [Figure 6])

are already binary (or dyadic) and hence, in a sense, intrinsically comparative (or relative); the fact that age can be brought in only a relative sense (variable and large sibling set sizes make an absolute feature, whether of age or birth order, too complicated as a way to deal with dyads); the possibility that the root gender perception is "like or unlike me" instead of "male or female"; and the fact that many of the social bases that might produce terminological sex distinctions among siblings are relative (as in same versus opposite sex) instead of absolute. In any event, Nerlove and Romney's relative sex feature certainly has the characteristics of the kind of relative feature I used in my classroom experiment (as opposed to the characteristics of the kind used by Bruner, Goodnow, and Austin), and their relative age feature seems likely to have those characteristics as well. Thus, their results for relative versus absolute features do parallel those of my classroom experiment; both show a somewhat smaller effect of the difference between relative and absolute features than Bruner, Goodnow, and Austin found in their work.

However, problems with complex relative features do show up when one considers the possibility of making an absolute judgment about a relative category, as one would have to if one used the feature contrasts of sex of elder or sex of younger. Such categorizations do not show up empirically, and there are good reasons to expect that they would not. They are complex, cognitively difficult features, even though conjunctively defined.

The results concerning marking will be discussed in chapter 8, where the distinction between marked and unmarked categories is addressed.

TABLE 6-3. Summary of Information from Table 6-2 with Factors that Distinguish Empirically Likely from Unlikely Categorizations (from Kronenfeld 1974:503 [Table 2])

Factor	Number of kinterms in a categorization								
	1	2	3	4	5	6	7	8	Totals
Total number of unique combinations	1	127	966	1,701	1,050	266	28	1	4,140
Disjunctively defined	0	121	923	1,589	886	169	10	0	3,698
Conjunctively defined	1	6	43	112	164	97	18	1	442 4,140
Sex-of-elder and sex-of-younger used as features	0	2	25	64	88	25	2	0	206
Sex-of-elder and sex-of-younger not used as features (my assumption 6)	1	4	18	48	76	72	16	1	236 442
Only absolute attributes used	1	2	4	1	0	0	0	0	8
≥ 1 relative attribute used	0	2	14	47	76	72	16	1	228 236
No distinctions made	1	0	0	0	0	0	0	0	1
Primary distinctions only used	0	4	0	4	0	0	0	1	9
Primary and secondary distinctions used only	0	0	18	12	8	16	0	0	54
Primary, secondary, and tertiary distinctions used	0	0	0	32	68	56	16	0	172 236
≥2 kintypes per term	1	4	18	16	0	0	0	0	39
< 2 kintypes per term	0	0	0	32	76	72	16	1	197 236

TABLE 6-4. Summary of Information from Table 6-2 with Factors that Distinguish Empirically Likely from Unlikely Categorizations (from Kronenfeld 1974:503 [Table 3])

						Empirically existent types	*Others not excluded*	*Totals*
Kronenfeld								
Assumption #, by which categorizations are excluded from empirical universe	5	1	2	4	7			
Categorizations with all categories containing two or more kintypes	14	1	8	2	4	12	0	39
Categorizations with at least one category that contains only one kintype	8	0	12	2	2	0	8	32
Totals	22	1	20	4	4	12	8	71

Reconciliation of Nerlove and Romney with Romney and D'Andrade

Our examination of Nerlove and Romney's demonstration of the strong importance of conjunctive definitions for human concepts serves to heighten the problem posed by Romney (the same) and D'Andrade's demonstration of the "psychological reality" (even if only weak and partial, as we suggested) of their disjunctively defined direct and collateral values on their direct/collateral feature. We dealt with part of the problem, involving their inclusion of siblings with lineals, with an appeal (a rather ad hoc one, unfortunately) to some more general notions of cognitive ease. Our present findings from Nerlove and Romney's sibling study do not change the Romney and D'Andrade picture, but they do explain why we want to take the conjunctivity requirement seriously as a psychological constraint and not leave it simply as a matter of mathematical elegance, and they do lend some support to the more general idea that the underlying psychological consideration in accounting for the shape of linguistic categories (behind the conjunctivity constraint, among others) is one of cognitive ease. Thus, finally, these new insights concerning the Romney and D'Andrade findings still leave us with the problem of precisely how to deal with their "direct versus collateral" distinction.

Nothing in Nerlove and Romney's analysis directly helps us with the additional problem in Romney and D'Andrade's analysis posed by the overlap, among their collaterals, of the range of *cousin* with the ranges of *uncle/aunt/nephew/niece*. However, a comparison of how the two studies approach their problem does suggest one insight. Nerlove and Romney limited themselves to what we have called (without yet

TABLE 6-5. The Empirical Effects of Conjunctivity (from Nerlove and Romney 1967:183 [Table 2])

Total number of terminologies examined	*245*
Number with conjunctive categorizations	240
Number with disjunctive categorizations	4
Number for which they did not make the determination	1

TABLE 6-6. Kronenfeld's Additional Subtypes Adding in Tertiary Distinctions to Nerlove and Romney's 12 (from Kronenfeld 1974:505 [Figure 7])

Number of Kintypes per Category	Major Ideal Type see Fig. 6-2	Tertiary Type Derived from Major Ideal Type	Reasons and Comments
	1,2,4,7	none possible	None of these contain any categories that have only 2 kintypes that could be divided by a tertiary distinction.
1-1-2-4	6,10,2	none possible	None of them have any categories that contain 4 kintypes as required by the division.
	3		See special case discussion *re:* assumption 7
	5		See special case discussion *re:* assumption 7
	8		If assumption 4 is not read as also barring the tertiary relative age distinction from the x side of relative sex.
	9		
	11		
1-1-2-2-2			
	3,5,8,9,11	none	Each has a category containing 4 kintypes which cannot be divided by a tertiary distinction.
	6		See special case distinction *re:* assumption 7.
	10		
	12		
1-1-1-1-2-2			
	3,5,8,9,11	none	
	6,10	none	Each uses two primary features leaving only one feature to subdivide; could only be done with use of secondary distinction.
	12		
IV-4 1-1-1-1-1-2			
	3,5,8,9,11	none	
	6,10	none	would require at least added secondary distinctions.

defining the term) "focal" referents (or ranges) of their sibling terms, while Romney and D'Andrade dealt with full (extended) ranges. Had Romney and D'Andrade limited their consideration to focal referents, the problem of the range of one term overlapping the componential definition of another[6] would not have arisen, and a componential view that split G0 and G1 each into close (that is, "direct") and distant (that is, "collateral") would have made some sense. In chapter 9 we will take up the systematic distinction between focal and extended referents of a term.

Notes

1. My characterization here, while sticking closely to Bruner, Goodnow, and Austin's original, does involve some reliance on clarifications I introduced in my article discussing Nerlove and Romney's work (Kronenfeld 1974). These few clarifications are explicated in my article.

2. Bruner, Goodnow, and Austin actually spoke of "relative concepts," which they contrasted with conjunctive and disjunctive ones. Their "relative concepts" were easier to learn than their "disjunctive" ones and harder than their "conjunctive" ones. Since their relative concepts were defined by a kind of feature (relative versus absolute), while their conjunctive and disjunctive ones were defined by the way features were combined (logical product versus sum), I chose in my discussion of their work, from which my present treatment is drawn (Kronenfeld 1974), to separate the two kinds of differences. At the same time, I should point out that since their relative concepts do involve a comparison of absolute features, there is a sense in which the cognitive operations involved in using relative features are not totally unlike those involved in forming concepts with absolute features.

3. My discussion here is based on both their article and my own reanalysis and extension of their work (Kronenfeld 1974). In order to get across the ideas, which I want to use as clearly as possible, I am not distinguishing the original form of their ideas and work from my own refinements of these. Accurate assessment of credit or blame for anything I say here can easily be made by comparing their article (Nerlove and Romney 1967) with my reanalysis (Kronenfeld 1974); anything from this discussion not found in either article is my further contribution for the present work. I speak in my discussion of Nerlove and Romney's work without modification by way of recognizing that the basic analytic insights were theirs.

4. Such stacking would be attained by artificially increasing the number of logical possibilities from which the same small number of accurate predictions would be made. Given the results, Nerlove and Romney's definition of the universe of logically possible sibling types is a very conservative one.

5. Durkheim (1938) cited "collective representations" as the (emergent) properties of society, the social facts that were irreducible to individual psychology and that thus justified a separate science of sociology (taken broadly to include, inter alia, modern linguistics and anthropology). For Durkheim, as for Saussure, who shared his interest in collective social phenomena (see, for example, Saussure [1916] 1959:6, 9, 11–14, 77–78) and who in some ways better explained such phenomena, language was the example par excellence of collective representations (see, for example, Durkheim 1938:2-8). The Nerlove and Romney demonstration is important for anthropology and sociology as a key example of the tight logical derivation of social facts (that is, of important aspects of collective representations) from findings of individual psychology. In an age in which chemistry has been reduced via physical chemistry to physics, I mention Nerlove and Romney's reduction not to denigrate Durkheim or his sociology but to illustrate the (generally unrecognized) importance of the Nerlove and Romney paper.

I will save for another occasion (see Kronenfeld and Kaus 1994) my more general solution to the problem of what Durkheim meant by "collective representations" and how such representations, as discussed both by him and by Saussure, can be reconciled to a world of individual minds without resorting to the kind of bland mysticism that too often tempts academics. That solution is illustrated with a simple computer simulation that actually generates Durkheimian collective phenomena from individual desires and actions operating in a social environment.

6. The problem is represented by the situation in which extended members of of one category—say, in English, "cousins" who are ego's parents' "first cousins"—fall into the componential definition of another category—in our English example, that of "uncles" or "aunts," defined as first generation, ascendant collateral. That is, while Romney and D'Andrade's componential analysis does correctly partition the set of focal relatives into kinterm categories, it does not deal so well with the extended ranges of the kinterms.

7

Marking

Greenberg (see esp. 1966) has been the major developer of marking theory, taking it from its Prague School origins in phonology and extending it to additional phonological phenomena, as well as to a wide range of morphological, syntactic, and semantic phenomena.

Prague Origins

The relationship between marked and unmarked categories was first described by Trubetzkoy[1] (see Trubetzkoy 1969, also Jakobson 1939). He noticed that in German the distinction between voiced and unvoiced stops disappeared (was "neutralized") in word final position. Thus the /d/ of *Bäder* contrasted with the /t/ of *beten* on the feature of voicing (/d/ being voiced and /t/ being unvoiced). But, in word final position, the /d/ of *Bad* had the same pronunciation as the /t/ of *bet*. Moreover, the common pronunciation of /d/ and /t/ in word-final positions was not some kind of average or random mix or random choice of the two word-medial pronunciations, but instead for all such pairs was consistent and predictable. In our example, the common pronunciation of /d/ and /t/, when their contrast was neutralized, was the pronunciation of /t/.

To understand why /t/ rather than /d/ or something else represented the neutralized pair, we need to briefly introduce a little information about Prague linguistic theory of the time and to look at the physical specification of our contrasting sounds in terms of that theory. We have already noted that componential analysis in American anthropology was borrowed from Prague School phonology, and in particular from Trubetzkoy's work. Instead of providing a universal list of phone types (i.e., sounds) in which all the sounds of any language could be described and then grouping these phone types into sets to describe the phonemic system of a particular language (in the manner of American linguistics of the period), Trubetzkoy and his colleague Jakobson described the phonemes of a language directly in terms of the distinctive features by which they contrasted with one another (or were distinguished one from the other). In Trubetzkoy's work, these were articulatory features, though later Jakobson switched to acoustic features; Jakobson, through his connections with Halle (Jakobson, Fant, and Halle 1951), provided the basis for modern transformational phonology.

Voicing was one of the feature contrasts used componentially to define German phonemes. Some feature contrasts, such as point of articulation/articulator, involved specific and differing articulatory actions for the production of each feature in the

89

contrast set. Others, however, such as voicing, aspiration, or nasalization, only contrasted the presence of an articulatory act with the absence of that act. Thus, /t/ and /d/ in German contrasted only on the feature of voicing; /d/ was identical to /t/ (as a labio-alveolar stop) except that /d/ was voiced (or entailed the action of voicing) where /t/ was not voiced (or did not entail the action of voicing). The opposition between /t/ and /d/, then, was an asymmetrical one, depending on the presence versus the absence of a given articulatory action. What Trubetzkoy noticed was that whenever the opposition between two sounds that differed only in the presence versus the absence of some specific articulation was neutralized, it was always the sound that lacked the specific articulation involved in the contrast that stood for (or instantiated) both the sounds. He spoke of the sound that had the articulation in question as the "marked" member of the opposition—marked by the added articulation—and he spoke of the sound that lacked the articulation on which the contrast was based as the "unmarked" member. The unmarked member was, thus, the more basic of the two, being defined *only* by all the attributes that the two shared; the marked member was derivative, being defined by all the attributes of the unmarked member *plus* the additional articulation/attribute by which the two sounds contrasted. His generalization was that whenever the contrast between a marked and an unmarked member of an opposition was neutralized, it was always the unmarked member (as the more basic member) that would stand for (or instantiate) them both.

Greenberg's Generalization

When Greenberg extended the idea of marking from the phonology of its Prague origins to other aspects of language, he had to find a more general criterion on which to base the opposition than the added articulation on which Trubetzkoy had based the phonological case. Greenberg began by detailing the attributes that covaried with marking in phonology. These attributes, where relevant differences existed, included the greater text frequency of the unmarked versus the marked, the greater amount of subphonemic variation in the unmarked than in the marked (for example, in English, we can see the distinction between aspirated and unaspirated /p/ versus the lack of any such difference for /b/), the use of the unmarked phoneme to represent both opposites when the opposition is neutralized (as in our *Bad, bet* example from German), and so forth. And, importantly, he found that these regularities of marked versus unmarked categories were not restricted to German but held true for all languages.

Greenberg's basic task was to find the set of attributes that, whenever present, invariably covaried with marking relations[2] (and thus also covaried with each other), which either singly or together could be used as reliable indicators of marking. A related but different issue concerned the causal connections between these attributes and the marking phenomenon. For phonology, because of the defining (or criterial) nature of the articulations involved, there seemed to be a clear case for accepting as basic Trubetzkoy's criterion, by which a marked phoneme contrasts with its unmarked equivalent by having an added articulation. The causal train by which the other attributes are linked to the added articulation involves the notion that, all other things being equal, people will choose the easier option more often than the more difficult (the "cognitive ease" assumption). It also involves the observation that the category, such as /d/, that involves the added articulation cannot develop prior to the category, such as /t/, that lacks it, because such a development would involve adding a new articulation, such as *voicing*, to a nonexistent articulatory base.[3]

Morphological analogs can sometimes appear to follow the phonological standard whereby an added articulation transforms an unmarked base into a marked alternative. An example is provided by the verb *cane*. In contexts in which the present tense/past tense opposition, *cane/caned*, is neutralized[4] (such as in the sentence, " 'Cane' is a regular verb"), it is the form lacking the added phonological substance (here, the past-tense morpheme *-ed*), that is, the present-tense form, *cane*, that stands for both.[5] However, there exist equivalent cases, such as *sing*, that feel the same morphologically, and that show the same evidence of tense marking (i.e., the present-tense form can stand for all forms when tense is neutralized), but where the marking relationship between tenses cannot be treated in the same way because the tense difference, *sing/sang* (and *sung*), is marked by a genuine alternation instead of a simple addition. Thus, in general for morphology, we cannot assign to such added phonological substance the basic causal role that added articulatory acts play in phonology; regarding the marking role of added phonological substance, we can only say that such added substance can serve as one indicator of a marked versus an unmarked category. Syntactic analogs exhibit the same properties regarding phonological substance as does morphology, while, on the *signified* side of Saussure's sign, the added articulation criterion is necessarily meaningless, even as an indicator, for semantic analogs.[6]

Greenberg (see his discussion in 1966) approached the problem of extending the applicability of marking in two ways. He first examined and developed the list of variables that correlated with the marked/unmarked distinction. His list included the greater text frequency of the unmarked; the potentially greater internal subdivision of the unmarked; the potentiality of the same marked member to contrast in two different places with two different unmarked members; and, finally, the ability of the unmarked to stand for both in contexts in which the contrast is neutralized. Second, he examined what was at issue in the distinction—the more basic or independent nature of the unmarked versus the relatively derivative and dependent nature of the marked—and considered what variable (from the preceding list) might play such a basic role in these other parts of language (morphology, syntax, and semantics) analogous to the role played by added articulatory action in phonology.

This question of what makes one member of an opposition more basic than the other breaks down into three subsidiary questions. (1) What perceptual experience or attribute (articulatory attribute, in the case of phonology) makes a language user treat or code one member of an opposition as more basic than the others? (2) In what way does this perceptual attribute function as the more basic member of the opposition? (3) What attributes of the domain in question produce the relevant perceptual situation? Greenberg did not explicitly separate out or address these questions. In picking text frequency[7] as his basic criterion for marking relations outside of phonology, he, in effect, dealt with our first perceptual question. I think the perceptual variable seemed the place to begin, both because it dealt more directly with available hard data and because it had a generality across domains that as we shall see, the particular attributes that produce it in a given domain do not have. We can also see—when we pose the questions explicitly—that one cannot effectively address the other questions without some prior understanding of the perceptual issue. The data that Greenberg provides, and his discussion of that data, also contain interesting implications concerning our second question of *how* the perceptual attribute functions as a more basic member.

The variable that seemed to Greenberg most likely to embody the basic nature of the unmarked (versus the derivative nature of the marked) member of an opposition—in the parts of language where phonic substance was not at issue, but where the issue of the logical relationship of the categories to one another still had to involve some substantive fact that could make one member of an opposition more basic than the other—was frequency of use. To understand why frequency plays this role, we have to go back to the observation that, in situations of neutralization, the unmarked member stands in for both. These neutralization situations provide instances of ambiguity, when we cannot be sure which of the contrasting items is actually meant; for example, when, in English, the nominal form "length" is used, neutralizing the distinction between "long" and "short." If we are in such an ambiguous situation, and if the frequency of occurrence of a term is a function of the frequency of occurrence of the situation that elicits it, then we will make fewer errors by assuming the more frequently occurring alternative than we would make by choosing the less frequent. So, whenever we experience the ambiguity, for whatever reason, in the absence of further information we are better off assuming the more frequent alternative than assuming the less frequent one (or neither); how much better off we are depends on how great the difference in frequencies.

At the same time, one of the reasons we experience or create such ambiguities is itself a function of frequency. Each linguistic distinction we make, of whatever sort, involves a certain amount of work. Often, in everyday speech, we avoid as much work as possible by eliding (or skipping over) material that is predictable; elisions that are made regularly and consistently enough for our children to learn them as part of their basic representation of langue thereby eventually enter langue.[8] This is the morphological process (not involving marking) by which, presumably, English's ancestral *menni* (compare German *Männer*) lost its trailing *-i*, which had been rendered redundant as a marker of plurality by the fronting (or umlauting) of the preceding *a*—and gave us the form that led to the modern *men*. Where we can save some work by leaving something out, and get away with it (in the sense of not overly impairing our communication), we often do so. Thus, in relation to marking, if one member of an opposition occurs much more rarely than the other, then a speaker can often get by without using (or even knowing) it; such partial knowledge produces a kind of de facto neutralization situation. Thus, children can live and converse for some time knowing "cow" but not "bull."

Frequency enters into children's learning of language in the sense that they will never learn elements (words, constructions, derivational rules, or whatever) they never hear, or that they don't hear and use with whatever combination of frequency and salience it takes to fix the elements in their minds (for understanding). More frequent terms are more likely to be heard by children than infrequent ones, more likely to be used repeatedly (and thus enter into patterns of feedback, reinforcement, rehearsal, etc.), and hence more likely to be learned, as opposed to repeatedly rederived (or re-created).

Of course, regularly derivable aspects of language (that is, "caned" from "cane," or "fiddled" from "fiddle") need not be individually learned, since once the relevant derivational apparatus (whether special machinery used for genuine derivations or just the normal deductive machinery used for regular inflectional forms) is learned, the forms can be easily generated. Such derivations must, of course, involve the producer taking a base form and doing something to it in order to arrive at the derived form. The "something done" can be something added (as in the regular inflections discussed above) or something changed; in either case, we have a clear basis for treating the base form as "more basic" and the derived form as more derivative or dependent. Since we figure out how to derive regularities from patterns found in what we know, the base form, in effect, becomes the first form typically learned—especially for those relevant linguistic objects encountered after the derivational rule has been learned and can thus be used to recognize derived forms.

For nonderivable alternative forms, such as *mouse* versus *mice* (which contrast grammatically on the feature of number), all else being equal, children will learn the more frequently heard term, *mouse*, first.[9] There will, then, exist a population of people who only know the more frequent term (*mouse*) but not the less frequent (*mice*); that is, who have not yet learned the second term (*mice*). When the people who lack the second term have to refer to instances of the term they do not know (*mice*), they will have to use the word they know (*mouse*), either with the regular derivational inflection (that is, *mouses*), if the inflection exists and if they know it, or uninflected (with or without paraphrastic modification, as in "three mouse")—depending on how important the feature involved in the contrast (the actual fact of plurality) is to the communication event (are we talking about a mouse eating seeds in a distant field, or about a bunch of them running over one's feet?).

Viewed in a general way, the frequency with which children encounter terms from some contrast set is a function of the frequency with which the terms are used and, therefore, of the frequency with which the situations referenced by the terms are at issue in conversation. Less confusion in a communicative situation will result from assuming the more frequently used member of a contrast, such as *mouse*—in the absence of specific knowledge concerning the attribute, such as number, on which the terms contrast—than would result from assuming the less frequent *mice*. If the disparity in frequency is great enough, then one can, in general, assume for that contrast set that the more frequently used term is meant, unless specific evidence to the contrary is presented.

It is in this sense of embodying the normally presumed member of the opposition—that is, the default expectation concerning which is more likely to occur—that the more frequently used member of an opposition can in the general case be considered the more basic. As the more basic, it has the potentiality of standing for the less basic or for exhibiting the other properties of unmarked categories; other factors enter into the determination of whether or not it actually so functions (and, if so, where and how).

When I was a graduate student, R. G. D'Andrade, then one of my teachers, pointed out that the idea of marking as described by Greenberg was a very powerful one, and was, especially, a great means of reducing cognitive workloads. Its power was attested, D'Andrade pointed out, by the fact that computer programmers had to independently reinvent it when they started developing standardized programs for general use ("canned" programs such as, particularly at that time, statistical packages). Such programs in general needed a series of instructions (also known as "parameter values" or some such) about how to structure any given run. Each instruction in the series could make a difference for a user's analytic purposes, and so had to be accessible to the user. But most of the instructions were irrelevant to most users, in the sense that there was a standard version of the instruction (parameter value) that was ordinarily used, and that most users did not know enough even to consider using an alternative value, anyway. At the inception of the use of such canned programs, a user had to go through a long list of parameters, setting each value for each run; such parameter-setting was laborious and tedious, and a big waste of time in any case, since mostly one just typed in values from a standard list. Eventually, however, some clever programmer got the idea of setting "default values" for these parameters—values that would always obtain unless the user made a specific decision to override them. The few parameter values that in fact had to vary—which were always specific to the given run—were not given default values, but were always left for the user to set in the old manner. Note that the usefulness of the default option in a program is a function of the frequency with which alternative choices must be made for the parameter in question—that is, to repeat our earlier phrasing, with the relative frequency with which the alternative items in the given contrast set are actually used in communicative events.

Marking relations provide us with the same kind of saving of mental labor in natural language that default options provide in computer programs. Marking promotes "cognitive ease," allowing us often to get away with learning only one or two terms instead of two or three, and by allowing us to avoid identifying features when we are unsure either about what we mean or what we are perceiving. Like the computer "default option," it provides an automatic specification of a set of parameter values that we either don't care about or don't know the correct settings for.

Marking provides us with a device for keeping in our language a rich set of potentially relevant defining features (and categories defined by these features) without having to think about them all the time. The default option of marking, in situations where it applies, provides us with a means of backgrounding features that are irrelevant to normal usage, while still keeping them available for use in those special situations in which they are needed.

Semantic Marking

Greenberg's general criterion bases marking relations on the relative frequency of the contrasting entities. But we still do not know what kinds of oppositions will exhibit marking relations or what kinds of factors will account for the underlying differences in frequencies on which marking is based. I would now like to turn to some examples from a few specific domains by means of which we can explore these questions. In these examples I will use data from a variety of classroom demonstrations and informal experiments to illustrate for at least some instances exactly how the phenomenon of marking works, what shapes it, and how it is used. I will, in most cases, be using neutralization—that is, the use of one term from a contrast set as a cover term for the whole set when the feature along which the terms differ is neutralized as my evidence (or criterion) for marking—rather than frequency as my criterion. This criterion is one of those Greenberg shows to covary with frequency, and is one of the alternative criteria he lists. I am using the neutralization criterion here because of its ready applicability, and because a focus on it serves to highlight some of the causal issues I want to raise.

Measurement Terms

I initially encountered these terms in connection with marking in a class taught by C. O. Frake that I took as a graduate student. These are adjectival terms of measurement like *big* vs. *small, large* vs. *small, long* vs. *short, tall* vs. *short, deep* vs. *shallow, high* vs. *low, thick* vs. *thin, fat* vs. *thin, broad* vs. *narrow, wide* vs. *narrow, fast* vs. *slow,* and so forth. Frake suggested at that time that for these terms it was universally (in all languages) the case that the left-side term (that is, the term from each contrast set signifying the greatest distance from a zero point) was always the unmarked one.[10] A sample of such relations is diagrammed in figure 7-1.

I will limit myself to English, but what similar evidence I am aware of for other languages is consistent with the picture for English. The evidence in English is various but consistent. Several of our marking criteria apply. For those contrast sets that have a derivationally related nominal form that refers to the dimension in question, such as *long/short: length, high/low: height, deep/shallow: depth,* and *broad/narrow: breadth,* it is always the left-side term to which the noun is related and that thus represents the pair when the contrast is neutralized. Greenberg (1966:53) cites word frequency as well as data in the indicated direction. We also see greater subdivision of the unmarked members of many of the oppositions; that is, we see several examples of different left-side terms being opposed to the same right-side term—*large* or *big* versus *small, long* or *tall* versus *short, thick* or *fat* versus *thin,* and *broad* or *wide* versus *narrow.*

In classroom experiments I have placed drawings like those shown in figure 7-2 on the chalkboard. These drawings were always in pairs; each pair consisted of two drawings of the same object, and within each pair one object was larger along one or more dimensions than was the other. For each object I asked the class to write on a sheet of paper (next to the number of the object) the word that went in the blank in the question, "How [click] is this [object name], where I am interested in its [indicated] dimension?" [click] refers to a clicking noise that I made to indicate the blank;

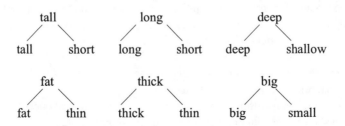

FIG. 7-1 Marking Relations for Measurement Adjectives

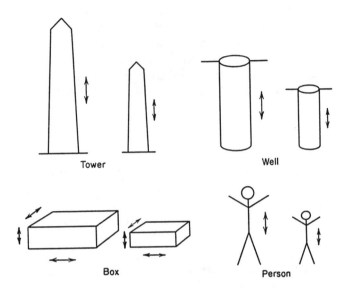

FIG. 7-2 Kronenfeld Drawings for Size Markedness Queries

[indicated] information either was provided by using a word such as "vertical" or by pointing. The object that was larger along the queried dimension would *always* get answers only from those terms on the left side of my pairs; for example, a (taller) tower might get "big," "high," or "tall" in the blank for the question about its vertical dimension, but never "small," "low," or "short." By contrast, the object that was smaller along the queried dimension would *always* get at least one term from each side, and in general would get at least a third of its responses from each; the shorter tower would, like the taller one, get some "big" or "high" or "tall" answers, as well as (unlike the taller one) some "small," "low," or "short" ones.

My explanation, though as yet unproven, for this phenomenon begins with the observation that all of these size evaluations consist of extension out from a zero point in a direction that is potentially infinite. This means that on each of these dimensions there exists an absolute minimum size but no absolute maximum. For any object, in any context (or in the absence of a particular context), one can ask how far it is from the zero point along the indicated dimension, and it is always the left-side term that queries extension out from the zero point (that is, deviation of the measurement from zero). Using the right-side term in a question queries extension *toward* the zero point, presumably (by implication) from some reference point along the dimension in question (that is, deviation of the measurement from some maximal value). Since there is no natural absolute maximum point (or maximum value) on any of these dimensions, any maximal reference point has to be a relative one, provided by the context in which the question is asked; without a relevant context, a question that queries a dimension relative to such a maximal point is necessarily meaningless.[11]

Thus, the left-side question—the "how large is it" sort—is more basic in its lack of any requirement for any comparative context, that is, in its lack of any presupposition concerning the scale of values at issue. The right-side, "how small is it" sort of question necessarily presupposes the prior existence of some object (or context) that fixes a relative "large-point" on the dimensional scale, and is in this sense a derivative judgment.

Another way of thinking about this relative-size question is as follows. We notice in these cases that each set of terms refers to an implicit scale running from a zero point on one end to infinity on the other. The unmarked term is always the one referring to distance from a zero point. The marked term always refers to a lesser distance, that is, in effect, to a distance back toward the zero point from some arbitrary non–zero point on the scale. Thus, "How big is it?" presumes nothing and simply asks about size, while "How short is it?" necessarily presumes that it is already (before the question is asked) short (i.e., shorter than some particular comparison standard) and asks how much so. Since this situation and its entailed logic is inherent in the world we live in and is not the product of any particular culture, these marking relations appear to be universal.

We have here an explanatory definition of the contrast between a "more basic" form and a more derivative one for at least one kind of semantic marking that is as clear and obvious as is the contrast defined by the idea of an additional articulation in Trubetzkoy's original phonological case. My classroom data shows that this special (local semantic) criterion (presence of an absolute versus only a relative reference point) correlates well with Greenberg's general frequency criterion. In this special case, the criterion actually explains the correlation, by showing why the one kind of term should occur in more contexts than the other, and thus, all other things being equal, more frequently. Meanwhile, this special criterion clearly has only a very limited range of applicability, which indicates why we still need Greenberg's general criterion.

Cows

For my next example of semantic marking I would like to examine some pairs of terms for males and females of various animal species. To begin with, let us look at cows (see figure 7-3). The word *cow* can refer either to any member of *Bos taurus* or to a female (versus a male) member of the species. *Cow*, meaning female, contrasts with *bull*, the term for a male; cow as the general term for the species includes both cows and bulls. Thus, we can say either "Yes, Johnny, that's a cow—it's a bull," or "No, Johnny, that's not a cow—it's a bull." *Cow* represents both *cow* and *bull* when the gender distinction is neutralized, and thus is the unmarked term by Greenberg's neutralization criterion.

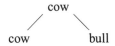

FIG. 7-3 Marking Relations for *Cows*

The reason for *cow*'s being the unmarked term (in the *cow*/*bull* contrast set) can be seen clearly in the American East, at least, where dairy cattle represent the major bovine industry.[12] Cows are more economically important than bulls, and they are much more frequently encountered. If one randomly encounters a bovine, and can't directly ascertain its sex, one will run little risk of mistake by referring to it as a cow. Cows are the kind of cow one normally encounters, and the kind one generally cares about. Where the most commonly encountered instance of the general category is one type versus the other, and where the one type is most central to the activity with which the category is associated, it is easy to see how the one type might stand for the whole category—that is, how cow could be used to refer to any bovine as well as to specifically female bovines.

Our bovine case offers us a semantic example of communication across different knowledge levels (compare our earlier discussion of *mouse* and *mice*). For nonderivable alternative forms, such as cow and bull (which contrast semantically on the feature of gender[13]), all else being equal, children will learn the more frequently heard term, cow, first. There will therefore exist a population of people who know only the more frequent term (*cow*) but not the less frequent (*bull*)—those who have not yet learned the second term (*bull*). When the people who lack the second term must refer to instances of the term they do not know (*bull*), they will have to use the word they know (*cow*), either with or without paraphrastic modification (as in "the daddy cow"), depending on how important the feature involved in the contrast (in this case, bovine gender) is to the communication event (that is, are we talking about a bovine eating a flower in a distant field, or about one trying to mount another?).

Cats and Dogs

For our next animal examples, let us take cats and dogs (see figure 7-4). Our basic marking relations in English are shown by the fact that we have a term, *bitch*, for a female dog, but no special term for a male dog, and by the fact that we have a term, *tomcat*, for a male cat, but no special term for a female cat. Thus, our unmarked *dog* is a male, and our unmarked *cat* is a female. That these conclusions, which follow from the linguistic code, are still psychologically active can be seen in sentence completion tasks, such as those I have given classes involving sentences like, "The cat hurt _____ paw," and "The dog wagged _____ tail." Overwhelmingly, one gets either "her" or "its" for the cat's paw and "his" or "its" for the dog's tail; since the little critters are not merely animate, but part of the family, and since English has no special *animate* neuter pronoun, "her" and "his" are more common than "its." As before, the marking relationship implies that we can say either "Yes, that's a dog; it's a bitch," or "No, that's not a dog, it's a bitch"—depending on whether the contextual focus is on

FIG. 7-4 Marking Relations for *Cats* and *Dogs*

the gender of the canine or only on the canine-ness. Similarly, a *tomcat* can either be an instance of a *cat* or be the (male) opposite of a (female) *cat*. The salience in my own family of the default genders was driven home to me when both guests and my immediate family persisted in referring to our dog as "he" and to our cat as "she" in spite of frequent reminders that the dog was a female and the cat a male.

The realm of cats and dogs becomes more curious when we turn our attention to potential reasons for the marking relations we have observed there. As far as I know, in our world of pets, both urban and rural, the two genders are present in approximately equal numbers, and there is no clear bias one way or the other regarding cats versus dogs. Thus, the kind of explanation of the observed marking relations that we accepted for cattle seems not to apply to our household pets.

I would like to suggest that the operative frequency/salience issue for the default gender of these pets has nothing to do with their gender at all—is a function neither of their observed gender frequencies nor the relative importance (to us) of the genders—but has instead to do with associations we have regarding their modes of behavior and, relatedly, the parts of our life-space with which we canonically associate them. We normally think of cats as *inside* pets. We see them as in control of their bodies, sure-footed, graceful, neat, and clean. On the other hand, we normally think of dogs as *outside* pets. They seem more rugged and excitable, more likely to knock something over, and less scrupulous about their own cleanliness.

I used the *inside*/*outside* contrast instead of the *indoors*/*outdoors* one, which perhaps seems more specifically accurate (to those of us who live in suburban America, at least) as a way of including another relationship. What is at issue is not simply whether the animal lives (or is felt to live) in or out of the house, but in whose realm—the wife's or the husband's—the animal lives. In America, at least, the household has traditionally been divided into wife's and husband's spheres according to location. The "inside" sphere has consistently been the wife's realm, while the "outside" sphere has been the husband's. What has varied across different environments has been the definition of *inside* and *outside* (see Mukhopadhyay 1980:chap. 3). On farms, the wife's *inside* realm has included not just the house, but also the farmyard and garden, while the husband's *outside* realm has included the barn and fields. In suburbia, her *inside* becomes the inside of the house (*indoors*), while his *outside* becomes the house's exterior, patio, and yard (*outdoors*). In urban apartments, her *inside* is the inside of the apartment, while his *outside* refers to public spaces such as halls; she puts the garbage in the kitchen can, and he carries it out to the hallway trash chute. It is to this wider universe of gender-marked spatial zones that I think our default genders for cats and dogs relate.

We describe cats in terms that are associated in our culture with women—in ways that reach far beyond the grace and bodily control required to avoid breaking china or furniture, which I suggested above as part of our "indoor" conception of cats, and which we sometimes associate with girls as opposed to boys. Cats are *slinky, careful* and *graceful, mysterious* and *hard to read*. Women are described in cat-like terms; they *purr*, have *sharp claws*, get into *catfights*. Dogs, on the other hand, like men, are *gruff* and *open, enthusiastic* and *energetic*, and sometimes too *rough* or *careless* around the furniture or fine china. Dogs and men are often *messy, careless* about keeping themselves clean, they *tramp mud about*, and so forth. Men *growl* and *bark* at folks, *raise their hackles* when crossed, and *act like puppies* when treated nicely. A *cathouse* is for (not nice) women, while it is the man who is *in the doghouse* for upsetting his wife.

I am assuredly not claiming that these portrayals are literally true of either cats and dogs or men and women. I am only claiming that they are parts of our cultural baggage of long-enough standing to have gotten fixed in our language. I offer them only by way of showing the pervasive linking in our culture and language of cats to women and dogs to men, and thus of showing why, I think, the default gender for cats is female and for dogs is male.

While it is not directly relevant to our immediate concern with marking, even if it is relevant to our larger theme of how we use language and how language presumes the basic regularities of culture, I would like explicitly to recognize the strong sexism that seems implicit in the linguistic codings we have been considering, and thus in the culture they reflect. In fact, I would like to provide some more evidence for it. A man gets in the *doghouse* by being forgetful (of, perhaps, a birthday) or by accidentally slipping up (by staying out a little too late with the "boys," or by breaking a favorite lamp); a woman gets in a *cathouse* by being deeply immoral and outside the bounds of polite society. There is something endearing about a man as an *old dog* (as in, "You old dog, you!"), while there is nothing endearing about a woman as a *cat*, old or otherwise.[14] Even similar activities are scored differently: a man who is *tomcatting around* is doing something similar to what a woman does in a *cathouse*, but his failing falls in the peccadillo range, while hers is in the serious moral problem area.[15] In the canine world, again, women lose. He, as an *old dog*, may be endearing, but she, as a *bitch*, assuredly is not. *Bitchiness* is inexplicable, petty[16] viciousness—a little like being *catty*, but worse and not limited (as *cattiness*) to being directed toward other women. When *bitch* isn't used to refer simply to a woman's nastiness, it can also be used to impugn her sexual morality—especially when expanded, as in *a bitch in heat*.

Using the *dog* term for her doesn't help. Calling her a *dog* merely asserts that she is nonfeminine—and, hence, in that way, masculine—versus the meanness or sluttiness of *bitch* or the petty (clawing-and-spitting) nastiness of cat. On those rare occasions when cat is used for him (as a reference to his "cat-like movements") the attitude seems positive.[17]

Again, I don't mean to have all of us English speakers agree with the views I have just detailed. But the above material does testify to the pervasiveness of the link of dogs and cats to men and women in our language and culture. Furthermore, it brings up a theme I have already touched on in my description of Saussure's theory, and which will play an important role later in this volume: that language is a tool people in a culture use in order to communicate about actual "stuff" in the world in which they live. The actual stuff may be physically there or "objectively" true about that world; or it may be "actually there" only in the sense of being "true" by social convention; or it may only be "there" in the sense of being part of the beliefs or presuppositions that inform people's perceptions and interpretations of events. Our use of language, including how we understand words, involves the understandings that we presuppose in our usage as much as it involves the literal meaning of the words or longer constructions that we use. How the systematic presuppositions we share as part of our "collective representation" of langue become linked to our signs and used in linguistic communication is a major concern of this volume.

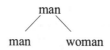

FIG. 7-5 Marking Relations for *Man* and *Woman*

Men and Women

For our third set of animal terms, let us take *man* and *woman* (figure 7-5). Phrases, such as that in the Declaration of Independence, that declare "All men are created equal" make it clear that, in situations in which the gender distinction between *man* and *woman* is neutralized, *man*, the male term, represents both. *Man*, therefore, is the unmarked category, and *woman* the marked. Our question concerns what it is that makes *man* more basic than *woman*. A cursory examination of the population around us makes clear that an argument about actual frequency of the referents in question, such as that we made for *cows* and *bulls*, will not work here.

The likely explanation emerges when we examine the practical effects that might have followed, say, at the time of the Declaration of Independence, from someone's actually confusing man in the sense of human being with man in the more restricted sense of a male human being. My sense is that what reduced the confusion, and thereby provided the substantive basis for the marking relation, was that *man* was used in its wider sense to refer, implicitly, to something like "people who count" or "people who matter," and it was clear that most of the people who counted most of the time, for most of the purposes at issue, were men. At the time of the Declaration of Independence it wasn't only women who were largely excluded from the group of people who counted, while ostensibly being included under the rubric of *men*; for many political, economic, and legal purposes, nonwhite men and nonproperty owning white men were in a similar situation.

Other, modern examples from English show us that the marking issue does not concern the existence of a general, all-purpose default gender for human beings per se; instead, the issue concerns the existence of a default gender for whatever specific purpose seems to be at hand. For example, we see that *nurses* are presumed to be female unless specified as *male nurses*, with the female term *nurse* as the unmarked term that stands for both when gender is not an issue. Similarly, in the other direction, we see that unmarked *doctors* are presumed male unless marked as *woman doctors*.[18] In these medical examples, the default gender clearly reflects practical realities of number in much the same way as it did for *cows* and *bulls*.[19]

The specific purpose at hand for our general *man*-versus-*woman* example seems to have been political and legal rights. In ancient Rome, a respectable woman remained a jural minor throughout her life, passing from her father's control to her husband's, and maybe even to her son's; she could not vote, hold property, or testify in court. The only women, apparently, who had such rights were women such as courtesans and prostitutes who were under no man's control. In the West, women's position seems to have changed only slowly. The French novelist George Sand, besides having to take a man's name in order to be published, could not control her own earnings, but had to work out a deal with her dependent and nonproductive ("shiftless," in my childhood vernacular) husband to get his permission to make some use of the money she earned. It is only in the last century in much of the West that women have gained the same basic political and economic rights as men.

Thus, for most political (social and economic) purposes, for most of our history in the West, using *man* to represent both male humans and humans in general carried no danger of any significant confusion. By "danger of significant confusion" I refer to the risk of making a mistake that entailed serious practical consequences. When the inclusion of women was specifically intended, clarity was ensured by use of a phrase such as "men and women" (or "ladies and gentlemen").

Nonetheless, the marking relationship between *man* and *woman*, with its male default, is still a contemporary fact of the English language. Thus, on the one hand, there is a sense in which those who take issue with complaints by supporters of women's liberation about the use of *man/men* in its non–gender-specific sense have a point. Such usage is a basic fact of the language, and thus its use by individuals does not necessarily represent any individual decision by the user to exclude women or condescend to them. On the other hand, however, we have seen that the linguistic usage does stem from and depend upon a cultural fact (in this case involving the relegation of women to a kind of second-class political and economic status) that might be seen as discriminatory or antiwoman. While these cultural and linguistic facts taken together may absolve some particular user of the unmarked *man* term of any active sexist intent (if not of insensitivity), they certainly do not support any complacent view to the effect that the conditions involved in the marked status of *woman* versus *man* are either neutral, innocent, or harmless.

The questions remaining concerning this issue are whether or not efforts to raise linguistic usage to consciousness have any effect on the cultural pattern, and whether or not linguistic usage tracks cultural facts closely enough (in time) to make current language usage any kind of valid measure of current culture. I have no data or observations to contribute toward an answer to the first question, I would like to see some data. I think the answer to the second question is yes. My thoughts on the question come from trying to fix the time of the change more closely and then looking at usage patterns for some words which have not, to my knowledge, been highlighted by the women's liberation movement. While basic legal equality for women in the United States seems to have been achieved by the 1920s, equality of access—to education, careers, jobs, pay, administrative positions, and the like—along with other social and legal preconditions for full equality were not even raised as an issue for the general public until the 1960s, and did not become a general presumption or expectation until the 1980s.[20] Given the recency of this change in the concrete activities one might expect actually to affect the practical mechanisms that, we have seen, drive the language, it is interesting to note the increasing use of unisex terms for close kin (*parent* instead of *father* or *mother*, *child* [or *kid*] for *son* or *daughter*, and *sibling* [borrowed into general usage only recently from anthropology, where it had been brought in as a technical term] for *brother* or *sister*)—where unisex terms per se have not been raised as a political issue. Of similar interest, though it has taken place in a context of greater political consciousness, is the declining salience of the *-ess* ending as a usable marker for female counterparts of what become, in effect, thereby unmarked male terms (i.e., the passing into disuse of terms such as *authoress, poetess, Jewess,* and *Negress*[21])—leaving the suffix only productive for animals (e.g., *tigress, lioness*[22], etc.) and only minimally so there.

I would like to conclude our discussion of marking relations among gender terms for animal species by pointing out that there need not be any marking relationship. A male horse is a *stallion* and a female is a *mare*; the cover term, *horse,* carries no presumption of any specific gender. For most purposes (pleasure riding, racing, and draft work) of which I am aware, stallions and mares seem more or less equally useful, and, I gather, the two genders show up in more or less equal numbers. *Horses* are outside the household spheres that give *dogs* and *cats* their default genders, and the considerations that obtain between *men* and *women* do not apply to them. Thus, there seems to exist no basis for assigning *horses* a default gender, and no reason to do so.

Marking Hierarchies

Let us now examine *man* and *woman* from a slightly different perspective. In particular, let us see what other oppositions these terms participate in, and what their marking status is in these other oppositions. We know that *men* and *women* are both kinds of *men,* as opposed to *animals,* and we know that *man* is, at the same time, a kind of *animal.* Going in the other direction, we know that *men* (vs. *women*) is divided into *men* and *boys,* and *women* into *women* and *girls;* going further, *men* (vs. *boys*) can be divided into *men* and "unmanly men" (for which a number of slang terms exist), and *women* (vs. *girls*) into *women* and "unwomanly women." Note that marking is relative to a specific opposition, not a permanent attribute of any term. *Man* is marked vs. *animal* and unmarked vs. *woman, boy,* and *wimp; woman* is marked vs. *man* and unmarked vs. *girl;* and so forth.

The cultural contexts in which these oppositions and their marking relations occur are varied. The science of zoology, as well as Twenty Questions' classification of the object to be guessed as "animal, mineral, or vegetable," provides a context in which *man* is an *animal.* We have already seen ordinary-language instances of *women*'s being kinds of *men. Boys* are seen as *men* in the allocation of public rest rooms, while *men,* in the sense that excludes *boys,* can be seen in the old sinking-ship instructions that ask *men* to wait for lifeboats until after the women and children have boarded—or in the notion that *boys* must become *men* (i.e., are not already there). Ads play to our notions of "real *men,*" while the Marines want "a few good *men*" (as opposed to wimpy, unmanly types).

These various, hierarchically structured usages of the same words constitute a "marking hierarchy"—a hierarchy of increasing or decreasing specification that allows us to use relatively few words for a great many subtle shadings of meaning (in appropriate contexts). This hierarchy is shown in figure 7-6.

The maximally specified sense of a term (e.g., *man*) in a marking hierarchy, that is, the sense that occurs at the bottom of the hierarchy, represents the attributes that users of the language will presume for a referent of the term in the absence of any contextual cues to the contrary. As such, it specifies a kind of default or core sense of the term. People will talk about *men* as if they are manly, adult males unless the cultural

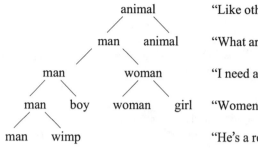

"Like other animals, we . .

"What are we, men or animals?"

"I need a men's room."

"Women and children first, men later."

"He's a real man, he uses Brut."

FIG. 7-6 Marking Hierarchy for *Man*

or linguistic context suggests otherwise. At the same time, I do not think that this default specification fully captures the sense in which, in ordinary usage, speakers typically *intend* their use of the term to be taken—or the sense hearers presume to have been intended or entailed. That is (even though I have no formal data on the question and so am only relying on my native speaker's intuition), I think that common, ordinary use of the term *man* entails an intended assertion that the conversation is about an adult male, but does not involve any particular concern with (or intended assertion about) the man's manliness. Speakers may implicitly presume that the man they are discussing is a manly one, but they do not care, and will not feel their discussion invalidated if he turns out not to be manly (by one measure or another). On the other hand, I suspect that many such discussions will be compromised if the *man* turns out to be a *boy* or a *woman*. The maximally unmarked, and hence—in a sense, at least—core sense (or referent) of a term may not be the one that is typically meant in conversation.

The questions of the relationship of marking defaults to definitional coreness or focality and of the relationship of both marking defaults and focality to what is typically *at issue* in a term's use represent important theoretical issues that need to be raised. We will not see these questions answered in this volume, but they will occasionally arise in the discussion of specific topics—as they did above.

The "default option" represented in natural language by marking relations provides various benefits. It allows speakers to get along with less vocabulary in relevant areas than would otherwise be the case. This reduction in necessary vocabulary reduces the learning load required for basic, entry-level communication, whether by children learning their mother tongue or by adults learning an additional one. The presence of such a default option allows easy and natural communication across broadly different information or interest levels. Dairy farmers, for instance, thus have an easy entry point for talking with city children about cattle by starting with "cows"; from there they can go on to develop the distinctions of gender, age, pregnancy and childbirth, and so forth that are central to their endeavor (and for which they have their own specialized technical vocabulary). Communication across the specialized worlds of experience entailed by the division of labor, such as that we discussed in connection with Berlin and Kay's work on basic color terms, is involved here; "robin's egg blue" can be seen as a marked alternative to an unmarked, basic *blue* category. In complex societies, wherein different individuals have widely diverse kinds of experiences and knowledge, marking relations provide a painless and largely invisible mechanism for conversing across much of that diversity.

Back to Siblings

Nerlove and Romney, in their study of characteristics that predict the structure of sibling terminologies we examined earlier when we discussed conjunctivity, used marking relations, as described by Greenberg, as an additional explanatory device. Greenberg (1966), in his discussion of marking criteria and properties, pointed out that if one member of an opposition or contrast set was more subdivided than the others, it would be the unmarked member. More generally, if a feature contrast had marked versus unmarked values, and if the categories distinguished by those contrasting features were further subdivided by any other feature, the markedness would limit the forms of subdivision that were possible. There was nothing to prevent the subdividing feature from dividing both sides of the original contrast equally, but if it only divided one side and not the other, that one side would have to be the unmarked side. For instance, if we take voicing (or its lack) as our initial division of stop consonant, noting that the unvoiced side is unmarked and the voiced side marked, and if we want then to examine languages in which one side of the voicing division (but not the other) is further subdivided by aspiration, we will find languages that have only the unvoiced stops (that is, not the voiced ones) subdivided by aspiration, but we will find none that have only the voiced stops (that is, not the unvoiced ones) thus subdivided.

Further on in his discussion of marking, Greenberg (1966:chap. 5) used an examination of Generation 1 (G^1) kinship terms to illustrate the application of marking theory to semantic features and to pose some empirical generalizations concerning marked and unmarked categories in kinship terminologies. Nerlove and Romney (1967) took Greenberg's generalization about subdivision (described above) and, treating his Generation 1 findings concerning which categories were marked and which unmarked as predictions/assertions about Generation 0 (that is, about a data set from which they were not derived), tested the explanatory power of marking in the same study in which they evaluated conjunctivity.

Based on Greenberg's findings, they concluded that the *senior* kin category of a pair of reciprocal terms was always unmarked relative to the *junior* category (which meant *elder* relative to *younger* for siblings, where generational differences were precluded). Gender, whether in one of its absolute forms (*sex of alter* or *sex of ego*) or in its relative form (*same sex* vs. *opposite sex*) showed no universal marking relations such as were required for Nerlove and Romney's research design, even though particular languages seemed often to have an unmarked gender. Their prediction, then, was that in no case should a feature subdivide a *younger* category without at the same time subdividing the matching *elder* one; the converse situation, in which an *elder* category could be subdivided without the matching *younger* one being similarly subdivided, was allowed.

TABLE 7-1.   The Empirical Effects of Marking
(from Nerlove and Romney 1967:182, 183 [Figure 1 and Table 2])

Total number of terminologies examined	245
Number with secondary subdivisions, to which marking is relevant	48
Number with a secondary division, where sex of relative is primary	5
Number for which the subdivision is on the predicted (male) side	3
on the opposite (female) side	2
Number with a secondary distinction, where relative age is primary	43
Number for which the subdivision is on the predicted (elder) side	40
on the opposite (younger) side	3

The results of the Nerlove and Romney study regarding marking are shown in table 7-1. The overall results are, again, clearly and strongly as predicted—even if less overwhelmingly so than was the case for conjunctivity and even if the scope of this part of the study (that is, the number of cases to which the marking prediction applies) is somewhat limited by the nature of the original research design.

More particularly, these results lead one to question Nerlove and Romney's assumption that *male* was universally the default sex for the sex-of-relative distinction. Other comparative materials (for example, Lounsbury 1964a:204 and Kronenfeld 1991:21) raise questions about Nerlove and Romney's assumption and, moreover, suggest that the default sex in marilineal systems is perhaps more likely to be female. On the other hand, Nerlove and Romney's other assumption—that *elder* will be unmarked relative to *junior*—seems well supported.

Berlin: Folk Taxonomies

Berlin (1972), continuing his ongoing interest in the evolution of vocabulary, and in relating vocabulary change to the technological development of society, has offered a model for the development of ethnobotanical nomenclature. He suggests that "*generic* names are fundamental and will appear first. These will be followed in time by major *life-form* names and *specific* names. At yet a later period, *intermediate* taxa and *varietal* taxa will be labeled. Finally, the last category to be lexically designated . . . will be the *unique beginner*" (1972:53). He diagrams the sequence as follows:

$$\text{generic} \rightarrow \left\{ \begin{array}{c} \text{life-form} \\ \text{specific} \end{array} \right\} \rightarrow \left\{ \begin{array}{c} \text{intermediate} \\ \text{varietal} \end{array} \right\} \rightarrow \text{unique beginner}$$

This order means that in any given section of any folk taxonomy, the levels historically would appear in this order, and thus it implies that at least one example of any level to the left of any arrow must occur before any examples of levels to the right of that arrow. Items such as *life-form* and *specific* that occur between the same pair of arrows have no specified order of appearance. Thus, any "language must have encoded *at least* one major life-form name and one specific name before the appearance of [any] intermediate and varietal named taxa" (p. 53). The categories—with the exception of *unique beginner*—are open classes, to which new items can continually be added throughout the history of the language; that is, a language can continue to add new *genera* even after it has developed *specifics, varietals,* and so forth.

In addition to noting the general progression described above, Berlin (1972:53) describes

> a regular sequence of lexical development for members *within each category.* Thus, given the appearance of the specific category, one may observe the further linguistic development of specific names from *lexically unmarked* to *lexically marked* expressions. The same observation holds for each category. This general feature suggests that languages may not only be rated in terms of the number of ethnobotanical nomenclatural categories encoded but can be ranked as well in terms of the extent to which members of particular categories have passed from an unmarked to a marked status.

In Berlin's picture,[23] generics represent natural categories in the sense that they represent naturally occurring segmentations of the botanic world (stemming from the functioning of Darwinian evolution), and in the sense that they represent units on scales of size and specificity that we are psychologically predisposed to recognize (because, perhaps, of our own evolutionary history). Ethnobotanical nomenclatures grow first by creating *generics,* that is, by recognizing and naming obvious (and presumably important) classes of plants. Subsequently they expand by creating new generics by analogy with old ones; for instance, by creating names like "poison ivy" on the model of "ivy" (where poison ivy is *not* a kind of ivy—and hence not a subordinate taxon).

The new additions are, initially, *lexically marked* categories, in contrast to the *lexically unmarked* original or central category. In general, by the process of elision we spoke of earlier, we would expect these longer expressions to be shortened and made derivationally opaque if and as they are used frequently; some, like *poison ivy* in English, do escape the process (whether for cognitive reasons or because it represents the occasional statistical sport).

Each generic label is tied to a typical type, the *type specific.* Berlin notes the history of typical species in biological systematics and in folk systems (p. 59). I want to point out that these labels are words, and that we have already in this volume begun considering the idea (based in part on Berlin's earlier work with Kay on color terms) that the referents of a term will be divided between focal ones that are tightly tied to the term and extended ones that have only a looser, secondary connection. In our terms, then, Berlin is saying that the focal referent of a folk *generic* will be a particular species (and, possibly, even a particular variety) that is common and important in the lives of the speakers.

Using Berlin's abstract example (pp. 64–65), but starting before Berlin's stage (a), in what we might call stage (pre-a), we have a *type-specific, x.* In our version, other related types (potential species) are referred to initially by the given *generic* term (as extended referents of it), with the usual possibilities of paraphrastic specification when specifications are needed.

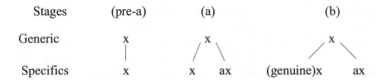

Stages	(pre-a)	(a)		(b)	
Generic	x	x		x	
Specifics	x	x	ax	(genuine)x	ax

In stage (a) of Berlin's example, the *nontypical specifics* are referred to as *ax*, where *a* is a conventional attributive. *x*, without modification, continues to refer to the *type-specific*. Generally speaking, as extended referents of a given category become important enough to rate their own categories, they are initially recognized as marked variants of the initial category and labeled by the addition of a standardized modifier to the *generic*, as in species such as "black oak." This is similar to the situation we have already seen in the marking of *lady doctors* as a specific, recognized subcategory of the *doctor* category and in the marking of *tomcats* as a specific, recognized subcategory of *cats*.[24] In stage (b), as any of these marked *ax*s become sufficiently salient to begin breaking down the totally routine presumption that a reference to the *generic* is automatically a reference to the *type-specific*, there comes an increasing need to gloss the type-specific with its own "type-marking" attributive (such as "genuine" or "real"), though such marking of the type-specific remains optional.[25]

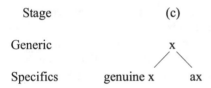

Stage		(c)	
Generic		x	
Specifics	genuine x		ax

In stage (c), the salience of the initially nonfocal species has risen enough (through economic change, geographical expansion, climate change, or whatever) to force the obligatory use of the type-marking attributive ("genuine"). This obligatory usage robs it of its special descriptive force (as a marker of the focal *type-specific*), and the binomial expression using it becomes just another binomial. Again, generally, if—and as—the second specific usage begins to approach the initial one in importance and frequency, the two labels will take on balanced forms. In the case of botanic species, that symmetry is achieved by making the initial specific into a binomial, usually by adding a modifier, such as "genuine" or "common," that recognizes its focal status. This botanical (or, more likely, biological) labeling process, by which *generic* categories are kept foregrounded via the maintenance of generic labels in the binomial expressions, is in this way somewhat different from the general process we see, for instance, in the balanced *monomial* lexical form of the *cow* vs. *bull* gender opposition. Normally, when paraphrastic descriptions become lexemes, they are reduced to one word. For biotic taxa, however, the evolutionary similarity of the specific forms (regarding structural relations and use) plus social use factors (relating to the division of labor) keep the generic term in use along with the specific terms, and thereby prevent the binomial expression's collapsing into a monomial—as would otherwise be the case. That is, a combination of social complexity and differing frequencies of use in different situations keep both generic ("oak") and relevant specific types ("black oak," "white oak") in the language as lexemes, *and* maintain the relevance of the generic in the binomial (that is, the "oakiness" of "black oaks"). The consistency of such binomial labels in folk taxonomies of living things is one piece of evidence in support of Berlin's notion that *genera* do represent a special kind of natural category for us. But, to my mind, the same kind of categorical approach and labeling seems also to be applied to some of our own creations, such as varieties of cars, that are produced (even if only in part) by a process of gradual historical differentiation.

Stages   (d)

Generic   x

Specifics   bx   ax

As a normal binomial expression, the label for the formerly focal *type-specific* is subject to the normal processes of linguistic drift. In stage (d) it may, through such processes, become derivationally opaque; or it may come to have a more mnemonically effective attribute (maybe some *b* chosen from the contrast set that includes *a*) substituted for the type-marking attributive "genuine." This stage would produce a balanced contrast situation among species labels, for example, "white oak," "black oak," and "live oak"—a binomial folk taxonomic situation analogous to our monomial gender distinction between "mares" and "stallions" (as kinds of "horses"). Berlin (p. 79) offers a model for the gain and loss of intermediate taxa that relies, in a similar manner, on marking, but that has the monomial properties of our earlier marking examples. Berlin's work with ethnobotanical nomenclature contains many important insights that are specific to the domain in question, as does his work with Kay on color terms. And, as with the color work, it is mostly these domain-specific insights that have attracted attention. The sense of (cognitively) natural categories that emerges from his ethnobotanical work is attracting wider attention from anthropologists interested in cognition (see, for example, Atran 1992).

However, our present purposes focus on the implications of Berlin's ethnobotanical work for our theory of the semantics of words. In this connection, we note the crucial role played by focal (versus extended) referents in thought about named categories and in the use of these categories under changing conditions. We note, also, Berlin's groundbreaking exploration of the relationship between marking and focality. He offers a systematic diachronic (as well as synchronic) treatment, for terms within his given domain, of the relationship between the unmarked member of an opposition and the focal referent of the supercategory that immediately includes the opposition. In his examples in the article we have been examining, he also implicitly recognizes the possibility that the level of contrast involving the maximally unmarked sense of a term may not be the most commonly or typically used level (compare our discussion earlier in this chapter of the marking hierarchy involving *man*).

Notes

1. Greenberg (1966:11) suggests "the first occurrence of the terminology marked and unmarked (in phonology)" was by Trubetzkoy in 1931, and the first "explicit use of this terminology for grammatical categories" was by Jakobson in 1932. Greenberg gives the citations.

2. A related issue for Greenberg concerned universals. He noticed that marking relations accounted for his universals, and, conversely, implicational universals provided evidence of marking. That is, his implicational relations in general held between unmarked and marked alternatives.

"All languages have a /p/ phoneme" is an assertion of an absolute universal; any existing language that lacks a /p/ is enough to disprove it. It applies to the entire universe of languages. The only relationship that can possibly exist among such absolute universals is equivalence of occurrence: where one occurs, all will occur.

"Any language which has an /m/ phoneme also has a /b/" is an example of a conditional assertion; that is, [the presence of /m/] → [the presence of /b/] ("→" means "logically implies"). It is an "implicational" universal because the assertion concerns an implicational relation. It is "conditional" because it applies not to the whole universe of languages, but only to the subset of that universe consisting of languages that have /m/. Implicational relations imply two-by-two contingency tables of a certain sort. If A and B are phonemes, and if we assign languages to a cell in the table according to their possession or lack of A or B, then B → A asserts that no languages will fall into the cell defined by +B and −A. Languages are presumed able to fall into any of the other three cells.

Thus:

		A	
		Present	Absent
B	Present	Ok	No
	Absent	Ok	Ok

The cell marked "No" should have a 0 in it in any real distributional study, and we speak of it as a "zero cell." A zero cell in an empirical study is evidence of an implicational relationship between the variables in question; the location of the zero cell tells us what nkind of implicational relationship. Implicational relations can be chained: /m/→/b/→/p/. Languages in each subset can be compared with those outside it, and diachronic change from one to another studied. Such distinguishing of permissible language states from impermissible ones and such relating of the possibility of one state to the presence of another allows one to construct an analytically powerful typology of languages. Implicational universals imply diachronic rules distinguishing possible changes from impossible ones. A language cannot have an /m/ unless it also has a /b/, which means that historically /b/s must develop before /m/s and, conversely, /m/s must be lost before /b/s. Any other chronological ordering would produce a synchronic distribution inconsistent with the universal. Thus a chain of implications defines a circumscribed matrix of possible historical transitions. In terms of marking, /m/ is a marked alternative to (or variant of) /b/, where the added articulation is the opening of the connection to the nasal passage; /b/ is a marked alternative to (or variant of) /p/, where the added articulation is the vibration of the vocal chords.

3. Since a /t/, for example, is *not* a /d/ made with a different kind of voicing, but is instead identical to a /d/ made without any kind of voicing articulation/feature at all, in the absence of the existence of /t/ there is no feature bundle to which voicing could be added to produce /d/. Figure 7-7 diagrams the transition possibilities for voiced and unvoiced labio-alveolar stops. The developmental consideration implies that one can have the unmarked member in situations that lack the marked, but not vice versa.

Given: the existence of other stops

Feature contrasts
  A: + stops exist; − stops do not exist
  B: + lab-alv articulation present; − it is absent
  C: + voicing contrast exists; − no voicing contrast

Conditions
  Possible
  1 : A+ B− C+or−   no /t/ and no /d/
  2 : A+ B+ C−   /t/ exists but no /d/
  3 : A+ B+ C+   /t/ and /d/ both exist
  Impossible
  4 :   /d/ exists but no /t/

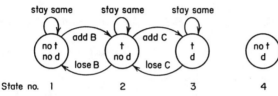

FIG. 7-7 Transition Possibilities: Labio-alveolar Stops

4. See also the situation in which, in the present tense, the first person/third person opposition, *cane/canes*, is neutralized, and the form without the suffix, *cane*, stands for both.

5. See "*Signe Zero*" by Trubetzkoy's colleague Roman Jakobson. Reprinted in Jakobson 1971:211–219.

6. I want to point out, additionally, that marking relations obtain both among the categories of language (i.e., /t/ vs. /d/ or *sing* vs. *sung*) and among the attributes or features that define categories or relations among categories (i.e., in the relationship between voicing and stop-ness, or among tenses and voices). The unmarked consonant is a stop and the unmarked stop is unvoiced; the unmarked vowel is voiced. The unmarked tense, in the languages I know, is present. Phonology examples show that marking relations can exist among feature contrasts as well as among the features of a single contrast set.

7. An early advocate of the importance of frequency phenomena for the shape of human language was George K. Zipf (1935). I should note also that Zipf, in the same work, anticipated our more general appeal to cognitive ease (see Zipf 1949), even if his version was not quite the same as our present one.

8. Remember that Frake's "Ethnographic Study of Cognitive Systems" (1962) demonstrates that more frequent usage results in shorter terms, which terms thereby become relatively unanalyzable and, hence, relatively primary semantic units. A strong version of this relationship was proposed by Zipf (1935:38–39) as the "Law of Abbreviation," commonly referred to as "Zipf's Law." Miller (1965:vi–ix) points out a mathematical weakness in Zipf's interpretation of his statistics, which vitiates Zipf's proof; however, Miller also notes (p. viii) that Zipf's behavioral principles, even if not proved by the findings he adduced, are still attractive. Some of the other linguistic evidence that Zipf adduced (pp. 30–37) is similar to some of our observations in the present volume regarding the histories of particular words.

9. The frequency with which the term *mouse* or *mice* is heard may be a function of the frequency with which the referents are encountered, but it may well instead depend on the frequency with which they appear important enough to talk about (as perhaps is the case with singular versus plural instances of the mouse in our ordinary experience). We will return to this issue later when we discuss semantic marking.

10. It was only a suggestion then, and I do not mean to claim that he stated it as a proven fact then or would necessarily assert it to be fact now. I do, however, want to make clear that I think his suggestion was correct—for reasons that will follow.

11. One way to test my hypothesis might be to give subjects a series of pictures of pairs of objects that are identical except for a difference along one of these size dimensions. The relevant dimensions on the pictures would be marked off in some sort of unlabeled scaler units. One might then ask the subjects to answer the question, "How X is this [figure]?" The prediction is that all subjects would answer the question about the unmarked figure with the number of units from zero that it measured. For the marked figure, one would expect some subjects to answer in terms of the number of units from zero, as for the unmarked figure, but one would expect other subjects to answer in terms of the number of units by which the marked figured differed from the unmarked.

12. The term *steer*, referring to a castrated male bovine raised for beef in the American West, raises other questions. The term *ox*, referring to the same creature raised as a draft animal in various places, also poses questions.

13. Derivable forms such as *tiger/tigress*, show their marking relations morphologically. Such derivational transparency suggests that the animals are only spoken of frequently enough to support one independently learned term; the other term, as it is needed, is re-created via a general derivational rule (which is now beginning to disappear). Since the gender marking, adding -*ess* to the male term, is built into the rule, I am not certain there is any special significance to be read into the fact that the unmarked *tiger* is the male.

14. As a *kitten*—or *sex kitten*—she is at least harmless and cute, if immature and childlike.

15. Although the fact that her sex is for pay while his is for fun renders the two not strictly comparable, it does not weaken the judgment implicit in the language. That is, it is the bad, "for-pay" sex that is coded in the language for her, while it is only the minor wink at morality for "a little fun" that is coded for him.

The real issue here probably concerns the greater (until recently, at least) social and legal consequences of women's sexual infidelity than of men's because Western society based inheritance rights on physiological parentage; in our bilateral system, both parents were relevant, but the identity of the mother was rarely in doubt; the biological father's identity was not obvious in the same way, and could only be guaranteed by denying the woman access to other men—giving us the famous "double standard."

16. Women are, in this linguistic instantiation of our collective unconscious, not weighty enough to have more than petty concerns. But they have none of the endearing, puppy-like openness that men show, even in their dislikes.

17. "Cat burglar" may be a negative case, but it feels more neutral to me. On the one hand we are praising his skill, but on the other hand we are labeling his activity as not a proper, manly one.

18. It is amusing to note that a man is apparently un*man*ned by being a nurse (he is only a "male"), while a woman suffers no such loss in joining the men as a doctor.

19. These numbers, of course, are currently in the process of approaching equality; as they do so, we would expect the marking relationship to disappear.

20. From the evidence I have seen, such equality is still fairly far from being an actual fact.

21. The remaining active terms from this set, such as *actress* and *laundress*, seem sufficiently fixed in the popular mind as independent entities as to be derivationally opaque to most users. Even so, they too seem to be fading from use.

22. The human terms from the set that *are* derivationally transparent and that seem to refer to what might be considered varieties of people have acquired even more negative associations through the foregrounding of the suffix as a marker for animals.

23. I am rephrasing his position according to my own understanding. For his own statements, see Berlin (1972, 1976).

24. However, as we shall see shortly, the situations are not identical because of the differing substantive natures of the entities being labeled.

25. For the examples of gender marking we discussed earlier, the substantive nature of the set of entities being labeled makes type specific attributives such as "genuine" or "real" inappropriate as distinguishing labels. For these gender cases—in situations in which the frequency with which the opposed terms are used are becoming more nearly equal—the options are either to mark both sides of the opposition with descriptive labels (as in "female nurse" or "male doctor"), or, more commonly, simply to drop the marking altogether (leaving all nurses as "nurse" and all doctors as "doctor").

In Berlin's biological cases, the default example represents the type first and/or most commonly encountered. In our gender example, the default does not represent a "type" at all (in this biosystematic sense), but rather the form that normally comes to mind or is normally presumed. General across such differences is our tendency to let the label for a default form (if such, in fact, exists)—the unmarked term—represent all members of the opposition, and, when necessary, our tendency to generate specific (not "species"!) labels for nondefault forms by adding some sort of descriptive modifier to the unmarked term—producing a kind of binomial marked term. As reference to such marked alternatives becomes more common, such binomial constructions can enter langue as the normal marked alternatives. As they enter langue, such constructions become subject to the same pressures toward shortening and derivational opacity as are other parts of langue. Different domains or situational contexts may differ in the degree to which they embody counter-pressures in the direction of maintaining binomial forms; it would be interesting to see a study of what such counter-pressures might be. Expressions such as "Ford Mustang" and "Olds Cutlass" are relevant. Trinomial forms seem generally too complex ever to enter langue.

8

Information Processing Limits

In this chapter we will examine the implications of Miller's "Magical Number 7 . . ." article[1] (1956) for semantic and decision structures of the sort studied by cognitive anthropology; in doing so, we will relate Miller's work to Bruner, Goodnow, and Austin's (1956:chap. 4) discussion of concept-formation strategies. We will be looking at limitations on our ability to process information, at the devices we utilize to get around such limitations, and on the relationship of these devices to the kinds of culturally standardized cognitive structures we have found within the semantics of natural language. I will suggest a cognitive structural explanation of a set of interrelated anthropological findings regarding the nature of complex semantic structures. We will see why early cognitive anthropologists (or ethnoscientists) kept finding one or the other of only two semantic structures: taxonomy-like tree structures (based on elaborated inclusion relations) and componential-like paradigmatic ones (based on elaborated contrast relations). We will explore the differences between the two structures in the relationship of attributes to categories, and we will explore the relative degree of foregrounding of the defining attributes versus the categories themselves in these alternative semantic structures. We will conclude by examining how the same explanation might apply to different kinds of linguistic and anthropological structures, including syntactic structures and the structures cognitive anthropologists have found to underlie a variety of culturally standardized natural decision processes.

Miller's Findings

I will now describe Miller's findings—in terms somewhat different from his—and then explore some of their implications for anthropology. A general problem anthropologists and others face when they try to generalize from conclusions reached in psychological laboratories to natural situations is to determine which findings represent robust conclusions about the world and which represent more narrow artifacts of the context in which the findings were produced. I am restating Miller's findings in order to separate what I see as his robust findings from experimental design artifacts. Much of the detail he reports seems to me to be an artifact of the experimental designs used in the work he draws on. Experimental contexts are tightly controlled to prevent contamination of the results by any variables beyond those being directly examined, but it is only rarely that these contexts are themselves examined to see if they are significantly shaping the experimental outcomes. I think Miller's particular statement of his findings is strongly affected by such experimental design artifacts.

The Problem: The Span of Absolute Judgment

Miller first explores the "span of absolute judgment"—the number of standards (or data items) differing along a single perceptual dimension that we can keep in mind for purposes of comparison with some new stimulus item chosen from that set of standards—and finds that we can only keep something like seven such standards, plus or minus two,[2] in our minds at any one time. The precise number of standards varies according to which perceptual dimension is being considered. When the span is exceeded, our ability to recognize (or identify) absolutely (versus relatively or approximately) an item from the set breaks down. He then turns to the means we have at our disposal to get around the limits imposed by this span, and finds that we can either start guessing, or we can increase our number of perceptual dimensions, or we can break the task down into a sequence of operations (on "recoded" or "chunked" units).

For a different but related task, Miller cites experimental work showing that people can recognize the absolute number of data items (for example, identical dots) in a flashed display if the number of data is less than seven; if the number is more than seven, then people have to guess. Miller terms the making of absolute judgments (of the number of items) in this context *subitizing*. Since he was primarily concerned with how to make absolute judgments above the seven threshold, Miller paid only minimal attention to this subitizing work and the guessing alternative that went with it. For similar reasons I will do so too.

Solution 1: Increasing Dimensionality

Miller's first (actually discussed) method of getting around the limit of seven categories or differing items per absolute recognition was to expand the number of perceptual dimensions involved. He found that adding dimensions did increase the number of categories that could be recognized, but also that as the number of dimensions went up the number of categories distinguished per dimension went down—and quickly approached two. For example, instead of distinguishing color by hue alone, we can also use both hue and brightness. Since we can distinguish approximately seven categories on a single dimension, we might expect to be able to distinguish seven times seven (that is, forty-nine) categories on two dimensions. However, it turns out that we can distinguish only ten or twelve categories on two dimensions; that is, the addition of our second dimension causes our categories per dimension to drop to three or four. The addition of a third dimension causes the categories per dimension to drop to two or three, and each successive new dimension brings the average number of discriminable categories per dimension closer to two—though there seems to be no evidence that this average need ever equal two precisely. Instead of talking of the number of categories or items, as we have been doing, Miller cast his discussion of the proceeding material in terms of the absolute amount of information (in bits, from information theory) per dimension, and he attributed some importance to the information-theory approach. We will see shortly why I chose not to follow his lead regarding the information-theory approach.

In addition to the decrease in the number of categories per dimension that accompanies the addition of each new dimension, Miller also found that there probably exists a "span of perceptual dimensionality," that is, a limit to the number of dimensions that can be added. He speculated that this maximum number of dimensions for the immediate, absolute recognition problems might be around ten, which would put the maximum number of immediately recognizable categories or items at a little over one thousand. Thus the maximum number of categories we can distinguish can be expanded from seven to about 1,024 (that is, 2^{10}) via the use of additional perceptual dimensions.

Solution 2: Sequencing

One thousand is a fairly big number, but we nevertheless are capable of dealing with much larger sets of items. For situations in which we need to recognize more than a thousand categories, or in which other constraints prevent us from utilizing so many perceptual dimensions, we need to turn to some other means of extending our range of potential discriminations. For such larger sets, Miller suggested that we "arrange the task in such a way that we make a sequence of several absolute judgments in a row." In the experiments dealing with such sequencing of absolute judgments, the subject was given a list of items and then told to repeat them from memory. Once again, Miller found that the number seven appeared—this time as the number, more or less, of items that subjects could immediately and absolutely remember. The number of remembrable items that he listed ranged from about nine binary digits to five monosyllabic English words (p. 259). Other examples included octal numbers, decimal numbers, nonsense syllables, and the like. But, where the seven (plus or minus two) items of the "span of absolute judgment" appeared to refer to an absolute amount of information (about 2.8 bits), this latter "span of immediate memory" did not refer to any absolute amount of information coded in about seven items or units. Somewhat fewer complex units (such as words) could be remembered than simple ones (such as binary digits), but the number of such remembered units never went far from seven. In spite of the recurrence of the number seven, Miller maintained that the "span of absolute judgment" dealt with an absolute amount of information, while the "span of immediate memory" dealt with the number of units ("chunks," as he called them), and thus that the two spans represented very different kinds of limitations.

In the previously discussed absolute-judgment situation, recognition of an item, whether unidimensional or multidimensional, is essentially instantaneous—all relevant perceptions are made at once and together. In the sequencing situation, on the other hand, one makes the relevant perceptions one at a time. Thus in a recognition task one might expect each of seven dimensions, considered sequentially, to be able to take its full seven values, and thus the total number of recognizable categories (through this sequencing device) to approach 7^7 (823,543).

But, for Miller, the gain here is not from sequencing alone; the seven items that can be held in immediate memory are different kinds of items from those represented in the absolute-judgment span. He phrased the absolute-judgment constraint in terms of the absolute amount of information (about 2.8 bits) contained in the choice among seven unanalyzable alternatives, while his immediate-memory constraint is seven items ("chunks") that may each be complex and hence decomposable into a great number of other units (though the number of chunks remembered does drop slightly as their complexity increases). For example, a sequence of seven decimal digits could be rewritten as a sequence of twenty-eight binary digits while a sequence of six three-letter nonsense syllables would also be a sequence of eighteen letters that might be represented by ninety binary digits (say, in a computer). Even two or three simple sentences might contain many more words, and hence could be decomposed into many more letters, decimal digits, or binary digits than could the seven decimal digits or the six nonsense syllables, and thus the three sentences would contain much more information than the seven decimal digits or the six nonsense syllables. Thus, by arranging our sequence of judgments hierarchically (for example, first, which sentence; then, which words in each sentence; then, which letters in each word; etc.) we can potentially recognize an almost infinite number of categories, although at the cost of the time required for the necessary calculations and memory searches.

This process of translating information from one form into another is called recoding. The process of forming stable, discrete (often labeled) cognitive units of such recoded information is called chunking. Through such recoding and chunking we can subsume a very large amount of information in a very few chunks, and it is thus that we get the perceptual richness that allows us to recognize the faces, houses, tools, cars, trees, and other objects that fill up the world around us.

Connecting Miller's Different Sevens

I suggest, contrary to Miller's assertion, that his two spans (of absolute judgment and of immediate memory) both reflect the same cognitive constraint, and that the apparent difference between them is an artifact of the design of the experiments he reported and on which he based his conclusions. In brief, Miller lost sight of the fact that both kinds of experiment rely equally on memory—since the absolute-judgment experiments require that the items being used as standards be rapidly assimilated and stored in memory in much the same manner as the immediate-memory experiments require the items being memorized to be assimilated and learned.

In the absolute-judgment experiments, subjects apparently are presented with a set of alternative values, which we can call "scale values,") on some perceptual attribute. Afterward they are presented with one of those values as a stimulus, and are asked to respond by indicating which value it is. Note that successful completion of the recognition, or "judgment," task presupposes the success of a prior memory task: subjects must remember the scale values. If the scale values were kept in front of the subject during exposure to the stimulus value, then the problem would be reduced to a trivial comparison of the stimulus value with the indicated scale values. Therefore we must conclude that the difficulty subjects have with the absolute-judgment experiments when more than seven or so scale values are involved must lie primarily in the memory task. The memory task, however, seems to be very much like the task of the immediate-memory experiments: a subject is presented with a series of similar items, or items drawn from a single, narrowly defined set; given a brief period of time to memorize them; and then asked to recall them by reproducing them in the immediate-memory experiments and by comparing them with the stimulus item in the absolute-judgment experiments.

There really are only two fairly minor differences between the two groups of experiments. First, in the immediate-memory experiments the items are to be repeated to the experimenter, while in the absolute-judgment experiments they are only recalled by the subject for purposes of comparison with the new stimulus item, after which only the matching is actually referred to. Second, the focus of the immediate-memory experiments is on the subject's memory of the items, while the focus of the absolute-judgment experiments is on the matching, and the memory task is considered inciden-tal—or passes unnoticed.

Miller supposes that the absolute-judgment experiments show an absolute infor-mational constraint, while the immediate-memory experiments do not. But this too is an artifact of the experimental designs used. In the absolute-judgment experiments, the stimuli were carefully controlled so that they differed from one another only along the single dimension that was being tested. They differed from one another in no other ways. In the related multidimensional experiments, too, the stimuli were allowed to vary only on the relevant dimensions. Therefore the stimuli did not contain any attributes (or variation) that were not relevant to the judgment task at hand, and thus that were potentially decomposable into additional information. On the other hand, in the immediate-memory experiment stimuli were used that were decomposable: hex-adecimal digits could be decomposed into binary digits (for example, "A1" into "10100001"); words could be decomposed into letters (for example, "cat" into C, A, T); and so forth. In all cases this "decomposable" information was irrelevant to the distinctions being made among the set of seven or so stimulus items, and therefore represented additional information transmitted by the item—information beyond that involved in the selection of one item out of the set. As we have seen, such decompos-ability was intentionally "designed out" of the absolute-judgment experiments.

In the immediate-memory experiments, subjects were allowed to try to memorize items that were linguistically coded and equivalent in culturally (or naturally) stan-dardized ways to other items (see the decompositions discussed above). The items had characteristics such that given some additional knowledge members of our culture might be expected to possess, they could be automatically translated into some other form that might contain information beyond the 2.8 bits represented by the distinction of seven items from one another.

In the absolute-judgment experiments, on the other hand, the items were neither linguistically coded nor culturally standardized, and there existed no cultural or natural basis for translating them in any automatic fashion into other kinds of items. Because of the ad hoc nature of the items and because experimental conditions did not allow the subjects to observe any structure within the set of scale items beyond the variation along the single attribute on which testing was taking place, there existed no logical basis for any recoding involving the items, and thus no way in which more than the 2.8 bits of information represented by the discriminations among the seven items could be dealt with. The absolute nature of the amount of information represented by the perceptual discriminations studied in the absolute-judgment experiments is thus an artifact of the way in which the experiments were designed. Had the scale items been culturally meaningful units, or perhaps even if the subjects had been enabled to learn standard associations with each of the scale items within a given set, some recoding would seem likely to have occurred here as well. For instance, since we do have standardized names for hues, I would expect that the subjects who recognized eight or nine hues (p. 249) could also have recognized the names and other words or phrases in which the name of the hue was embedded (such as "redhead" or "blue blood"—assuming those colors were included in the set of hues, and assuming the differences were on the scale of primary color differences). It is true, however, that as long as the specific task requirement is instantaneous recognition, we will of necessity not have to accomplish recoding (since we have described recoding as involving additional mental operations that take real time—however little it may be), and the amount of information contained in our set of seven items will necessarily be limited to the 2.8 bits represented by their distinction from one another. I would suggest, though, that if the experiments had been designed so as to allow subjects to focus serially, on one attribute at a time (for example, first identifying the hue of a line, and then attending to its thickness or length)—and possibly so as to allow subjects to use attributes that were clearly distinct from one another (such as hue and length)—a noticeably greater number of judgments would have been made, as was indicated, if indirectly, by Miller himself.

Kronenfeld's Restatement of Miller's Findings

My claim is that the absolute-judgment constraint is not seven items' worth of information bits at all, but is the same seven "chunks" that Miller found to constitute the immediate-memory constraint. The constraint can be restated as follows: We can hold in our immediate memories no more than about seven items that differ from one another along a single variable. We can increase the number of items by increasing the number of variables along which the items contrast, but only at the cost of rapidly decreasing the number of ways in which items can contrast with one another along any one of those variables. Instead of the absolute information constraint Miller ascribed to the absolute judgment span, we have a relative information constraint that deals with only the information directly represented by the alternatives before us in the given stimulus set, regardless of whatever additional information these stimulus items can or cannot be decomposed into.

What is meant by "variable" here is somewhat complex. The contrast between a single variable and several variables is a function of what we have learned to treat as a variable as much as it is a function of the objective attributes of the stimuli being remembered.

In general, one cannot speak of a single dimension or a single attribute along which items differ, as was done for the absolute judgment experiments, because such cognitively complex knowledge as that involved in the memory experiments does not seem to have the kind of obvious dimensionality that many perceptual judgments do. In what sense might a series of numbers, or nonsense syllables, or words be considered unidimensional or multidimensional? Are the color words of English, for instance, to be considered one- (or two-) dimensional because of the nature of the physical reality they label, or of greater dimensionality because of the many ways in which their shapes, derivations, and connotations differ from one another? Or are they to be considered one-dimensional because of the fact that they represent different values along a single attribute of "meaningful combinations of letters"? Psychological experimentation on the nature of memory and the structure of recall has done much to refine this problem, but I am not aware of any solution. It is this problem with dimensionality that makes it hard to speak in any precise way of what an analog of the multidimensional absolute-judgment experiments would be in the immediate memory experiments.

Let us assume that there are something like seven "current attention registers"[3] that can be dedicated by the brain to alternative values on some single cognitive variable (that is, on one attribute dimension, or from one "closely related set"). Additional sets of seven such "registers" could be added for additional cognitive variables (up to, say, Miller's ten such sets), but the proportion of each set of seven that had to be dedicated to cross-referencing the other sets would increase with the addition of each new set. If we assume that some process roughly like this is taking place in our brains, then in the unidimensional absolute-judgment experiments the first set of seven "registers" would be filled with the scale values; in the multidimensional absolute-judgment experiments, more sets of seven "registers" would be used, but the requirements of cross-referencing would leave fewer "registers"—in each set of seven available for scale values. In the immediate-memory experiments, the initial set of seven "registers" would be filled with the items being remembered; we are, for the time being, leaving open the question of how the additional sets of seven might be used.

In the subitizing experiments there is no (salient) basis on which the subject can organize the stimulus materials into groups, sets, variables, and so forth, and so the subject is compelled simply to assign one dot per "register" as long as there are enough "registers" available. When the number of dots exceeds the number of "registers," but also when the lack of any system in the arrangement of the dots prevents the subject from any effective recoding, there can be no precise pattern to the assignment of dots to "registers" and thus no way of recording the precise number of dots. In this case, the subject can only make gross judgments as to whether there are a few, or some, or many (or maybe even something like "six or seven") dots per "register," and so can only produce estimates.

On the basis of the effects of added dimensionality in the absolute judgment experiments, I would guess that if a mixture of dots and some saliently different shape (such as, for example, stars) were used as stimuli in the subitizing experiments, subjects would be able to subitize for numbers somewhat greater than seven—say, around eleven or twelve. And, similarly, I would expect the addition of some third shape to increase the number a little further.

Miller Summary

In general, I am suggesting that all of Miller's encounters with the "magical number seven" have to do with a single cognitive constraint, the number of related items we can keep in our short-term working memory—however memory might actually be constituted (see Vera and Simon 1993:44)—at one time while also keeping in mind the specific nature of their interrelatedness. If we use only a single basis for assessing relatedness, then we can keep only about seven such items in mind while we work on them. If we have more than seven such items to attend to, then we have Miller's three choices concerning how to get around the limit of seven. (1) We can abandon a precise characterization of our items or of their interrelationships and start using approximations or "guesstimates." (2) We can use additional bases for assessing relatedness (that is, additional dimensions or attributes), but only up to a limit (about ten) and only at the cost of being able to make fewer distinctions per basis (that is, per dimension or attribute). (3) We can attend to our items sequentially, by considering only one basis of relatedness at a time (or, at a higher cost in cognitive effort, a very few bases); at any given time, we would have in our short-term working memory only the small set of items that pertain to the one basis of relatedness we have chosen (dimension, attribute, variable, or whatever). Since the constraints on our longer term storage are less stringent that those on our short-term working memory, we can in this manner attend to a considerably larger number and variety of items. However, such increases do entail costs: the time it takes us to consider a given set of items increases with the number of items (beyond the actual computing time it takes to solve whatever problem we are working on, there is the "bookkeeping" time it takes to keep moving items in and out of short-term memory and to keep searching long-term storage) and the success of the strategy depends in an increasing manner on the organization, speed, and precision of our system of information storage and retrieval.

If we combine the making of sequential judgments with recoding, then we can obtain cognitive control over an extremely wide range (and large volume) of information. Our sequencing, then, need not be simply among alternative, equally fine-grained bases of relatedness, but instead can be hierarchical, focusing ever more closely on the specific set of items that is of interest to us. Such hierarchical focussing is what we use when we play the game "Twenty Questions"—at least, when we can play it correctly. Not all cognitive information processing problems require such focusing. (Later we will briefly examine some cultural information processing problems that do not.) But where its use is appropriate, the device of recoding can be very powerful, and one of the kinds of organization of terms in some linguistic domains that we want to get to depends on such hierarchical focusing. It should be noted that we are not limiting the use of recoding to only the particular task used in the immediate memory experiments, but are generalizing it to Miller's other related tasks. In particular, we are suggesting that recoding can perfectly well apply to the remembered set of scale values with which some observed (or imagined) item is compared in a recognition task. In other words, we can recode a list of alternative possibilities (in linguistic parlance, a paradigmatic set) as easily as we can a list of concurrent items (a syntagmatic set).

Bruner, Goodnow, and Austin's Version

In the fourth chapter of *A Study of Thinking* (1956), Bruner, Goodnow, and Austin discuss selection strategies in concept attainment—that is, the strategies subjects use in selecting possible instances of a concept for examination in order to determine what the concept is. The general set of experiments on which their discussion is based is built on the deck of eighty-one cards that we described in chapter 6 in connection with with Bruner et al.'s conjunctivity experiments; the cards differ from one another on one or more of four attributes (shape of figure: circle, square or cross; color of figure: green, red, or black; number of figures: one, two, or three; and number of lines around edge of card: one, two, or three), and every possible combination of the different values of the four attributes appears on a card. The experimenter forms a concept (for example, a single black square) and asks the subject to find out what the concept is. The subject then selects a succession of cards, one at a time, and for each in turn is told whether or not the attribute combination on the card fits into the concept; when ready, the subject guesses at what the concept is.

Bruner et al. describe the alternative kinds of strategies subjects use at one time or another in selecting cards to ask about. They discuss the experimental factors that lead to one or another strategy (for example, whether or not there is a cost attached to wrong guesses; whether or not there is a reward for the speed with which the concept is attained; whether or not there is a limit to the number of cards that can be examined, and, if so, what it is; and so forth).

For our purposes, however, we want to concentrate only on the alternative strategies themselves, and not worry about the factors that encourage one or another strategy in particular, specific experimental contexts. We will consider some general information processing constraints on strategy selection and what these have to say about the general conditions under which one or another strategy will or can be adopted. We will see that Bruner et al.'s strategies can be explained in terms of Miller's spans and his devices for getting around these, and we shall see that Miller's spans explain under what conditions, in a concept formation task, a high information/high cognitive load strategy becomes practicable. This discussion will give us some idea of the generality of the cognitive/information processing constraints we have deduced from Miller's paper.

Bruner, Goodnow, and Austin's Experiments and Findings

Bruner et al.'s four alternative search strategies are simultaneous scanning, successive scanning, conservative focusing, and focus gambling. After briefly describing each strategy as Bruner et al. see it, I shall re-present those findings within the terms of the conceptual framework I have evolved from Miller's article. Before proceeding to the findings, however, I shall detail a few facts about the concepts that subjects are in the process of seeking. These concepts are each conjunctively defined by the intersection of positive values with one or more of the attributes previously described; thus, "red figures," "red squares," "pairs of red squares," and "pairs of red squares with a single edge-line" are all possible concepts, while "black and green figures," "nonred figures," and "squares or pairs" are not possible. In the present experiments, subjects were given this information concerning which kinds of concepts were possible and which were not.

In Bruner et al.'s *simultaneous scanning* strategy, the subject keeps all possible hypotheses in mind at once, and selects a card to be examined that is most informative—that is, that comes closest to eliminating half the hypotheses if the card is in the concept, and half if it is not in it. When the number of possible hypotheses is at all large, this strategy places a very heavy load on memory (or other information storage facilities) and requires a heavy computational effort to find the best next card, since the status of many different kinds of hypotheses must be remembered, and each of these hypotheses has to reevaluated for each card. The subject selects cards so as to quickly winnow out the potentially incorrect hypotheses until there is only the one correct hypothesis remaining.

In the *conservative focusing* strategy, the subject first searches (however he or she chooses) for a positive instance—that is, for a card that belongs to the concept. Whenever the subject finds a positive instance the subject tests for the relevance of each attribute of that positive instance (or "focus" card) one attribute at a time. Because of the conjunctive nature of all of the potential concepts, when the subject has determined which attributes of the positive instance card are relevant to the concept, the subject will then be able to form the concept by using the intersection of the values the relevant attributes have on the focus card. This strategy does not directly attack the question of how to locate the initial correct instance. Since the subject is not "simultaneous-scanning," however, this initial search process will be in some manner sequential. And, once such an instance is located, the strategy places only a small load on memory (remembering the focus card and which of its attributes have been tested so far), and requires only minimal computational effort (permuting the values of one attribute at a time and afterward forming the intersection of relevant values).

In *focus gambling*, as in conservative focusing, the subject first finds a positive instance of "focus" and then tests for the relevance of the attributes on the focus card. However, this time, the subject permutes more than one attribute at a time. The multiple permutations can range from the simple varying of a couple of attributes at a time (instead of the single attribute that would be varied in conservative focusing) all the way to the systematic and simultaneous testing of all hypotheses consistent with the positive focus.

Each permutation that does not move one out of the concept eliminates several attributes at a time, and so moves the subject toward a solution more speedily than does conservative focusing. However, when a permutation is made that does move the subject out of the concept, then the subject must perform further tests to determine which attribute or attributes was responsible for the move (as opposed to the situation in conservative focusing, where the single permuted attribute is automatically responsible for the move and thus significant for the concept). Until a permutation is reached that moves the subject out of the concept, this strategy has memory requirements comparable to those of conservative focusing; once such an instance is reached, the memory and computational load increases while one assesses the cause of that movement and considers the various remaining hypotheses. Depending on how the subject chooses to sort out the remaining hypotheses, the memory and computational load may not subside again once the subject has identified the attributes responsible for the move. Thus this strategy requires somewhat more mental effort than conservative focusing, but considerably less than simultaneous scanning.

Successive scanning, like simultaneous scanning, is a strategy based on hypotheses instead of on attributes. However, instead of trying to eliminate hypotheses systematically, the subject simply forms one hypothesis after another until he or she manages to guess the correct concept. In a variant of this strategy the subject at least tries to remember past guesses so as not to repeat them, and the subject may even try to make minimal deductions about the status of a few hypotheses other than that being directly tested, but the subject performs no systematic search. In the "lazy" variant the subject remembers nothing. This strategy, unlike the other three, does not ever guarantee a correct solution. The lazy variant places no appreciable memory or computational load on the subject, but does invite the subject to go in circles. The more memory-reliant variant method has memory and computational requirements that can approach those for simultaneous scanning, but does not have simultaneous scanning's advantages of the systematic search to which these memory and computational resources are addressed.

Discussion of Bruner, Goodnow, and Austin

Bruner et al.'s specific experimental design imposes special constraints on the subject's choice of concept formation strategies (as, indeed, does any specific design). In order to generalize the experimental results, we must look beyond these constraints and their specific effects to the general notions implicit in the various strategies. The problem is that, as was the case for the experiments that Miller reported, these experimental design constraints are narrow enough to make it difficult for us to be carefully deductive when we attempt to generalize the findings even to the limited world of our present discussion, let alone to the "real" world in which we live. The generalizations that follow, thus, are necessarily speculative, and would benefit from the kind of probing and refinement that experimental evaluations of them would produce. Meanwhile, as anthropologists and linguists, we have to work with what the psychologists have given us.

Simultaneous scanning amounts to doing everything at once—that is, to keeping a multidimensional universe (or paradigm) of attributes and hypotheses in one's head at the same time. Because of our information processing limitations, we can use such a strategy only where we have just a few items to deal with or where we have some external "bookkeeping" devices. Such a strategy does require that we know the universe of attributes that may possibly pertain to our sought-after concept, but it does not require that we have a positive instance in hand before we begin our search. It is the concept formation equivalent of Miller's notion of getting around the span of absolute judgment by adding additional attributes and transforming the unidimensional process into a multidimensional one. Let us call this a paradigmatic form of mental operation (that is, of information processing, or concept formation, or concept identification).

Conservative focusing amounts to proceeding one attribute at a time—that is, mentally fastening on a succession of attributes or dimensions one at a time. This technique is useful with large numbers of items. In situations like Bruner et al.'s concept formation experiments, this method does require that the subject have in mind a positive instance of the concept in question—as well as a knowledge of the universe of potential attributes—before it can be utilized; in situations that do not meet the latter requirement, it may be more time-consuming than a multidimensional strategy. It is the concept formation equivalent of Miller's notion of getting around the span of absolute judgments by making a sequence or succession of unidimensional absolute judgments. Let us call this a sequential form of mental operation (or information processing, or concept formation, or concept identification).

It is true even for simultaneous scanning that, by virtue of the experiment's design, the data on the basis of which the correct hypothesis is selected comes sequentially, but the cognitive process involved requires more or less simultaneous attention to a variety of attributes. As such, that process is opposed to the sequential attending to attributes that underlies conservative focusing. I suggest that the cognitive skills necessitated by adoption of a simultaneous scanning strategy include (but are not restricted to) those needed for Miller's multidimensional absolute-judgment experiments, while the cognitive skills required by a conservative-focusing strategy are essentially those of sequentially ordered unidimensional absolute judgments. The potentiality for successfully adopting a simultaneous scanning strategy, then, is at least limited by the constraints on information processing identified by Miller for multidimensional absolute-judgment situations. With four attributes, people should not be able to utilize much more than an average of two values per attribute; the complicated calculations required for arranging and evaluating the separate hypotheses involved should reduce both the average number of values possible per dimension and the maximal possible number of dimensions even further. That is, in principal, we should expect a strategy such as simultaneous scanning to be possible only where a subject has just two values apiece on only a very few attributes. Conservative focusing, on the other hand, has much broader limits of applicability.

Focus gambling is a mixed strategy. Like conservative focusing, it uses a sequential process to find an initial positive instance and thereby to simplify the problem. In attending, then, to the simplified problem, it becomes more like simultaneous scanning in its attention to several hypotheses at once. Its speed and efficiency vary, as does its memory and calculating load, according to how ambitious the user is about maximizing the multiple hypotheses being simultaneously considered, but its memory load and calculating load will fall somewhere between that of conservative focusing and simultaneous scanning.

Additionally, and more interesting, at least to me, focus gambling has the potential to represent a compromise between simultaneous scanning and conservative focusing in another way. For problems (unlike those built into Bruner et al.'s experimental designs) where simultaneous scanning would represent a logically preferable strategy if only it were mentally possible, but where the memory and computational loads are too great, focus gambling might represent a useful compromise. Such a problem might be one in which the attributes have interactional effects that finally prevent their being evaluated one at a time. In such a situation, focus gambling might be thought of as a strategy that winnows out irrelevant attributes in much the same way as conservative focusing, but which then uses something like simultaneous scanning for the final examination of the much reduced (and absolutely small) universe of likely-to-be-relevant attributes. In Miller's terms, this would amount to using a sequential strategy to reduce the information processing problem to a size small enough for a multidimensional direct solution to be cognitively feasible. Later on, we will briefly look at a cultural decision-making problem—house-buying—that seems often to be handled in this manner.

One should be able partially to get around the information processing limits of simultaneous scanning by recoding one's universe of potential hypotheses into a structured arrangement. Thus one could keep track of which single-attribute hypotheses were eliminated, which double-attribute ones, and so forth. Such a plan might not manage to simplify things enough to allow the use of a full simultaneous scanning strategy, but it might contribute to achieving a conservative focusing solution by allowing one to search for an initial positive instance in a manner sufficiently systematic to leave one with some useful information when one finally found that positive instance.

The first positive instance is important, because it becomes the focus of both focusing strategies. Once one has such a focus for Bruner et al.'s very limited experimental card decks, an easy route to an assured and fairly quick solution is to use conservative focusing to evaluate the role of any attributes not already understood at the time the focus is found. For a focus card with four attributes, the maximum number of additional cards one would have to examine (under the conjunctivity assumption) in order to necessarily reach a conclusion in the absence of any other information about the concept would be between four and six (one for each attribute that only allowed for absolute values, and two for those that also had the potentiality for relative values). In the limited universe of such a card deck, it is hard for any other strategy to do much better than the preceding one (and, thus, than conservative focusing) in determining the minimal number of additional cards needed to guarantee an assured solution once a focus card has been found. In a real-world situation with more variables and more kinds of variation, sharper advantages over conservative focusing would quickly emerge for even a minimal form of focus gambling in the phase after the initial positive instance or focus was found. By "minimal" I mean a form of focus gambling that considered even just a few variables at a time—that is, one that fell considerably short of a fully efficient simultaneous scanning approach to the focal subproblem (in which all possible hypotheses were simultaneously considered).

Even with Bruner et al.'s limited card deck, even the minimal version of focus gambling, considering only two or three attributes at a time, enables one to possibly reach a solution more quickly than one would with conservative focusing—since variations from the focus that do not move one out of the concept eliminate two or more potential attributes at a time from further consideration. However, the cost of this minimal version is that variations that do move one out of the concept then require additional searching in order to find which variations are relevant to the concept. This additional searching requires additional data (that is, the examination of additional cards). Thus, the number of cards that need to be examined within Bruner et al.'s severely limited universe for a guaranteed solution is larger for focus gambling than for conservative focusing, but the number typically needed may, in general, be less (especially if the probability of any given attribute's being irrelevant to the concept is sufficiently higher than fifty–fifty). Such probabilities occur in situations where the typical concept is extremely likely to be defined by a single attribute; if the concept being sought is not in fact defined by such a single attribute, even the most easily structured version of simultaneous scanning is highly likely to establish that fact quite quickly.

Bruner et al. do discuss how various aspects of the experimental situation other than those we have been considering can affect choice of strategy. An absolute constraint on the number of cases that can be examined (in this case, cards) may preclude waiting for a focus to occur, and so force an attempt at some form of simultaneous scanning, or may make the subject give up and turn to successive scanning—that is, guessing. A limit on the number of cases that can be examined after a focus has been found might make a focused gambling strategy (with its potential for a quick solution) preferable to conservative focusing. If the attributes have any significance for the subject prior to the experiment, the subject's expectations about the attribute's relative probability for significance may affect the choice of strategies, and so forth.

Successive scanning is, at its simplest, the stab-in-the-dark type of guessing that we turn to when we do not know how to begin, or when we do not know what the potentially relevant attributes are, or when we lack the time (or number of instances) we would need to successfully pursue any strategy. It seems possible that there might be "ballpark" strategy variants of such guessing that might link it up with Miller's third device for getting around the "seven" constraint—for example, making rough estimates—but I have as yet no precise notion of how this might work.

In sum, then, Bruner, Goodnow, and Austin's simultaneous scanning strategy is equivalent to Miller's multidimensional strategy of information processing—and breaks down when the size of the problem exceeds Miller's limits. Conservative focusing is equivalent to Miller's sequential structure, and has the slowness associated with it. Focus gambling represents a combination of the two, using a sequential strategy when the problem is big and a multidimensional strategy when the problem has been sufficiently simplified. Successive scanning is equivalent to neither of Miller's strategies, though it may relate in some way to the "guesstimating" alternative that he and we have not explored.

Background: Taxonomies versus Paradigms in Anthropology

Let us now turn our attention to anthropological and linguistic findings. The way toward connecting findings in these disciplines to Miller's work was first pointed to by Miller himself, when he observed that phonemic systems appeared to be an example of his multidimensional absolute judgments (see the following section) and to stay within the limits he had described for such judgments. His observation seems particularly apropos to the componential analysis approach of the Prague School (as well as to phonological system of transformational linguistics that subsequently developed out of Prague phonology), since the issue concerns the recognition of entities formed by the intersection of defining features.

Componential analysis in anthropology, as developed by Lounsbury (1956) and Goodenough (1956), was modeled directly on the Prague School's componential analysis of phonemic systems. In semantic componential analysis one looked for the semantic features (significata, that is, attributes of the denotata of words) that distinguished the denotata of one word from the denotata of another. A minimal set of such features that distinguished a given domain (set of related terms) from other domains and that distinguished the words in the domain from one another constituted a componential analysis of the domain. An ideal solution was one in which every word was conjunctively defined by the intersection of values of each of the features, and in which every such intersection was represented by a word; that is, one in which every feature was expected to be relevant to every word, and in which there were no "holes" in the paradigm.

Such perfect paradigms have been hard to find in natural language, but nearly complete ones have been found in a number of domains, especially in kinship terminologies. Many anthropologists at the time of Lounsbury and Goodenough felt that the special susceptibility of kinship to componential analysis was based on anthropologists' possessing an a priori set of potentially distinctive features, that is, an "etic grid" (deriving from the nature of genealogical relationships and analogous to the International Phonetic Alphabet in phonemic analysis) in terms of which the domain could be analyzed. It was felt that the rest of language would become susceptible to componential analysis as such "etic girds" were developed for other domains (see figure 8-1).

Somewhat later, in the early 1960s, a slightly younger group of linguistic anthropologists (Conklin 1962, Frake 1961, Metzger and Williams 1963, 1966) began systematically describing folk taxonomies. At first the relation of these analyses of folk taxonomies to componential analysis was not clear; some analysts talked as if they were simply another variety of componential analysis, while others treated them as quite different. Gradually (see Lounsbury 1964a:205–206 and Kay 1966) the differences between the two became clear. In folk taxonomies each distinctive feature normally was used only to distinguish a single set of terms. The various distinctions made by the various features were arranged hierarchically, such that only the first distinction pertained to the whole domain; the second distinction pertained only to one of the sections distinguished in the first, and so forth (see figure 8-2). Terms at the same level of distinction were related to each other by opposition (as alternatives, in a sense) in much the way terms in a componentially analyzed paradigm were related to one another; but terms on different levels could also be related by inclusion, which could not happen in a componential paradigm. Finally, for folk taxonomies, the shape of the described semantic structure was determined by the inclusion relations among the various terms in the domain, while the shape of the described semantic structure

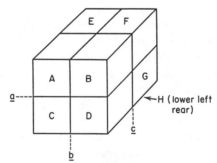

Key Lower case letters label features
     Upper case letters label categories
     Underlining indicates relative importance

FIG. 8-1 Ideal Componential/Paradigmatic Structure

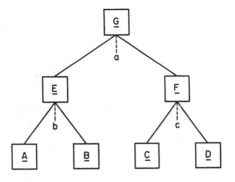

Key   Lower case letters label features
Upper case letters label categories
Underlining indicates relative importance
A, B, C, and D are terminal taxa

FIG. 8-2 Ideal Taxonomic Structure

in a componential analysis was determined by the values the various terms took on the different defining features.

Of course, componential (or paradigmatic) structures can be embedded in taxonomic ones, and vice versa, but each kind of structure still remains clear and distinct from the other. The only point at which the distinction between the two becomes ambiguous is in the case of a small set of terms being distinguished from one another along a single dimension—and we shall see that this is the null case of both kinds of classification.

In the present discussion of semantic structures, I am treating taxonomies in particular as the alternative to componential paradigms, since these were the primary hierarchically arranged sequential structures that early cognitive anthropology dealt with. However, the discussion pertains as well to other hierarchical sequential structures, such as partinomies, that have been discussed in the literature.

Implications of Miller's Work for Anthropology

Taxonomies and Paradigms: Implications of Miller's Findings

If we now attempt to place these kinds of semantic structures, which anthropologists found, into the context of the information processing strategies we found in Miller's work, we can begin to make sense of them. Componential paradigms are culturally standardized versions of the multidimensional, everything-at-once, paradigmatic kind of information processing structure. Componential paradigms are normally described in terms of relatively few features (i.e., well within Miller's rough limit of ten such features) and normally have few values per feature (most often two, sometimes three; apparent cases with more—for example, Wallace and Atkins' [1960] five generations—often seem cognitively to be broken down into a couple of smaller valued dimensions [cf. Romney and D'Andrade 1964]). Informant recognition of an item from a componential set normally seems to be instantaneous. When not instantaneous, such recognition seems to be in terms of checking off features. Componentially analyzable sets of terms seem to be in relatively high-frequency use, which aids in making instantaneous terminological assignments.

Miller's limit on the number of values per feature, where the number of features is more than three or so, appears to explain the tendency for componential paradigms to have mostly binary features. That tendency accounts for the kind of observations that led Jakobson to raise binariness to a kind of first principle (as in Jakobson, Fant, and Halle 1951, Jakobson and Halle 1956; see also Jakobson 1952). Miller's findings imply that Jakobson overstated the case. Since via Lévi-Strauss (see, for example, 1963:101, and see Leach 1970:126) the Jakobsonian overstatement—that is, the idea that oppositions should *always* be binary—became widely accepted in some parts of anthropology (see, e.g., Leach 1976:63), it seems worth pointing out that Miller's psychological evidence only suggests a strong *predominance* of binary oppositions and only then in multifeature (or multidimensional) paradigms. The fact that Miller's average number of values per feature (or dimension) is always greater than two (even if by only a small amount, and even if that amount decreases with increasing dimensionality) means that in his data there is always some contrast (or opposition) that contains more than two values.[4]

Obviously, a child is not born knowing paradigmatic structures. They are learned in conversations, particularly those involving misuses.

Child: "Danny's my sister."
Parent: "No, Danny's a boy. He's your *brother*."

From such interchanges the child learns that "brothers" are boys and "sisters" girls.

Child: "Daddy's my brother."
Big Brother: "No, dummy, Daddy's a man—he's your daddy!"

And so forth. The features, the values of the various objects on the features, and so forth are gradually learned. Since there is at this time no primary object to use as a base line in these componentially organized sets of terms (as there is in taxonomic learning, as we shall see), the contrasts are learned as they are pertinent to immediate perceptions (rather than as step-wise deductive processes).

Taxonomic (or, more properly, tree-like) semantic structures are culturally standardized versions of the sequential information-processing alternative in which a sequence of simple decisions is made. In the case of such tree structures, the sequence of information-processing decisions are arranged hierarchically so as to allow one to start with a broad, immediately recognized or known unit and gradually narrow down to the desired concept or information. Such structures can be very deep and can contain many terms that are of low frequency and that are known well only by few people in a society; they are well adapted to large universes of terms and to situations in which different people work with different aspects of the domain in question. Since such hierarchically arranged structures are based on successive chunkings of low-level detailed terms and recodings of these into fewer higher-level terms, and since distinctive features only pertain to the internal arrangement of each chunk, we can see why distinctive features are relatively unsalient in taxonomic or tree structures, and why there is no particular cognitive pressure to repeat the features of one chunk in some other chunk.[5]

Let us imagine a few conversations that will illustrate how the sequential hierarchical process works in the use and development of a taxonomic structure.

I. Q: What is a lion?
    A: A big cat from Africa that is tawny; males have manes.

II. Q: What's that?
    A: A cat.
    Q: Huh?
    A: A big, spotted one.
    Q: And—?
    A: A leopard.

Conversation I is between two people, say, parent and child, and illustrates both how one learns the taxonomy and how one uses the taxonomy to increase one's knowledge of the world. Conversation II could simply be with oneself; it illustrates the process of identifying an object one knows but does not know familiarly enough to have its name on the tip of one's tongue. It is the sequential search procedure in which one first "recognizes" the object as a member of a high-level class with which one is readily familiar, then decomposes that class into its subclasses and identifies the subclass to which the object belongs, and then similarly decomposes that subclass. Thus one uses long-term memory and does not rely on instant recognition. The immediately recognized classes are familiar categories with whose members one interacts frequently, and the unmarked members of these classes are the particular members with which one interacts frequently (cf. Greenberg 1966)—in this case, cats. In the case of "Scratchy," one's pet *Felis domestica*, the process thus would be considerably shortened:

III. Joey: What's that?
     Bill: A cat.
     Joey: Oh, yeah.

As we have seen in chapter 7, these general considerations of the uses of depth do appear to explain some part of why Berlin's folk taxonomies universally evolve as they do (Berlin 1972). As long as everybody in the culture does the same things, taxonomies are not needed because everyone deals with the same objects as everyone else, and does so with the same frequency as everyone else. But with increasing division of labor, people's activities begin differing from one another, and different people begin dealing with different objects with different frequencies. At this point, they need general ("generic") terms for classes at a high enough level for all to use them frequently enough to learn and remember them, and they need devices for relating these high-level classes to the various specific objects they each separately deal with—hence the question, What kind is it? and the attendant development of taxonomic structures. This relationship between the division of labor and taxonomic depth (in relevant areas of culture) is a suggestion I first heard from Frake in 1965 in a classroom conversation, and that seems to be borne out by the work of Berlin and others.

Thus, a child learning language first learns the labels for a large number of objects around her- or himself as discrete instances—almost as proper names: "Joey, *cat!*" Then categories are separated from names: "Annie, this is a cat," and "Billy, Scratchy is a cat." Then, later on, the child begins to learn about other objects as belonging to named categories that are like those he already knows—except for the addition of alteration or certain specified features. Thus:

> Lion   =   Cat + big, tawny, African
> Jaguar =   Car + sporty, British, expensive
> Quill   =   Pen + made from feather, old

Such taxonomic connections, however, are not exclusive. The same object (and/or label) can (and is likely to) participate in several structures at once—and so our structures become, in effect, cross-linked.

> Lion   =   Noble + in animal world
> Jaguar =   Cat + big, yellow with black spots, South American
> Quill   =   Feather + long, stiff, from large bird

The separate semantic structures—kinds of cats, kinds of cars, kinds of feathers, animal exemplars of human social roles, and so forth—remain distinct from one another; the shared words do not cause the structures to merge. But the different individual words do carry some overtones or an aura from one context into the other. We do think of a "Jag" (that is, a Jaguar car) as purring, having a lot of energy waiting to be released in a breathtaking spring forward, and all that. A knowledge of quill pens does cause us to fasten our attention on a different aspect of a goose's primary wing feathers than the aspect we attend to when examining other feathers (such as, perhaps, its pin feathers).

The same kind of frequency/cognitive ease considerations that can produce the marking relationship between a particular species and its genus—in which the species name also stands for genus—can also apply to use relations, in which an object is most frequently experienced in a single use (as, for example, in the past, in the use of quills for writing), or to part/whole relations, where, in some context at least, a particular part is all of the whole that matters (as in "hired hands"). I only mention these cases as examples of not strictly metaphoric processes by which one word comes to appear in a variety of places. Metaphoric extension itself (see chapters 10 and 11) obviously represents another example—especially if one of the metaphoric extensions comes to be used with particular frequency.

In the same way that taxonomies can be cross-referenced by overlapping words, paradigms can be cross-referenced with each other and with taxonomies. That is, the same word can appear in a number of otherwise unrelated semantic structures, or even several words can so appear. "Hands" and "heads" belong to a semantic structure of body parts but also to another semantic structure that refers to members of a work crew (whence they came, presumably via metaphoric extension).

There also exists a further, more systematic way in which taxonomic and paradigmatic structures can be interrelated (see Wexler 1970, on which much of this immediate discussion is based). Each node in a taxonomy is a contrast set (cf. Frake 1962);

so far we have been talking as if each such set consisted of seven or fewer items contrasting along a single dimension. However, it is also possible that the contrast set at such a node might be a multidimensional one— that is, a paradigm—in which case we would have a paradigmatic structure embedded in a taxonomic one. Similarly, the items of a paradigmatic structure would be head terms for further taxonomic elaboration, in which case we would have a taxonomic structure embedded in a paradigmatic one. Note that the same frequency-of-use constraints and Miller-derived size constraints would apply to the paradigmatic parts of such complex structures as we have described for freestanding paradigms; and, furthermore, the successive taxonomic levels would make the same time and information retrieval demands that are made by pure taxonomic structures. Keeping track of where one is in the hierarchical structure might also be expected to impose some additional cognitive load that would further constrain potential recourse to paradigmatic substructures. For the preceding reasons, such mixed structures might be expected to be unlikely for specific semantic domains. Where one has higher level structures (though possibly less agreed on and less elaborated) that relate separate domains to one another (e.g., a general social role macro-domain that relates kinterms, job roles, civic roles, etc.), the net effect seems highly likely to be some such complex structure.

It still seems to me, even considering the possibility of such mixed structures, that the distinctions between paradigmatic type structures and taxonomic type ones are clear. These distinctions are: a focus on relations of terms to features versus on inclusion relations among terms; an expectation that every feature will appear in the definition of every term versus that each feature only pertains to the subdivision of a single term and thus only to a subset of the total set of terms; and instantaneous recognition among a complex set of alternatives versus a sequence of recognitions among successive simple sets of alternatives. Any switching within a taxonomic structure to an embedded paradigmatic one would thus require a conscious shifting of mental gears. Furthermore, one always seems clear about which kind of structure one is in, in the sense of aware of among what kinds of alternatives one is choosing among (that is, alternative categories that are mutually exclusive versus those that represent alternative levels of inclusion) and whether or not a current choice stands alone or is linked to some train of other choices.

There is no logical sense in which any one of the contrasts between taxonomic and componential structures listed above necessarily implies the others. We do, for instance, have higher order terms for subsets of componential paradigms; for instance, "parent" includes both "mother" and "father," and could be defined within the componential paradigm for English kinterms. What is interesting is that terms like "parent" are not normally defined within such paradigms but are treated as if they are part of some alternative, overlapping structure. I will shortly suggest why such exclusions are not accidental, but represent good analytic judgments. Similarly, there is no a priori reason we could not repeat the use of a single feature in several different branches of a taxonomic tree. It is true that, in particular cases, empirical facts about the items being categorized might preclude such repetition, but even where the repetition is possible and could be done, ordinary language users show no particular inclination to do it—in spite of the local cognitive economies that might seem to accrue to users if the features represented the major cognitive load of such arrangements. The reason appears to be that such potential repetitions of distinctive features are far enough apart in the overall taxonomic structure to be part of different substructures, which must be independently learned in any event; and so the postulated economy is only apparent (as long as the attributes actually used are not too strange and thus expensive to learn). Finally, there seems to be no logical reason we (whether natives or anthropologists) could not see taxonomic structures as a relationship among features instead of among terms.

Taxonomies and Paradigms: Other Factors

Let us now step back and look at where our attempt to use Miller's findings to account for the shape of the semantic structures found by cognitive anthropologists now stands. We are concerned with why the various cognitive structures anthropologists have found in different cultures have the specific shapes they do. I have suggested that one major aspect of those shapes concerns whether they are paradigmatically organized or hierarchically (taxonomically) organized. I have proposed that the informational constraints described by Miller explain why such structures, once they achieve any complexity at all, must have one of these two kinds of shapes, and I have suggested informational factors about the domain being structured that push it in the direction of one or the other kind of structure. What I would now like to do is quickly sketch out some other factors that will also affect the shape of the resultant structure. My goal at present is not to elaborate or detail these separate arguments, but only to indicate other kinds of explanatory considerations that I regard as complementary to (rather than contradictory to) the argument I am developing out of Miller's discussion.

Obviously, the *substantive nature* of the referents of a verbal domain can favor one kind of structure over another. In our examples the important attributes of kinsmen (e.g., age, sex, lineality) really do cross-cut the domain, while the world of animal species really is arranged "taxonomically"—that is what Darwinian evolution is all about.[6]

However, in the latter case, there are places in which componential structurings would be possible but seem to be avoided. I gather that folk always put dolphins, bats, and such in only one place in their folk taxonomies, even if they are aware of reasons for cross-referencing. And a series such as that shown in figure 8-3 is not often described as a componential paradigm, though it would seem that it could be.

Similarly, categories like *ancestor, descendent, parent, child, grandparent, grandchild*, and so forth indicate that a hierarchical or taxonomic organization of the

Equine		Bovine		Ovine		Caprine			
stallion	mare	bull	cow	ram	ewe	billy	nanny	Adult	Subcategory
colt	filly	calf		lamb		kid		Young	
horse		cow		sheep		goat		Category	
Male	Female								

FIG. 8-3 Example of a Taxonomic-shaped Structure That Could Be Paradigmatic, but Is Not (Note: For simplicity's sake, I am ignoring neutered males, such as gelding, steer, and ox.)

terminological domain of kinsmen is not absolutely precluded by the nature of the substantive or pragmatic domain, that is, of how we sometimes talk about it.

Thus, I do not claim that the substantive nature of the realm of referents of a verbal domain is irrelevant to the shape of the verbal structure by which a language codes the domain; such substantive natures clearly do play a role.[7] What I do claim, though, is that such substantive natures are never by themselves sufficient to determine the verbal structure of the domain. It is important to recall that we are not talking about individual people's perceptions or the conceptual structures they might create from those perceptions, nor are we talking about such perceptions or conceptual structures that might be statistically common in some population; instead, we are talking in particular about those conceptual structures that enter into the collective representation that is langue. Important for the shaping of these collective conceptual structures are the cognitive processes that fix categories in our minds and the social and communicative conditions that provide the situations in which those cognitive processes become operative.

There seem to be at least three ways in which *frequency phenomena* affect the kinds of structures we are considering in this section. The first refers to the frequency of usage required to keep a word in the language. People learning a language must hear a word often enough to learn it, or they will coin new words or constructions to cover the referents of the word when they do need it. And they must use the word themselves often enough to have their misuses corrected; my children learned that it is "men," not "mans," long before they learned that it is "fish" instead of "fishes."

The second place where frequency phenomena enter in concerns the frequency with which groupings of terms within a domain are made. If only one grouping of a given set of terms is used frequently enough to be standardized, then we have a piece of a taxonomic structure; if alternative groupings are regularly used, then we have the basis for learning the cross-cutting attributes of a paradigmatic structure.

The kinds of conjunctivity considerations described by Nerlove and Romney (1967) and Kronenfeld (1973) lead people to try to apply their categorizing attributes as completely as possible throughout the domain and thus to create whatever indicated categories do not already exist; the lack of sufficient frequency of use of particular terms (or categories) to maintain (or create terms for) them produces gaps in the paradigm and represents a pressure toward the elimination of attributes. The process is the same panchronic one Greenberg has described for changes in phonemic systems. However, for the moment, we are looking only for the sources of incompleteness in our paradigmatic structures.

Our third recourse to frequency phenomena concerns the frequency of interaction with the substantial referents of a term that is required to maintain instant recognition of the terminological category. This concern is important because I have proposed that paradigmatic structures permit instant recognition of the item once the domain has been called to mind, while hierarchical or taxonomic structures are devices for arranging the recognition task sequentially and thereby allowing search-and-retrieval operations involving other memory stores to come into play.

The particular semantic structures we find in "nature" are organizing devices based on functional needs and constraints, both cognitive and pragmatic. The cognitive constraints described by Miller force such structures into one of the two kinds of information arrangement.

Anthropological Studies of Decision Making

I would now like to turn briefly to the area of natural decision making, in which a number of anthropologists have worked (see Quinn 1975 for an early overview; more recent work includes Young 1980, Franzel 1984, Gladwin and Murtaugh 1984, Mukhopadhyay 1984, and Plattner 1984). At a symposium at the Mexico City meeting of the American Anthropological Association in November 1974, Quinn commented to the effect that what all studies of such decision processes seem to have in common is the breaking up of a single complex decision into a sequence of steps. Our discussion of Miller's work suggests why this should be so, and implies that we should be able to say a little more than that about the shape of the decision-making process by which different problems are handled. With this expectation in mind I would like to look more closely at a few examples of natural decision making discussed by Quinn.

In a study of house-buying decisions in Hawaii (1971), Quinn has described the process her informants went through in terms of "elimination by aspects" (a notion borrowed from Tversky). In this process, her informants first considered all the features of a house that might affect their purchase (such as price, location, number of bedrooms, etc.). For each feature they established absolute bounds within which they felt they had to stay, and then limited their search to houses within those bounds. They considered such houses in terms of one feature at a time, gradually eliminating those that were less desirable on successive features; this process involved ordering features according to importance. In this process explicit trade-offs were made between values of one feature and values of another as the range of possibilities became clear, but such trade-offs were between isolated features. Her point was that buyers never attempted to deal explicitly with the entire gestalten of the house they were considering, but instead attended to the houses one feature at a time.

Since there are a large number of attributes that can affect one's purchase of a house, and since many of these attributes can take a great many values, I propose that the sequential search procedure Quinn found follows necessarily from Miller's work (as we have refined it), and closely parallels Bruner, Goodnow, and Austin's findings concerning "decisions" about a sought-after concept in a complex universe of potential concepts. The house-buying problem can be seen as a kind of concept formation problem in which nature has defined the best combination of house attributes for our buyer, and our buyer is trying—by looking at particular instances of related concepts (i.e., other houses)—to arrive at that concept. The strategy Quinn's informants have been following appears basically to be Bruner et al.'s conservative focussing strategy, though with occasional excursions into something like focus gambling. Conservative focussing, also, given the differences in the pragmatic nature of the problems being dealt with, seems to be what elimination by aspects represents. If we conceptualize the house selection problem in terms of our interpretation of Bruner et al.'s findings, we might predict that when the problem is sufficiently simplified (i.e., the range of possibilities sufficiently narrowed down), Quinn's informants might switch strategies. We might expect that they would switch to a simultaneous scanning type strategy. A simultaneous scanning strategy would be an example of Miller's paradigmatic information-processing alternative, and so might be expected to be relatively instantaneous and hence relatively subconscious (since it lacks the more conscious searching of long-term memory that his syntagmatic alternative can involve).

It is with interest, then, that I recall Quinn's comment, when she first presented the paper on house buying, to the effect that her informants, having proceeded via elimination by aspects to gradually select a specific house as their best choice, would often, at the end of that process, look at the house and then impulsively settle instead on some other house. What I suspect is that their attribute-by-attribute searching allowed them to considerably simplify the problem by eliminating many attributes as essentially irrelevant to their decision, and to rule out many values on many other attributes as unacceptable. For the simplified attribute universe that remained, they found that they were able to make a net comparison (considering everything at once) of the small set of houses that remained potentially acceptable. The apparent "logical" decision to settle on some other house appeared to be the trigger that made them step back from the attribute-by-attribute comparison and consider the small set of whole gestalten left in the universe—often producing the observed change in decision. Since this latter process was an instantaneous, everything-at-once comparison, Quinn's informants were unaware of any decision-making process, and so felt their change of mind to be an impulsive one. Of course, as Quinn has pointed out, once they settle on a decision, all kinds of dissonance-reduction processes take over, which rapidly make the final decision into the only possible or desirable alternative.

In terms of our discussion of Miller's information-processing strategies, we would say that the process Quinn described as "elimination by aspects" is a sequential one with the various decisions at least partially arranged hierarchically—so that the "correct" decision is gradually homed in on. The hierarchy, in this case, is not the hierarchy of applicability of the attributes we saw in our semantic example of taxonomies; here, every attribute does pertain to every house. Instead, the hierarchy is one of importance; the more crucial factors are considered before the less crucial ones.

In a study of Mfantsi litigation (1976) Quinn has shown that, rather than sit down with the charges and evidence and decide directly on a verdict, Mfantsi elders (in local, informal court cases) take each aspect of the charges and relevant evidence one at a time and separately calculate the effect of each on the final "pacification" (the fee that is paid by the losing party to the winning party). In this case the number of factors that might affect the pacification is too large (and complex) to be considered all together, and so the syntagmatic or sequential information-processing strategy is used. The factors are considered, according to Quinn, in no particular order, and each factor can only have the effect of driving the "pacification" up or down. Since the factors thus each act in a parallel manner on the same entity, and since the consideration of one in no way depends on the prior consideration of the other, there is no sense in which the elders home in on a decision. Thus the sequential process is not arranged hierarchically. Instead, they use the pacification level as a kind of marker or counter that is simply adjusted in turn for each factor they consider; their final verdict is the point to which the counter is pointing after the last factor has been considered. (I should point out, though, that one separate factor can at some point in the process be a comparison of the tentative level of pacification with more generalized feelings about what it should be.)

Syntactic Structures

It is tempting to consider the syntactic structure of sentences as another example of such hierarchically organized sequential information processing systems, in which each node represents a chunking of the items it immediately dominates. I will now briefly sketch a version of this idea I presented in an earlier paper, and will limit myself to aspects relevant to our present discussion of sequential recoding strategies. A fuller exploration and explication of this idea would have to deal with a variety of syntactic and child language development issues that would take us far afield from the topic of this volume. Those issues were raised in a programmatic form in my earlier paper (1979), and interested readers may consult that discussion to see how I approached them.

Kronenfeld 1979 offered an approach to the phylogeny and ontology of human syntax that seemed capable of accounting for adult human syntax of the sort characterized by transformational, generative grammars while also respecting the biological constraints described in my discussion of claims about innate capabilities in the introduction to this volume. This approach aimed at making language both learnable in the time that human children have available to learn syntax and evolvable in the time that human beings have had since our phylogenetic divergence from our nearest anthropoid relatives.

The approach deals with the relevant learning and evolutionary problems by breaking the learning problem into separate cognitive components, as many of which as possible are designed to be basic parts of general cognitive functioning rather than specific to syntax or language. Such general components could be the products, then, of a much longer period of evolution than that involved in the latest human/ape split, and, accordingly, such components might be expected to show up in homologous forms in related species. The goal of this breakdown was to make the specifically human (and human language) component as small and as simple as possible; it should represent a small evolutionary step (even if one with large and important consequences) and it should not be so far removed from ape capabilities as to be impossible for apes to manage, at least minimally (even if crudely and with difficulty). Thus my approach represented a shift from a general and vague characterization of language as simply "innate" to a more complex but specific characterization in which I tried to be much more specific concernining what exactly about language *was* innate and which particular innate elements were to be considered specific to humans.

This approach to the development of syntax is pertinent to our present concerns because it involves hierarchically organized "chunking" of a form similar to that we have seen in taxonomic structures. One important component of this approach to syntax—a component neither specific to humans nor specific to syntax or grammar—consists of recoding. Sequences of contextually delineated but relatively undifferentiated binary nodes from a relatively deep but homogeneous structure are recoded as nodes in a shallower structure whose nodes are more multinary, complicated, and distinctive. The point of offering the example now is to illustrate the potential relevance of hierarchically structured chunking to a wider universe of cognitive structures beyond taxonomies and their like.

The approach consists of six stages. Each stage represents a type of cognitive operation performed by a child who is learning language, that is, forming her or his internal representation of langue. Each stage is dependent on the one before it. The first stage is *naming*. This is the only distinctively human stage, and presumably does represent some innate human disposition. That is, it seems almost impossible to keep human children from attaching names to things (objects, actions, and so forth), while closely related animals such as chimpanzees can only be taught to do so with difficulty; at the same time, it is noteworthy that chimpanzees can be taught the activity of naming, even if it seems not to come naturally to them. The second operation consists of using names in one-word utterances. That is, in this stage, the child uses a name in a context and with an intonation that suggests a definite communicative intent. For instance, the child says "bottle" in a situation in which the parent knows that the child wants her bottle and in another situation in which the parent knows the child is showing off his partially drunk bottle. This is the kind of utterance that in "rich interpretation" is analytically expanded into some kind of simple sentence. However, I do not think the child necessarily intends the syntactic structure we adults would use if we were communicating the presumed message (that is, to take the preceding examples, either "Bring me the bottle!" or "Look at what I drank from the bottle!"). I do presume, though, that the child intends the message that adults would use the fuller sentence (one of those just given) to communicate. The third stage involves the child's using a minimal form of syntax. The child joins two words in a construction in which one word is the focus and the other a modifier. Here we might have utterances such as "*mommy* bottle" or "bottle *me*." The relationship between the two words is signaled by intonational features such as stress or loudness; the word made more salient is the focus. The words themselves are not syntactically or inflectionally differentiated, and so we are not speaking of parts of speech or syntactic roles; we are instead talking about functional semantic roles. As with stage two, I would argue that the child intends the message but not the syntax of the expanded sentence an adult would use for a similar communication. The fourth stage is embedding, and is already implicit in the previous stage. That is, if two words can be combined to form a single, more complex utterance, and if that complex utterance is used by a child as if it were a single word, then there is nothing to prevent that complex "word" from being joined with some other word to form an even larger and more complex, three or more word "single" utterance. Thus, we may have "mommy-bottle me," perhaps in a situation that suggests that the child wants the mother to bring the bottle to the child, or "mommy bottle-me" in a situation in which the child wants the mother to admire what that child is doing with the bottle. There is still no syntax per se; information about the relation of the words to one another and to the conversational and phenomenal contexts is still carried only by intonation and the directing of attention.

Through all these stages the child is getting feedback from adults in the form both of responses to requests or observations embodied in the communication and of repetitions by adults of slightly expanded versions of the child's utterances. The child first sees whether or not the communication has succeeded in its goal, and then gets some indication of what a slightly fuller and better phrasing might be (or might not be, in the case of a failed communication).

The fifth stage involves the recognition of recurrent patterns and the ability to extract regular frames from these patterns—thus "mommy hand," "daddy hand," "doggie hand," and so forth. The child seems to guess at bases of generalization, and to continually modify such guesses on the basis of feedback. This operation seems to represent the classification basis from which word classes initially evolve, and thus to represent a first minimal step toward actual syntax. A later classification of such classifications would seem to be involved in the child's working out of more general parts of speech (such as nouns and verbs, or things and actions). But, at this stage, there are still no grammatical markers, and so all syntactic information is carried only by relative intonation features such as stress or loudness.

The sixth operation is recoding or "chunking." A simple multiword sentence of the sort produced by stage four can be seen as a two-word sentence in which one (or both) of the words is in turn decomposed into another two-word sentence, and so forth. A structural tree diagram of such a sentence would consist of a relatively deep hierarchy of binary nodes. "Chunking" would recode pieces of such trees into shallower, multinary nodes, and would introduce grammatical function words (or morphemes) as markers of sentence slots (from stage four) and thus of syntactic roles.

In effect, stages two through five produce a kind of phrase-structure grammar. The great depth of a structure produced by such a grammar, the purely relative marking of the relationship between items in each node at all levels, and the lack of any differentiation of elements from one another are all features that make this kind of structure hard to hold in mind, hard to follow in use, and hard to comprehend. Some sort of transformation operations are necessary to render it processible. The complexity and opacity of such a structure explain why we never see untransformed sentences (that is, utterances based directly on "deep structure") at any level of language use beyond the very simplest. Children do not first learn phrase structure representations and then how to transform them; instead, they start utilizing stage six operations as soon as untransformed structures become at all hard to follow—which is to say, very early in their learning process. From then on, it is transformed "surface structures" that children build on and elaborate in further language learning. As relatively simple surface structures become too extended and elaborated for easy processing or comprehension, they too are further transformed—into newer, more complex, but better marked and delineated syntactic structures.

The hierarchical structures represented by successive "chunking" operations are not merely summaries of knowledge gained in some other fashion; they are instead powerful tools for actively facilitating the process of complex thought, including complex juxtapositions of various ideas.

For a somewhat more fully explained presentation of this approach see Kronenfeld (1979:218–227), from which this sketchy version has been taken. Again, I want to reiterate that my goal in offering this account here is not to convince readers of its ultimate truth or accuracy; it is instead primarily to illustrate the kind of wider usefulness I see for hierarchically organized sequences of "chunking" or recoding operations. I also offer it as an illustration of how I would attack the innatism problem I raised in the introduction.

Successive "chunking" is not unlike what happens when we learn to drive a car with a manual transmission. We first learn elaborate, self-consciously applied rules about the timing and juxtaposition of brake, clutch, accelerator, and steering wheel—rules that are too complicated to be totally followed in practice in a self-conscious manner. We mostly are not taught the rules directly, but have to infer them from a combination of our mistakes and what we are told. With practice, we gradually begin to automate our actions and decisions, first at the simplest levels and then at more complicated levels—and, as we do so, we lose conscious sight of what operations we are in fact executing and what cues we are using to trigger the operations. We develop a "braking" chunk that relates clutch and brake use to speed, motor sound, and so forth, and a "gear shift" chunk that relates shift lever use to clutch, speed, and motor sound. These simple chunks then become parts of larger chunks such as "gearing down for a turn," "stopping for a light without burning out the brakes," and so forth. These larger chunks become themselves automated in the same way; they too come to be thoughtlessly and automatically executed. But, even as our simple "braking" chunk becomes submerged in a larger "turning" chunk, it still remains available to us for direct, conscious use when needed. Note that these chunks, once they are learned, are performed automatically, with only a minimum of conscious thought, and are in this sense habitual. But they are not habits in the sense of being automatically executed in some fixed form once triggered. Within the various chunks we, as drivers, are constantly making decisions and tuning our operations to our goals (for instance, reacting to the sound of the motor and the feeling of acceleration in deciding when to turn; taking a turn more slowly than usual to avoid upsetting the groceries in the trunk, and so forth).

Our driving chunks, like our language chunks, come to make up a hierarchical structure of successively decomposable nodes: turning includes slowing down, which includes applying the brake and using the clutch if the speed becomes slow enough or if one needs to downshift. This insight—that the structure of language at this abstract level is the same as the structure of action, and that both structures consist of tree structures that are operated upon by rules that transform one tree structure into another by altering nodes at various levels—is not a new one; it forms a fundamental part of Lashley's 1951 article "The Problem of Serial Order in Behavior" (even though he placed more stress on the kinds of problems of temporal and spatial integration that are now rising to the fore in work on distributed computing).

Summary

I am suggesting that it is not by accident that ethnoscientists found only the two kinds of semantic structures, taxonomically shaped ones and paradigms. Miller described two exact ways (and one approximate way) of getting around the limitations imposed by our inability to keep more than seven or so items that differed along a single dimension actively in our minds at a time. One way was to increase the number of dimensions along which items could differ from one another. But he pointed out that as we increased the number of dimensions the number of distinctions per dimension we could make dropped rapidly, and he pointed out that there was probably an upper limit of something like ten dimensions that we could thus handle. I would like to add that there is much mental effort involved in learning and maintaining such a large multidimensional mental structure, especially if the items being dealt with are themselves complex recoded chunks; this heavy cognitive load would suggest that the bigger the structure the greater the frequency of use necessary to maintain it in people's minds. Miller's second way of getting around the "magical number seven" was for subjects not to keep all relevant items in mind at once, but instead to deal with them sequentially; that is, we could mentally deal with successive sets of seven items arranged so that whatever more complex problem we were trying to solve was dealt with gradually. The processes of chunking together bunches of relatively simple items and recoding each such chunk as a single more complex item allow us in many situations to arrange our sequence of sets of items hierarchically, and so to gradually narrow our focus of attention (much as one does in the game of "Twenty Questions"). The limitation involved in this alternative is that the sequential process takes time (the longer the sequence, the more time), and problems of information storage and retrieval in long-term memory are raised. The effort required to learn the chunking represents another limitation. There is, however, no obvious limit to the number of items that can be handled this way. Miller's third way of getting around the limitation of seven was to switch from absolute to probabilistic information processing. This process does not concern us at present, since we are here dealing with absolute identifications and decisions, but we might note that it, too, seems well represented in normal cultural operations.

Notes

1. I am using this source in particular because it is one of the defining documents of the currently dominant paradigm in cognitive psychology. As such its findings still stand, even if they have been somewhat refined in the intervening years. Meanwhile, no subsequent work has laid out the problem so generally and so untechnically.

2. The actual mean over all the studies Miller reports is 6.5; one standard deviation includes between 4 and 10; and the range is 3 to 15 categories (p. 250).

3. The quotation marks are by way of making clear that this is a metaphor for something not yet well enough understood to be treated precisely or directly.

4. These findings provide support for Ohnuki-Tierney's (1981:454) observations, which she credits to Needham, regarding the predominance of binary oppositions, but also noting the presence of trinary and greater oppositions.

5. Presumably, the features, being nonrepetitive, are in this case less salient than the indicated forms they distinguish; that is, they are simply "whatever it takes to distinguish X from Y."

6. Hunn (1976, especially pp. 515–517) offers a particularly insightful argument concerning one factor (perceptual distance) which might push people strongly to see some part of the world as taxonomically organized. His example nicely illustrates how general cognitive capabilities, joined with regularities in the experienced world, might produce the kind of cross-system regularities that sometimes are felt necessarily to imply more specific innate mechanisms (see my discussion of innatism and universals in chapter 2). His discussion of the factors which might push for defining-attribute versus *gestalt* definitions of taxonomic entities (pp. 513–514) is similarly insightful and stimulating. Hunn's argument involves an appeal to cognitive ease, and is based in part on Bruner, Goodnow, and Austin's discussion of how people reduce the work involved in processing complex multi-attribute concepts (1956:47).

7. Hunn 1982 suggests that cultural knowledge, and the uses people have for the materials being classified affect their linguistic classifications of biota. In this respect, Hunn is arguing that people's classifications of living things are not totally unlike their classifications of cultural artifacts, and so represents one of the views with which Atran 1990 is disagreeing (see also

Atran 1985 and Hunn 1987). I want to point out that the issue of whether or not there exists any special biological basis for our perception of living things is irrelevant to our present linguistic purposes.

Hunn is also raising the issue of general purpose versus special purpose classifications. This distinction, as I have argued elsewhere (Kronenfeld 1985), is important for biological systematics and for scientific classification in general. For classifications coded in natural language, as well as for ones implicit in other bodies of more or less standardized cultural knowledge, the issue seems to work out differently. The frequency conditions that govern the continuance of any given sign in natural language would seem in general to work against the presence of distinct special purpose classifications in natural language; instead, one would expect a variety of relevant information to be attached to whatever classification had the frequency needed for survival, and one would expect the nature of that classification to be affected by such attachments. (See Anderson 1987 for a discussion of the utility of one such cultural knowledge system.)

Hunn's own position on these issues is more complicated than what is suggested by the preceding dichotomies. He is specifically proposing "a taxonomic hierarchy model . . . based on the contrast between a general purpose, biologically natural taxonomic core and special purpose, biologically artificial peripheral taxa" (1982:830). In one sense, the disagreement between people like Hunn and Atran can be reduced to the question of whether the natural part of biological classification is "natural" because it is in the substance of the material being classified or because it is in some way preprogrammed in our minds. In terms of our present concern with language as a collective representation and as a tool (which we use to communicate with each other about our thoughts), it does not matter whether the categorizations and structure of the thoughts we communicate come from the world around us, from the nature of our minds, or from some more unique confluence of history, accident, and individual creation; the processes by which we create and maintain signs, infer core referents, and flexibly extend reference remain more or less the same.

IV

SEMANTIC EXTENSION

In this part we will examine extensionist approaches to semantics. Chapter 9 begins with a review of the major approaches to the semantics of word meaning within anthropology and related disciplines. Each type of approach is briefly sketched out, analyzed, and its limitations shown. The remainder of the chapter examines work within the ethnoscience tradition prior to the present theory. Extensionist models are introduced via the classic analyses by Lounsbury of Crow- and Omaha-type terminologies and by Berlin and Kay of basic color terms. The final sections of chapter 9 look at three more recent examples (from my work on Fanti kinship, Kempton's work with *ollas*, and Basso's work on Western Apache use of horse partinomy terms for pickup trucks) that illustrate specific points concerning data collection, variability (both within an individual's usage and among the individuals of a community), and the logic of extension. Chapter 10 presents the actual theory. The theory's concepts are described and applied to a variety of illustrative problems.

9

Prior Extensionist Work

Why an Extensionist Theory Is Needed

In order to see how an extensionist approach contains the power but not the limitations of earlier semantic models, we will explore how traditional componential analysis (see Lounsbury 1964a, Goodenough 1956) can be treated as a special case of graded category membership analysis, which in turn can be treated as a special case of prototype/extension analysis (see Rosch 1973, Rosch et al. 1976, Coleman and Kay 1981). We then will show that there are semantic situations with which the first two kinds of analysis cannot deal, although the third can. Finally, we will sketch the outlines of what a general semantic theory of word meaning based on prototypes and extension will look like. That sketch will include a discussion of kinds of extension.

Limitations of Componential Analysis

In a componential analysis, semantic space, or some particular region of it, is divided by a matrix of attributes or features into a set of clearly defined and sharply demarcated boxes. In such a representation of semantic space each region of meaning is defined by the intersection of relevant features, such that each term or referent under consideration falls into one and only one box of the matrix (see Lounsbury 1969:21).

However, Berlin and Kay have shown that, in the case of color terms, contrasting terms label categories that are not sharply bounded but instead, grade into one another. Similarly, in classroom experiments we have shown that some objects are clearly glasses and others clearly cups, although yet others will be called cups one time and glasses another time, depending on context. Examples such as these involving color terms and drinking containers suggest that the componential view is inadequate in at least one way: the boundaries between boxes cannot be volumeless planes, but must be thick regions that can themselves contain the things (that is, potential referents) that do not unambiguously belong to either of the two boxes they separate.

Limitations of the Category Grading Variant

A semantic space with thick boundaries represents a "category grading" or "fuzzy boundary" model. Since the thickness of the boundaries can vary from one region (or domain) to another, the limiting case is obviously one in which the boundaries are so thin as to become volumeless; thus the componential model can be seen as a special case of the category grading model.

However, there remain some situations with which the category grading model as described is incapable of dealing. First of all, it does not entirely account for the structure that informants produce within the set of clear members of a category (see Lounsbury 1969:22). For instance, in Fanti, father's brother is clearly and unambiguously a member of the kinterm category that may be glossed in English as "father," and belongs to no other kinterm category (see Kronenfeld 1973). However, father's brother is, just as clearly, not as good an exemplar to Fanti speakers of the *father* category as is real father. Father's brother would clearly seem to lie inside the Fanti *father* box (that is, unambiguously inside the father category), and not in the thick border region around that box (where it would be if there were some ambiguity about its membership); yet it clearly has a derivative structured relationship to another, more prototypic exemplar of the *father* category, that is, real father.

A second limitation with category grading becomes apparent when one examines the relationship of verbal categories to their functional bases. The Fanti *uncle* category (see Kronenfeld 1973) includes mother's brother, mother's mother's sister's son, and mother's father's brother's son, among other relatives. Mother's brother is, preeminently, the relative from whom one expects to inherit. But only rarely does any property last long enough (that is, two generations after its original creator) for one to be able to inherit from one's mother's mother's sister's son; and one can never inherit, for example, from another denotatively correct referent, namely, one's mother's father's brother's son, since that relative is not necessarily or normally a member of one's lineage or clan.

The essential functional basis of the uncle-sibling relationship in Fanti—that is, the social fact that occasions the terminological categories—is (potential) inheritance (see Kronenfeld 1973); yet that functional basis is, in the normal course of events, likely to be implemented only with one kintype—the kernel, or the prototype or core—out of the range of kintypes that make up the set of denotatively correct referents for the *uncle* term. That functional basis absolutely cannot occur with at least one other denotatively correct referent.

Any reasonable semantic theory should isolate and specify the focal referents of a term, that is, referents that participate both in the term's essential semantic relations (i.e. functional bases) and in the pragmatic relations that engender the category represented by the term. By any reasonable version of the category grading model, mother's brother, mother's mother's sister's son, and mother's father's brother's son would in Fanti all have to be clearly in the box within semantic space that defines the Fanti *uncle* term. And yet only a single kintype out of that larger set is in fact relevant to the essential semantic relations or functional basis described above. This fact forces one to turn seriously to Lounsbury's assertion (1964a:1088) that even close-to-the-kernel, denotatively correct referents of kinterms are best considered as metaphoric extensions of the kernel referents of such terms. That is, at least, in the domain of kinship, Lounsbury's assertion suggests the need for a different kind of semantic theory—one in which semantic space looks more like a constellation of stars than a matrix of boxes defined by distinctive features. In this space the stars are the small set of things that have their own special labels—that is, the referents to which the essential semantic relations of the relevant terms apply. Things falling elsewhere in the space are called by the label of the star in whose gravitational field they fall—that is, by the label to which they are closest or most similar in some relevant way.

A third kind of problem in the category grading model involves communicative function. In Fanti the contrast between the *father* and *uncle* categories divides the class of nurturant, to-be-respected parental-generation males into those from whom one can inherit (the *uncle* category), and those from who one cannot inherit (the *father* category). The *uncle* category is marked (by one's potential inheritance of one's uncle's property), and contrasts with the unmarked *father* category. Informants told me that one could call one's uncle "father" (as a sign of respect), but not vice versa. The potential inheritance relationship is sharply limited to a particular genealogically defined subclass of kinsmen, while the nurturance and respect relations appropriate to *father* apply to a greater or lesser degree to all appropriately aged men in the community. Thus the *father* term is connotatively extended to nonkinsmen, while the *uncle* term is not. The use of either term implies a relationship of nurturance and respect, but the use of the *uncle* term carries the additional assertion of an inheritance relationship. Calling an uncle by the *father* term, then, by downplaying the inheritance relationship, emphasizes the respect aspect. The relations between items (here, various kintypes) and attitudes (here, respect) that underlie such communicative functions do not in any way derive from or even relate to the full ranges of the terminological categories. Empirically, these essential relations focus on prototypic members of the categories, but do not extend according to category membership in the smoothly diminishing manner a category grading model would imply.

We have laid out this information concerning the causal basis and communicative import of these two Fanti terms in order to examine the denotative semantics of the *uncle* term. More generally, we can see in Fanti kinship clear reasons for analytically separating definitions of prototypic or kernel members from definitions of mechanisms for extension. A single set of verbal labels can be shown to refer to a single set of kernel kintypes, but at the same time to be involved in three alternative patterns (or systems) of extension from the kernels (that is, skewed, unskewed, and courtesy; see Kronenfeld 1973). Only the prototype/extension model of word meaning allows us to describe the separate extension patterns in a way that directly explains the relations among the patterns.

As we have already noted, the kinship version of the prototype/extension theory we have just characterized derives from the work of Lounsbury, who has limited his own work to kinship terminologies. Generalizing from kinship is hard, since the relative product mechanism by which semantic extension takes place in kinship seems (at least insofar as we are aware) to have no obvious parallel in any other domain. However, we do want to assert that a prototype/extension theory, incorporating heterogeneous means of extension, is the correct one on which to base a general theory of referential semantics. Even if the actual mechanisms of extension are different, the semantic considerations (which necessitate the choice of a prototype/extension theory for kinship) apply equally to many other domains (see Lounsbury 1969:21–22).

A General Look at the Prototype/Extension View

In the prototype/extension theory, focal types—the stars in our model of semantic space—are defined in terms of attributes, features, or *Gestalten*. Extension mechanisms may also be defined in terms of features. In the special case in which there is only one pattern of extension, the prototype/extension theory reduces to the category grading theory, and thus any domain that can be covered by the category grading theory can also be covered by the prototype/extension one.

In general, in nonmetaphoric usage, an item that does not have its own label is called by the label to whose focal member it is closest or most similar. In situations of actual use, degree of similarity will not always be absolute, but will be biased or weighted by various kinds of context and by the cultural implications of the use of one label versus another. Many of the stars in our version of semantic space have, as it were, variable gravitational fields. For instance, a cup-like object will have to be much more similar to the focal cup in order to be referred to as "the cup" in a set of cup-like objects than it will in order to be referred to as "the cup" in a set of glass-like objects. A slightly sick American (with a single given set of symptoms) is likely to say "It's a cold" when he wants to go to a ball game and "It's the flu" when he wants not to go to work—even though "cold" and "flu" seem pretty clearly to be contrasting categories.

In our stellar model of semantic space, marking relations will give us something like subsidiary bodies, that is, planets. For example, *mug* is a category (as opposed to the *cup* category) that has its own focal type and its own force field; at the same time, the entire *mug* category, including the focal type, lies within the *cup* force field—that is, almost any mug[1] is a kind of cup (when *cup* is opposed to *glass*).

As we shall see for the domains of Fanti kinship and English, Japanese, and Hebrew drinking vessels, the relationship among denotative definitions, functional relations, and derivational history is only clear and only explicable in connection with core referents of terms (as opposed to the full, extended sets of referents). This special significance of core referents gives them a crucially different role in a prototype/extension theory than they have in a category grading (or fuzzy boundary) theory. The kind of imputation of primary semantic processes to the full extended range of term referents implied by the category grading view underlies both the "language-determines-thought" and the "language-simply-maps-thought" versions of theories about language/thought isomorphisms.[2] The problems we find with category grading show why such isomorphism theories have never seemed satisfactory.

The prototype/extension view allows us to see how language can be the flexible tool it in fact appears to be. It allows us to see how language can be used to talk about things (as filtered and shaped by cognitive structures) in a reasonably precise way, even in the absence of any simple language/thought isomorphism. Language has enough referential connections to enable users to know what they are talking about, but it is also free enough from any referential lock to enable them constantly to use existing language categories to talk about novel entities, or to focus on novel features of existing entities.

Semantic Extension: Basics

In his Crow and Omaha article (1964b) Lounsbury opened up a radically new approach to anthropological semantics. Instead of looking for a distinctive feature definition that applied uniformly to the full range of referents of a term, he split the defining process into two stages. He restricted his distinctive feature definition to a small set of focal referents for each term (in a contrast set), and then used another set of operations (rewrite rules, in the case of his kinship example) to connect other potential referents to the focal referents of the categories. These extended referents fell into the terminological category of the focal member to which they were connected.

In using multiple definitions to delineate the denotata of any single term Lounsbury was opting for disjunctive definitions of these extended categories. We want to consider what reasons justified paying this price (in the view of this scholar's adamance concerning the importance of conjunctivity), and what other considerations mitigated or eased the pain of this price. When we have satisfied ourselves about the better fit of this new approach to native speaker behavior, to the understandings implicit in that behavior, and to the terminological products of that behavior, we want to go on to ask what it is about natural language communication that leads natives (including us) to opt for such an approach versus the supposedly simpler, one-step distinctive feature one. After we have fully explored this new approach in its specific kinship and color applications, we will then want to consider whether it applies generally to all words in all domains, or only more narrowly to domains such as kinship or color with certain particular characteristics.

In this chapter we will examine two early cases of semantic extension in detail. Because the material is simpler and more readily accessible to readers lacking specific technical expertise, and because its mechanisms are more generally relevant, I will first consider Berlin and Kay's *Basic Color Terms* (1969). With that example fresh in the reader's mind I will then turn to Lounsbury's original kinship terminology example.

Berlin and Kay: Basic Color Terms

Structural linguistics texts (see, for example, Gleason 1961:4) classically used color terms as the prime example of how languages varied absolutely from one another in how they carved up the world, and thus of the impossibility of an easy translation from one language into another. Many anthropologists and linguists had initially interpreted the Whorfian Hypothesis as asserting that perception and thought were structured by language, and thus that people speaking languages that coded the color universe differently perceived colors differently. Lenneberg, in two coauthored articles (Brown and Lenneberg 1954, Lenneberg and Roberts 1956) disposed of the perceptual issue by showing that perception of color differences was much more fine-grained than any language's coding, and that such perceptions were uniform across cultural and linguistic lines. Lenneberg's work, however, still left open a cognitive version of that Whorfian interpretation, by which the way people conceptualized their colors (that is, categorized them nonverbally or thought about them) derived from their linguistic codings.

Conklin, in his article on Hanunóo color terms, carried the position that language represented thought and that speakers of each language concepualized the color domain differently a step further when he showed that in Hanunóo (a northern Philippine language) the same "color" (by our color systems) would take one of two alternative labels or terms, depending on whether the object possessing the color was fresh and succulent or dry and dessicated; that is, he asserted that dryness/dessication was a component of their color domain. That meant that even our higher level analytic categories ("domains" denoted by words like "color" or "kinsman") were not absolute, but varied from culture to culture.

In a graduate seminar at the University of California at Berkeley in the mid-1960s, Berlin and Kay decided to explore those color differences among languages more systematically, and somewhat differently, than had previous researchers on color terminologies. They had members of the seminar go out and collect color terms and their referents from speakers of a variety of different languages in the Berkeley area. They and others have since validated (and extended and fine-tuned) their findings with monolingual speakers of several of these (and other) languages in field situations.

To keep the task easy, and to guarantee that they were dealing with concepts widely shared within a language community, they limited themselves to "basic" color terms, that is, to color terms elicited from their native speaking informants that were not considered by these native speakers to be a "kind of" some other color. In general, though not exclusively, these were the words that the language had evolved for talking about color per se directly (such as, for example, "blue," in English), as opposed to by means of reference to the color of something else (such as, again, in an English example, "robin's egg blue"). They kept the eliciting task simple by using as a stimulus a two-dimensional sheet (that is, a cylinder laid flat) of color chips drawn from the three-dimensional perceptual color solid (as represented in the Munsell color system), on which hue and brightness varied while saturation was held constant. They covered the sheet with clear plastic, and asked informants to draw (with a grease pen) a circle around all the chips to which the color term in question applied (in our English example, for instance, around all the "blue" chips).

They added one novel task to the preceding fairly routine one. They also asked informants to draw a second circle around the chips that were the very best examples of, for instance, "blue." This new task represents a behavioral analog in the domain of color for the analytic distinction that Lounsbury (1964b) had made in kinship between "kernel" or "core" referents of terms and "extended" members.

They found that the circles around full ranges (that is, around "all the blue chips") were as variable from language to language as the literature had led them to expect. In addition they found that these circles varied just as much from one speaker of English (or of any other language) to another as they did from language to language. This finding, in isolation, might make it very hard to understand how we communicate at all. But they also found extremely tight agreement among speakers of English concerning the best, or what we will now call "core," examples of each color. This agreement extended as well to speakers of all the other languages. That is, any language that had a core in the area of English "red" had as that core precisely the chips that English speakers identified as core "red"; and the same held for every other color. Some languages lacked color categories that other languages had, but any languages that had any given color category had, as core referents for that category, the same chips as had any other language that had those categories. The semantics of color term reference were universal; the number of color terms varied from language to language but their definitions did not.[3]

Berlin and Kay found, additionally, that they could predict which colors any given language had basic terms for from the total number of basic color terms the language had; that is, the terms appeared in a specific order. Any language which had red necessarily also had black and white; any language which had blue/green necessarily also had red; and so forth. This regularity amounted to a chain of "implicational universals" of the sort explored by Greenberg; mathematically, it is referred to as a "partial ordering" ("partial" because is is possible for some items to be tied, or to share the same rank). Such a partial ordering, as Greenberg has noted also in connection with other sets of terms, has diachronic implications: it means that languages can only add (and lose) color terms in a specific order. Thus, Berlin and Kay chose to speak of the "evolution" of color terminologies.

Berlin and Kay next noticed that the order of languages they had found on the basis of number of basic color terms possessed represented at the same time an ordering of the cultures or societies in which those languages were spoken on the basis of degree of technological development. This equivalence explains Berlin's tendency in several places to adopt phrasings that echo the evolutionary phrasings of Lewis Henry Morgan.

Reaching such conclusions required comparability of not only the stimulus objects (the color chips) but also of the color terms. In other words, how could one be sure that *azul* in Spanish was indeed the *same* "color" as *blue* in English? The way that appeared reasonable[4] to Berlin and Kay was to match the referents of the words. But a comparison of the full ranges of color terms did not provide terribly secure matches. To some degree, languages with fewer terms broadened the reference of those terms to cover pretty much the same range of chips that another language used more terms to cover. A language from New Guinea might use one term to cover the ranges of *black, blue, purple*, and part of *green* in English; with which English term was the New Guinea language's term to be linked, and on what basis? Even among languages with approximately the same number of terms there was considerable variation from one language to the next in the full range of chips covered by the various color terms.

Order and comparability were found, however, when one considered the data on "best examples." The color from the New Guinea language, above, clearly matched English *black*, and not the other English colors, when one compared its best example chips with the best example chips of English's *black*. The best example of *azul* matched very closely the best example of *blue*. The Berlin and Kay findings, then, depended not only on their use of a standard color stimulus set but also on their distinguishing best examples from full ranges of referents for these colors. These best examples are what we speak of as "focal" referents.

My acceptance of the semantic implications entailed by the word "focal," and the crucial definitional importance that is implied for focal referents in the above discussion, comes in part from the pattern of results described above. But it also comes in response to another finding of Berlin and Kay's: the variation among speakers of a single language (say, English) was as great for the full ranges of referents of color terms as was the variation among languages for those full ranges; it was only on best examples that speakers of a single language agreed among themselves. This last meant that the use of a basic color term in conversations between speakers of a single given language (in the absence of contextual information) only reliably communicated information about the focal referents of the term. In a rough way, we might say that only focal referents were directly tied to the terms (or signs); other referents were linked to the terms only more loosely through their relationship to the focal referents. The key referential relations of language, at least in the domain of color terms, clearly could be seen to pertain specifically to core referents rather than to the full extended ranges; this finding constituted a major advance in study of the semantics of word reference.

My own view of the process by which nonfocal colors are labeled is, roughly, that they are labeled by whatever color term best combines being closest to them with distinguishing them from the other colors with which they are being contrasted in the given situation of use. My sense is that the inter-speaker variation that Berlin and Kay found was, in part at least, the result of different speakers' confronting the stimulus chips with differing implicit contexts in mind. However, the Berlin and Kay data lack the contextual information required for confirmation of my suppositions. I have myself conducted some very informal experiments in classes in which I could get students reliably to pick out a given shirt (of, say, a sort of red-orange color) by either referring to it as the "red" one or the "orange" one, depending on whether the other shirts in the group from which it was being picked were oranger or redder than it was. We will return to situations like this when we get to my general semantic theory.

Berlin and Kay's work has attracted attention primarily because of the universal partial order among color terms that they found, because of the grounding of the order of appearance of color terms in the physiology of the eye (particularly, the nature and frequency of different kinds of color receptors) that they suggested and which Kay subsequently has tightly demonstrated in work with other researchers (see, for example, Kay and McDaniel 1978), and because of the correlation they found between the number of basic color terms a language had and the level of technological development shown by the culture to which speakers of the language belonged.[5]

For our present purposes, though, what is important is the need Berlin and Kay found to find, define, and separate out focal referents from the full range of referents (or denotata) of a set of terms. An important set of empirical findings about a set of terms could only be made with focal referents and could not be seen or demonstrated in full (or extended) ranges. Thus, they provide important evidence for the usefulness of the distinction between focal and extended referents and for the utility of considering focal referents as the more basic and extended referents as only secondarily pertaining to the terms in question.

Lounsbury: Crow and Omaha

Lounsbury, after his early work on componential analysis of (Iroquois-type) kinship terminologies, turned his attention to Crow- and Omaha-type terminologies (1964b, 1965). These are terminologies which, inter alia, contain terminological categories that cut across generations, such as, for example, Fanti, in which one's father, father's brother, father's sister's son, father's sister's daughter's son, father's mother's sister's son, father's father's brother's son, and father's father's brother's daughter's son, among others, are all included in one's "father" category. It is difficult (though not impossible, as Atkins 1974 has shown) to construct conjunctive definitions for the full ranges of such categories, and the conjunctive definitions that anthropologists have managed to come up with for such categories seem very cognitively complex (and thus tend to cancel the cognitive advantage to native users conferred by conjunctivity).

Lounsbury's novel solution to the problem posed by such systems was to give up on the idea of a single (conjunctive) definition of the full range of denotata (referents) of each kinterm, and instead to offer simple, conjunctive definitions of core or "kernel" denotata (referents) for each term plus a simple set of equivalence rules for each system that would allow other kintypes to be set as equal (terminologically) to kernel kintypes of kinterms and thus to be identified as denotata of those kinterms. He initially instantiated his equivalence rules as reduction rules,[6] in which an expression to the left of a left-to-right arrow could be rewritten as (reduced to) the shorter expression to the right of the arrow. The rules applied to genealogical strings, and applied to any string in which the expression on the left side of the rule could be found; contextual constraints as well as genealogical nodes were included in the left- and right-side expressions. The rules were repeatedly applied, as long as the left-side expression of any rule could be found in the string being reduced; when they could no longer be applied one was left with kernel strings. Figure 9-1 includes an example of a set of such rules and their application to a number of kintype expressions; the example is of a Crow-type system and is taken from Fanti data of mine.

In figure 9-1 I have stated the left- and right-side expressions of the rules in three different forms: as diagrammed genealogical strings, as representations of the strings in the Romney notational scheme used elsewhere in this volume, and as the kind of relative product strings of primary terms (the way in which Lounsbury stated them). Relative products are algebraic products defined such that the order of the items matters (that is, where x·y does not equal y·x)—as, for example, in kinship strings in which "father's brother" is not the same relative as "brother's father." Because of Lounsbury's use of relative products, and because his relative products (though not the equations he builds from them) are very similar to our ordinary language definitions of kinterms, his rule system is often spoken of as a relative product calculus. We do want to note that, while the rules do not require relative products per se for their operations, they do require literal representations (of some sort) of the relevant genealogical strings, and that as such they operate on entities of a very different sort than the features that are involved in a componential definition.

Lounsbury's kinship analysis, like Berlin and Kay's color one, has attracted anthropological attention primarily because of certain cross-cultural substantive regularities that it showed or depended on logically for its success. Such regularities for kinship included the basing of kinterm calculations on genealogical strings which were in turn modeled on a biologically based model of reproduction and family makeup; the utilization by all genealogically skewed systems of only a few variant forms of the same few rules; a Greenbergian implicational universal (see Greenberg 1966) relating the Lounsburian skewing operation to the merging one; and a focus of kinterm categories on nuclear family and other genealogically very close relatives.[7] As

FIG. 9-1 Lounsbury's Reduction Rules for Crow-type Kinship Terminologies

Merging Rule

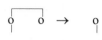

Somebody's mother's sister is equivalent
    to that somebody's mother, and reciprocally,
some woman's sister's descendant is equivalent
    to that woman's own decendant
i.e., ...MoSi → ...Mo
and   ♀ Si... →   ♀ ...

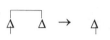

Somebody's father's brother is equivalent
    to that somebody's father, and reciprocally
some man's brother's descendent is equivalent
    to that man's own decendent
i.e., ...FaBr → ...Fa
and   ♂ Br... →   ♂ ...

/+fof/ → /+f/
/+mom/ → /+m/

Skewing Rule (Crow-type, Type I):

Somebody's mother's brother's child is equivalent
    to that somebody's own brother's child,
        and, reciprocally,
somebody's father's sister's child is equivalent
    to that somebody's father's sibling
i.e., ...MoBr... → ...Br...
and ...FaSi... → ...FaBr... or ...FaSi...

/+fom–/ → /om–/

---

previously, for color, I want to endorse the importance of these domain-specific findings—here, for kinship studies—but focus our present attention on the semantic mechanisms that were required for the findings to emerge.

Lounsbury's newer procedure for analyzing kinship terminological systems seems to have provided the model for Berlin and Kay's distinction between core and extended referents of a term. Like Berlin and Kay's color term analysis, Lounsbury's analysis involved a direct definition of the paradigmatic or oppositional relations among terminological categories and of the referential meaning of the terminological categories in terms of core referents, and a secondary assignment of other (potential) referents to terminological categories (as extended referents of those terminological categories) on the basis of their relations to the core referents. The relationship between an extended referent and the core referent to which it related was calculated in different ways for each of the two domains (kinterms and color terms), and each form of calculation seemed, in part at least, to depend on specific, substantive properties of

Half-sibling Rule:

Somebody's mother's child is equivalent
to that somebody's full sibling
i.e., ...MoSo... → ...Br...
and ...MoDa... → ...Si...

Somebody's father's child is equivalent
to that somebody's full sibling
i.e., ...FaSo... → ...Br...
and ...FaDa... → ...Si...

+f– → o
+m– → o

Notes

1. In Romney's notation system "m" represents a male person; "f" represents a female person; "a" represents a person of either sex; "b" . . . "b" represents a pair of persons of either sex, but where both are the same sex; "b" . . . "b̄" represents a pair of persons of either sex, but where the two are of opposite sexes. "+" indicates a child-to-parent link; "–" indicates a parent to child link; "o" indicates a sibling-to-sibling link. An expression enclosed in slashes refers both to the indicated expression and to its reciprocal. A "." following a person symbol indicates that the symbol must be a terminal one; if a person symbol in a rule is not followed by a link or a "." it means that the rule applies to any expression in which the indicated expression is embedded; a " . . . " following a person symbol means that some link must be there; i.e., that the person symbol cannot be the terminal symbol in the kintype. These last conventions are taken from Lounsbury 1964b.

2. In the traditional notation system: "Fa" represents a father; "Mo" represents a mother; "Si" represents a sister; "Br" represents a brother; "So" represents a son; and "Da" represents a daughter. A "." following a person symbol indicates that the symbol must be a terminal one; if a person symbol in a rule is not followed by a link or a "." it means that the rule applies to any expression in which the indicated expression is embedded; a " . . . " following a person symbol means that some link must be there; i.e., that the person symbol cannot be the terminal symbol in the kintype. These last conventions are taken from Lounsbury 1964b.

---

the phenomena being categorized. The color similarities are based on the distance of the extended referent from alternative cores as calculated mathematically in the three-dimensional space defined by the three continuous variables that define color hues (but where these values may be weighted or biased or skewed by context). The kintype similarities are based on the equivalences implied by the rewrite rules that we have just described, whereas the equivalence rules are dependent on specific logical properties of genealogical space.

Whither Conjunctivity?

The Berlin and Kay definitions of focal (or core) ranges can be stated conjunctively, as can, if only approximately, Berlin and Kay's definitions of any given single informant's extended or full range. Since Berlin and Kay's average or mean extended ranges for each of their languages are based on the overlap of individual ranges, these can be characterized more or less conjunctively. But the variability of extended ranges makes it impossible (for Berlin and Kay or for anyone opposed to their position) to characterize all that variation in the application of any single color term with a single conjunctive definition based on values of the dimensions of the color solid—the characterization that can be made for focal ranges. In the Berlin and Kay analysis, some disjunctivity necessarily comes from breaking the definition of the range of referents for a color term into two stages: first, the definition of core values in terms of defining features, and, second, the definition of extensions from those cores in terms of similarity calculated on the three continuous feature dimensions in terms of which the core referents are defined, but where the resulting values may then be weighted or biased by other contextual information.

The Lounsbury kinterm data does not show the individual variability shown by the Berlin and Kay data. In part this lack of individual variability comes from Lounsbury's use of published data for kinterm systems; that is, data that had already been cleansed of individual variation. However, my own field experience among the Fanti, in which I did find some significant variation in definition (of extended ranges, though not of cores) and considerable variation in usage (see Kronenfeld 1973 and 1980a), suggests that, even given the variation I found, the genealogically structured nature of kinship categories and calculations leaves considerably less room for individual variation than does the spatial nature of the color domain. Instead of any free-ranging individual variability in extended category ranges, I found for my Fanti kinterm case three alternative patterns of extension (used by everybody) that were all based on the same common set of core (or kernel) referents of the common set of categories, and which were related to one another by differences in the amount of information that went into calculations of similarity. This is another instance, along with the means of calculating similarity, of the domain-specific nature of various semantic findings.

Like our Berlin and Kay example, our Lounsbury example does involve conjunc-tively defined cores and simple bases for extension out from those cores. While the Lounsburian equivalence rules themselves may be conjunctively defined (depending on whose version one takes and on how one considers definitions; see Kronenfeld 1980a:601–602) the iterated application of them is not. One is tempted to claim that the beautiful simplicity of the rules and their uncomplicated applicability—at any time, of any rule that fits—makes up in cognitive ease for the cognitive cost of the disjunctivity. I am not sure how analytically to treat this trade-off between the cognitively easy disjunctivity of Lounsbury's rewrite analysis and the harder con-junctivity involved in a componential approach to skewed terminological systems. My uncertainty comes in part because the native speaker operations (for calculating kinterm assignments of relatives) that Lounsbury's rules represent have in actual practice a very different form from that of those rules; in native speaker operations I have studied, relative products are used to map relations *among* terminological categories instead of within categories (as they are used in Lounsbury's rules), and native speaker operations I have studied do not normally involve the same kind of iterated or repeated operations as do Lounsbury's rules. See Kronenfeld (1980b) for a formal description of this native system of kinterm calculation, a discussion of its relationship to Lounsburian analysis, and a discussion of some of the issues concerning conjunctivity it raises.

We have earlier shown that people find conjunctively defined conceptual categories much easier to form and maintain than disjunctively defined ones. Now we are trying to discover, by means of the Berlin and Kay color study and Lounsbury's work on Crow- and Omaha-type kinship terminologies, what the units of word meaning are to which these considerations apply. In other words, we are trying to see which kinds of word meaning units are learned as (basic) concepts and which are calculated from these in what manner (through conjunctively defined rules, it is hoped). We are exploring the theory that it is only core or focal referents that are necessarily conjunctive, and that there are relatively simple ways (simple in terms of our wider notion of cognitive ease, which extends beyond conjunctivity alone) of relating other potential referents to these cores. Part of the evidence for this view is the difficulty we found, for both color terms and kinterms, in coming up with conjunctive definitions of the extended ranges (especially taking account of the variability shown by extended ranges).

MORE RECENT SEMANTIC EXTENSION

In this section we will briefly examine some further examples of semantic extension, published after the work of Lounsbury and of Berlin and Kay, that contribute to the background of the semantic theory being presented in this volume. We will examine the mechanisms involved in each of these examples, the ways in which the terms and the mechanisms of extension function in communication, and the substantive conditions that shape each. The examples will be Kronenfeld's work on skewed kinship terminological systems, Basso's discussion of the Western Apache use of their horse partinomy for pickup trucks, and Kempton's work on Mexican ollas.

Kronenfeld: Fanti Kinship

In a series of articles (1973, 1975, 1980a, 1980b, and 1991) I have described and analyzed the kinship terminological system of the Fanti. The Fanti are a cultural group on the coast of Ghana in West Africa who speak the Fanti dialect of the Akan language (the language, also, of the Ashanti and other related groups in Ghana and the Ivory Coast). The Fanti are matrilineal, with exogamous corporate lineages that "own" and control the inheritance of property use rights, organize funerals, and are linked to an Akan-wide system of putatively related clans.

Fanti kinship terminology consists of the terms shown with rough English glosses in table 9-1. The paradigm of kernel or core referents (or denotata) of each term are shown with the distinctive features (or significata) by which they contrast with one another. There are three alternative patterns of extension by which these categories are extended from their core referents out to other referents. These three patterns are related to one another as a kind of marking hierarchy in which the extensional basis of the relatively unmarked pattern is used in conjunction with some additional information in the relatively marked pattern.

TABLE 9-1. Fanti Kernal Consanguineal Kintypes, with Glosses,
by Distinctive Features (from Kronenfeld 1973:1579)

	Nuclear Family	Both	Lineage
For Female Ego			
G^{+2}		nana grandrelative /a+a+a/	
G^{+1}	egya "father" a+m	na "mother" a+f	wofa maternal "uncle" (i.e. mother's brother) a+fom
G^{0}		nua "sibling" aoa	
G^{-1}		ba "child" a−a	
G^{-2}		nana grandrelative /a+a+a/	
For Male Ego			
G^{+2}		nana grandrelative /a+a+a/	
G^{+1}	egya "father" a+m	na "mother" a+f	wofa maternal "uncle" (i.e., mother's brother) a + fom
G^{0}	nua "sibling" aoa	akyɛrɛba male's "sister" mof	
G^{-1}	ba "child" a−a		awofasi matrilineal "nibling" (i.e., male's sister's child) mof−a
G^{-2}		nana grandrelative /a+a+a/	

Key: See table 8-2, note 3 for the notational scheme for kintypes.

Kernel kintypes are the focal or primary kinsmen in the different terminological classes. The set of consanguineal kernel kintypes consists of one kinterm for each generation of the nuclear family, and a separate kinterm for the nearest matrilineage member of that generation if that kinsman is not in the nuclear family. Sex of alter is not a distinctive feature except where the nuclear family member of one sex in a generation is in the lineage while the one of the other sex is not; in this case the kernel kintypes are distinguished independently for each sex. For example, in G^{+1}, "mother" is in the lineage, but "father" is not, so there is a term for "maternal uncle" who is in the lineage, but there is no corresponding female "aunt" term. In G^{0}, siblings are in the lineage, and so there is only a sibling term in this generation. In G^{-1}, a female ego's children are in the lineage, so she needs only a "child" term; a male ego's children are not in the lineage, and so he has both the "child" term and a "maternal nibling" term for his sister's children who are in the lineage. Because she is his link to his "niblings," a man also has a special optional term for his sister which is particularly apropos when speaking of her children. Finally the parents of G^{+1} kernel relatives and the children of G^{1-} ones are all grouped together in a "grandrelative" term. These consanguineal kernels are presented according to their distinctive features in Table [9-1]. Non-consanguineal kernels are not discussed here, but can be shown to be generated in the same manner as the lineage ones are here ([see Kronenfeld 1980a]). Kronenfeld 1973:1578

The most unmarked (and most commonly used in ordinary conversation) pattern of extension, which (for convenience) I call the "courtesy" pattern, extends the kinterms in a somewhat metaphoric manner,[8] to people on the basis of relative age (in particular, the direction of the difference and the approximate amount of difference) and gender, without any genealogical information. Since the side of the family information by which lineage-based terminological categories are distinguished from nuclear family–based categories in genealogical reckoning has no meaning without a genealogy, the lineage-based terms are not extended in this courtesy pattern. The lack of genealogical specification means that this extension pattern is not restricted to actual kin but is based on a loose and general extension of nuclear family roles to the wider community.

The next, "unskewed" pattern is distinguished from the courtesy pattern by the addition of the information entailed in genealogical specifications. This genealogical information restricts the pattern to actual kin, enables the use of side-of-the-family information to distinguish lineage-based terms from nuclear family–based ones, and enables generation to be distinguished from relative age. Extension in this unskewed pattern is, in effect, along the components of generation, relative age, gender, and side of the family that are implicit in the paradigm of kernels. This pattern represents genealogical extension on the basis of the general parenting roles of the nuclear family; the genealogical constraint means that distinctions involving side of the family and gender on the basis of lineage membership in the paradigm of kernels are preserved in this pattern of extension, even though lineage relations are not an issue here. The precise pattern of extension is defined by the set of Lounsburian equivalence rules presented in table 9-2. The unskewed Fanti pattern represents a Hawaiian-type (or generational) terminology with certain Dravidian-type–like modifications.

The most marked pattern (and the least commonly used) is the skewed one. It is distinguished from the unskewed pattern by the addition of a Crow-type skewing rule to the set of extension rules, giving us the skewed set shown in table 9-2. The skewing rule represents the addition of an equation informants self-consciously held, and which they added to the generational base of the unskewed pattern; they explained this equation by saying that the "nibling" (that is, sister's son) will inherit from the "uncle" (mother's brother). The skewing rule depends on the lineage categories that are distinguished from nuclear family categories in the paradigm of kernels. The skewed Fanti pattern represents a Type 1 Crow-type terminological system.

The key points of the Fanti example for our semantic theory—at the level of Saussure's langue—are the use of a common set of kernels (focal referents) for a variety of alternative extension patterns, the use of a variety of alternative patterns of

TABLE 9-2.   Reduction Rules for Fanti Consanguineal Kintypes
(from Kronenfeld 1973:1589)

1. Check to see if expression is a kernel kintype.
2. Skewing Rule
    $/+mof-/ \rightarrow /+m+f-/$
3. Merging Rule
    $/+bob/ \rightarrow /+b/$
4. Half-sibling Rule
    $+a- \rightarrow o$
5. Cross/Parallel Neutralization Rule
    $/+bo\overline{b}/ \rightarrow /+\overline{b}/$
6. Generations Extension Rule
    $/+a1+a2+a3/ \rightarrow /+a1+a2/$

Notes

1. The rules are an ordered set that accounts for both the skewed and unskewed extension patterns. For the unskewed pattern, rule 2, the skewing rule, is not used. The operative rules are applied to any kintype expression in the order they are listed; the first rule that applies is the one used. After a rule has been applied to an expression, then one starts again at the top of the list of rules. The process is finished when no reduction rule is applicable—that is, when one has reduced the given expression to a kernel expression.

2. The same rules can be used for expansions, with the following understandings: (a) Reverse the direction of the arrows. (b) No expression may be expanded into the kernel expression of another kinterm; this is the expansion equivalent of rule 1. (c) No expansion other than that of rule 6 can apply to /+a+/. (d) If rule 2, the skewing rule, is being used, then rule 5 cannot be applied to /+a–/.

3. Romney's notation system has been used. An "m" represents a male person; "f" represents a female person; "a" represents a person of either sex; "b" . . . "b" represents a pair of persons of either sex, but where both are of the same sex; "b" . . . "b" represents a pair of persons of either sex, but where the two are of opposite sexes. "+" indicates a child-to-parent link; "–" indicates a parent-to-child link; "o" indicates a sibling-to-sibling link. An expression enclosed in slashes refers both to the indicated expression and to its reciprocal. A "." following a person symbol indicates that the symbol must be a terminal one; if a person symbol in a rule is not followed by a link or a "." it means that the rule applies to any expression in which the indicated expression is embedded; a " . . . " following a person symbol means that some link must be there—i.e., that the person symbol cannot be the terminal symbol in the kintype. These last conventions are taken from Lounsbury 1964b.

extension, and the inclusion in the single kernel set of all the kinds of information that will be needed for any of the extension patterns (or, conversely, the limitation of all expansion patterns to reliance on information that is in the one kernel paradigm).

This example allows us to reconcile the old Kroeber (1909) versus Rivers and Radcliffe-Brown (see esp. 1940, 1941) debate about whether kinterms are to be seen primarily as linguistic entities or as indicators of social roles. On the linguistic side, we see that these terms *do* function (are used) as words in conversation, and we see that their extended ranges do not correlate with social categories, nor, as shown in Kronenfeld 1975, do they correlate with the behavioral patterns speakers feel pertain to the social roles in question. But, on the social side, we also see that key social roles in nuclear family and lineage have played a basic structuring role in the paradigmatic distinctions among kernel kintypes and that they loom important in the form of the extension rules.[9]

In terms of usage and communication—Saussure's parole—we note that the use of particular patterns of extension is not limited to the social contexts that occasion them, but rather that every pattern is available at all times (though with different probabilities of being used in different social contexts). Terms are selected for use in conversation from the full range made available by the kernel definitions and by the alternative semantic rules for extension according to what they communicate (including connotations and overtones, implicit intentions, and the like) in the given context. Within a given conversation, different speakers may use terms from different extension patterns—that is, may use terms nonreciprocally—even if the one person's usage becomes part of the context for the other person's choice of term.

Thus the terminology with its variant forms as a part of langue provides sets of regularities, that is, patterns, which speakers are free to use as suits their purposes. This point was brought home to me when I observed a pair of Fanti cross-cousins nonreciprocally addressing each other—as "father" in one direction, and as "brother" in the other (see Kronenfeld 1969:104–107). I knew from other interviews with them that both men knew (and stated) that the "correct" reciprocal of "father" was "child" and of "brother" was "brother"; thus the usage I observed did not result from any lack of awareness of the pattern or from any resistance to it. Further investigation revealed that since they were close kin they felt they had to use kinterms in genealogically correct forms, instead of the nongenealogical mode of the courtesy pattern; such genealogically correct usage also emphasized the genealogical link, which, I gather, they wanted to do. At the same time, since they liked and respected each other, each man was anxious to show the other as much respect as he could—and so each man, in addressing the other, picked the highest status term out of the set available to him for that genealogical position. Thus, one man picked "father" (from the skewed extension pattern) over "brother" (from the unskewed pattern), while the other man picked "brother" (from the unskewed pattern) over "son" (from the skewed pattern). Their goal in this conversation was not to be correct, but to communicate their messages as effectively as possible with the resources that their language afforded them.

The courtesy pattern extends the kinterms connotatively (and mildly metaphorically) to other relatives and townspeople on the basis of the patterning of the behaviors and behavioral relations connoted by the terms. Since these behaviors are, in general, patterned by contrasts of gender and relative age (here subsuming generation), this pattern of extension amounts to extension of the terms to nonnuclear family members (and, especially, to nonkin) on the basis of age differences and gender.

Kronenfeld: Kinship Comparison

The Fanti data showed fixed and constant focal (or kernel) kintypes joined to alternative patterns of extension in which the kinterm categories defined by those kernels were variably extended to other kintypes. The Fanti case raises the possibility that such a pattern might hold cross-culturally for kinship terminological systems in general—that the kernel referents of kinterm categories, as defined in Lounsbury's extension work, are definitionally primary and relatively fixed (temporally or across subcultural variation), while nonkernel referents are defined only secondarily and derivatively in relation to the kernel ones, and show more variability (among alternative patterns) in their assignment to kinterm categories. I want to offer some comparative evidence in support of this supposition.

When one examines data on kin terminologies for a large number of related languages and cultures—as is assembled, for example, in Morgan's data on the Dakota Indian groups (within his Ganowanian "family" [1871: Table—Appendix to Part II, pp. 281–382])—the following facts emerge. Since the languages are closely related in terms of their diachronic linguistic family tree, it is not surprising that they use similar, that is, cognate, signifiers. But the relationship that signifiers have to signifieds within signs, as well as the linked sound/meaning criteria that historical linguists use for recognizing cognates, should mean that the signifieds for these various signifiers also match. Yet, if we use the full (that is, extended) range of referents (denotata) of these terms to infer their signifieds (related to their significata) we find a very bad match, since the languages show very different patterns of extension. Some of the languages have patrilineally skewed Omaha-type terminologies; some have matrilineally skewed Crow-type terminologies; and some have unskewed Iroquois-type terminologies.[10] Indeed, the actual Omaha Indians and Crow Indians, for whom the two opposed types of skewing are named, are closely related members of a Dakota subgroup that also includes the Yankton and Oglalla Dakota (Sioux) Indians, who have unskewed terminologies. However, contrary to the picture we get for extended ranges, when we limit our comparison to kernel or focal kintype referents we find an extremely good match across the whole Dakota group. The componential paradigms of these kernels match similarly well.

Since the languages involved are fairly closely related, we know that they have each relatively recently developed out of a single, common ancestral language. The period of time involved has not been sufficient for the terminological labels (signifiers) or the focal referents (pointed to by the signifieds linked to each of these signifiers) to drift very far apart. But that same period of time has been quite adequate for great changes to occur in the extended ranges and thus in the extension operations (or rules) that produce these ranges (that is, extend them from the kernels). Thus we have diachronically based comparative data that supports the same contrast between relatively fixed, constant focal referents and more variable extended ranges that we found synchronically within the single Fanti system.[11]

The above comparison is completed by the inclusion of the Fanti skewed pattern. The languages, that is, the Fanti versus the Dakota, are unrelated (at least in any traceable way) and have very different signifiers, differently defined focal referents,[12] and very different kernel paradigms. The Fanti extension rules, on the other hand, are very similar to those of the Crow Indians, and accordingly different from those of the Omaha or the Yankton or Oglalla Dakota.[13]

The independence of kinterm extension patterns from kernel paradigms is further illustrated by a computer program I wrote in 1965–66, which produced Lounsburian-type rewrite rule analyses of kinship terminologies (Kronenfeld 1976). The program, where appropriate, reduced the full range of a given kintype to (or sometimes almost[14] to) a single kernel kintype, and listed the rules it used to effect the reductions. To test the accuracy of its rule determinations it used the rules it had identified to reexpand from the kernel(s) to the full range. The program operated successfully without any information about the componential features that defined the term in question or about the other terms with which it contrasted. The independence of the extension pattern from any reliance on immediately contrasting terms is possibly peculiar to kinship, because of the unique relative product mechanism by which the similarity of potentially extended kintypes to kernels is assessed (without any attention to contrasting terms) for genealogically traced kin. However, the potentiality for calculating extension by means of mechanisms, features, or devices that are independent from the features by which focal referents are distinguished from one another (and, thus, on which the terminological categories contrast with one another) does appear to apply more generally to domains other than kinship terminologies.

Basso: Apache Pickup Partinomy

Basso (1967) offers a particularly nice illustration of the flexibility of semantic extension, and of the referential power we gain through this flexibility. Basso shows how the Western Apache dealt with the problem of how to refer to the parts of a novel cultural artifact, the pickup truck. They could have created a new vocabulary, as we sometimes do, with the aid of Latin or Greek roots, for new domains in English (for example, see terms such as "television" and "pneumatic"); or they could have developed paraphrastic descriptive vocabulary into a new set of linguistic signs, as we have for "computers" (from the term for "something that computes") and "calculators" (from "something that calculates") in English; or they could have borrowed the vocabulary along with the artifact, as we borrowed our English roulette-wheel vocabulary from French. Instead, though, they used the set of terms they already had for the parts of an old 'artifact', the horse,[15] to the new pickup (Basso 1967:473). They took what would initially have been a metaphoric extension (within parole) and seem rapidly to have automatized it, or made it part of the linguistic code (langue).

What is interesting here, for our present purposes, is that we have no trouble understanding their references—at least, of course, once the horse terms are translated into English. The connection between the Apache word for "hoof" and the concept of a truck *tire* is, in and of itself, a good example of Saussure's arbitrary relationship between signifier and signified. However, the Apache word for "hoof" is already conventionally related to their concept of a horse's hoof, and so they (or we, with our English versions) can use the *hoof-tire* conceptual connection in their (our) effort to decode the pickup part reference for "hoof." But that connection, too, by itself seems fairly arbitrary; the objects look different, are made of different material, work differently, and so forth. It is only when we factor in the context provided by the other, contrasting terms in the set, and understand that "parts of a horse" terms are being applied to a pickup truck, that the connection becomes more obvious. We are talking about "hooves" versus "eyes" or "backs" or "mouths" or some other anatomical part. Those contrasts may not focus us down to a single, unique referent, but they do focus us enough for a reasonable guess to be made—especially in the added situational context provided by the rest of the sentence in which the term is used and by the communication situation.

There is nothing that forces one to use a horse partinomy to speak of the parts of a pickup truck, but if one does decide to do so, gross facts about the shape and use of horses and pickups do considerably constrain the referential possibilities.[16] An important part of our communicative use of extension depends on the paradigmatic (in Saussure's wide sense) context provided by the contrast relations in which our terms or signs participate and by the semantic category to which the terms belong. In effect, it is not just a term that is extended, but the contrast set to which the term belongs. Also important, but more obviously so, is the syntagmatic context provided by the communicative situation, the particular sentence, and so forth.

Kempton: Mexican Ollas

Kempton, in an exceedingly careful and thorough study (1981), has, inter alia, examined the reference of terms for categories of vessels (*olla*, or big stew pot, and contrasting terms) in Mexican Spanish. He has modeled his primary experimental design closely on that used by Berlin and Kay for their study of color terms. He conducted extensive interviews in which he elicited terms and explored the definitions, contrast and inclusion relations, and salience of the elicited terms. One of his primary field techniques involved the use of line drawings. He produced a matrix of drawings of vessels that gradually varied along dimensions of height and width and that showed categorical variation in the number of handles (none, one, two) and the presence or absence of a spout. He had informants circle all the drawings that were examples of, for instance, *ollas*, all the drawings that were best examples, and those that were "sort of" members. His results, like Berlin and Kay's, showed a clear dependence of extended ranges on focal instances.

His experimental design allowed him to carefully explore the effect of continuous variables having to do with the dimensions of the pots. In doing so he also demonstrated the practicability of generalizing the Berlin and Kay research design. The drawings seemed less useful (or insightful) for dealing with discrete features such as presence or absence of a handle, although through other techniques Kempton established the fact that these attributes functioned as all-or-nothing (as opposed to continuous) variables for his informants. Like Berlin and Kay's original, Kempton's design did not provide him with the tools for formally exploring the effects of situational context, intended usage, and presumed shared knowledge; it did not involve extensive study of the relationship of vessels to conventional (possibly named) subcategories and to marking relations among such categories. Finally, while Kempton's study contains interesting information about the functions of the various vessels, it does not systematically study such functions.

Kempton's study is important for our present exploration because of its careful and rigorous demonstration of the relevance of Berlin and Kay's findings to the classification of culturally specific, artifactual domains as well as universal, physiologically based domains such as color. It is also important to see that, where appropriate, the continuous distance metric for assessing similarity that was shown to be used for color (whereby one color differs from another by virtue of differing values on continuous, ratio-scale attributes) can also be used for other kinds of cultural categories.

Notes

1. For some people large German beer steins are a kind of *mug* but not of *cup*.

2. A typology of past views of the language/thought relationship that have influenced anthropological thinking will be presented in chapter 9, when we examine the cups-and-glasses application. Those views will at that time be contrasted with the view embodied in the present theory.

3. This set of shared cores provides a basis for denotative, if not connotative, translation. Conklin's Hanunóo findings concerning alternative labelings of the same color can be seen in this light to pertain to alternative contextual biasing of extension, not to core definitions. While the relationship between "core concepts" and "unmarked referents" is not totally clear, we will not go too wrong by thinking of core referents as the most unmarked referents of the terms. The relationship of marking to coreness will be discussed in later chapters.

4. Obviously, when one compares terms from different languages taken out of context and from different sized contrast sets, one has already given up on any exact match in terms of sense or oppositional meaning (in terms, that is, of Saussure's linguistic value in a language's system of values. An approximate match of sense meanings might be approached by examining terms that fall under matching cover terms in the various languages. Matching words such as "color" in the various languages would be relevant here, where we are dealing with "kinds of colors," but Berlin and Kay do not provide us with data of this sort.

The tension between oppositional meaning and referential meaning is, as noted earlier, a longstanding one in linguistics. Saussure (see his discussion of linguistic value [1959:111–122], and see Kronenfeld and Decker 1979:506–507) accepted the notion that underlying continua in the physical world we perceive (such as, I would claim, the physiological domain of color used by Berlin and Kay) structure and constrain our linguistic categories in important ways. Saussure's position was bracketed on the one side by the Prague linguists Jakobson and Trubetzkoy, who wanted to ascribe a much more important structuring role to the (nonlinguistic) physical substance of language—primarily, in their case, phonological substance—and its relationship to the world to which language referred, and on the other side by purer structuralists such as Hjelmslev and his Copenhagen School, members of which wanted to consider language totally as a system of relations without even the underlying structuring role that Saussure accorded substance (in various places other than the "radically arbitrary" link between signifier and signified).

The comparisons needed to provide empirical evidence of substantive universals must, for lack of any other option, rely on referential meanings—and, in a sense, must remain vulnerable to any problems entailed by such reliance. On the other hand, comparative results as overwhelmingly systematic as those of Berlin and Kay (or of Greenberg 1966), even without the physiological evidence later adduced by Kay and others, makes it hard for one not to accept (and believe) that one is dealing with units that are meaningful within the languages involved.

5. The problem of why such a correlation should exist is an interesting one, though outside the primary focus of this volume. Relevant here is Frake's argument referred to in chapter 4: that the number of terms (whether basic or otherwise) a language has within a domain reflects the degree of cultural interest in the domain, while the taxonomic depth, and thus the number of superordinate terms (which tend to be "basic" terms, in the Berlin and Kay sense), reflects the range of different experiences people in a culture have and thus their need for a special vocabulary that is not tied to particular experiences.

In a rough way, and drawing on insights of Berlin and Kay as well as of Frake, I would suggest that more technological development entails a greater division of labor. A greater division of labor entails a greater divergence of primary sensory experiences—for example, the color of a farmer's fresh shoots versus that of a fisherman's shallow coastal waters—to which reference can be made in a conversation in which, for example, one is attempting to convey information about a certain shade of green. This divergence entails a greater usefulness for relatively context-free (that is, "basic") terms, for example, colors, and a potentially greater frequency of use for such terms. A farmer can convey a specific bit of color information to another farmer by referring to the color of freshly sprouted hay in early morning light, but that kind of instancing breaks down when he starts talking to a fisherman about the color. With the fisherman he will need to be able to talk about things such as "a very yellow green."

Such variable experiences within a speech community push for a larger number of "basic" terms specific to analytic or abstract domains such as color. But if they are to be maintained in the language, such terms must be used frequently enough for children to learn of, pin down, and remember them. Thus the frequency with which these basic abstract terms are used in conversation represents a limit on their proliferation.

Separate from the question of the number of basic terms in a language is that of the order in which these terms develop—which is constant across language for the case of color. For the particular color case, Berlin and Kay's work suggests that the order in which successive colors present themselves as candidates for frequency of use is a function of their salience to speakers. Subsequent work by others (see esp. Kay and McDaniel 1978, but see MacLaury 1992 for a differing view) suggested that a major aspect of their salience is determined by the physiology of the eye, and particularly by the relative density of receptors tuned to one or the other color. I would expect that aspects of frequent communication situations would also affect salience.

6. Lounsbury initially focused on the reduction form (versus expansions) (Lounsbury 1964b:356–7,362) perhaps in part because of difficulties in properly limiting the context of expansions. Subsequent work (see Kronenfeld 1976 and 1980a), joined with the use of notational schemes that better represent genealogical relations (such as the Romney scheme used in this volume), has eliminated this problem, and current forms of Lounsburian equivalence rules for such kinship terminologies can be easily used, either for expansion or reduction.

7. The debate about the relationship of Lounsbury's rules to Malinowski's extension of sentiment theory arises here. I would only point out that, while Lounsbury's demonstration of semantic extension does increase the likelihood that Malinowski's theory is also correct, neither is logically dependent on the other. Elsewhere (Kronenfeld 1973, 1975) I have shown that patterns of kinship "behavior" (taken in a broad enough sense to include sentiment) relate to, but do not closely match, patterns of terminological extension; in my Fanti example both behavior and terminology were extended, but through very different mechanisms.

8. See Lounsbury's discussion (1969) of degrees of metaphoricity in kinship terminological systems.

9. The relationship of patterns of kinship behavior to kinship categories, and of these patterns and categories to the work of various important kinship theorists (including Kroeber, Radcliffe-Brown, and Leach) is treated in Kronenfeld (1975); the relationship of Lounsburian rewrite rules (and my treatment of them) to the positions of Kroeber and Radcliffe-Brown is sketched out in Kronenfeld (1976:914).

10. The data for this discussion come from Morgan's compendium, in which these unskewed examples are all Iroquois-type. Kronenfeld (1989) throws some doubt on the definition of the cross/parallel distinction implicit in Morgan's data. That discussion suggests some substantial problems with Morgan's description of his skewed systems and raises the possibility that Morgan's unskewed cases might have actually been Dravidian-type instead of Iroquois-type. But that argument does not affect the present point.

11. In the Fanti example, as I have already indicated, the difference between the skewed and the unskewed variants reduces to a single rule. That skewing rule, unlike the other Fanti rules, is a self-consciously held one that is very self-consciously tied to particular matrilineal inheritance facts (see Kronenfeld 1973:1579,1581; 1980a:600,604–605). If the Fanti were to change their inheritance pattern to a patrilineal one, the logic they use for Crow-type skewing would allow them easily to switch to Omaha-type.

The kind of variation seen in Morgan's data could easily result from a Fanti-like situation in the language immediately ancestral to Morgan's Crow and Omaha if some, but not all, of the descendent groups had subsequently changed the unilineal emphasis of their primary inheritance pattern. Going further, it seems possible, in fact, that such variation was present even within the groups Morgan was describing—and that it may even be a common although often unreported feature of skewed terminologies.

My own guess, for reasons I lack space to go into at this time (but which are discussed in Kronenfeld n.d.), is that the Fanti situation *is* more common than the ethnographic record would indicate. I suspect that most ethnographers attributed such variation in their data to contamination from outside sources (e.g., European languages), took their informants' assertions that the most marked system was the "correct" one, and reported only that one; I discuss such evidence from the Fanti, and my reasons for interpreting it as I do, in Kronenfeld 1973:1583; 1980a:605–606.

12. The focal referents are not totally dissimilar, of course, because of the relevant universal considerations discussed above in conjunction with Lounsbury's Crow and Omaha work.

13. The actual comparison is complicated by systematic errors in Morgan's data (see Kronenfeld 1989, in which these errors are described and systematically analyzed and the evidence for calling them "errors" is presented).

The reason for using Morgan's data for comparative purposes remains the fact that no comparable comparative corpus has been put together anywhere else by anyone else. Readers for whom my characterization of Morgan's errors raises doubts concerning my comparison of Fanti extension rules with the rules of Morgan's Crow-type Dakota systems should reassure themselves by comparing my Fanti rules (Kronenfeld 1980a, 1980b) with the rules described for other Crow-type systems by Lounsbury in his basic work on skewed systems (1964b).

14. The program was primarily concerned with skewing, and built in only other rules that were required for correct identification of relevant skewing. Some cases of failure to reduce to a single kernel were attributable to the omission of certain other elementary rules. Other cases derived from a combination of my reluctance to resort to ad hoc procedures and problems concerning how best to define kintypes and rule domains in one or another variant of the Romney notational scheme.

15. Basso characterizes the general anatomical set as applying to a wide range of entities that are capable of moving themselves (1967:475–476), including humans (p. 473). His only discusssion of a particular model for the application to pickup trucks was his observation (p. 473) that some informants name the horse as the particular model for the application. For rhetorical purposes I am taking Basso's informants' suggestion regarding the horse as the model in my discussion, but I should point out that my use of the example is not affected by the difference between the horse or humans as specific models or that between such specific models and the more general model represented by the full Apache set of self-moving entities.

16. This is an example of what I have sometimes called a "natural convention"—that is, a representation whose use is itself arbitrary, but which carries with it (for whatever reasons) strong substantive (and hence nonarbitrary) constraints on how the representation is to be made. The idea, and the basic examples, come from Gombrich's *Art and Illusion* (1960).

The ancient Egyptians were in no way constrained to use size to represent importance in their art. But once they elected to do so, they do seem to have been constrained to link "big" with "important" and "small" with "unimportant." Such a connection between size and importance is a common linguistic one—as in New Guinea "big men" (political leaders), "big chiefs," "all the little people," and so forth: "big" is always more important. I suspect that the reason relates to the fact that our eyes, while moving around, dwell more on important people than unimportant ones—and that makes it so these important people fill up more of our retina, in much the same way that big objects as opposed to small ones do (controling for distance); however, I would be prepared to accept a more mundane explanation such as the possibility that big people are more likely to win old-fashioned fights than small ones, all else being equal; in any event, the regularity is there.

Our own convention—that size (in art) represents distance—seems natural (even photographic) to us. But then there is the fact Gombrich notes (1960:53) that technologically isolated people who were unfamiliar with the convention and who had never seen photographs or the like, when shown photographs, were not automatically able to read them. Gombrich indicated that learning to read the convention, though, came quite rapidly. For example, I gather, when presented with a picture of a person in the foreground aiming a spear at an elephant in the background, viewers unfamiliar with photographs reacted with some comment about the big man aiming at the small elephant. They learned quickly how to read the photographs, and did not make such mistakes for long. (See Deregowski 1972 for a description of some related experimental work; Deregowski emphasizes more long-lived effects of cultural differences on perception. It is clear that reading the photographic convention of size for distance, where "bigger" is "closer," was no more automatic or "natural" than reading the Egyptian art. The link of size to distance, of course, does (more clearly than our previous example) relate to the retinal size of the image. Gombrich also (1960:44–48) discusses the conventional use of the light-dark continuum to represent distance.

10

The Theory

A semantic theory that accounts only for the denotative meaning of terms and that offers no insight into the connotative or metaphoric use of those same terms is seriously lacking. A theory that has to treat "chair" (what we sit on) as being totally unrelated to the "chair" (the leader of our meeting) is obviously inadequate as a theory of our semantic competence. We do not necessarily have to settle for inadequate theories. The shape of a reasonable semantic theory is already beginning to emerge in work on extensionist semantics. I want now to lay out a version of what such a reasonable theory might look like. What follows is not proven and is not always spelled out well enough to be formally testable, but it does represent a set of empirical propositions that deal with the problems raised in our discussion of componential models and that accord well with a wide variety of formal and informal observations about our use of language.

This theoretical approach will allow us to explore category prototypes and extensions within culturally variable domains, such as books and drinking vessels, that do not seem especially dependent on physical, physiological, social, or cognitive universals for their structuring. It will enable us to avoid the kind of circle Rosch gets into (for example, see 1973:182, 187; also see Rosch and Mervis 1975:576, 598–99) when she defines category membership as being relative to prototypes, while defining prototypes as the best examples of categories. Instead, it will let us see functional and interactive relations as producing categories by causing what will become focal items to get labels. External form attributes of those focal items will be seen as providing the normal basis on which the category is extended to nonfocal items.

For reasons of brevity and focus, we will speak throughout the following dicussion about the referents of words as if they were simply things. However, I do want to emphasize that I agree with the suggestion of Gladwin (1974), Kay (1978:81), and others that verbal categories, or the features that define them, can often be based on cognitive schemes rather than on precise, physically defined features of their referents, and I intend our discussion to be taken in that light. This view is implicit in Saussure's distinguishing his "signified" (a concept) from the thing—external to language and the minds of language users—we call the "referent," even though at the time of Saussure's work psychologists had not yet spoken of cognitive schemes. Such notions as "functional relationship" and "functionally relevant, but external, form features," which will come into our discussion later, obviously refer to cognitive structures.

Cores and Universals

The distinction between core and extended referents is based on Berlin and Kay's (1969) distinction between focal and nonfocal examples of colors and on Lounsbury's (1964b, 1965) distinction between kernel and nonkernel referents of kinterms. Cores in general seem relatively fixed within any single linguistic community, but extended ranges and mechanisms of extension seem much more variable. The mechanism of extension in the kinship systems described by Lounsbury is unambiguous in the sense that it places extended referents (or members of a kinterm category) clearly in one and only one category. However, the extension described by Berlin and Kay exhibits much greater variability in terminological assignment: informants agree among themselves about core exemplars, but show considerable variation (across individuals, times, contexts, etc.) in their assignment of instances as extended members of color categories. My own work on Fanti kinship, utilizing a wider range of data than that used by Lounsbury, shows considerable variation in the extension of kinterms, even if of a more structured kind than that seen in Berlin and Kay's data.

Kinship and color both are terminological domains in which noncultural and, to some degree, universal factors shape the determination of core exemplars—even if to varying degrees and in different ways. Other domains exist where similar forms of extension occur but where cores clearly are not universal. For example, in both Kempton's work on *ollas* that we just examined (Kempton 1981) and my own work on cups and glasses (taken up later in this chapter and previously described in Kronenfeld et al. 1985), a distinction similar to that in Berlin and Kay's color example was found between core (or best) exemplars (which were unambiguous in their category membership) and extended exemplars (which were often much more ambiguously or variably members of the category in question).

Within Lounsbury's kinship analysis and Berlin and Kay's analysis of color, cores, then, are "fixed" in two senses: they are stable and unvarying within a speech or language community and they are stable (or universal) across languages. For purposes of the general semantic theory we are developing, though, we want to separate the two senses. The former sense—the stability of cores within a language community—is central to the theory being presented here, while the latter sense—the stability of cores across languages—obviously does not apply to many areas of vocabulary, and so cannot be central to any general theory of word semantics. As we shall shortly see, by my theory, the in-language stability results from how we conceptualize words and anchor their communicative use; the in-language stability is *not* the result of any kind of universality of the domains in question, and does not depend on any universal or innately predisposed cores.

The Importance of Cores

Focal (or core) referents of terms are crucially important in my theory because they are the referents that determine the attributes normally associated with the various terms. That is, core referents represent the particular entities through which the two parts of meaning—sense relations and reference—are tied together. It is for core referents that what we might call a "referential lock" exists; it is this referential lock with core referents that protects us from the infinite regress situation implied by Wittgenstein's "family resemblances" and by Rosch's circularity. It is the relations among core referents of the terms in any given paradigm (or contrast set) that define the dimensions or sets of components along which the terms (or categories) of the paradigm contrast with one another. These are thus the dimensions or sets of components on which are specified the defining attributes (or other criterial attributes) of the different members of the contrast set (or componential paradigm). According to the theory, the specification of other, nondefining (in the sense of not serving to distinguish members of the contrast set from one another) attributes that are typically or normally possessed by the core referents or exemplars (and which thereby come to be associated with the category) comes secondarily.

Out of context, focal referents are absolute in the sense that they belong to the category and exemplify the category without comparison to any other referent of their own or other categories. (Berlin and Kay's canonical "red" is an example of such an absolute core.) However, if any particular context is common enough and stable enough for some set of people to have standard or canonical expectations about it, secondary or context-specific cores can develop that, in that context, can temporarily override the general core and become the focal anchor or reference point for discussions in that context that involve the vocabulary in question. (The shade of crimson some of us associate with Harvard might be an example of such a derivative subcore.) This process by which derivative cores (or context specific subcores) can emerge is not restricted to a single instance for any given category. Alternative contexts can produce alternative context-specific cores, and a hierarchy of successively more specific contexts (each of which is included in the next higher, more general level) can produce a hierarchy of context-specific cores. Such a hierarchy can become a kind of marking hierarchy (see chapter 7 and Greenberg's work on marking theory, 1966, 1968), and thereby lead to the emergence of new terminological categories (see Berlin 1972, 1976).

Denotative and connotative extensions are made within the domain (area of discourse) to which the core or focal item belongs and within the context of the set of paradigmatic oppositions in which the core items participate. Metaphoric extension is made to an item outside this domain (or to one having some unusual kind of position within it). I am speaking of metaphoric extension in a general sense that includes metonymy and synecdoche, since I think the same thought patterns and usage mechanisms underlie all nonliteral extension.

Learning Langue: Core Senses and Extension

Speakers of a language induce coreness for particular referents of a term from a combination of factors, including the functions associated with the category, the relative facility with which alternative members of the category accomplish (or epitomize) the category's functions, the temporal priority of speakers' contact with alternative members, and the relative salience (perceptual and interactive) of alternative members.[1] The set of core referents thus induced becomes the source of the various alternative bases along which extension takes place. Form attributes provide the basis for denotative extension from the core ("denotative" in the sense of extension through "technically correct" definitions) and are taken from descriptive characteristics of core members. Functional[2] attributes of the category provide the basis for "connotative" extension (that is, extension based, e.g., on how one feels about the exemplar or what one does to it). Attributes can be either continuous (for example, shape, volume, etc.) or discrete (for example, presence of some particular material or appendage or some common use). Attributes of a given category can vary in their importance or salience relative to one another in two ways. First, they can vary according to paradigmatic context. For example, different attributes are used to distinguish a cup from a mug than are used to distinguish a cup from a glass. Second, attributes can vary according to the context of their use. For example, different attributes are used to select a "glass" from a set of glass-like objects than are used to select a "glass" from a set of cup-like objects. Some particular category may grade into another along some particular attribute, while a similar attribute might produce a discrete boundary between another pair of categories. For example, the transition from glass material to nonglass for a glass-shaped object moves one immediately out of the glass category, while the reverse transition for a cup-shaped object only moves one somewhat away from the prototype.

Denotatively "correct" extension of a category to noncore items is defined in terms of form attributes. Denotatively "correct" extended members of a category are items that fit the "definition" of the category in terms of form but differ noticeably from the specific form of the category's exemplars. An example might occur when the word "glass" is used for an unusually shaped (even if functionally appropriate) glass such as a goblet; a more extreme example might be the extension of the term "glass" to an object correct in form but inappropriate in function, such as an Irish coffee glass. Connotatively extended members of a category are items that function similarly to the category's exemplars but differ from those exemplars along some significant form attribute(s), as, for example, a plastic cup referred to as a "glass."

A core pen, defined according to the functional basis of the category, will be something with which one can write in ink (with an implication, stemming from the contrast with erasable pencil, of permanence). But a core exemplar of a category is not (normally, at least, and not for such concrete items) such a pure, platonic abstraction; for each of us a core pen has a shape, a type of point and ink-supply mechanism, a color of ink, and perhaps a color itself. There is a sense in which the use of ink can be said to be an "essential" feature of the pen, and thus present in the core schema for each of us; aspects of the shape—which have to do with how we are to hold it—are probably similarly essential. Other aspects of shape are essential only if we take into account additional constraints such as portability, including how we are to keep it in our pocket or purse, and so forth—and ink-supply mechanism. For many of us, especially those of us who are older, our core "pen" (the one we picture in our minds' eyes when we think of the word, or the one we answer questions about "pens" in terms of) is a fountain pen—with a nib point and a refillable ink supply. We "fountain pen-ists" recognize another kind of pen, a ballpoint pen, as an extended member of the pen category; it is a genuine member of the category because it has the essential feature of writing with ink and the quasiessential feature of portability. Most of us recognize also that it is now used much more commonly than the fountain pen. In fact, for many others of us—the younger ones—the (nonrefillable) ballpoint is the core exemplar of the pen category; for "ballpoint-ists," the fountain pen is a slightly archaic extended member of the category.

We can see, with the pen example, that denotative form attributes that define core exemplars depend in part on the form we experience that best fulfills the function implicit in the lexicalization of the category. The shifts in core referents of the pen category over time, for instance from a quill—the pinion feather (of a goose or turkey) from which the word derives—to a stick pen with a metal nib (which was dipped in an ink well, as was a quill pen), to a fountain pen, to today's ballpoint, and possibly to tomorrow's felt-tipped pen show us that core exemplars are normal or typical ones, and coreness changes as the population of exemplars changes. At the same time, the fact that some of us persist in maintaining "archaic" cores suggests that the population of exemplars does not have its effect on us constantly, but rather primarily when we are learning the term in question. Fountain pens were the most frequently used kind of pen (and also the most prestigious and best working) when I learned about pens, and so were established as my core exemplars. (Salience is probably the central issue here, but frequency of interaction seems to me to play a special role in the determination of relative salience.) I recognize the subsequent shift toward ballpoints by recognizing them as the prime subcategory, and the normal selection of convenience, but my core exemplar of the pen category remains the one I first learned—the fountain pen. I do not want to claim that cores are immutable even for individual speakers, but only that early learning generates a tremendous amount of inertia, and that it takes exceptional conditions of interaction with the things in question, and perhaps some exceptional importance attached to using one versus an other exemplar, to overcome that inertia.[3]

If we assume that coreness is part of our modern version of Saussurean langue, then we see that different parts of our speech community can have slightly variant forms of langue—as long as communication is not unduly impaired.[4] We also can see how language changes (or linguistic drift occurs) within a Saussurean model through the existence of slight variations in langue among different parts of a wider community, and through a gradual shift over time in the (relative) populations of the parts.

A pertinent example of why we want to separate denotative extension from core membership (as well as from connotative extension) is provided within the domain of books, magazines, and so forth, where books are functionally distinguished (from, say, magazines, pamphlets, or booklets) as substantial, nonephemeral collections of textual material. The actual form of books has evolved over time and varies across cultures. We denotatively define our books as having a large number of bound pages and hard covers (and we presume their size to be within a canonical range). In this domain, an example of a denotatively correct (form) extension of the term that is connotatively (or functionally) wrong would be the "write your own" books that are "published" in the United States; they look just like any other book, except that the pages are blank. They are usable as diaries, but are not in any way organized for such use and are not sold as such. Conversely, the scrolls of the Torah constitute a functionally correct use of the word "book" (even of "The Book") that nonetheless does not fit our current denotative definition of a book. A similar problem is presented, though perhaps in a more emotionally convincing form, by a tape recording—say, for the blind—of *A Tale of Two Cities*.

Several kinds of structural ambiguity concerning category membership are possible. Taxonomic relations can include situations in which the core item of one category is a denotatively extended member of another category (for example, a *mug* is a kind of *cup*). Two taxonomically related categories can overlap so that a single item can be a denotatively extended member of both—or a connotatively extended member of both (as seen in the relationship of soup mugs to *mug* and *bowl* categories). We will examine in chapter 11 the case of the plastic cup in American English, a situation in which an item (or a whole subcategory of items) is denotatively a member of one category while connotatively a member of another.

Form and Function

From what we have so far seen in a number of domains, "denotatively correct usage" refers to use of a category label that is consistent with functionally relevant but external form features, while "connotative usage" refers to use that is consistent with the functional relationship on which the terminological isolation of the focal item is based but inconsistent with some aspect of the external form features. Operationally, it seems to me that what has traditionally been called "denotative usage" refers to usage for which informants will say, "Yes, that *really* is a book," or "Yes, he *really* is my uncle,"[5] while "connotative usage" occurs when informants say something like, "No, it's not really a book exactly, but its contents are like a books," or "No, he's not really my uncle, I just call him that out of respect and because I like him." Metaphoric usage is not correct to informants in any literal sense, but does convey something about the broader meaning involved; "the thought" *is* "father to the deed," even if thoughts are too inanimate to have kin or to behave in a fatherly fashion.

Folk definitions typically are not created to convey abstract, existential truth but to communicate useful definitional information in the kinds of situations in which such information typically is needed but not present (in the minds of all those involved). Our understanding of the import of folk definitions depends on our understanding of why and how they are created and used. Typically, *in referential situations*, folk definitions are needed and created (in answer to a "What is an X?"–type question) in order for someone to tell someone else how to recognize an instance of the category being defined. In such a situation, keying the primary definition to function would not help, although identifying a form does help. The functional question ("What is X used for?" or "What does X do?" or even, in the appropriate conversational context, the functional version of "What is an X?") is normally dealt with at the sign level (that is, as a signified, without any direct concern with reference); if the object in question is unknown, the function question ("What does it do?") is preceded with an identification one ("What is that?").

The Domain of Books: a Brief Example

Some of the concerns at issue in the form/function (denotative/connotative) distinction can be further explored in a brief consideration of some examples drawn from the domain of books and magazines mentioned earlier in this chapter. After briefly sketching out, in outline form, the interrelationship of terms in this domain, I will use the domain to disucss some aspects of the form/function contrast.

In my sketch I will first provide a tree diagram of the contrast and inclusion relations (indicating for relevant entries some of the structuring attributes). Following that diagram I will offer a few illustrative observations concerning particular categories and then some observations regarding form, funciton, prototypicality, and extension for the term "book" itself. Finally, I will lay out some of the principle marking relations.

Summary of Book Domain

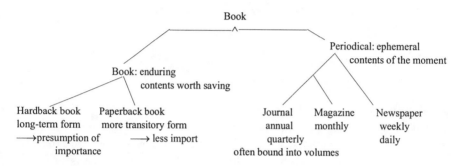

Observations:

Some anomalous forms:

1. A "comic book" feels like a periodical because of its trivial nature.

2. *American Heritage* was once published as a hardcover periodical; it seemed to be aiming for the patina of a thing to keep—even if the ploy seems not to have worked.

The verb form of "book" seems to derive from the noun form: that is, it means something like to "put into a (authoritative, legal, enduring) book" (cf. ledger—official register).

The sense of "book" taken in the verb also seems involved in the expression "to throw the book at," which entails hitting someone with the full, authoritative, complete, detailed, and enduring verson of the law.

Form, function, core, and extension:

Core function: preserving important words in a permanent and authoritative form

Core form: bound sheets of quality paper, with printed material, a substantial number of pages, and hard covers

A prototype: "The Book" (i.e., the Bible)

The Bible, as "The Book," exists (in one tradition) in an earlier form, now noncanonical, as scrolls. Scrolls are now an example of connotative extension on basis of function without form.

There exist other examples of function without form: "talking books" for the blind (on tape); "books" on computer disks.

Taking the idea of the importance of the content without the rest of the form, we get the "blue books," in which examinations are written.

If we look at extension based on form without function, we get:

Close to the core: ledgers (permanent, but filled in, not printed)

More distant, but still in the domain of stored information: "write-your-own" books of blank pages

Out of the domain—extension between function and metaphor: "books" of matches

Marking:

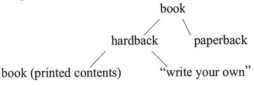

The distinction of concern here is that between extension from a focal sense that is based on function (characterized by attributes such as the relatiave permanence of a book's contents vs. the relatively ephemeral contents of a magazine), and extension from a focal sense that is based on form (characterized by attributes such as the nature of the bindings). Form and function come together in focal books or magazines, but have to be separated into two different systems of semantic extension in order to account for people's inconsistencies in their classification of certain subtypes (for instance, classifications based on function, where the form does not fit—such as calling "ledgers" or "notebooks" kinds of "books"), for judgments they make about ambiguous bases, and for reasons they adduce for these judgments.

Assessing Similarity

In the domains with which we[6] and others have so far experimented, several different ways of assessing the similarity or contiguity on which extension is based have emerged. In denotative extensions of kinterms we and others have demonstrated the kind of relative product calculus that is represented by Lounsbury's rules and embedded in a Fanti speaker's assertion that someone is his father because that person is his father's brother. In the domain of color terms, Berlin and Kay (1969) and others have shown that extension is based on values along the dimensions that structure the three-dimensional color solid, as represented physiologically in the retina's opponent system (see, particularly, Kay and McDaniel 1978, but also see MacLaury for another view). In the world of pens and pencils, similarity seems to be based on the number of discrete attributes that are shared (such as yellow wood vs. other casing and lead vs. ink in writing utensils). In the world of cups and glasses, similarity seems to be based on the number of discrete attributes involving materials and appendages. It is important to note that the similarity is relative and, to a degree, ad hoc, depending on the context of use, the level of opposition, and the nature of what is being communicated. In a sense it is a matter of using whatever works.

Paradigmatic Relations

In the kind of semantic theory we are proposing, paradigmatic or "sense" relations among terms would be generated by relations among focal types, and would be defined in terms of the attributes or features by which those focal types contrast with one another. Considerations of paradigmatic consistency, conjunctivity, and the like would constitute the same kind of influence on category definition—and pressure toward the addition or deletion of categories—that they are felt to constitute in componential theories (see Nerlove and Romney 1967, Kronenfeld 1974), but these influences would apply directly only to the focal types. In effect, one would have a componential analysis that often would not cover a large part of the denotative range of the terms it included. In our semantic space, such a curtailed componential analysis would apply only to the "stars" themselves, not to other objects caught in the stars' gravitational fields.

For our book domain, we see the following kinds of paradigmatic contrast relations. "Book" contrasts with "pamphlet" on denotative features such as style of binding (sewn vs. stapled), covers (hard vs. soft), and amount of material (thick vs. thin); connotative features of contrast include presumed duration of interest (enduring vs. ephemeral). "Magazine" is similar to "pamphlet," but with the added feature of regular, periodic (vs. one-time-only) emergence—a feature by which "magazine" also contrasts with "book." "Periodical" is a kind of magazine,[7] but one that is, functionally, on the enduring (vs. ephemeral) side of the duration-of-interest feature—and thus, denotatively, more substantially bound. Paperbacks are kinds of books[8]—a subcategory whose core is distinguished from the core book denotatively by its binding (which falls between that of a proper book and that of a magazine) and its cover ("soft"), and connotatively by a presumption of less duration of interest than a book (even if greater than that of a magazine).

Metaphor

Metaphoric extension is a key aspect of our use of language. It is one traditional semantic theories have ignored and which some modern theorists cite as evidence of the inapplicability of formal analytic procedures to the study of language. Before providing some illustrative examples of metaphoric extension and its explication in my theory, let me quickly sketch out the general way in which the theory deals with metaphor. In metaphoric extension an individual term is not extended by itself, in isolation, or on the basis of its attributes alone (or their match with attributes of the item to which it is potentially being extended). Instead, the term is extended along with the entire set of paradigmatic oppositions in which it participates in its home domain.[9] Its attributes (or features) do get matched against those of the target item, but not absolutely—that is, not without comparison to the attributes of the terms to which it is opposed. In metaphoric extension, a paradigm—that is, a set of contrasting (or opposed) terms—is extended to the domain or universe containing the target item. The differences among items in the target domain are lined up with (or oriented along) the attributes or features along which terms in the extended paradigm contrast with one another; then, the term that, relative to the others, best matches the target item—relative to the items from which it is being distinguished—is used to refer to that item.

The relative similarity of the target item to the source signified and its core referent can be in terms of form or shape, of function, or of things it is normally associated with. Similarities of shape can be based on the item itself (seeing the shape of a car's floor gear shift lever as being somewhat similar to that of a tail) or on the relation of the shape of the item to its location in the larger framework (seeing the car's grill as similar to a mouth or its exhaust pipe to a penis). Relationships of function can be based on similarity of function (in the sense that a T.V. camera sees as does an eye), on contribution to function (in the sense that a car's headlight helps us to see), or on assistance to function (in the sense that we see through a car's windshield). The connection can be a kind of superficial form of the function (as in the sense that a car's door, like a "mouth," can be said to "swallow" its passengers—especially, perhaps, if the passengers thereby disappear from the arena of our interaction with them).

The point here is that these matches of attributes are not made in any absolutely predetermined manner or according to any rigid or fixed formulae, but are instead made probabilistically according to whatever determinable basis seems likely to best isolate the item in question (or the desired sense of the item). The basis itself need not, and does not always, absolutely uniquely isolate the item in question; all it need do is narrow down the possibilities enough for the hearer (or receiver of the message) to quickly use other contextual criteria to make the identification. All we really need are the kinds of connections we make use of in the game of charades, and, as in that game, the less ambiguous the better—but better any connection than none. Thus, the "mouth" of a car could refer either, on the basis of shape and location, to the car's grill, or, on the basis of function, to the car's gas intake, but it cannot refer to much else on the car, and certainly not to its roof, wheels, seats, windshield, and so forth.

This flexibility of potential comparison allows us to commonly and comfortably use old words for new items or situations with some assurance, nonetheless, that we will be understood. It is this flexibility that enables a finite, if fairly large, set of words to be used to talk about a potentially infinite variety of new things.

Metaphors range in their "liveness" from fresh and original ones that someone creates to strikingly convey a new thought to the totally conventionalized ones that show up in dictionaries as alternative senses of the word in question. This continuum represents the result of the natural process by which some metaphors strike people other than their initial users as particularly useful and apropos, and so are reused by them. As more and more people use them, older metaphors are increasingly treated as part of the established communicative resources of the language (rather than as the fresh and ad hoc visions they originally represented).

When a new generation of language users experience some established, older metaphor as a part of the regularities from which they infer langue, then that metaphoric usage enters langue, and comes to represent a secondary and derivative sense of the term. This sense is secondary to and derivative from the primary sense represented by the source of the metaphor, and has its own secondary core referents. Presumably, such a process is involved in the emergence of usages such as "department *head*." When the metaphoric usage becomes sufficiently well established and salient relative to the original source of the metaphor, then its psychological dependency on the source can be lost, and the usage (the now-"dead" metaphor) comes to represent simply an alternative primary sense of the word in question; an example is seen in the present lack of a relationship between the *table* in "table of random numbers" and the table upon which we eat—but here, a "table" of something such as figures once represented a metaphoric extension from table of the sort on which we eat.[10]

Polysemy such as the preceding differs from homonymy, where the alternative words (as in "dear" and "deer") are connected by no known or felt link at all, except that they are pronounced the same way.

This process of domesticating wild metaphors represents one way by which languages develop new resources. It is part of the process, discussed later in this chapter, by which secondary cores develop, and as such parallels what we have seen in chapter 4 regarding the growth of taxonomies. As with new taxonomic nodes, the information represented by higher level connections of a metaphor's source provides a framework by which those who use the new resource (or the new secondary core represented by the routinized metaphor) can quickly and efficiently convey what they mean by such usage to those who do not know the usage, such as children learning the language or strangers from other places.

I have been describing a process for metaphoric extension in which the knowledge structures evoked by the source paradigm are fleshed out in context of the distinctions relevant to the target domain and then used for making inferences about communicative intent or meaning. Within one's own language and culture, this fleshing out of knowledge structures and use of the fleshed-out knowledge structures in making communicative inferences is so routine and subconsciously automatic that we are unaware of doing it; and the relationships thus specified seem too obvious to necessitate any explanation. It is only when learning a really foreign language and culture, or when trying to teach a computer to converse, that we are forced to raise these processes to consciousness. The semantic theory, thus, is in some ways explaining what seems obvious to native speakers, but the real point is to explain what it is—the process of foregrounding and inference—that makes the "obvious" so obvious to us.

As an example of the kind of reasoning involved in metaphoric extension, consider our use in English of the term "father." The term has several senses, and refers to a number of attributes. It is denotatively defined as some person's physiological genitor. In the absence of other information we normally presume that the "father" is the husband of the person's mother (or genetrix). The term normally carries connotations of loving interest in the person and solidarity and support; of responsibility for feeding, training, and educating the person while young; and of bequeathing possessions to the person. The term often connotes, also, a certain amount of authority and need for respect or distance. A core "father," then, is one to whom all of these conditions apply. A physiological genitor who takes no further interest in his child is "technically" that child's "father," but not really a proper or "genuine" father to the child—and is, therefore, in my theory an example of denotative extension. On the other hand, a person who, without the biological relationship and without any legal obligation, raises a child is "like a father" or "really a father" to that child—and an example of connotative extension. An adoptive father can, depending on his behavior, be connotatively a father to the child, and is in some, but not all, senses denotatively the child's father; an adoptive father thus can be close to our core notion of "father," but necessarily lacks one attribute of the full core concept. A priest is a person with an interest in us that is generally father-like (in that it involves concern on the part of a senior—"senior," that is, in terms of authority and relevant knowledge rather than of age—for the training and general well-being of juniors). However, his interest in us is different in its details (i.e., in the nature of his residential and financial relations with us, the source of his authority and interest, the nature of the sanctions he commands, and the sense in which we are junior to him) from the specifically father-like concerns of a connotative "father." Thus, a priest can be a "father" in a more metaphorically extended sense.

When, in ordinary conversation, we hear someone speak of his or her "father," without being given any specific information about the sense in which the term is meant, we normally assume that a core father (with all the above attributes, both connotative and denotative) is meant. If information about some particular noncore attribute is given—either by being explicitly mentioned or by being implicit in either the conversation or the context—then we modify our view of only the attribute in question, but barring other information to the contrary, still assume canonical values for the remaining attributes. For example, reference to "my stepfather" necessarily means a mother's husband who is not my genitor and probably means one who has not adopted me, as well. But we still assume father-like behavior and responsibility unless something (such as, perhaps, the prefix "evil," or, more subtly, some special stress on the "step" morpheme) indicates otherwise. In this sense the core referent or exemplar of a category can be seen as the "default" or unmarked referent or exemplar, and represents the sense of the category that is normally used in reasoning about the category vis-a-vis other related categories. While the essence of my argument is that this usage (including the presumed default or unmarked sense) is quite reasonable in the sense of not representing any claim that clashes unduly with our normal native-speaker understandings, I do want to point out that it is not tautologically forced. One could imagine a radically different view in which only information explicitly present was presumed; much past semantic theorizing seems to have entailed this presumption. Among views involving the presumption of a more complete picture than that which is explicitly given, one could imagine a position in which, in the absence of further information, the *least* central or core exemplar was normally presumed—on the basis of being least inclusive of particular incidental details of the core. Alternatively, one might have a position in which the most statistically common exemplar (whether in absolute frequency or in frequency relative to some particular set of relevant situations or contexts) was normally presumed, or a position in which some kind of middle exemplar within the range of possibilities was presumed.

The fact that speakers of a language (in normal usage) implicitly presume core exemplars of verbal categories seems too special to exist simply by chance or as the result of some sort of historical accident. Such a fact seems much more likely to have a functional basis. In particular, this presumption of core exemplars seems crucial to the way in which we use a limited vocabulary to communicate fairly precisely (as precisely, in fact, as we—with increasing paraphrastic elaboration—choose to take the time and effort to communicate) about a seeming infinity of novel and special situations and nuances of meaning. This use of core referents and their paradigmatic oppositions accomplishes this communicative aim by telling us how words are to be taken in the absence of further specification, and by directing us to where further specification (or modification) is most needed.

In order to consider the effects of relations among core referents of related terms within a given paradigm (or contrast set) on our reasoning about noncore (and noncanonical, in the sense of being different from the normal presumption entailed by the use of the term) exemplars, let us look at why priests are, metaphorically, "fathers" instead of "uncles" (as are senior family friends). There is a general sense in which priests seem more avuncular to us than paternal—they are friendly and warm, they care about us without being part of our actual nuclear family, and have an interest in molding our behavior without actually being our parents. To understand the "father" usage we have to understand that the basic decision is to extend a kinterm to the priest; the decision concerning which kinterm is only a secondary one. We see first that the use of a kinterm (versus, for example, a term from the domains of friendship, community roles, or business relations) entails an intrinsic, natural, and enduring (and, thus, noncontingent and non–ad hoc) solidary relationship. We next turn to what is at issue in the contrast among the core exemplars of the various kinterms. When speakers refer to a priest as "father," they are asserting that, as opposed to a brother, he is senior to them; that, as opposed to a mother, he is male; and that, as opposed to a grandfather, he is proximate. What remains is the contrast with "uncle." We see that the basic denotative contrast between core "father" and core "uncle" is between two genealogical paths, and understand that this distinction is irrelevant to priests because they are not related to us through any genealogical path at all. The next most salient, connotative difference is that fathers are directly responsible for our well-being and training (in which connection we owe them respect and obedience), and are normal sources of inheritance for us, while uncles are not; that is, fathers are like uncles, but with these additional properties. Our cultural knowledge rules out the inheritance connection, and so we understand that priests are supposed to have a parent-like responsibility for watching over us and training us (in moral and theological issues in particular); by calling a priest "father" we accept and foreground that sense of direct personal responsibility and the reciprocal obligations of respect and obedience. Even if the usage is metaphoric, and thus the central feature that defines the domain (for example, +kinsman; see Lounsbury 1969:25) is missing, the term's relationship to those terms with which it contrasts remains, and the semantic bases of those contrasts remain. Such paradigmatic contrasts are utilized regardless of whether a speaker is using a metaphor to make a statement about an object (as in our priest example) or simply in order to identify the object.

Every category has attributes and associations that are incidental to its denotation and that relate only thinly to its functional entailments. Such attributes and associations can be based on consequences of functional entailments or on incidental characteristics of salient exemplars. People are creative, and can seize on any such implied or "accidental" attributes or associations as a basis for metaphoric extension. As long as the relevant aspects of the source of the metaphor and of the target to which it is being applied are well enough understood, pragmatically, by speaker and hearer, and as long as there is sufficient context to allow them to deduce which aspects are at issue, people can understand the metaphor. People understand the reference, whether it is to an object itself, to a use or quality of an object, or to some other connection of the object. Language itself provides speakers and hearers with one essential part of this necessary context through the paradigmatic or contrastive relations that words have with other words in their immediate domain (as well as through the normal syntagmatic associations of the words). These paradigmatic relations, as we saw in our priest example, reflect functionally important distinctions of use as well as cognitively important distinctions of form. Thus, when Basso's Western Apache (1967) extend the word for a horse's eye to the headlight of a pickup truck, they are extending that word not in limbo but as part of a set that entails contrasts with the words for a horse's leg, mouth, back, and so forth. These contrasts, which necessarily come automatically with the use of any word, help speakers to quickly isolate the relevant aspects of the object referred to and thus to quickly identify that object. Even if there is more than one such contrast set to which a given word belongs, there are only a few such sets, and the focusing role of the paradigmatic contrast remains operative.

For example, in the fifties, one could get a cheap laugh in some circles with any slightly pompous intonation of the line, "Today I am a fountain pen . . . ." The joke amounted to a wry comment on a confounding of moral issues with material ones. It derived from the then-common practice of giving fountain pens as Bar Mitzvah presents, from the convention of the Bar Mitzvah boy's speech/sermon, and from the high salience of the incoming gifts to many of the boys in question. Here, the fountain pen derived its metaphoric meaning from the combination of its accidental identification as a common Bar Mitzvah gift with the incidental fact that the rising use of ballpoint pens (while it had not yet rendered fountain pens irrelevant—as they are today) was already leading to the perception of fountain pens as *luxury* writing implements, and causing normal or typical examples of fountain pens to therefore be made of (or made to look as if they were made of) more precious materials than had previously been the case.[11] This metaphoric use of the word "fountain pen" depended primarily on the nonessential (to pen-ness) fact of what typical examples (in the gift context) were made of, rather than on any essential denotative or connotative feature.

Throughout this volume I have maintained that any reasonable semantic theory of reference should account for the broadest metaphoric usage as well as for more narrow denotative or connotative usages. We have seen now that metaphoric extension is not intrinsically different from more narrow or direct kinds of extension; only the kinds of attributes of the focal item on which the extension is based differ. We see that an integrated semantic theory encompassing both literal and metaphoric usage in natural language can be built on a basis of prototypic cores and varied means of extension.

Creating New Langue

Separate from the question of how a person learning a language induces the cores of already existent categories is the question of the origins of semantic categories and the initial determination of focal items.

Functional relations interact with the kinds of salience considerations that account for marking relations (such as initially encountered types, frequency of use, perceptual salience, and so forth) to produce a focal item and its attendant label, which in turn isolates a signified, for which a signifier is created (through borrowing, derivational rules, elision of a paraphrastic description, and so forth). A canonical referent is recognized from which denotative definitional features are abstracted. Connotative features are taken directly from the function.

The new categories emerge within a paradigm, and displace or rearrange other items (that is, change their "values," to use Saussure's terminology) within that paradigm. That is, the signified of the new sign forms a new set of contrasts with the other signifieds of the paradigm, and those contrasts either are fitted to an existing structure of oppositions (that is, framework of interacting features) or inclusions, or become the disturbance that causes a new structure (arrangement of features) to be created.

Zipf's law (see Zipf 1935) refers to the inverse correlation between the frequency of use of an expression and the length of the expression—that is, its phonemic and morphemic complexity. Such a correlation comes from the process of elision and pronunciation changes by which initially derivationally transparent or paraphrastic constructions lose redundant phonologic substance and thereby lose their exocentricity and/or intralanguage motivation (that is, their ability to have their meanings predicted from their parts). When the separate signifiers of the constituent signs of such a construction become unrecognizable and merge together into a new and arbitrary signifier, then a new sign has been created whose signified is the instantiation of the formerly derived or constructed signified that was involved in the new usage and whose core referent is the exemplar whose frequent use produced the elision. For example, see the proposed etymologies for "sister" in Indo-European (Friedrich 1966:7,9) versus the term's opacity in modern English.[12]

The degree to which the new signified replaces an old one from which it has been split off and the resulting potential for confusion of the new sign with prior existing signs has an effect on the pace and shape of the process of sign formation. If there is no such confusion, then the new signified replaces the old—as in the case of "pen," where, since the old core served no special purpose, focality easily shifted—from feather to staff pen to fountain pen to ballpoint. If the potential for confusion does exist—that is, if the old core retains its importance—then what happens depends on the effects of the elision process on the signifier—that is, on the relationship of the evolving signifier to other significant signifiers. Consider the "paper cup": It is important in and of itself. When the context is clear it can be called "cup," but does not replace teacup as the focal "cup," since teacup retains its own separate importance. Ordinarily it might collapse into "paper," but that signifier is already taken up by our newspaper (which occurs in enough contexts shared with paper cups to pose too great a potentiality for confusion). It could acquire a distinctive (nonextended) signifier by shortening its constituent parts into something like "papecu," but such shortening seems strange enough as an English elision to be difficult for native speakers—and thus, so far, "paper cup" has resisted any Zipf's law pressures.

The signs of newly created items (newly created signifieds with created signifiers) that get enough use move into the language—and out of control of their creators. "Kleenex," "Coke," and "Xerox" all represent made-up proper (derivationally opaque) names that, through a process similar to the one described by Berlin for folk taxonomies which we examined in chapter 7, have become generic names—to the partial discomfort of their creators, because of copyright issues). "High-fidelity phonograph," which was a descriptive paraphrase, has been successfully Zipf-ed down to a new sign, "hi-fi." "Television" and "telephone" were made-up, derivationally opaque (in English) names that retain their long forms in formal speech but which have been Zipf-ed down to "T.V." (or, in England, "telly") and "phone" in informal speech.

Even when they are not used frequently enough to be maintained in the language, we still see the continuing use of derivational procedures, descriptive labels, and made-up names. But then they constantly must be newly derived, described, or made up. The coined terms do not stick; Zipf's law does not shorten them; and we constantly produce new ones.

In sum, new categories emerge when noncore objects in some verbal category function importantly enough and frequently enough to acquire and maintain their own labels. The particular sound-images come into being as a result of any of a variety of mechanisms that are not relevant here. The objects in question then become the core referents of these new labels, and thus the core members of new verbal categories.

Computers present an interesting recent example of how something new has become important enough to rate a terminological category of its own. Computers split off from the calculator/calculating machine clump and became perhaps more important than the parent category, but calculators remained useful and important— and clearly different from computers. The sound image came from a derived form of the verb *to compute*, a synonym of *to calculate* (that is, similar, but different); in dictionaries published as recently as the early 1960s one can see that the signifier had already existed as a derivational form with a general agentive meaning (a person or thing that computes[13]).

Derivational histories or etymologies (both real and merely felt) are highly relevant to native speakers' senses of word meanings, and thus essential to any full theory of referential semantics. In our treatment of specific domains, including that of drinking vessels, in chapter 11 we will be compelled to call upon diachronic consid- erations—even if our appeal to such considerations will be relatively simple and unworked-out.

Brown and Witkowski's (1981:608) suggestion concerning the usefulness and feasibility of constructing "a thesaurus of regular semantic change paths" is an interesting one, and would, as they suggest, be highly useful for semantic studies, including the kind of theory being developed in the present volume. Examples of figurative language that they offer, such as the derivation of the Spanish word *músculo* ("muscle") from the Latin word *musculus*, the diminuitive of *mus* ("mouse") (p. 608), and the argument concerning basic regularities of perception and reasoning they offer (p. 606–7) to explain such usage seem interesting and important in their own right, and accord well with the semantic theory of the present volume.

Etymologies and Culture History

The histories of old extensions—that is, the histories of lexicalized things (including actions) and their associations through time in a language, in the various and succes- sive speech communities that use, define, and redefine the language—are what is coded in etymologies. The one-to-many nature of language drift, as one speech community grows and splits into several, means that what are related but separate languages today made up a single one in the past.

One can work back through these separate historical tracks to triangulate old meanings. One can look for generalizations about what directions of change are more or less likely when two daughter languages have different meanings for what is historically the same word. One can look at complexes of oppositions in a given domain to see which interpretations make sense.

For example, let us examine "uncle"/"nephew" in English:

> uncle < Latin *avunculus* < Latin *avus* (grandfather)
>   cf. *avia* (grandmother)
>   (*avunculus* looks to be "little grandfather"
> nephew < Latin *nepos* (nephew, grandson)

And, for comparison, also
>   aunt < Latin *amita* (paternal aunt)
>   cousin < Latin *consobrinus* (maternal first cousin)
>   (*sobrinus* - maternal cousin)

In considering such a set of terms we can use our synchronic comparative knowledge to frame a series of questions (and hypothesized answers) concerning the social conditions that are likely to have produced the observed pattern. For our kinship example, we can ask, In what kind of universe are uncles and grandfathers likely to be brought together (or confounded)? Was the range of these terms likely to have applied to all grandfathers? (Based on general regularities of kinship terminologies, the likely answer seems to be no.) Did they apply to all uncles? (Again, the likely answer seems to be no.) If not, which were included and which not? (Most likely to be included would be male forebears on the maternal side; most likely not to be included would be those on the paternal side.) What would the others have been called? (It seems likely that paternal uncles would have been called "father," and paternal grandfathers by some sort of "grandfather" construction.) What would cause the *avunculus* term, especially in light of its primary sense as grandfather to attach to the uncle category? If, hypothetically, the (patri-) lineage or other reasons for coding according to side of the family—maternal versus paternal—in the kin terminology had broken down, with a shift in emphasis toward the distinction between lineal and nonlineal relatives, what might have happened? It would seem that the "grandfather" sense of *avunculus*, or mother's father, was assimilated to the other, matching "grand-father" terminological category, which had applied to the sociologically more basic (in the prior patrilineal system) father's father. Fathers' brothers, in the old system, had no separate category into which mothers' brothers could have been assimilated, while mothers' brothers had the *avunculus* category (alone, once the mother's father had moved over to "grandfather"); the merger of the two kinds of colineals into the *uncle* category, with the "uncle" label, would then be fairly natural; the maintenance of the "not in my primary kin group, but close" sense of the *avunculus*/"uncle" category might also be relevant. Thus, a transition from an Omaha type system to an Eskimo type system can make sense of changes such as those we see in our etymologies, and can thereby give us some basis for thinking about the past extensions from which current usage is derived.

The preceding gets even more interesting when we realize that the Indo-European roots for the basic direct/lineal terms (father, mother, brother, sister, son, daughter) are really well attested (for example, all six are clear in English; see Friedrich 1966:7) while there are not such widely attested roots for the collateral set of terms, as well as, in general, much confusion and variability among the daughter languages regarding these terms, as, for example, the English borrowings from Latin which we just examined.

Functional Relations and Knowledge Structures

Linguistic signs—which are primarily, in the present work, words—have two different sorts of relationships to one another: formal and functional. Formal relations include the various kinds of paradigmatic and syntagmatic relations that Saussure sketches out for signs, and which include, under his paradigmatic heading, the semantic relations of contrast and inclusion identified by Frake (1962). Syntagmatic relations include grammatical relations and other aspects of the arrangement of words that affect how their meaning is understood.

In the present theory, functional relations refer to the relationships among the functional attributes of the terms in the given domain.[14] They include what is at issue in the contrast between opposed terms (for example, the use of chairs for sitting on versus that of tables for putting things on), functional groupings within the domain (as, for instance, the fact that chairs typically are used with tables), and functional interactions among referents of related words (for example, how a chair relates to a table in various situations of use), and so forth. Within the theory, then, funcitonal relations among signs represent the knowledge structures involving entities and actions in the world external to language, to which given signs are linked and in terms of which the functional attributes of signs are defined. Such knowledge structures are psychological entities, and thus individual; at the same time, the functional constraints of language force all members of a speech community to develop very similar versions of these particular knowledge structures. There exist within psychology a number of approaches to the study and description of such knowledge structures; any theory of knowledge that accomplishes the tasks described in this chapter would serve the purposes of my semantic theory. Although I am not a psychologist and am not in the position of being able to determine the best such theory, my characterization of relevant knowledge structures has to be cast in some sort of terms, and so I have chosen Piagetian-type schemas for this purpose. In the context of the psychological theory I know, the Piagetian approach seems most directly and clearly (and convincingly) to describe the kinds of learning and knowing processes that I see the semantic theory requiring. My reasons for preferring the Piagetian type of schema are explained in the appendix.[15]

If we ground our discussion in a Piagetian framework, then functional relations among signs refer to the Piagetian schemas, by means of which the presumed referents of the various relevant terms are understood (or presumed) to interact. That is, these schemas (which we might call defining functional schemas) represent cultural knowledge (or suppositions) about how the entities prototypically referred to by signs' signifieds are presumed to interact. In the conversational use of words (whether regarding the speaker's decision concerning which term might best label some action or entity, or regarding the hearer's decision concerning the most likely intended referent of the linguistic expression in question), the interactions entailed by the schemas can be compared with observed interactions in the phenomenal world to which the terms are being applied, or with other knowledge regarding the entities at issue (deductions, presuppositions, beliefs, imaginings, etc.), depending on the nature and topics of the discourse. The goal of the comparison is a first plausible fit that can then quickly be tested against the rest of the conversation (see the famous example in Lashley 1951:513); the goal is not some maximally ideal fit, nor the exercise in logic that would be required for such maximization. The functional schemas within a set of signs (or the paradigm of kernel referents of that set), then, form a kind of template that can in turn be compared with sets of things in the nonlinguistic world—whether the "things" be natural things, cultural things, substantial things, or things of the imagination, and whether they be objects, actions, or attitudes.[16]

I want in particular to draw attention to the difference between the paradigmatic formal/semantic relations of contrast and inclusion, by which signs are related to one another in language,[17] and the functional schemas by which the referents of the signs in question are presumed to interact in the phenomenal world.[18] Such functional schemas embrace, for example, all the kinds of relations discussed by Frake (1964) regarding "Notes on Queries . . . ," such as what something is used for, what it is made out of, who uses it, and so forth. From our present perspective, we can see Frake's methodological discussion (1964) as addressing ways of eliciting the functional relations among segregates (that is, signifieds) in a language—as opposed to the formal relations of inclusion and contrast that he discussed in his earlier "Ethnographic Study of Cognitive Systems" (1962). A failure to make (and be clear about) the distinction between formal and functional relationships has led to some muddiness and occasional confusion in the anthropological literature concerning linguistic structures and related cognitive structures (as in Quinn 1982:775). See Colby, Fernandez, and Kronenfeld 1981:428–429 for my own contribution to the muddiness. See Dougherty and Keller 1982 for an illustration of the problem produced by the confusion; their clear delineation of the issues contributed importantly to my current understanding.

Signifieds participate in linguistic knowledge structures (that is, schemas embodying the functional relations among signifieds—the functional schemas referred to in the preceding paragraph), which, in turn, outside of language, link to pragmatic knowledge structures (schemas about the world—what we might for now call "world schemas"). "Linguistic schemas" concern the relation of signifieds to one another. They include our folk definitions (what makes something properly an X), our knowledge of why Xs are distinguished from other related or similar things, and our expectations regarding what X should do, be, and so forth. "World schemas" refer to our representations or conceptualizations of things in the world outside of the linguistic forms we are using—what we know of the "what" that is being talked about. They represent our knowledge of what we are talking about,[19] regardless of whether that knowledge has come through linguistically coded forms, from direct experience, or through some nonlinguistic coding.

We can see the relationship between the present discussion of schemas and the basic units of the theory by recasting our characterization of "core," "denotative extension," and "connotation extension" in terms of these functional schemas. The link between the linguistic schema that includes the signified face of a sign and the relevant world schema that includes the referent we are using the sign to label represents coreness if the world schema essentially matches the linguistic schema. The link represents denotative extension if the world schema fits our definition (what we say an X is), but is in some other way significantly divergent from the linguistic schema. The link represents connotation if the world schema fits our sense of what X does or of why X is distinguished, but is in some other way significantly divergent from the linguistic schema. If the world schema fits neither our definition of X nor our sense of what X actually does nor why X is distinguished, but if some aspect of the relationship between X and opposed entities in the linguistic schema matches some set of relations in the world schema, then the link is a metaphoric one.

In effect, my theory embodies a claim that our understanding of conversations or discourse is not based narrowly on only the literal attributes of the words used nor only on the claims explicitly made, but instead is based on the schemas—richly filled-in constructions in the Piagetian sense—of possible situations (that is, things and actions we can talk about) that our language and culture provide for us, which our linguistic signs evoke (situations of the sort described, for example, by Langacker 1987), and which must be shared (and are known or presumed to be shared; see D'Andrade 1987:112–113) in order for communication to take place. That is, we do not simply interpret (and reason from) the literal semantic attributes, narrowly inferred, of the words we hear or read, but we instead interpret (and reason from) the schemas they evoke. My semantic theory explains part of how these schemas are constructed by individuals and shared among them. It does so by describing the role of core exemplars, the selection of core exemplars, and the process by which core exemplars and paradigmatic relations among core exemplars are used—in the context provided by the conversational situation and by the topic of the conversation—to flesh out in regular and understandable ways the picture evoked by the words themselves (and by our cultural associations with these pictures). In elaborating this role for schemas in the semantic theory I am asserting that words, as used in ordinary natural language, cannot be understood through any more simple or direct way, that is, by direct use of defining features or reference relations.

Some Remaining Questions

As the theory stands, there are several processes involved in the development of semantic categories that require further attention. First, I want to explore more fully the process by which classes of things (whether physical or mental) come to be the referents of new signs. That is, I want a better understanding of how something "function[s] importantly enough and frequently enough to acquire and maintain [its] own label[]." Our distinguishing of Saussure's "signified"—the concept within the sign the "signifier" (or sound image) isolates and to which it, in a sense, refers—from the referents of the sign, the classes of things (whether physical or mental) in the world to which the sign points within the context of langue, will be important here.

Additionally, the theory needs further development regarding the process by which focal exemplars come to be singled out by a person learning a language from the fuller class of things to which the sign points and to be understood as such (especially considering the social and passive nature of langue). Similarly, further development is needed regarding the process by which signs (and their respective signifieds) are linked into particular paradigmatic sets, the process by which a particular set of defining features is abstracted from the focal exemplars of a sign, and the related process by which relevant functional oppositions are defined within a paradigm. For all of these processes it is important to better understand the interlinked but sometimes opposed roles played, on the one hand, by the specific, actual structure of the universe of referents itself and, on the other hand, by the structuring effects of the interaction of cognitive processes and cognitive limitations with the frequency and nature of usage—as represented, in part, by our three explanatory principles (conjunctivity, marking, and information processing constraints).

Notes

1. The following briefly outlines some of the basic factors that appear to make various senses of a word more or less basic to native speakers of a language, and which thereby shape the definition or determination of coreness.

    A. Developmental factors: Learning order, the order in which various referents are encountered; but this order can vary from individual to individual or from time to time.

    B. Cognitive factors: Basic vs. extended senses that are learned in some order by adult speakers or inferred in some order by adult speakers from relations among forms or usage; but this order can vary from individual to individual or from time to time (even for a single given individual).

    C. Historical: The actual historical facts may be fixed but can be cognitively irrelevant as awareness of the connections is lost.

       i. In terms of the history of the language, as senses of a word grow apart, the effects on coreness of relations among such senses can be lost—for example, for words such as "base" or "mean":

         —"base [vs. noble] metal" in relation to "home base" or "military base"

         —"meanie" as in "mean person" (cruel and nasty < ungenteel < low), from "mean and sure estate" (mean as low/at the bottom < average [vs. exceptional])

       ii. In terms of the life history of the individual, the order in which senses are learned: for example,

        the above senses of "mean," seem

        —first to be learned as unrelated synonyms;

        —and then some speakers later learn the ways in which the different senses are related to one another;

        —and only later still do some of them learn the historical core/extension relations among the senses.

       And, for example, with the senses of "cup"

        —first, again, the separate senses seem learned as unrelated synonyms,

        —then "paper cup" seems to be pulled out as basic,

        —then later the ceramic teacup comes to be recognized as basic.

D.   False etymologies can provide some insight into cognitive senses of words. Such pseudo history can give more insight into cognitive processes than real history because there exists only one likely explanation of the false etymology (the pull of cognitive pattern), while real etymologies may only be historically real without having any cognitive reality. Consider "filly"—it feels French (cf. "*fille*"), but has a true-blue Old English history.

2. Miller 1978 discusses the form/function contrast and its relationship to semantic extension in terms not unrelated to the present usage. Friedrich (1970:6–8) introduces a denotative/connotative distinction that is similar to mine, although with some significant differences.

3. For some people my age with experience somewhat comparable to mine, the replacement of fountain pens with ballpoints has been total enough and long-lived enough to have caused their core exemplar for the pen category to shift from the former to the latter. My point is only that such shifts do require massive and long-lived shifts in experience—and thus that it is harder to shift an existing core than to form a new one.

4. Kronenfeld and Decker (1979:508) discussed Saussure's fiction of synchronic stasis as follows:

It should also be pointed out that Saussure was aware that the synchronic stasis between moves was a fictional construct abstracted from a continuing process of change ([Saussure 1959:]101–2) which was only approximated ([Greenberg 1970:]347). This working fiction could only be avoided after the distinction between *langue* and *parole*, and the process by which regularities in *parole* gradually came to be incorporated as changes in *langue*, were well understood (cf. [Greenberg 1978]). That a language over time represented a succession of frozen states and that changes between states were instantaneous (as in the chess analogy) was the major aspect of Saussure's *Course* that troubled Meillet in his review of the Course ([Meillet 1916]).

It is the fact that speakers act as if there is a single, shared *system* that made Saussure's fiction so important and useful. And it was Saussure's grasp of the importance of this synchronic system (see also Saussure 1959:77–78), which explains his importance for subsequent linguistic theory; Meillet appeared to lack Saussure's awareness of the ways in which langue was a system. In this sense, Saussure's insight seems deeper than that of Meillet, his former student.

5. This use of "really" is similar to Kay's "technically" hedge (1987:73–74). I do want to raise the possibility that "technically," as a hedge, might have more to do with precise, narrow meanings in the speaker's knowledge (i.e., my denotative form definitions) that with reference to some outside expertise (as Kay suggests).

6. "We," here, refers to Armstrong, Wilmoth, and me—in the context of our cups-and-glasses research.

7. Although I have been speaking of contrast sets, and thus explicitly of terms related only by contrast (or opposition), I do want to point out that relations of inclusion do indirectly become relevant—especially via oppositions between marked and unmarked terms. Thus, in my usage, "magazine" contrasts with "book" and includes "periodical"; but under the general sense of "magazine," "periodical" (as a kind of magazine that contains materials presumed not to be of only passing interest) contrasts with another, more specific sense of "magazine" (containing material presumed to be ephemeral).

Marked categories, such as "bull," relate (at least often) to their unmarked counterparts such as "cow," simultaneously, through both contrast ("No, Johnny, that's not a cow, it's a bull") and inclusion ("Yes, Johnny, that's a cow; it's a bull"). This duality, in which "cow" in one sense (as our folk term for the species) includes "bull" as a male "cow," but in another sense (as an explicitly female one) contrasts with "bull," is what Greenberg (1966:26) speaks of as the ambiguous nature of the unmarked category.

"Periodical" thus is a marked (for nonephemerality) category, versus the unmarked "magazine" (which can be ephemeral or not, but which in the absence of specific information to the contrary is presumed to be ephemeral).

8. "Paperbacks" are a marked category vis-a-vis the unmarked "books" category in the same way "periodicals" are relative to "magazines."

9. Keller and Lehman 1991:276 make a similar observation, but tie it to the "classical distinction between literal and figurative meaning." I see "department head" as figurative, but I am less sure about the "table of random numbers." The table of random numbers still seems to me, though, to represent a case of polysemy rather than homonymy because, while its psychological *dependency* on ordinary tables has been lost, there remains some native-speaker sense that the two usages are related.

10. The role of such paradigmatic relations in semantic extension was pointed to by Friedrich in his discussion of his version of connotative extension (1970:8).

11. A wry cultural variant, and commentary, was introduced in the early sixties by changing the line to "Today I am a cuff link . . . ." The wryness was that, as luxury items went, fountain pens had at least better associations than the cuff links that had begun to replace them: better (to some of us future academics) conspicuous consumption of a symbol of learning than of a symbol of the business or professional world in which cuff links were useful.

12. This elision and simplification seems the same as the process by which pidgin grammars are constructed—that is, through a process in which content words (such as, for a hypothetical example, terms such as "tomorrow" or "many") become elided into grammatical particles (signaling, in the case of our hypothetical example, future action or plurality).

13. It seems possible that, had calculators not already emerged and preempted the "calculator" signifier, computers might have been called "calculators" since (from the naive user's perspective, if not from the perspective of the engineers who design them and their languages) they do more that simply compute, and since the verb "to calculate" has a somewhat broader sense than does "to compute."

14. Miller's (1978:313) distinction between a person's practical and lexical knowledge is relevant to our present distinction, but not identical to it. Part of the difference has to do with the fact that in the present theory functional relationships are among signifieds—and thus are distinct from nonlinguistic knowledge of the world.

15. I want to reiterate, however, that I am neither offering nor logically relying on nor making a psychological case for one particular theory of the structuring of knowledge versus another. My theory does *not* depend on Piagetian schemas versus some other kind of knowledge structure. It does, though, assuredly assert and thus depend on the kinds of knowledge described and on our ability to use that knowledge in the ways described. That is, my theory takes such structured knowledge as a given and then explores the reasoning by which we relate words to that knowledge and use words to address it.

16. The knowledge included in our internal representations of the paradigmatic relations among signifieds and their core referents within a contrast set and of the functional relations those referents enter into allows us to "recognize" extended referents as instances of terms from the set. That is, we do not apply some abstract definition of the term to the thing we are trying to label, and we do not systematically detail the features of this thing. Instead we match the template implicit in our representation of the set of signifieds with our picture of the thing and what it relates to in context, and then we pick the best match as the label or term to apply to the thing. That is, we leap from the minimal set of clues that, *in context*, seem to allow for a reasonable interpretation—this, for example, can be seen in our responses to optical illusions, as examined within gestalt psychology (for the theory, see, for example, Koffka 1935, Köhler 1947; for specific illustrations see Attneave 1971): all at once we see a picture (that is, recognize it) and we interpret everything in the stimulus as congruent with the picture (that is, there exist no "mixed" pictures), wherein potentially

divergent elements are seen as indicating variations or details of the basic theme and not as negative or disconfirming evidence.

From another anthropological perspective on perception and knowledge, see Ohnuki-Tierney pp. 455–458, Gombrich, *Art and Illusion* (1960—p. 64, which Ohnuki-Tierney cites, but also the whole section, titled "Truth and the Stereotype" from which the quote comes), and Bartlett (1932), on which Gombrich draws (see Gombrich 1960:74).

For some different cognitive science views of how recognition works and how it relates to "direct perception," see the discussion of Gibsonian "affordances," on the one side by Vera and Simon (1993:41), and on the other by Greeno and Moore (1993:51–52, drawing on papers of Neisser's). Since my semantic theory deals particularly with explicit categories in a symbol system, the cognitive science debate does not affect our argument; by either side's view, our recognition of the referents of linguistic signs works more or less the same way.

Relevant here is the issue of "conscious awareness." In addition to the knowledge that we consciously know and self-consciously apply, there presumably exists knowledge that we have (e.g., of how to carry out some activity such as, for many of us, using our body language to keep somebody talking) but which we are unaware of having and unaware of using (when we apply it). Miller's discussion of "chunking" (1956:293–295) suggests that there exists yet other knowledge that we have learned self-consciously and, thus, have been aware of, but which subsequent to learning we automated and thereby pushed into subconsciousness (cf. Vera and Simon 1993:18–21). Much of our semantic knowledge—like our knowledge of how to manipulate the brake and clutch while driving a car with a manual transmission—seems to be in the latter category. Such knowledge normally is exercised by us without our awareness, but can be raised to consciousness when abnormal conditions arise (such as using the motor to brake the car, or dealing with a skid). In a sense, we seem to use our conscious attention for making decisions and for analyzing problems; mental activities that are automatic (here, automated)— such as orchestrating the brake and clutch while coming to a stop at a stop sign—appear to work more smoothly and faster if they are carried out without our conscious intervention.

My suggestion would be that the knowledge we use in recognizing the referents of signs is of this "chunked" kind, which can be raised to consciousness.

17. As Hutchins shows (1980:19–42), the traditional ethnoscience classifications and information structures do have their uses (i.e., showing the categorical relations that his informants are reasoning with), even in contemporary cognitive presentations.

18. The distinction between formal and functional relations I am making here is similar to Keller and Lehman's (1991:289) distinction between "formal specification" and "conceptual embedding" as "the two facets of concept definition." But see Keller and Lehman (1993:88), where they seem to opt more exclusively for something like my functional relations.

19. The key point is that "schemas about the world," in referring to what we are talking about, are functionally or situationally defined. Thus, in the extreme recursive case "what we are talking about" can be the very linguistic schemas we use to talk about the world—as is the case for the present text.

V

EXTENDED APPLICATIONS

Having described the theory and illustrated its operation with a variety of local examples, I would now like to offer some more extended applications—involving first the mundane domain of cups and glasses, and then more problematic domains that include political and religious oppositions, domestic task allocation, and ethnic groupings. In these examples we will see how the theory applies to a domain and how it helps us understand what appear otherwise to be anomalous facts about the domain.

11

Examples

Drinking Vessel Study

For my first example of a systematic application of the theory to a cultural domain, I would like to explore the domain of "cups" and "glasses" in English, and to compare it with similar domains in Hebrew and Japanese. This study was carried out and described in cooperation with James D. Armstrong and Stan Wilmoth, who were also coauthors of the paper (Kronenfeld, Armstrong, and Wilmoth 1985) from which this discussion is drawn. Uses of the pronoun "we" that do not obviously refer to the author and reader together refer to my coworkers and myself.

Framework

Our experimental design was set up to compare our extensionist view with three alternative idealized views of language/thought relations, and to allow us to then evaluate how well our data accorded with these various views.

First, according to a strong Whorfian view, language determines perception. The structure of similarity relations among verbal categories should vary from one language community to the next, and there should be a simple, direct relationship between people's verbal categories and their structuring of relations among the objects to which the words refer. Therefore, the structure of similarity relations among actual objects should differ from one language community to the next in ways that parallel the ways the structure of similarity relations among verbal categories differ among these communities.

Second, according to a strongly pragmatic theory, language directly reflects the way objects are substantively dealt with. A simple, direct relationship should occur between structuring sets of actual objects and structuring the verbal categories into which they fall. Therefore, the structure of similarity relations among verbal categories should be similar from one language community to the next.

Third, according to the traditional version of the nonisomorphism position—a kind of "neo-Harrisian"[1] view—people are expected to deal directly with actual objects on the basis of their functional characteristics (which, in our drinking vessel domain, are more or less uniform across languages). In such a view language would have no particular relationship to objective functional categorizations. In this case, one should expect the structuring of similarity relations among actual objects to be similar across languages, while one should expect the structuring of similarity relations among verbal categories to differ from language to language. It follows that there should be no overall similarity from one language to the next in the assignment of objects to verbal categories.

The theory on which this chapter is based uses the distinction between core and extended referents of labels to establish a *limited* isomorphism between the universe of referents and the universe of the verbal categories that refer to the referents. The limitation is that the isomorphism applies *only* to core referents and *not* to extended ones. In a domain such as the one under consideration, we expect similarity relations among verbal categories to parallel those that obtain among the functionally relevant aspects of the actual objects—but only for those objects that represent core referents. Since the objects in our present domain function similarly across the cultures and languages we are considering, we expect similarity relations among verbal categories to be similar for these languages. The three language communities do differ, however, in their histories of contact with the actual objects under discussion and in the sources from which they took their signs, and so we do allow for the possibility of significant differences among the languages in their patterns of extension—that is, in their assignment of (noncore) objects to categories.

Design

Native speakers of Hebrew, English, and Japanese were interviewed about the labels they apply to a collection of objects we call drinking vessels in English.[2] The interviews were conducted in the language of the speaker for the Hebrew and English groups, and in English with the aid of an interpreter for the Japanese group. Twenty-three university students, ranging in age from their early twenties to early forties, served as the English-speaking informants. Ten native-born Israelis served as the Hebrew-speaking informants. Twenty-one Japanese students were drawn from the English as a Second Language (ESL) program at the University of California at Riverside. The Israelis ranged in age from twenty-five to forty, while the Japanese were all in their early twenties. Approximately the same number of females and males were interviewed.

The set of objects contained thirty-five items for Japanese and English-speaking informants. Because the interviews in Hebrew were conducted in the field, a smaller subset of objects was used. With the help of two Israeli informants in the United States, this subset of eleven items had been chosen to provide a set of objects that included a comparable range of both core items and extended referents.

Initially, the subjects were asked, in a general, discursive way, to label each item in our collection of drinking vessels and to discuss the relation among the objects, their labels, and so forth. The set of objects comprised cups, mugs, and glasses varying in size, shape, material, and use. These interviews were intended to determine the range of terms applied to "drinking vessels" in the various languages, to explore the structure of the domain of the labels applied to these objects, and to identify core or prototypical objects in the set.

Subsequently, the informants sorted the collection of objects into groups based on inter-item similarity. After performing the sorting task, the informants were asked to describe the attributes of the objects that determined inclusion in any given subgroup.

The next task in our research was to have the informants sort a set of words referring to drinking vessels like those in our set of objects into groups based on the similarity inherent in the meaning of the words. The two sorting tasks are the basis for our multidimensional scaling (MDS) plots, which provide a means for comparing similarity relations among objects with similarity relations among verbal categories as well as for comparing each kind of relation across the languages.

The final task was to investigate the labeling of the objects. In this phase we asked our informants to classify the set of "drinking vessels" into groups based on the major category labels determined in the exploratory sessions (i.e., "cups" and "glasses" in English; "koppu," "kappu," and "gurasu" in Japanese; and "cosot" and "sefalim" in Hebrew). For example, the English-speaking informants were instructed to sort all the items in the collection into one group of things called "glasses" and another group of things called "cups." The informants had the option of excluding items from member-ship in the specific categories mentioned for each language. No informant participated in more than one task during any given interviewing session.

Results

The data from the object-sort task for speakers of each language were used to calculate pairwise similarity matrices that were then used for multidimensional scaling. The MDS plots show us how the different language communities structured the domain and provide us with a means of evaluating differences among them (see Figures 11-1, 11-2, and 11-3). We found a high degree of interlanguage-community similarity. The plots for each group of informants identify three clusters of objects: cups, glasses, and disposables (objects made of nontraditional material). The Japanese speakers have tighter clusters for each of the three subsets than have the English or Hebrew speakers. Both English and Hebrew speakers place the handled paper cup somewhere between the clusters of disposables and cups, while the Japanese include this item with other paper cups. English speakers place the nondisposable plastic cup (called "tumbler" in the figures) between glasses and disposable cups. Calculating Pearson's *R* on the interpoint distances gives a rough measure of interplot congruence. *R*s ranging from .81 to .89 indicate a high degree of congruence among the three plots.

Discussion

Our preliminary interviews suggested there were important and interesting differences among the languages in their verbal segmentation of the domain. Subconsciously assuming language/thought isomorphism, we had naively expected the MDS analysis of object-object similarities to produce greater interlanguage-group differences than appear in figures 11-1 to 11-3. But we found, as Kronenfeld had already found for Fanti kinship, that informants are perfectly capable of thinking about objects with only a minimum of interference from linguistic categories.

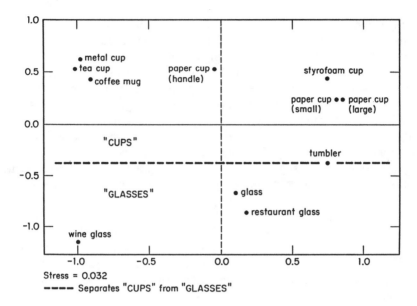

FIG. 11-1 Two Dimensional MDS Plot from object sort for drinking vessels by English speaking informants

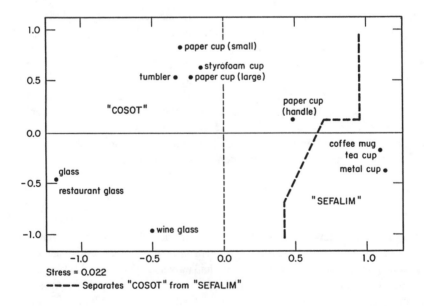

FIG. 11-2 Two Dimensional MDS Plot of Similarity Data from object sort for drinking vessels by Hebrew speaking informants.

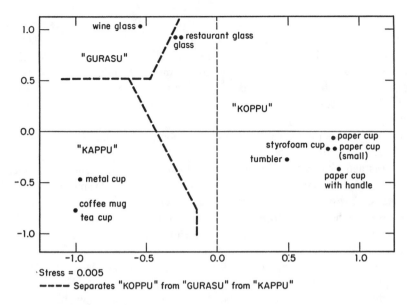

FIG. 11-3 Two Dimensional MDS Plot of Similarity Data from object sort for drinking vessels by Japanese informants

While conducting this research in Israel, the sharp differences between what is tapped by the sorting tasks and what is tapped by the object-label assignment task were driven home to Armstrong. His Israeli informants professed not to understand how there could be any differences between Americans and Israelis in the verbal classification of the items. In order to demonstrate to his informants the great variation between the linguistic categorizations of the two languages, Armstrong had an American partition the set of objects into "cups" and "glasses." Even though the prototypic "cup" in English was the same as the prototypic "sefel" in Hebrew (and the two terms were thus reasonable translation equivalents), nonprototypic items were classified quite differently. The American classified all things called "cup" in English together (paper cup, mug, plastic cup, tea cup, etc.), producing a group that made little sense to the Israelis. In contrast, Israelis classified a number of objects that in English are extended referents from cup (paper cup, mug, plastic cup, etc.) with the Hebrew equivalent of the English "glass" (*cos*) in Hebrew.

By combining the data from our initial interviews with the data from the labeling task, we are able to describe the drinking vessel domains for each language. In English this domain is divided into two subgroups, one based on the core concept of cup-ness and the other on the core concept of glass-ness. The concept of cup-ness predominantly involves a squat hemispherical shape, but includes opaque material and a handle, and typically implies use for hot drinks. The concept of glass-ness focuses on the material—glass—but also involves a tall cylindrical shape without a handle, and typically implies use for cold drinks.

In Hebrew the entire drinking vessel domain is referred to as *cosot*. The item identified as the core "cos" by Israelis is the same item identified by English speakers as the core "glass." However, the salient attribute(s) determining coreness are not the same. Whereas the overriding determinant for glass-ness in English is material, in Hebrew it is cylindrical shape. The Israelis have a subgroup of *cosot* called *sefalim*, which are the equivalent of our "real" cups and mugs. In this Hebrew case coreness is determined by the attributes that mark a particular function (e.g., a handle for insulation, in the case of cups). In the same way that a mug is a kind of cup in English, a sefal is a kind of cos in Hebrew.

In Japanese the domain is segmented into three subgroups: *kappu*, *gurasu* and *koppu*. The core *kappu* is the same item as the core *cup* for Americans and the core *sefal* for Israelis; it is defined by the same attributes as cups and sefalim, although the Japanese place more emphasis on the presence of handles than do speakers of the other languages. *Gurasu* are noncylindrical, usually stemmed objects made of glass. The core *gurasu* is best exemplified by what we would call a "brandy snifter" in our collection of drinking vessels. The most salient attribute for this group is shape. *Koppu* is the category of drinking vessels containing all the items made of nontraditional materials; their most salient attribute is cylindrical shape. The Japanese identified a nondisposable plastic cup as the core item for this group.

By distinguishing core from extended referents and by distinguishing form from function attributes, our theory allows us to deal with some situations in which either objects or subcategories are seen as ambiguous regarding their membership in one or the other of two opposed categories, but are not perceived as simply being on some gradient between the two categories. In so doing, our theory makes sense of certain common informant responses that other theories (e.g., componential analysis or category grading) seem unable to handle. For instance, many Americans will say that a nondisposable plastic item shaped like a glass is "really" a "cup," even though it seems to them more like a "glass." For these people this item shares with the cup category the particular form-class attribute—namely nonglass, opaque material—that is essential in English to the distinction between cup and glass, even though this item is far removed from the core *cup*. Hence it is denotatively an extended "cup." However, the object's function (for cold drinks), as well as several salient but noncriterial form attributes such as shape and durability, pull the object moderately close to the core "glass" (for which category both informant behavior and statements showed material to be the criterial attribute). This proximity to "glass," especially regarding function, accounts for the connotative extension of the "glass" term to the object and also for people's strong feelings that it ought to be a "glass."

Other American informants place the glass-like plastic object clearly in the *glass* category by reducing the special criteriality of material as opposed to shape or durability. Historically, the movement seems to be in the direction of this shift in criteriality—we think in response to the strong functional pull of the glass category in conjunction with the relative increase in the use of plastic glass-like objects. We suspect that once the drinking glass category is generally uncoupled from the glass as a material, the core referent of the category will rapidly shift to a plastic object in response to the relative frequency with which people encounter the two.

In Japanese we found a similar example of structural ambiguity. Cylindrically shaped objects made of glass were called "koppu" by some informants and "gurasu" by others. These items possess the material that determines inclusion in the *gurasu* subset and the shape and function central to the *koppu* subset, and are therefore ambiguous. Slightly more than 50 percent of the Japanese informants labeled such items "koppu," and the remainder called them "gurasu." Another example of an ambiguous object (from Japanese) is the handled paper cup, which possesses attributes from both the *koppu* and *kappu* subgrouping. Slightly more than 50 percent of the informants classed this object with the *kappu*.[3]

Our theory indicates that a handled paper cup should be ambiguous for Israelis, since it possesses salient attributes from both the *cosot* and *sefalim* subcategories. As with plastic cup in English, the form attributes of this object tend to push it in one direction (i.e., toward *cos*), while functional attributes tend to push it toward another (i.e., toward *sefel*). However, all the Israelis interviewed said this item was a kind of *cos*, and only one informant said that it might be called a *sefel*. The reason for the absence of ambiguity in this case reveals something more about the nature of function in our theory. Function is seen not simply to be a matter of the kind of use but also to involve experience, which depends on frequency of use. Paper drinking vessels have never been commonly used in Israel, and only recently have disposable plastic drinking vessels been introduced. In Hebrew there were no ambiguous items, because the domain structure of the language and history combine to preclude this possibility.

Blackfeet "Full Bloods" versus "Mixed Bloods"

Having outlined the theory using a relatively concrete domain as an example, I would now like to turn to three more abstract domains. My major goal in these examples is to show how some problems of conflicting usage—that is, situations in which different people seem to be using the same term(s) to apply to opposed conditions, or in which different terms seem to be used for identical conditions—can be resolved with the aid of a semantic theory such as that which I am proposing. Within the theory, I want to focus on the ways in which several aspects of the semantic structure guide how we think about the entieties being labeled. These aspects include paradigmatic or componential relations among core referents within a contrast set, the inclusion of contrast sets under individual terms (or categories) at next higher levels of contrast, and marking relations among members of contrast sets. I want, in particular, to show how conclusions that are not strictly logically entailed by the explicitly posited entities (in some particular discourse), or by explicit attributes of these entities, can be strongly implied by the semantic structure of the domain to which the entities belong. In particular, such implications follow if we assume the following: (1) that the given contrast set (to which the words used to refer to the entities belong) exhausts (or partitions) the relevant universe; (2) that (for purposes of deduction and extrapolation) the entities possess all the attributes of the core exemplars of the words used to refer to them (except for those explicitly denied); and (3) that the choice by speakers of words (and contrast sets) used to refer to the entities serves to foreground the attributes that are at issue in the discussion of those entities.

For my first example of a more abstract domain I would like to examine Blackfeet Indian uses of the concepts (or ideas of) "full blood" and "mixed blood" in tribal political discourse. This discussion is drawn from work by Doctor Stan Wilmoth

(1987), but includes a fair amount of interpretive explication by me—for any inaccuracies in which Wilmoth should not be blamed.

I want especially to explore the nature of core exemplars of the terms in question, the nature and implications of the contrast sets in which they participate, the relationship of these contrast sets to the terms at the next higher levels of inclusion (which include them), and the strands of reasoning foregrounded and made to seem obvious by this semantic structure. The kind of reasoning I am referring to is that exemplified in chapter 10 in my discussion of the senses in which the term "father" can be and is taken.

In particular, our problem concerns the apparently frequent free-floating usage by Blackfeet of the terms "full blood" and "mixed blood," while the terms nonetheless are used in Blackfeet political debate as if they label very obvious and concrete differences in values and position. By "free-floating usage" I mean that a given person may be spoken of as a full blood in one context and as a mixed blood in another—without any (apparent) assertion that he has changed either his ancestry or his political alignment in the interim. Similarly, I mean that a particular political position can, on one occasion, be addressed as a full-blood position, but on another occasion be considered a mixed-blood one. The problem is not simply that the Blackfeet people use the terms inconsistently—after all, were it the case that they either did not know what they were talking about or did not care, then we would have an interesting ethnographic situation but hardly an interesting semantic problem. Rather, it is that they use the terms to label politically (and thus cognitively) important distinctions, and that they seem to have no trouble understanding what is meant or referred to in the usage I have described in spite of its apparent inconsistencies and in spite of disagreements about specific usages. In other words, a semantic theory that is to account for their linguistic behavior here must allow for flexibility of reference—but in some sort of interpretative framework that allows the flexibility to be easily understood or decoded. The extensionist theory I am developing, by referring understanding and interpretation to core referents or exemplars, and by utilizing consistent rules of extension of terms, in context, to noncore referents, easily and straightforwardly accounts for such usage in a way that other semantic theories do not. What is at issue is not the mere presence of cores as kinds of Platonic essences, but the ways in which cores are defined, the ways in which relations among cores foreground particular topics, and the ways in which categories are extended out from the cores.

An important semantic, as well as sociopolitical, context for the concepts "full blood" and "mixed blood" is provided by the basic framing contrast between "Indian" and "white"—that is, by the contrast set involving the item (Indian) that includes them. In the universe we are considering (the white-controlled world in the United States, where Indians exist in relation to whites), white-ness is the unmarked category, the conceptual default that applies to people not otherwise marked for another category. Indian-ness is implicitly defined as a marked contrastive category, and hence relevant attributes or gradations of Indian-ness pertain primarily to locations along an Indian-white continuum. More specific concepts, such as "Blackfeet," while very important to Blackfeet people and maybe to anthropologists, lose their specific ethnic significance (for whites, and, perhaps to a lesser degree, for Blackfeet as well), and become almost synonymous with "Indian" in this wider racial/political linguistic context—

even though there exist particular political and economic situations where being Blackfeet versus some other kind of Indian becomes quite important. Thus, in our Blackfeet context, the unmarked Indian is Blackfeet, and core Indian is normally understood as core Blackfeet. The basic role of the Indian versus white polarity means that not-Indian automatically entails white-ness. The primacy of that opposition means that not being Blackfeet similarly entails being White rather than being some other kind of Indian.[4] Both the Indian-white polarity and that of full blood versus mixed blood can be used to frame more or less continuous gradations—in the sense that being "less" Indian entails being "more" white, and so forth.

The notion of biological ancestry, as measured by "blood," was introduced as an indicator of degree of Indian-ness by the U.S. government as a way of allocating the various (alleged) rights, privileges, and benefits that were provided to Indian groups in response to their loss of land and freedom, and to their position as wards of the U.S. government.

The term "blood quantum" was introduced by whites as a measure of someone's percentage of Indian ancestry. "Full blood" originally referred to totally Indian ancestry, and thereby to full entitlement to all benefits (and restrictions) that pertained to Indians; more particularly, "full-blood Blackfeet" referred to total Blackfeet ancestry and entailed full rights in official Blackfeet tribal political and economic activities. "Mixed blood" referred to mixed ancestry, and entailed partial rights or fractional benefits. The basic polarity remains one of degrees of Indian-ness (specifically, of full versus partial), even though the technical definitions of the categories (what percentage defines "full"; how relevant the difference between Blackfeet and any other Indian blood is) have varied over time (in response to changed conditions) and across situations (according to who was doing the defining for what purposes). The conditions that have occasioned these shifts, while interesting and relevant, are beyond the scope of the present discussion.

Using blood quantum in this manner as a measure of legitimacy and an index to rights led to the use of the word "blood" as a marker of genuineness. "Full blood," then, connotes a "real" Indian—as opposed to "mixed blood," which connotes an attenuated or compromised Indian-ness.

Ancestry, at least to the whites who designed the blood quantum system, referred to "racial" characteristics. Full bloods, most marked as Indians conceptually, were also, in principal, marked physically. The less white one looked, the more Indian (by implication) one must look, and so dark ("red" to Whites, though not to Blackfeet) skin and dark (straight) hair become attributes of Indian versus white, and hence of full blood versus mixed, identity. The conceptual opposition between full blood and mixed blood can be used in an extended sense in reference to these supposedly ancestral features, even in the absence of the denotatively defining information. The biological (here, genetic) versus cultural (ranging from time spent in the sun to style of dress) aspects of appearance are often not clearly distinguished by non-anthropologists (both because of confusion concerning their basis and because of the feeling that what you get from your parents is "ancestral" regardless of whether you were born with it or have learned it). It is not surprising that extension of the full-blood versus mixed-blood opposition on the basis of appearance should stretch to include, as bases, attributes such as clothing and grooming style—and maybe more general features of life-style as well.

Another kind of very important, but nonbiological, ancestry is represented by language. The language one speaks is important as a symbolic marker, both because of its salience and ease and clarity of recognition, and because it cannot be as casually acquired as can clothing or style. Furthermore, native-speaker fluency (especially in a minority language) is tied up closely enough with growing up in the relevant speech community—a cultural community that often is also relatively biologically homogeneous—for it to feel equivalent to biological ancestry to many Indians and non-Indians. Second-language fluency (in Blackfeet or English) represents an important enough commitment of time and effort, or an important enough period of intimate interaction, to have important identificational implications. The implications regarding cultural contact and interest of even second-language use are serious enough to cause a person in a full-blood context and/or seeking a full-blood identification to be very leery of using English; conversely, whites who use Blackfeet are understood to be asserting a strong pro-Indian stance.

Since Indian ancestry was used as a measure of Indian-ness (or, in our present case, of Blackfeet-ness), full bloods were thought of as more clearly and thoroughly Indian, and hence more traditional in their Indian ways. Mixed bloods, on the other hand, being of mixed (Indian-white) ancestry, were seen as culturally mixed, and hence more assimilated or acculturated to white society.

Thus, the full-blood versus mixed-blood contrast connotes traditional Indian versus assimilated Indian, and one simple and basic extension of the terms (and, therefore, of the contrast set in which they participate, including the implicit third—polar—term, white)[5] is to situations in which the terms are applied on the basis of these connotations, rather than on the denotative basis of literal biological ancestry. Such connotative extension is strongly tempting (and hence common and basic), because it makes the concepts more culturally relevant and useful than does the strict denotative criterion, and because it subtly (and perhaps subconsciously) undermines the authority of the externally created and applied definition of who is an Indian (or a Blackfeet). This first kind of culturally based extension of the conceptual opposition provides the basis for most other connotative usage.

In the area of politics, the "traditional Indian" end of the continuum refers most directly to traditional political forms, means of making collective decisions, and so forth. But, since these traditional Indian forms exist in contrast to a white norm of individualistic, "one man, one vote" expression of narrow self-interest, the Indian or full-blood side of the opposition can come (within Blackfeet political discourse) to connote communally motivated (or implemented) values or actions, in contrast to individual ones—even in a Plains Indian culture that greatly emphasizes individual experience. And, in the same context, "communal" action can contrast with "democratic" action, where the former is Indian or full blood and the latter white or mixed blood.

Since white culture is considered (by most whites and many Indians) to be more modern (technologically, but, by inference, often also politically and culturally), the idea of the traditional Indian is linked with the idea not just of cultural conservatism, but also with the more general sense of "conservative" that implies opposition to change, adaptation, and modernizing (that is, "conservative" as "stick-in-the-mud"). By this extension, full blood versus mixed blood can come to imply "opposed to" versus "supportive of" modernization (whether of political forms—for example, elected councils—or of economic ones—for example, newer forms of land management).

"Culturally conservative," in the context in which whites are associated with technological power, implies nontechnological and thus natural. Since being an Indian means (to both Indians and whites) having less technological control over nature, Indians are associated with the "natural" end of the natural versus man-made opposition. And hence "Indian" (and thus "full blood") comes to signify (or to be usable as a label for) a pro-nature or pro–unspoiled wilderness position, in opposition to "white" (or "mixed blood"), which signifies, in this context, techno-logical intervention.

Regarding specific economic or political issues, we now have several bases on which the full-blood versus mixed-blood opposition can be extended: (1) The mixed-blood label can be applied to those in favor of some innovative (or "progressive") technique or management scheme, as opposed to those (full bloods) who are pushing maintenance of "the traditional way." (2) The mixed-blood label can be applied to those who are supporting some program backed by whites, versus "full bloods" who oppose the program. "Whites" can refer either to local whites or to the white establishment—especially as embodied in the government. The Bureau of Indian Affairs, on the one hand, as an arm of the government, can be "white," but on the other hand, as the Indian representative in government and as the government agency itself most populated with Indians, it can be "Indian," especially in a context in which it is opposed to some other part of the white establishment. Thus, depending on context, backers of the BIA can thereby be labeled as either full bloods or mixed bloods.[6] 3) Any issue which is in fact backed by people generally known as full-blood leaders can become a full-blood issue; other people taking the same position can, then, by extension, be labeled as full bloods. Those taking the opposite position become, in this context, mixed bloods. The same applies, vice versa, for issues espoused by clearly recognized mixed-blood leaders.

In terms of the general idea of core versus extended concepts, we can say that a core Indian is a person of completely Indian biological ancestry who speaks an Indian language, and looks physically and dresses like an Indian. This core Indian espouses traditional Indian values, including respect for nature and respect for traditional Indian forms of leadership and collective action. This core Indian contrasts with a core white, who is of European descent and northern European appearance, who speaks English, is technologically adept and school educated, and who believes in individual desires and actions being impersonally amalgamated to produce collective action when necessary.

While the attributes summarized in the preceding paragraph are definitely not of equal weight, in general, the more of one or the other set of attributes a person possesses, the more unarguably and unnegotiably the person is presumed (in the context of reservation political discourse) to belong to one or the other opposed categories. On the other hand, in an appropriate context, any one of the attributes can put a person (on an ad hoc basis) in one or the other category—in opposition to other persons who have a contrasting attribute on the relevant feature. People who have attributes from both sets are freer to move back and forth between the two identities, but are seen as belonging less convincingly to either.

In terms of marking considerations, the unmarked, or default, person is a white—and so, in the absence of relevant information about a person, one presumes him or her to be white. If any particular relevant attribute is known (in the absence of others), an identification is made on that basis and core values appropriate to that identification are presumed.

In the context of the preceding white/Indian opposition, the category of Indians is subdivided into more or less Indian-y Indians, and is coded, dichotomously, as a full-blood versus mixed-blood opposition. The default category, of Indian-y Indians, is the full bloods. The mixed-blood category is defined by its contrast with (difference from) the full-blood one. But since white versus Indian is the context, and since Indian is defined, in a sense, as maximally non-white, non–Indian-y Indians can only differ from Indian-y ones in the direction of Whites, and so mixed bloods become relatively white-y Indians.[7]

Core full bloods, then, are core Indians. Core mixed bloods represent a more complicated notion. They are maximally white-like Indians who are nonetheless Indians. That is, they are Indians who have some white ancestry and a somewhat white appearance, who speak English, and who try to live like whites while claiming Indian-ness. Since Indians are a marked category distinguished racially (and hence by virtue of birth) from whites, and since they are in some ways a lower-status (or even stigmatized) group, there is a kind of residual presumption that they cannot actually become white and hence that even the most white-like of Indians will be only imperfectly white (or imperfectly accepted as white, by either whites or Indians). The mixed-blood core will therefore fall somewhere in between the Indian core and the White core.

As an in-between, "neither fish nor fowl" category, the mixed-blood category has the potential for denigration that impure categories seem always to risk. On the other hand, it carries the positive connotations evoked by the idea of "hybrid vigor," a kind of genetic metaphor perhaps made particularly salient (to us, at least) by the use of the "blood" descent idiom.

The core referents of a term (or concept) represent the truest members of the category, and are the presumed referents of any usage of the term in the absence of further specification or contextual information. Since the core referents are defined by (or implied by) some set of attributes, these attributes are presumed present in the absence of specification or implication otherwise. For example, a reference to an Indian (in the Blackfeet political context we have been considering) presumes a full blood with all the attributes of core full bloods (that is, ancestry, coloring, language, clothing, mode of making a living, etc.).

If some particular noncore attribute is mentioned—for example, an Indian person is mentioned as speaking English—the presumption is still that the remaining non-specified attributes of that person are core (that is, Indian, in our example)—with the exception of those implied by the specified attribute in context. If the Indian is described as dressed like a white and as being at a meeting with important government officials, then fluency in or use of English speech might also be inferred by members of the local universe.

The primary point of using the Blackfeet example is to illustrate how the framing opposition (Indian vs. white)—its definition, and the logic of its related conditions, joined with the way in which the subsidiary opposition between full blood and mixed blood was initially defined—closely constrains the ways in which the subsidiary (full-blood v. mixed-blood) opposition can be extended or taken. The core full blood has to rest on the core Indian, and the opposed concept has to differ in the direction of whiteness; the rest follows.

Various other attributes that signal full blood versus mixed have been discussed in this section. They function connotatively, marking someone as acting as if full or mixed in some given context, and providing a basis for the use of the "full" or "mixed" label to communicate or be understood in that context, even in the absence of the denotatively defining attributes. These connotative attributes are not defined by fiat, and are not learned as any kind of rote list, but rather are derived (in the manner illustrated earlier in this section) from the pattern of oppositions, the pragmatic givens, the communicative force of the opposition, and denotative definitions—as well as from the uses of political rhetoric.

The sets of oppositions that we are looking at here, unlike those involved in our cups and glasses, kinship, books, and pens examples, involve contrasted social identities or groups that are politically opposed to one another and which may each have a different perspective on the nature of the semantic contrast or the proper definition of its opposed concepts. Even so, the freedom of the opposed groups to define concepts as they might want is severely limited. The kind of communicative situation involved in our examples, in which the opposed groups are using the concepts/labels in question in their communications with each other, and the entailed necessity of largely equivalent referential use, severely constrain the ways in which the different groups' definitions can differ from each other.

In the Blackfeet example, the politically dominant group in the framing opposition (the whites) has provided the denotative definition of full-blood and mixed-blood Indians, has defined Indian as the marked category opposed to white, and has defined full blood as the unmarked Indian. The whites have also specified much of what makes for a core (and hence full-blood) Indian. The Indians have not, in intergroup communication, much challenged these definitions, though they have sometimes among themselves used somewhat variant denotative definitions and core specifications; more often, they have manipulated the assignment of defining attributes for category membership to individuals when they have wanted to control those individuals' categorical assignment.

In the English religious example that follows, both the default values of the categories and the labeling of defining features as denotative versus connotative seem at issue between the two groups—perhaps because neither group is fully under the political or economic control of the other.

Protestants and Catholics, Puritans and Anglicans: Religious Controversy in Reformation England

In this section I want to exemplify the semantic theory's application to complex and problematic domains (in a manner similar to the exemplification provided by the Blackfeet example) by addressing the terms in which an opposition—conceptual, but also political and social—between certain religious groups was understood by the opposed parties. In this example, unlike the Blackfeet one, the definitions of the core concepts that epitomize the opposed groups are themselves at issue.[8]

My discussion is based on two articles of J. Z. Kronenfeld (1983 and 1989). J. Z. Kronenfeld (1983) examined a particular poem of George Herbert's ("The Windows"). She was particularly concerned with the question of how, on the one hand, a critic such as W. H. Auden could take the poem as evidence of Herbert's preference for a decorated church relying on visible signs as opposed to a bare church relying on speech alone (that is, sermons), while, on the other hand, a critic such as Sheridan D. Blau could use the very same lines of the very same poem to support the opposite interpretation. In her analysis, J. Z. Kronenfeld concentrates on the alternative sets of oppositions that the crucial sets of terms participated in (that is, "decorated as opposed to what" and "bare as opposed to what"), and on the contextual clues to Herbert's meaning that his contemporaries would have recognized. In that discussion she points up some of the complexities of position and some of the contradictory doctrinal strains that characterized the Church of England at the time in question. J. Z. Kronenfeld (1989) provides, among other things, further discussion of these issues.

My intention is to examine how my semantic theory might account for some of the complexities and contradictions that J. Z. Kronenfeld describes. I mean to "account for" the complexities and contradictions by showing how they are entailed by the nature of the opposition (Catholic and Calvinist/Protestant) and of the core signifieds of the opposed categories that provided the context within which the Church of England emerged as a marked variant of the Protestant category. This examination will serve to illustrate the application of my theory to universes in which the definition of core referents is itself contested.

My discussion is based on J. Z. Kronenfeld's study. However, in order to make my argument, I have had to adduce information beyond that which she provides; and, in order to keep my argument clear and succinct (as it has to be to successfully illustrate the point about contested cores), I have made simpler assertions about these complex matters than a scholar in either religious studies or Renaissance English history or literature would make. Thus, J. Z. Kronenfeld is responsible neither for the use I have made of her study nor for the additional religious and historical observations I have brought into the discussion.

The facts about the religious groups, their theologies, and their controversies I am discussing should, however, represent standard knowledge—I am neither a historian nor a specialist in religious studies and aim at no substantive contribution of new knowledge to such studies. I want to use these standard facts to illustrate how signifieds and the core referents implicit in the cognitive structures that relate these signifieds to one another are organized in a contested and ideological domain such as this. I want to show how the nature of other semantic information, such as the nature of the framing opposition, structures the way in which the opposed terms are interpreted. And I want to show how the process of reasoning from core referents to an interpretation of noncore referents works as it did with the Blackfeet, even when the makeup or definition of the cores is contested.

In speaking of "cores" being "put together," I refer to the assemblage of the attributes that characterize the core representations (or, in cases like this, *Gestalten*) of the terms in question. The problem at hand in this section particularly encourages our distinguishing "essential" from "basic" (and "accidental") attributes. The assemblage seems to be a mixture of attributes that are logically required by the terms of contrast between the opposed entities (what might be called essential attributes); of other attributes that, while not themselves logically required by the contrast, seem culturally to follow from those required attributes (what might be called basic attributes); and still other attributes that accrue to the cores from our need for the cores to be fleshed-out representations, and that are based on attributes of experienced referents that are most prototypical (what could be called accidental attributes). The way in which opposed or contrasting terms are interpreted is systematically influenced by the framing opposition—that is, the opposition participated in by the term whose category is subdivided by the opposition under consideration. The framing opposition influences the ways in which the terms in question are free to vary, and affects how such variation is likely to be interpreted; it constrains the valences and instantiations that traditionally attach to various of the attributes under consideration; and it shapes cultural expectations about extensions of attributes out from defining instances.

The particular oppositions I want to address are those between Catholics and Protestants during the Reformation in Western Europe and, among Protestants, the derivative and analogous opposition in England between what we would today call Anglicans and Puritans or nonconformists. The latter opposition has had different historical incarnations, of course. In the latter part of the sixteenth century, for example, it would have involved the split between conforming members of the established church (which later on came to be called Anglican) and those who wished to purify or reform it further, particularly Presbyterians who wished to do away with the Episcopal form of church government. Closer to the time of the seventeenth-century civil wars, as "Anglicans" and Puritans became more distinctly and politically polarized, the opposition was, of course, exemplified by that split.

I will be talking about religious cultures, which are an amalgam of doctrine, forms, and general knowledge. Polemical relations among the groups being talked about at any particular time can involve issues either of religious doctrine or of church form, and that form can refer either to the organizational form of the church or to the liturgical form of its worship.

The general problem I want to address concerns the way in which the use of certain terms (such as Catholic, Protestant, Anglican, and Puritan) and their associated concepts seemed fairly consistently to evoke certain derivative conceptual associations and implications of relevant doctrine in the minds of hearers and readers at that time, and does now as well. These associations and implications were entailments that *advocates* of the positions thus labeled did not always want to assert or espouse—and, in fact, sometimes went to some lengths to deny (such ascribed positions, as we shall shortly see, included "being idolatrous" or "being opposed to secular authority"). Similarly, in people's minds at the time, opposition to positions such as Catholic or Protestant seemed necessarily to entail the espousing of conceptual associations and implications that seem to a modern observer not to be automatically implied by the strict logic of the assertions themselves. The line in situations such as this between religious doctrine per se (which is not a question of semantics) and the semantic entailments of terms used in discussions of such doctrine does get particularly muddy.

However, it still has some meaning, insofar as religious labels (as we have just suggested) have some consistent entailments for disputants and the wider community alike, and as these entailments are sometimes not of the sort preferred by a disputant who nonetheless recognizes them (at least, in the sense that he or she feels constrained to explicitly admit their salience by denying them). I want to show here how these entailments follow from the nature of our use of core referents of terms in our reasoning about entities referred to by the terms. We will see how positions are fleshed out with a variety of details that are neither explicitly specified in doctrine nor logically implied by doctrine; we will see that this fleshing out of positions is particularly a consequence of presuming (and casting arguments in terms of) core exemplars or referents of key terms and then of reasoning from these cores, rather than from the specific (and noncore) forms or exemplars that are explicitly espoused by the actual disputants in some specific controversy.

What Semantics Can and Cannot Do

Religious groups, like other political groups, struggle for a variety of reasons, whether power, wealth, prestige, or even morality or ideology—but not very often, I suspect, for semantic reasons. A semantic theory cannot provide much help in explaining why these conflicts arise, but it can help us understand how the conflicts are coded or stated, and can even help us understand which doctrinal or ancillary issues will rise to the fore in any given case. The semantic theory can help us understand where each group is perceived (by the relevant speech community) to be conceptually or ideologically vulnerable, in general, and where, in any conflict between two groups, each is specifically vulnerable vis-à-vis the other. The semantic theory does this by helping us to reason from an understanding of the primary real and substantive differences (or issues) between the groups to a fuller understanding of what the full or elaborated positions of the two groups will be in a given context, of how the positions of one group will match up against that of the other, and thus of where each will perceive the weaknesses of the other (relative to itself) to be. Semantics is relevant in this way because, even though individual leaders try to construct positions that support their claims and that are secure from criticism, their constructions are understood by members of a wider community in terms of the ideological baggage they in turn bring to the conflict—including assumptions about what is normally opposed to what, about what defines a position or value as good or bad, and about what reasoning processes apply when one is evaluating the implications of one or another position. The parties to the debate are not able to change this overall contextual framework—at least not more than a little—because, in their debate, they are speaking to a larger community and trying to win by convincing those not already in—or securely in—one camp or the other.[9] (Of course, this may not be true when only their armies are "debating.") Such convincing can come only through an appeal to underlying values that are shared by the wider society, and appeals to such values—including the logic by which one claim is understood to imply another, and to violate or accord with some value—have to be made in understandable, shared language, where the language includes the moral shadings of terms, the propositions or positions they imply, and so forth. To the degree that by common accord certain consequences necessarily follow from aspects of the basic position of some group, the group is stuck with dealing with these consequences repeatedly throughout history, even if it doesn't like them and tries to construct a counterargument by which the consequences do not follow from this basic position.

I want to argue that it was through such a culturally patterned reasoning process, embedded in the semantics of language, that Catholicism had throughout the period in question to defend itself against Protestant accusations of idolatry, while being unable to convincingly mount the same charge in the opposite direction. Similarly, Protestant groups seemed more vulnerable to accusations regarding excessive pride than did Catholic groups. Developed Anglicanism eventually emerged as a Protestant variant that avoided vulnerability to the "pride" charge, but only at the expense of adopting forms that left it looking only ambiguously Protestant; the interplay of politics in its foundation and in its forms left it, also, with the feel—if not the doctrine—of a national "Catholic" church (as opposed to the Roman Catholic Church), and thereby also contributed to its ambiguity. The process by which Anglicanism became caught in the middle was not simply one of formal logical deduction from doctrinal principles, or merely of recognition of some social fact concerning the church's membership or position. That process also had to do with the contradictory inferences concerning the wider religious, social, and political alignments of the Anglican Church that could be made on the basis of various non–doctrinally significant aspects of its structure and public presentation (and with how these aspects matched with comparable aspects of the Catholic Church, on the one side, and of more prototypical Protestant churches on the other). I will show how the semantics proper and the shared (pragmatic) cultural understandings that were embodied in the semantic structure of the language—particularly in the elements built into their core definitions—contribute to an understanding of why Catholics (and Anglicans) kept insisting on hierarchy and on marks of status and rank within their churches. Conversely, I will show some of the similar pressures toward core Protestant denial of such marks, and show something of why Presbyterian or certain more severe forms of Calvinist Protestantism were repeatedly felt by monarchs to pose a threat to their civil position—whatever the Protestants in question claimed to the contrary. Finally, the feature of human equality under God that was built into the general Protestant core contributed, when juxtaposed with the Anglican Church's building into its religious governance markers of rank that extended into the civil sphere, to the whipsawed situation that Anglicans continually found themselves in. The good Protestant virtues of spiritual egalitarianism and the downplaying of marks of position pointed one way (politically); the religious implications of the monarchal need for hierarchy and marks of status—in a church that had a secular monarch as its titular head, and an episcopate—pointed another.

The Structure and Content of the Oppositions

The framing opposition (that is, the contrast set that includes the items under consideration, which here are Catholic versus Protestant, and analogous oppositions within the Protestant side) for the semantics example with which we are concerned in this section is Christian versus pagan. Anything that is not Christian is pagan, and to the degree that something moves away from Christianity it moves toward paganism. The key defining attributes of "Christian" are a belief in one God and a belief in his incarnation in Christ, who is the route to salvation. In contrast—from the Christian perspective—pagans believe in (many) false gods, which are often embodied in visible images called idols. Particular gods were understood (even by Christian viewers of pagans) as having particular areas of influence (such as war, the sea, wisdom, the hunt, etc.), as in the Roman and Greek pantheons.

Up to the Reformation period with which we are concerned, Christianity in Western Europe was unitary in its conceptual opposition to pagan beliefs, and was embodied in a single, universal Roman Catholic Church. The church derived its authority from Christ through direct transmission to his disciples, who became its founders. The church held that sacerdotal powers were specifically transmitted through the ceremony by which a priest was ordained and in which the authority of the church was recognized. As a hierarchical structure on earth, the church embodied a hierarchical view of the rest of existence, and as people at the bottom of the hierarchy (laity) needed intermediaries (priests) to deal with the top of the earthly hierarchy (the pope), so too they needed intermediaries (people, called saints, who had led particularly blessed lives, and who had demonstrated their heavenly effectiveness) through whom to deal with the heavenly authority, God. Saints often had individual areas of particular concern or effectiveness, and were often represented by standardized images as an aid to the illiterate faithful. It is also relevant to our concerns that this hierarchical structure was known to have developed (at least on earth) somewhat after Christ's death, and in a context involving the political model of the Roman Empire and the hierarchically ordered intellectual model of Aristotelian thought.

Protestantism, and especially Calvinism—the version that seems most relevant to Tudor England—developed in political, religious, and especially conceptual opposition to Catholicism (see Lake 1989:73–75). Since the primary anterior conceptual frame was Christian versus pagan, in order for Protestantism to be opposed to Catholicism without itself being pagan, it had to show that Catholicism had deviated from ideal Christianity in the direction of paganism. It did this by opposing the historical accretions of the Church to Christ's own simpler Christianity. Hence, Protestantism was against the idea of a hierarchy of religious authority (which is not to say that there was absolutely no authority of elders or equivalents within relevant religious communities—see the next section). No hierarchy meant no need for intermediaries on earth or in heaven, and no special transmission of sacerdotal power. Religious authority derived directly from God and resided in the consciences of believers; the faithful dealt directly with God. Saints, since they could not be legitimate intermediaries, were seen as false claimants to divine power, and hence (given their embodiment in images and their areas of specific responsibility) necessarily as idols.

The lack of hierarchy and of intermediaries meant that Protestant believers, in principle, were responsible directly to God and had to rely on their own consciences to assess the sinfulness—or lack of it—of their actions. On the basis of early Christianity (but perhaps also because of more immediate political and religious traditions), however, Protestants held the idea that religion inhered as much in a community of believers as in individuals. This religious community had coercive power, was responsible for aiding the salvation of its members by helping to refine their beliefs and protect their morals, and was needed to confer legitimacy on political institutions. Thus, a derivative religious authority did reside in the community; however, it rested not on any legitimacy granted from external religious authorities to its leaders but instead on the collective consciences of its membership. It had leaders, but in general they derived their position from their ability to appeal to the consciences of their communities or congregations.

How Religious Cores Get Their Political Overtones: Church Structure and Politics

From a Catholic point of view, the Protestant emphasis on individual conscience makes the Catholic versus Protestant opposition one of order and structure versus anarchy and chaos. But Protestants seem mostly to have shared the Catholic fear of (religious) anarchy, and so used a more democratically based authority to tie individual conscience to collective action.[10] And Protestant democracy (at least at its inception) was not a philosophically based political or social democracy, but rather a specific practical device to allow members of a religious community to deal directly with their God; that is, Protestants did not necessarily believe in social equality, even though their opponents often ascribed such a belief to them.

While the preceding discussion refers to religious governance, the positions outlined can be—and often were—seen as concordant with the approval of certain forms of secular political organization. The secular implications of Catholicism at the time were all for a hierarchically ordered state with a king at the top. The Protestant model was more ambiguous; it could be read as an argument for monarchy or democracy. On the one hand, if an earthly realm were modeled on the heavenly one, it would have a king at its head, albeit one who dealt more directly with his subjects than did the king in the hierarchical Catholic model; on the other hand, the relations among members of the religious community on earth would suggest a more demo-cratic, if theocratic, model for political relations.

The Catholic church, as a complicated hierarchical structure, had (not surprisingly to us, as modern anthropologists), attired its functionaries in visible markers (uni-forms) of their position in its hierarchy. Richness of material and workmanship were traditionally the markers of importance in Western culture, and so the Church made extensive use of these tangible symbols of its importance and the importance of its functionaries and structures. In denying the legitimacy of the hierarchy, the Protestants necessarily had to deny the legitimacy of its symbols. This criticism of richness of attire was modeled on the poverty of Christ's own ministry (which ministry they took as the basis for their own legitimacy as "true Christians" as opposed to "pagans").

The Protestant (or Puritan, or nonconformist) emphasis on conscience versus church authority was seen by Protestants themselves as a reliance on inner truth as opposed to on external forms or appearances. Clothing as a form of external presen-tation—especially the apparel of ministers, but also clothing in general, in a context where standards of ministerial apparel were sometimes seen as having wider im-plications—represented a kind of potential distraction from truth (or snare for fleshly eyes). Nakedness was not the answer, however, since naked bodies were themselves (as a result of the original loss of innocence in Eden) seen as potent earthly distractions from religion and morality. Hence, clothing was necessary, but it had to be modest and bland enough not to distract believers from their pursuit of inner truth. For the Protestant (or Puritan), rich and showy attire was in many ways similar, at least in its effects, to wanton nakedness, both being fleshly snares; for the Catholic, however, plain clothing shared with nakedness the failure to provide the necessary dignified and visible markers of legitimacy, authority, and rank. Neither group espoused nakedness, but the idea of nakedness had different primary resonances for the two groups.[11]

For the Protestants the Catholics were pagan-like, particularly in the sense of their being idolaters who worshiped both images and human substitutes instead of God himself. For the Catholics, the Christianity of Protestants was fatally compromised by virtue of their denial of the Church that God established and thereby of the authority by which the purity of the faith was maintained; Protestants were sinners not for worshiping idols, but for putting their faith in themselves instead of in God (and, by implication, in the church that he had established as his vehicle for the expression of his will). Idolatry was the charge that Protestants hurled at Catholics, while the countercharge hurled at Protestants by Catholics was heresy involving self-indulgence and pride or lack of humility.

To summarize our picture of the Catholic/Protestant opposition: Unlike the case in our Blackfeet example, the two sides did not agree on the core definition of the framing concept that embraced their opposition (Christianity, in this case), or on their definitions of their two opposed categories (Catholic and Protestant), or on the default presumptions regarding the concomitants of those definitions. At the inception of the opposition, the unmarked or default form of Christianity was Catholicism, and the Protestants were marked by their rejection of the forms accreted since Christ's death. The members of the marked category, the Protestants, were trying to redefine that default and present themselves as the basic form of Christianity—and hence to leave the Catholics as less centrally Christian and therefore, given the framework, necessarily more pagan-like.

The preceding provides the Catholic versus Protestant framing situation within which the Church of England emerges. In denying the authority of the pope, it of course became, in doctrine, Protestant versus Catholic. At the same time, by substituting the king of England for the pope as supreme earthly authority, it remained hierarchical (and thus rather Catholic in its form of governance). Insofar as (in these nondoctrinal matters) it represented a marked, nonprototypical form of doctrinally Calvinist Protestantism, its keeping of more Catholic forms than did prototypical (Calvinist) Protestantism guaranteed that it would be seen (by Protestants[12]) as relatively more Catholic and hence less purely Protestant—in a context where "more Catholic" meant "more pagan." And, by the substitution of king for pope, the Church of England made sure that any discussion of religious symbols or legitimacy would necessarily have secular political overtones. In particular, any truly Protestant denial of religious hierarchy and its symbols did necessarily have secular political overtones in an England where the head of the secular state occupied the apex of the church hierarchy, and where the religious officers, the episcopate, also sat in the House of Lords.

The Church of England was, then, from the time of its break with Rome, in a contradictory position. Denial of papal authority defined it, by Catholic lights, as Protestant, and hence heretical. At the same time, by Protestant lights, its maintenance of hierarchy and of the symbols of hierarchy made it look very Catholic—with the pagan overtones that entailed for more prototypic Protestants. It could not easily give up on hierarchy because of the nature of its particular tie to the monarchy and its concomitant role as protector of order and position. From the Catholic point of view, it was denotatively Protestant, though with most of the connotations of Catholicism, while from the Protestant perspective it was partially Protestant (via its denial of papal authority and its espousal of Calvinist doctrine) but only incompletely Protestant by reason of its forms. The line between denotative and connotative definitions was less sharply drawn for Protestantism; attributes such as those involving the symbols of hierarchy that were only connotative for Catholics partook of some real denotative force for many Protestants. The Church of England was also Catholic in its emphasis on forms as the institutional vehicle of God's grace, while the Protestants emphasized individual conscience and scriptural study. It wanted, for what started out as political reasons, to deny the key denotative definition of Catholic Christianity, while maintaining all the connotative forms and ancillary mechanisms of Catholicism.

The Church of England thus arose within a framing opposition between Catholicism and Protestantism (in its more severely Calvinist forms). From the perspective of each of these framing extremes, the early Church of England's intrinsic defining attributes were those that characterized the opposition, and thus were evaluated negatively. This problem with the early Church of England's definition constituted a pressure on the church toward the rapid evolution of some kind of third pole, and a rationale for that position, that would leave the Church of England with some kind of positive characterization that did not automatically taint it. The later evolution of new signifiers, such as "Anglican," eventually gave it a kind of independent definitional status of its own. In a context in which the Protestant disavowal of religious authority (and distancing from secular authority) eventually became the basis for a variety of different Protestant churches, the Anglican Church, having been founded by Henry VIII for political rather than doctrinal reasons, and only later having taken on its Calvinist doctrine, adapted to its anomalous Protestant position both by emphasizing its status as an established national church and by emphasizing that its hierarchy of authority was a matter more of "mere" administrative and political form than of doctrinal significance. Because of this more secular focus, it allowed more doctrinal latitude than either end of the Protestant/Catholic opposition that framed it.

The example on which we have focused, Renaissance religion, illustrates something about the relationship between essential features and oppositions. As was initially indicated, "essential features" are aspects of the external (pragmatic) situation to which the linguistic opposition is created to refer. A pragmatic reason or issue arises that produces the differentiation of a set of opposed or contrasting categories, and which becomes an essential feature of the meaning of the opposed categories. In our present religious example, such pragmatic reasons include a feeling that human institutions had gotten in the way of God's worship and of salvation, and that this state of affairs was being maintained by the authority of the pope and the religious hierarchy through which the faithful were expected to deal with God. Views on the authority of the pope and the directness of the worshiper's approach to God are foregrounded by this dispute as essential features of the opposed categories. The logic of the framing situation (involving shared purposes, uses, or descriptions of the newly opposed categories) then entails certain other features of contrast between them, which may be called basic. Such basic features in our contrast include the Protestant insistence that worshipers could and should understand God's will directly from the Bible and from God's appeal to their individual consciences, instead of through the intermediary role of the Church hierarchy (which follows from the Protestant rejection of papal authority and the religious role of the hierarchy the pope heads and through which he claims to exercise Christ's authority); instead, there was an emphasis, modeled on the early church, on the community of believers and on the lack of religious differentiation within that community. There was also a tendency to downplay the effects on salvation of acts in this world (related to the beliefs in predestination and the importance of being called by Christ). Finally, and most importantly for our purposes here, primary exemplars of two opposed categories will, as they emerge, be found to regularly (at least, at some particular moment in time) differ from each other in consistent ways that are, however, neither essential nor basic; these features of difference may be called accidental. One example of such an accidental feature would be the Protestant tendency toward either Presbyterian or congregationally based systems of church governance that, while not doctrinally required, serve to maximize the contrast with Catholic forms. Another example regards clothing; special clerical vestments, as symbols of the special sacred powers of priests, were viewed with suspicion by Protestants and rejected by most. Concomitantly, there was a tendency to extend the concerns regarding clerical vestments to the clothing of members of the congregation in general—partially because the removal of the intermediary role of the priest or minister lessens the difference between him and his congregants and partially because the resulting symbolic emphasis on modesty and simplicity and on the unity of the congregation reinforces the identification with early Christianity.

To summarize, then: Essential features are those that are actually at issue in the contrast; basic features are those that have some intrinsic logical connection to the essential ones. Other features, which I have labeled above as accidental, are not logically required (or universally held) but go into the contrasting cores (on the basis of salient exemplars and of a sense of psychological and cultural consistency) as a way of fleshing out the opposition and of giving members of the culture fuller gestalten to hold in their minds as core exemplars.

My argument is that instead of narrow lists of doctrinally asserted positions, it is these filled-out cores that go into people's default expectations regarding the religious categories in question and that structure their thinking about and reasoning about these categories. It is this tendency to anchor our thinking in such cores that makes it difficult for doctrinally acceptable but culturally divergent variants (that is, variants that diverge on their "accidental" features) of these religious positions to be evaluated in terms of their asserted positions—that is, to avoid the unwanted conceptual baggage that others keep imputing to their position and judging them in terms of.

"Men's Work" versus "Women's Work" in Los Angeles

My final example is drawn from Carol Mukhopadhyay's (1980) study of a population of households in Los Angeles in which the resident wives were nurses working at a local hospital. As with my other examples, I am taking liberties of interpretation and explication for which the source should not be blamed; I am also adding some of my own ethnographic observations and interpretations with which Mukhopadhyay might not always agree.

Mukhopadhyay described and analyzed the sexual division of labor for household tasks in families in which both spouses were employed. Her data came from eighteen families of residents of a community in a suburb of Los Angeles. She picked a set of families (from a middle to lower middle class neighborhood) with employed wives, in order to ensure that work demands outside the home were approximately balanced for both spouses. Her focus was on the processes that generate the sexual division of labor and she used a decision-making approach. Her initial concern was with who actually did what in the house. But since she could not observe the family for twenty-four hours a day (over a single day, let alone over any extended period), and since her presence altered what was happening, she had to get her informants to tell her what various members of the family did. In the course of her study, as she interviewed informants and related what they told her (at one time or in one situation) to what else they told her (at some other time or in some other situation) and to what she herself observed, she was forced to separate—as did her informants, apparent action in some area from primary responsibility for that area; she had to determine what, in various conversational contexts, "doing the job" meant with regard to the question of action versus responsibility, and what "doing the job" meant from the different points of view of the various actors.

In her informants' discussions of cultural models, and in their discussions of their own practice, tasks were apportioned out into cluster areas (such as meal preparation, child care, yard work, care of cars, and so forth); primary responsibility for the cluster of tasks could be the wife's, the husband's, or joint. Within a given cluster (such as, for example, meal preparation) the person with primary responsibility (here, the wife) would be responsible for most of the tasks, but the other spouse might well also have some responsibilities (such as, in our meal preparation example, the husband's responsibility for barbecuing). Attributes of tasks or task clusters that were relevant to negotiations included such things as heaviness and danger, which went with males, such things as gracefulness and nurturance on the female side, and such things as relevant skill or finding the task rewarding, which could go either way. Activity zones such as inside the house (female) versus outside (male) also came up. Mukhopadhyay also discussed the process by which people acquired their "cultural precedents" (see below), and the general historical and conceptual features that shaped this acquisition process. However, since these issues do not concern our present discussion, I will leave them aside.

In order to gain a productive analytic description (versus one that simply summed up previously observed events), Mukhopadhyay attempted to construct a model of the decision process by which families actually worked out, or negotiated, who was to do what. This collective family decision process included taking some account of at least the outcome (and sometimes the process) of individual decisions about individual goals, and some account of the rules of the negotiation process by which individuals or their arguments were able to shape the collective decision.[13] In those negotiations appeals were often made to "cultural precedents." Such precedents were sometimes taken as applying directly to the task in question; the task was simply known to be *men*'s or *women*'s work. On other occasions—commonly, when there was some disagreement between the spouses concerning who should do the job—the precedent was taken as applying to attributes of the task; the task was claimed to have some attribute that, by common knowledge, clearly implied it to be *men*'s or *women*'s work. Obviously, such appeals were constructed to encourage the decision to come out the "right" way (from the point of view of the person making the appeal). But, to be effective, the appeals also had to meet another constraint; they had to be plausible in terms of the common system of knowledge and values that was shared by the negotiators, and they had to have the moral force needed to make one of the parties acquiesce to a decision that went against her or his desires.

That is, the act in question (for example, carrying the T.V. into another room) had to be a sufficiently unambiguous exemplar of the cited concept (for example, "heavy"—hence, men's work) for the other party (for example, the husband) to admit the applicability of the concept and hence the appropriateness of the implication for action (that is, he carries the set). "Sufficiently unambiguous" can mean absolutely applicable, but, normally, in the situations where such debates develop (that is, situations that are felt to be debatable in the first place), "sufficiently unambiguous" means relatively applicable—that is, more applicable than the counter-concept proposed by the other party. In the case of carrying the T.V., such a counter-concept might be, say, "indoor work" or "housework"—concepts that would imply women's work, and hence the wife's doing the carrying. The argument, then, often reduces to a debate concerning how close the act in question is to the central meaning of the cited concepts. In the hypothetical case I have been developing, the husband might point out that the wife often carries something heavier (that is, their three-year-old child); she might respond by saying by saying that carrying the kid is indeed killing her back, but in that case (*unlike* the T.V. case) her important maternal responsibility to nurture her child overrides all else. She might go on to point out that husbands are always expected to help their wives with heavy jobs in the house. By now, of course, she has him nailed to the wall—and he does the job! I want to emphasize, though, that what is at issue is not some idle word game, but rather a kind of contest to see who can find the more applicable cultural standard or rule. In a sense, he winds up doing the job for moral reasons; that is, he cannot reasonably pretend that the job does not more closely match the core definition of the standard she cited (which has him doing it) than it does the standard he cited (which would have had her doing it). It is worth noting that he does the job even though he does not want to, even though he may be physically powerful enough to prevent her from forcing him to do it, and even though there is no external authority to which she could appeal to force him to do it.[14]

Mukhopadhyay's work, in addition to its immediate and direct importance as an exemplar of the application of the study of natural decision-making to a new kind of area, speaks importantly to such Durkheimian questions as the nature, role, and functioning of the moral order in society. But for now I want to put all these interesting questions aside and only look at how the concepts she uses in her study exemplify, and show the usefulness of, the kind of core/extension approach to meaning (of words and the concepts they entail—and even of concepts that lack simple verbal labels) that I am developing in this volume.

The Cultural Frame

In contemporary America, we have cultural norms concerning which activity spheres, kinds of work, and concerns, activities, and skills are men's, which are women's, and which can belong to either.[15] The home is regarded as primarily the woman's domain of responsibility. Overlapping with the home in these cultural norms, but separate, is child care. We have an expectation that the woman be more nurturant and more knowledgeable about questions of nurturance (including emotional support and nutrition). Men are expected to work outside the home at a "job." Men's home responsibilities traditionally include "outside" work (such as yard work and barbecuing), mechanical work related to job skills (such as home repairs), and heavy work requiring strength (such as moving furniture). Men are often (though not always) physically bigger and often have more muscle tissue (and whatever strength that entails). Men are more likely to take (or be expected to take) physical risks, and more trained in interpersonal violence. While such physical coercion is not approved by the culture, there is an understanding and/or fear within the culture that his greater strength and combative skills have the potential of being turned on her. Perhaps related to the coercion issue, or perhaps related to the man's position of supposedly dealing more frequently with outsiders or strangers, is the "traditional" ascription to the male of the "head of the household" role and, as a consequence, of some sort of special authority.

The "home" versus "out" opposition in our culture represents a general "in" versus "out" opposition relative to the home. In suburbia, the wife's domestic domain is the house and the husband's is the yard and garage or workroom. In city apartments, her "in" becomes the apartment proper, while his "out" becomes, for example, the region from the apartment door to the building's trash chute down the hall. On farms, I gather, her "in" is not just the house but the farm yard around it, while his "out" is the fields. This in versus out opposition has been maintained, even though, over time or space, the physical conditions that instantiated one or the other have changed. The in versus out contrast would seem likely to have had something to do with why, at the beginning of modern industrial society, men went out to "jobs" while women stayed home an did "housework."[16] In contemporary America, there is a tendency, perhaps aimed at emphasizing male importance, to reserve the word "work" for jobs and to exclude housework from such "work"; as more women have gotten jobs, there has been some tendency to transfer the husband/wife asymmetry from "work" to "careers."

The work versus nonwork opposition is sometimes realized as work versus inactivity, sometimes as work versus play, and sometimes as paid versus unpaid activity. The "work" that men were supposed to go out and do counted on all three measures, while homemaking activities assigned to women did not count on the pay measure. Since pay was seen as the major source of food, lodging, clothing, and so forth for the industrial-age family, it provided a salient measure of work. Men had paid jobs, and hence worked, while women, in principle, did not. There are some ways in which the preceding tended to produce an inference that whatever women did, ipso facto, was not work; but I want to leave that issue aside and look at the effects of jobs on the allocation of household tasks.

In particular, domestic labor at one's own home did not count as work. Since the initial industrial idea had been that women did the home maintenance and child care work while men went out and got jobs in order to "bring home the bacon" or be breadwinners, women received (and pretty much still have) the lion's share of jobs in the allocation of domestic tasks and responsibilities. However, since men had some domestic tasks (represented today by such tasks as furniture moving, lawn mowing, and barbecuing) there was a kind of conceptual balance that permitted claims of parity—and gave Mukhopadhyay's nurses' husbands a basis for claiming, as some did, that the fact that their wives had jobs (were working) did not necessitate any change in their normal, or in the traditional, division of domestic labor. Sometimes this asymmetry was accounted for by calling (or making) his job a "career," while hers was left as "just work" (or as only "helping out" with the family income); more often, in Mukhopadhyay's sample, the asymmetry was not explicitly recognized by husbands, who rested content with the idea that she should do the traditional women's work around the house while he did the men's; even those men who recognized the asymmetry were either optimistic or naive in their assessment of the degree to which their undertaking additional tasks (or hiring help) was sufficient to redress the balance. The women mostly accepted this imbalance as given; even women who felt overworked, and who recognized the imbalance, insisted only on more help, not on real parity. The effect of the preceding considerations regarding domestic labor was that the basic imbalance itself did not represent an effective argument for the wife. She could claim absolute overwork as a reason for seeking some relief, or she could point to scheduling conflicts between her job and certain household tasks (mostly involving meal preparation),[17] or she could plead temporary illness.

So our oppositional structure between men's work and women's work entails a preference for his working away, at a job, and for her staying at home and doing domestic work there. At home it entails his doing the dangerous or heavy work and having primary responsibility for outside tasks, and entails her being in charge of nurturance and having primary responsibility for inside tasks. By extension, all the inside, nurturant jobs such as cooking, cleaning, and child care fall to her domain. And our oppositional structure entails a situation in which she remains responsible for the lion's share of domestic tasks.

Reasoning and Negotiating about Tasks

The closer a given task can be shown to come to the core male (or female) task definition, the more convincingly male (or female) it is. The closer task is, in general, the one with more male and fewer female attributes (or vice versa). However, attributes may not be equally weighted. For example, in a particular situation (such as moving furniture around in the house), more functionally important attributes such as "heavy" (implying male) may take precedence over background attributes such as "indoors" (implying female); on the other hand, if one of the parties has task-relevant experience and skill (for example, knowing how to hang drapes), such experience may affect the relative weights of the attributes (in the direction of making that party more likely to get the task, regardless of sex).

An important determinant of the significance or convincingness of an attribute will be the relative closeness of the instance under discussion to the core class of instances of that attribute. For example, something (like a big T.V. set) that—literally—weighs a lot will be more convincingly "heavy," and thus imply a male task, than will something hard (such as income tax preparation), which is only metaphorically "heavy."[18] In the absence of a more convincing attribute, even a thinly appropriate one will be better than none at all: one woman in Mukhopadhyay's sample did use the "heavy" characterization as a device to justify the fact that her husband did the taxes!

Coreness (regarding the defining attributes or gestalt of a concept) and centrality (of some attributes to the major functional basis of a concept) are notions that operate at several levels. That is, one can evaluate the centrality (or importance to the core definition of the male or female task area) of one attribute vs. another (for example, "nurturance" vs. "indoors" to female tasks, or "heaviness" vs. "mechanical" to male tasks), but one can also evaluate the centrality (nearness to the core attribute definition) of one instance of an attribute vs. another instance (for example, literal vs. metaphoric "weight" to "heaviness").

Let us take men's and women's task areas as our focus, and look at the centrality of various attributes of those areas. The involvement of lifting heavy weights in a task (such as moving a big TV set) is an attribute that makes the task—other things being equal—a male one. But, if the task is lifting a child, the female attribute of "nurturance" may outweigh "heaviness" in relevance to the task (in some situations, at least)—since "nurturance" is more central to the basic conception of women's work than is "lifting heavy objects" to the basic conception of men's. Alternatively, we can take this attribute as our focus and look at various instances of "heaviness" in order to evaluate their closeness to our canonical notion of "heaviness": lifting the T.V. set outranks lifting the food processor. In the same way, "lifting a hurt child to calm her" may outrank "carrying her because she doesn't want to walk" on the "nurturance" scale. In negotiations, both the degree of relevance of the attribute to the core sense of men's (or women's) work and the degree of centrality of the given instance to the core sense of the attribute come into play.

One can even go further and repeat the process with the $attributes_2$ which define an $attribute_1$, that is, with the $attributes_2$ of an instance which make it more or less central to an $attribute_1$. For example, the importance of an action (say, kissing a child's bruised hand versus seeing that a cut is properly cared for) to one's child's health and safety is an $attribute_2$ that makes an instance of "nurturance"—an $attribute_1$ of women's work—more or less central to the core cultural sense of nurturance. And one can repeat the process with a consideration of what makes an action important to the child's health and safety.

The potentiality of infinite regress is forestalled in normal life by our effective practice, as natives, of learning certain primary core instances of certain concepts directly as *gestalten*—even if we later learn to map attributes or features off these *gestalten*. These primary *gestalten* are instances such as the definition of the core "mother" and "father" I spoke of in my work on Fanti kinship (Kronenfeld 1973, 1980a) which were, for Fanti speakers, direct or primary categories, as opposed to the core "sibling" or "uncle," which was defined by Fanti speakers in terms of relations through mothers and fathers.

Two general points emerge from our consideration of male and female tasks. First, since we are speaking of concepts, we have to realize that concepts are themselves often specified in terms of other concepts. Second, as we have seen in our working women example, various levels of the hierarchy of categories and attributes can be accessed and used in the process of negotiation, especially when the negotiation involves socially important categories such as "men's work" (or "full blood").

Some Thoughts on Ethnicity

I would like now to briefly explore some of the implications of this book's semantic theory for our understanding of ethnicity and of ethnic groups. This exploration primarily grows out of our Blackfeet example, which, in its consideration of contending groups or positions that were primarily contrasted in terms of their degree of Blackfeet-ness, largely dealt with questions of ethnic identification and with ways in which such identification could be used in political mobilization. But I want to include in our consideration what we have seen in our English religious controversy example regarding contending conceptions of the defining attributes of opposed groups and what we have seen in our Los Angeles working family example of negotiations regarding the convincingness of alternative ways of assessing the relevance and weight of the various attributes that make up a category.

The problem I am concerned with is the great confusion that seems to enter into any attempt to define the characteristics of some particular ethnic group, to define the membership of such a group, or, indeed, to define the nature of ethnicity itself. This problem splits into a definitional one and a social one: first, How do we know members of an ethnic group or markers of one when we see them? Second, In what social groups or communities are actually located the shared conceptualizations—the collective representations—of ethnic groups?

Regarding the definitional question, I want first to suggest that the mechanisms— with their variability and plasticity—that we saw used to extend "full blood" status, and thus Blackfeet-ness, to a wide variety of people and issues characterize our ordinary-language use of ethnic group labels in general. This conversational fact means, in turn, that ethnic groups are *not* clearly defined and bounded social entities— *even though* they often feel to us as if they are. Instead, I want to suggest that we—the members of a speech community and a culture—share the linguistic signs that refer to various ethnic groups, and thus the signifieds that, with their implicit prototypic referents, specify a pure and complete version of what a member of such a group should be. This sharing of cores is subject, I might add, to the same temporal slippage we have seen with core "pens" and to a comparable "spatial" slippage as well, as we move from local speech community to local speech community. This sharing is also subject to the same kinds of contestation (between insiders and outsiders, or between contending insiders, or, even, between contending outsiders) regarding key attributes that we have seen in our religious controversy example.

Ethnic groups represent a sort of folk taxonomy of the "kinds of" people that exist, and, as such, their taxonomy has some of the same characteristics as our folk taxonomies of kinds of animals or plants. Such groups are contrastively perceived relative to other such groups, and lower level groups can be included, hierarchically, in higher level groups. For example, "Blackfeet" contrast with "Crow," while both together belong to the category of "Native Americans"—which contrasts with "whites." The taxonomy of kinds of people can include marking relations, as in our present example, where Blackfeet is understood as the unmarked Indian.

Significant problems that come up in discussions of ethnicity and ethnic groups (whether in the broad sense of "race" or in the narrower sense of culture or nationality of origin) come up, as well, in discussions of class, of occupational groupings (such as academic, businessman/woman, student), of regions (as in "the South" or "the West"), and of religious groups. The various overlapping communities to which one belongs are the social units in which inhere the "collective representations" (langue-like codes) that define and are defined by ethnic and other kinds of social groups. Both self-conceived community membership (as in "I am a _____" or "As a _____, I . . .") and interactively defined "communities" of which participants may even be unaware can be loci for such collective representations.

The alternative kinds of groupings represented by ethnicity, occupation, class, region, and religion are (largely)[19] logically unrelated to one another. But there often are strong statistical associations—which often produce default expectations or marking relations. For example, "academic" implies "Anglo" (if, it is hoped, to a lessening degree); "black" implies lower socioeconomic class (if, again, with the hope of decreasing degree); and "Anglican" implies "English." As natives, we do not usually know the statistics, but we do build such associations into our collective representations—often over-starkly, as stereotypes that suppress our awareness of variability, and often as kinds of primordial facts that suppress our sensitivity to historical causes as well as our understanding of possibilities for future change.

Relations among the various communities (of some single sort, such as ethnic) can be those of opposition, consonance, or "ships passing in the night"; the relationships thus categorized can be either social/political relations among groups or conceptual relations among categories (as held by membes of some community). Compare oppositional pairings such as black-white, Hispanic-Anglo, or (until recently) Italian-Jewish, with more consonant pairings such as Alsatian-Scottish or Ukrainian-Polish, and compare both with less traditionally conceptualized pairings such as Anglo-Slovenian or Japanese-French or Black-Irish as characterizations of mixed ancestry in the United States and of the affiliations that might result. The fact that two groups are opposed, whether conceptually or politically, does not prevent me from simultaneously having the potentiality of being in each. Sometimes they, or the dynamics of the situation, force me to choose between such alternatives; at other times, I can belong to both while situationally foregrounding one or the other.

Both kinds of overlap (that is, between different kinds of groupings and between different groups within one kind) together create questions concerning the *specific makeup* of the *actual community* or group that forms the locus of the collective representations that make up the beliefs or knowledge of some particular ethnic group. Are these collective representations to be understood as inhering in the collection of people that claims the affiliation in question, in the collection of people that exhibits it in some clear or salient fashion, or only in the group (or a group) that actually meets or interacts as an instantiation of the ethnicity in question? Or, conversely, are the collective representations to be understood as inhering in the wider society (within which the ethnicity in question is located) but with some sort of marking indicating their ascription to (people of) the particular ethnicity? *Insofar* as collective representations are accepted as "objectively" real, and insofar as they are considered to inhere in groups, these questions become centrally important.

On the other hand, if collective representations are *not* seen as actually existing directly, but only—on the model of langue—as the fiction each of us (as an individual) presumes when we each form our separate, individual internal representations of what we see as the collective understandings held by others, then the problem of where they reside eases considerably. By this understanding of collective representations, the various groups do not have to be real or discrete; we as individuals can form a representation of the understandings held any collection of people that we sense to be a group and that others we interact with seem also to treat as a group. The existence of a name for the group in our language guarantees such overlap and provides a mechanism for keeping our various individual representations more or less aligned.

Identification

However, ethnic labels are not just terms used in conversation; they are categories in terms of which people sometimes construct their self-identifications and, thus, categories that can be used for political mobilization. These further facts pose again the issue of the sense in which we understand ethnic groups to be groups and of the sense in which people belong to such groups. How are ethnic groups to be seen as actually constituting functioning social groups, and by what mechanisms are such groups formed? By what mechanisms are such groups perceived or understood by their members as groups?

The question of identification is central to any collective functioning of ethnic groups. The more deeply people identify with a group, the more likely they are to be mobilizable by it (that is, by *what they perceive as* its interests or its leaders or its social consensus). In this case, their degree of identification is likely to depend on the degree to which they themselves embody the core defining attributes of the group (relative to other groups), as well as on other kinds of attributes, such as the status or power of the group. Perhaps, sometimes, identification with the group in the absence of any of the core features can lead people to mobilize with a group, too; but such participants often will face suspicion about their motives or conviction. On the other hand, as happened with many Jews in Hitler's Europe, the more people are identified with an ethnic group by the wider society, regardless of their own feelings, the more likely they are to see (or be forced to see) themselves as functioning in that ethnic capacity. Such identifications are not ever simply objective facts; they are always somebody's choice and are always made on the basis of somebody's criterion. On the other hand, the credibility of such identifications is always constrained by more objective facts about the person claiming such identifications (or being imputed them by others). We are not free simply to be what we want—unlike, by contrast, the characters in the attractive fictional world Marge Piercy constructs in *Woman on the Edge of Time* (1976), in which ethnic identities are put on as easily as tempting kinds of ethnic foods might be eaten.

People's choices regarding their own group identifications and affiliations foreground, in turn, questions of primary identification or basic underlying loyalties, and then of the nature of the "self" itself. How does one decide to what person or to what group one's primary loyalty goes?[20] Does one's primary loyalty go to a leader (and if so, which one), to a local community, to an ethnicity (or race or language), to a religion, to a class? People seem to pick these primary loyalties in various ways, and not always as social scientists would have it. Marxists have called it "false consciousness" when people address their loyalties to communities or other vertical segments of society rather than to their horizontally drawn economic class. But, nonetheless, people do in fact seem capable of investing themselves heavily in ethnic identities. As the popularity and income of Reverend Ike (or Adam Clayton Powell) showed, when members of a social segment feel their group to be really denigrated, they can wind up feeling a lot of pride in (and loyalty to) one of theirs who has made it—even if he or she has made it by turning his or her hard-earned gifts into conspicuous consumption. Ethnicity does seem to provide a powerful device for mobilizing social groups. Of the kinds of group definitions or identifications that cut across local communities, ethnicity seems perhaps the most powerful—though religion can sometimes compete. Class almost never seems to do it. Often, of course, these memberships covary significantly, and then serve to reinforce each other.

The conceptual categories of ethnic groups—labels and their signifieds—have clear boundaries, but individual affiliations can be overlapping or muddy. In some situations, such as a mobilization issue or a conflict between the *two* groups with which some individual identifies, the boundary issue can be raised or foregrounded, and the individual can either be forced to choose or society may choose for the person (as the American South did, in former times, for anyone with any Black ancestry, and as the Nazis did for Jews in their empire). Boundaries within actual populations of people always seem to represent a kind of imposition (and hence a social and psychological stress), since reproduction and affiliation never in fact seem to segregate themselves so neatly.

How are competing loyalties traded off? What happens when I am forced to choose? Do I dodge, mediate, or pick? What factors (locally and/or generally) affect/bias/stack the question of how I deal and, if I pick, whom I pick?

Regarding the relative primacy of loyalty to an ethnic group versus loyalty to other kinds of social groups, my sense is that several different variables each play a separate role. The final result seems something like the sum of these different variables' separate effects. I refer to variables such as the following. The more the wider society labels ethnicity (or race or . . .) as a key social definer, the more likely one's primary loyalty is to be with such a group. If ethnicity is important in a society, then, the more overwhelmingly one's relevant attributes match some ethnic core, the more likely one's loyalty/identification goes to that ethnic category over other types of groupings, such as class or local community. The more one's livelihood depends on the ethnic group, the greater is the probability of primary loyalty going there.

The loyalty question[21] shades into the identity question. Who am I? That is, what category of person am I? Do I see myself primarily as a member/part of Group X, or do I see myself as a person belonging to many different groups (and hence defined by none of them)?

The question of the nature of the "self" is posed here: Is it the overlap (intersection) of the communities (not just ethnic ones) to which the individual belongs, or is it the central, personal "thing" that responds to those various communities and to the various contexts of participation? Communities are more than just roles. They are the contexts within which roles are defined. Roles exist within them, but sometimes, in varying ways, also define them.

The interactive relationship between the "self" and the communities that define the codes, values, and loyalties of that "self" poses a kind of conundrum: (1) I negotiate my use of—and, thus, membership in and loyalty to—the various communities or categories to which I have whatever degree of access in order that I man "win." (2) But "win" implies winning relative to some values (and maybe by some rules). (3) And values (and rules) are social constructions that inhere in communities—even if, as with langue, we each internalize some representation of them. At issue here are not only choices among conceptually opposed entities of a single sort (such as ethnic identifications), but also choices concerning which kind of entity to foreground—for example, "Jew" vs. "Southerner," "black" vs. "middle class," "Catholic" vs. "anthropologist," and so forth.

I am not presently proposing solutions for these problems, but I do want to suggest that the theory I am developing and the approach embodied in it, as illustrated in the examples of this chapter, are relevant to such important social issues and do offer significant contributions toward their analysis.

Notes

1. Marvin Harris (the anthropologist), not Zellig Harris (the linguist), is the model.

2. Our awareness of cups and glasses as an interesting domain for study probably derives from Kronenfeld's experiences in C. O. Frake's classes in the mid-1960s. Other researchers have also used cups or cups and glasses for investigating category boundaries and category inclusion (cf. Labov 1973, Andersen 1974, Kempton 1978). Andersen's work with childhood development of "fuzzy" category boundaries is especially relevant and is generally consistent with our findings.

3. It might seem that nontraditional material, rather than cylindrical shape, is the most salient attribute of *koppu*. However, most of our informants stated that most of those materials are not often encountered in Japan (e.g., "Hapo styro no koppe"). Hence, we conclude that material is less functionally salient in this case than is shape. Our transliteration of Japanese terms are those we got from our informants; they may not be the normal Roman alphabet spellings.

There remain questions about indigenous Japanese drinking vessels (e.g., *sakizuki* and *younomi chawam*). These items were usually initially grouped with *kappu*. However, all informants found this arrangement uncomfortable, because the traditional items lacked handles. This lack pushed them away from *kappu*, even though the presence of all other traditional form attributes pulled them toward the category. The more ritualized use of these items increased this feeling of discomfort with the *kappu* grouping of these objects. Most informants felt that these items actually belonged to a separate and somewhat isolated category based on ritual use attributes. There appear to be differences between males and females in terms of their perceptions of these traditional items.

4. Historically, whites in the United States represented an amalgam of a number of former nationalities who were joining an expanding polity. The only neighboring polity (in the north) was Canada, which seemed socially and culturally similar. Hence, whites, in their relations with Indians, saw the basic *we* versus *they* contrast in racial terms, as one between whites and Indians.

Most Indian groups saw themselves—nonracially—as cultural, political, and social units vis-à-vis other such units. These other units were initially other Indian groups, but eventually came to include white groups.

Let us consider an example. Northern Ute children with whom I worked and lived in the summer of 1962 saw the world as Ute versus others, where others included Sioux, Cheyenne, Comanche, United States-ians, and so forth. That is, they did not see it in racial terms. For those children (in a tribal group that had not been subjected to the outrages many others had), the status of the Comanche (who were linguistically closely related and culturally similar up until the advent of the horse) as their traditional enemies outweighed any feelings of white injustices to Indians in general. This insight hit me when I was watching a Western movie in which the cavalry was fighting the Comanche, and realized that the Ute children were rooting for the cavalry—because the Indians were Comanche!

It is only very recently, after long, and intensively racist treatment by whites, that Indians have been forced to begin evolving a pan-Indian (ethnic) self-identity. As I understand Wilmoth's work, the Blackfeet are similar to the Utes in this regard; from their point of view, the basic opposition is Blackfeet vs. other, and not Indian vs. white. However, our full-blood vs. mixed-blood opposition refers to Blackfeet people in terms of a continuum between Blackfeet and whites, and in a situation where whites control power and thereby structure political and economic relations. The Blackfeet, in this situation, are forced to live within at least the gross shape of white conceptualizations, including the white-Indian opposition; even within the Blackfeet's own conceptual scheme, for related reasons, the whites loom now as the most salient others, and thus as the prototype of non-Blackfeet—giving the Blackfeet their own, if only local, version of the basic white v. Indian opposition. In this Blackfeet view, other Indian groups, being "others" but also being somewhat more Blackfeet-like than the whites, fall somewhat ambiguously between the two prototypes, and thus can, depending on context, be situationally assimilated to either.

5. White is the category that contrasts with the Indian category (which includes full blood and mixed blood) at the next higher level of contrast. It is also the category that represents the opposite end of the polar continuum that is anchored at one end by full-blood Indian and along which mixed-blood Indian differs from full-blood Indian. As such it is always implicit in any use of the full blood versus mixed blood paradigm/opposition.

6. Wilmoth, in a personal communication, says that a history of differential co-optation has confused, complicated, or confounded the application of the labels to supporters of programs because, even though mixed bloods run "programs," "the council," and so forth, and even though full bloods have a long history of low level jobs (e.g., maintenance work) and are most exploited, controlled, and so forth, it is still the case that full bloods support the BIA as a means of countering the mixed-blood–dominated council and because of their economic dependence on it.

7. An exception is found in the rhetoric of a national Indian movement—The American Indian Movement (AIM)—that redefined "Indian" in a way that benefited the mixed-blood elite in the 1960s and 1970s.

8. For a political example of contested core definitions, see Vike's 1991 analysis of rival groupings within the Norwegian Labor Party in a small industrial community.

9. Even if one side is strong enough to win without such neutrals, it still has the problem of maintaining the loyalty of its supporters in the face of attempts by the opposition to woo them away.

10. These views of order and anarchy also apply, respectively, to conformist "Anglicans" and Presbyterians in their opposition to each other during the late sixteenth century.

11. Nothing in their preference for plainness, incidentally, prevented individual Protestants from competing for who could have the most appropriate dress or for who could show the best taste and quality of materials in their nondistracting plainness.

12. For Catholics, the key issue was papal authority, and so the Church of England remained purely and heretically Protestant.

13. In the usual situation, both areas of responsibility and specific task actions were not actively "decided" or negotiated, but were determined on the basis of how the people in question (or their families) had done it in the past—that is, on the basis of what Mukhopadhyay calls "cultural precedents." New situations were treated in ways that seemed consistent with explicit cultural precedents or with actors' inferences about implied precedents. New decisions had to be worked out, or negotiated, when novel situations arose (especially, perhaps, in new families) for which the spouses' separate (natal) family cultural precedents differed or for which some outside model intruded. For established families, negotiations were needed when family conditions changed significantly in ways that one, the other, or both spouses thought relevant, or when new topics arose for which existing cultural precedents seemed ambiguous. In general, areas of responsibility were more stable—less often reconsidered—than actual action allocations, and so most actual negotiations involved specific activities rather than areas of responsibility.

14. He does it, of course, in part, to maintain the amicable continuation of their little society; but since this concern applies equally to her, it does not account for why on this occasion it was he and not she who gave in.

15. The "men's work" versus "women's work" opposition develops from some aspect of the physical, social, economic, or political contrast between men and women; the underlying issues are currently the subject of much debate. The basic human sexual division of labor has traditionally made women primarily responsible for child care and related in-the-home family maintenance activities, and men particularly responsible for dangerous activities or activities requiring short bursts of strength, especially outside the home or family. My own guess would be that this package develops as much from childbearing and breast-feeding as from anything else. The nature of male and female differences in contributions to reproduction meant that the loss of a woman hurt the reproductive potential of a group much more than did the loss of a man. The combination of relative protection from danger and relative contribution to nurturance tended to keep women relatively more at home (whether it be camp, house, or whatever), and to make that more their domain. This relative expendability of men left them freer for dangerous jobs like defense and hunting. (The danger to women involved in childbirth only made the possibility of losing them to other, avoidable, dangers even worse.) What physical sexual dimorphism we have seems related to these basic role divisions; greater male body size presumably entailed certain kinds of additional strength. The point of my scenario is not, at this time, to argue its correctness, but only to indicate something of the kinds of issues that are involved in the general conceptions of male and female work that lie behind the particular cultural values and norms which, in turn, frame the local issues that Mukhopadhyay is concerned with.

16. The in versus out opposition, the still-significant dependence on breast feeding, and, perhaps, attitudes toward danger all seem to me to have contributed to the fact that, when the industrial age came, it was the men who were supposed to go out to work, while the women, if they could afford to, were supposed to stay (work?) at home. Women did, of course, in fact, work in factories. Since they (and children) were considered more vulnerable and hence less able to protect themselves than their husbands or fathers, it is not inconsistent to think that factories (or sweatshops) might thereby have preferred to hire them—as a more malleable and cheaper workforce. Thus I am not saying that women did not go out and work, but only that, ideally, they were not supposed to—and were not normally thought of in ideal cultural models as doing so. The culture had other, additional reasons for keeping women at home if possible. At least one such reason involved protecting the husband's (and society's) interests in the legitimacy of their children—and thereby entailed the husband's control of his wife's sexuality and the father's control of his daughter's (in the interest of getting her a good husband).

17. Some of the women even owned up to intentionally arranging their job schedules to produce such conflicts as a way of forcing their husbands to assume some of the home work.

18. "Heavy" objects are difficult or hard to move. From that focal basis, a difficult task can be labeled as "heavy."

19. There do exist, of course, some more logical entailments—for example, that between occupation and class. For example, street sweeper implies lower class (given the economic component in class and given the low pay of street sweepers)—but, on the other hand, a businessman can be in any of several social classes.

20. Here, I am specifically referring to one's penultimate loyalty—what one sees as the primary loyalty after loyalty to the society/state itself; but I think the same considerations enter into the loyalty question when it becomes the prior question of loyalty to the state versus to something else. I am also leaving out personal loyalties to family and friends, even though these loyalties do interact in important ways with the more sociocentric group ones I am considering.

21. I am speaking here of loyalty to groups. Loyalty to an individual, while probably not unrelated, does introduce other kinds of issues not related to our current topic.

12

Toward a Theory of the
Semantics of Words

The semantic theory described in the present volume offers a way to account for the well-attested flexibility with which words are used in ordinary discourse, while at the same time making clear the shared anchors to experience and the shared systematic framework that make it possible for us to understand each others' creative usages. The theory, in the tradition of Saussure and Durkheim, situates language clearly as a collective phenomenon; clearly as an entity that inheres not in isolated individuals, but in a community. The theory, then, is concerned not only with the individual experiences and understandings that shape the learning and use of words, but, also with the social processes by which the knowledge and usage of individuals is tied together and meshed into a single collective system. This social framework not only embraces the regularities of normal established usage but also, perhaps more importantly, the conceptual means by which novel individual creations are structured and understood and by which the collective system changes over time—whether the change represent adaptation to changed external material circumstances or to interior changes of style, interest, or perception.

The semantic theory applies to individual words (or terms)—entities that have the properties of Saussurean "signs" and of Frakean "segregates." A group of words that in some context relate more closely to each other than to words outside the group, or a group of words that all refer to aspects of the same situation, can be spoken of as a "domain."

Words are conceptual entities. They participate in semantic relations and pragmatic cognitive relations. Semantic relations include both the sense relations of words (or terms) to other words and the reference relations of words to whatever it is that we are using words to talk about. Sense relations are those aspects of meaning which pertain to the relations of opposition and inclusion among words—what something is not, and what it is a kind of. Reference relations include both the internal (in the mind) relationship of a word (Saussurean sign) to its signified (the conceptual face of the Saussurean sign) and the external relationship of the word to the actual referents, whether real or imaginary, that the word is being used to talk about in a specific discourse. Actual referents of words are divided into prototypic or core referents and extended referents. Core referents are tied directly to the primary sense meanings of terms, and relations among core referents have much to do with the structuring of sense relations among terms. Extended referents are tied to words' signifieds (and attendant conceptual meanings) and to sense relations among terms only through their similarity or contiguity to core referents. Signifieds are based on core referents. Pragmatic cognitive relations include the conceptual schemas that interior referents of terms are normally presumed to participate in; especially important are those schemas that encompass the pragmatic functional situations that were frequently enough referred to in discourse to produce the distinct signs in question (the "defining functional schemas" of the relevant terms).

Extension can either be based, denotatively, on the "form" features by which referents of words are recognized or, connotatively, on the "function" attributes that represent what it was about the referents of the term that made them salient enough in discourse to merit separate terms in the language. Extension can also be based, metaphorically, on the semantic relationship of a term to other terms in its contrast set or domain, or on the pragmatic relationship of the internal referent of a term to the internal referents of other terms in its defining functional schema.

Thus, the kinds of paradigmatic relations among terms that are produced by componential analyses define part of the sense "meaning" of the terms and relate that sense meaning to core referents. By this theory, componential analysis is only properly applied to sets of core referents, and any success such an analysis has in delimiting extended referents is, for the general case, accidental; in specific cases, in which componential analysis does seem to work well for the extended referents of a complete set of terms, that success probably says something about the kind of extension being used in the domain in question. That is, extension can be made on the basis of features already used to distinguish contrasting categories from one another, or it can be made on the basis of other attributes of core referents; information about the use of terms in the domain and the use of the entities to which the terms refer can be gleaned from the kinds of extension of the given terms that normally occur in one situation or another in the language in question. In componential paradigms, it is normally the features of contrast—as opposed to the relations (of contrast) among terms defined by those features—that are foregrounded (or salient) to speakers. Thus, a "brother" who becomes a "female" thereby changes into a "sister"; the features are crucial.

Taxonomic structures also represent part of the sense relationships among terms. By the present theory, taxonomic relations in ordinary language should only strictly apply to core referents of terms in the taxonomy. Insofar as such taxonomic relations do apply, in some domain, to extended referents of the terms of the domain, that success tells us something interesting about the extension processes being used (as noted above for componential relations). In taxonomic structures, it is normally the relations of contrast and inclusion among terms—as opposed to the features on which contrasting terms differ—that are foregrounded. Here, a "horse" born with five toes remains a "horse," if an odd one; the features can be useful, but it is basic underlying processes or *Gestalten* (depending on the domain and language in question) that are determinative.

In order to account for variations in usage within a speech community, the theory has to attend to what it is that keeps a word active in a person's vocabulary—including the term itself, its primary referent, its denotative and connotative features, and its major semantic and conceptual connections. One key feature seems to be the frequency with which the term is used—and the frequency with which it is applied to one or another referent, and with which it is used in one or another applicational/conceptional context and conversational context. These frequencies, along with other kinds of salience considerations, shape our individual senses of which referents, which situations, and which attributes are crucial to any given term. Insofar as these aspects that a term or its use or associations enter into the communicative use of the terms, then the relevant experiences have to be common enough in the relevant speech community to be maintained in more or less similar forms by a substantial number of members of that community; aspects that are important for what members are trying to communicate will be shaped in each individual (in the direction of a common form) by feedback from other individuals.

In a general way, the theory presumes that things (whether actual objects, or actions, or attitudes, or attributes, or something else) that are important enough in people's lives for them to talk about frequently enough for the terms they use to be maintained in their language will enter their language. The physical shape of the new word (its Saussurean signifier) will arise through processes that lie outside our present range of concerns. The core referent will be the most commonly encountered exemplar of the concept. The denotative features of the term will be based on the features of the core referent, especially on those features that distinguish it from core referents of other terms. Connotative features will include the primary function (that is, the usefulness of the signified concept, whether conversational or practical, that accounted for the term's frequency of use in discourse) and the attributes that are central to that function. For some purposes, at least, features important to the functional attributes (what might be called "essential features") will be distinguished from more incidental ones. Speakers of the language will infer internal referents from these features of cores, and will infer defining functional schemas from the core referent and its interaction with related concepts in the situation in which the primary function occurs. Since conversational use of the term and conversational extension of the term by a speaker is based on these internal referents and schemas, significant divergences by a speaker from community norms in these areas will produce confusion; such confusion will result in feedback that will lead the speaker to refine her or his concepts in the direction of community norms—at least in areas or aspects of usage that pertain to the communicative aims of the speaker. All of the attributes and features of the internal referent or the core referent of the new term, including form and function, become available for use in metaphoric extension, as do all the relationships entered into by the new term, including semantic ones of contrast and inclusion, conceptual ones of the defining functional schema, and any information entailed by routine extensions.

In the course of the presentation, we have utilized a number of extended examples or cases. We have examined in varying detail the examples used in the work on which the present theory is based—that of Lounsbury (and others) on kinship terms, that of Berlin and Kay on color terms, and that of Berlin (and others) on folk biological taxonomies. We have separated the process of semantic extension out from more specific details of the given domains—including issues of universal (cross-cultural and/or cross-language) patterning and of possibly universal perceptual or social features. Differences in mechanisms of extension in those source domains forced us to separate the general attributes of semantic extension from the particular mechanisms that may be used in one or another specific domain (by participants in one or another linguistic or cultural community). We used work on kinship by Lounsbury and by Nerlove and Romney to explore our first explanatory principle, conjunctivity. We used Berlin's work on folk taxonomies to explore the application of Greenberg's work on marking relations to our present concerns. We turned to general ethnoscience work on componential paradigms and folk taxonomies to explore our third explanatory principle, cognitive limits on our ability to process information.

We have used several elaborated examples of semantic extension to illustrate various aspects of the semantic theory. Our first example—an extensive exploration of the metaphoric extension of terms relating to cats and dogs to the realm of human women and men—came in our discussion of marking relations (even before we introduced the idea of extension). We were focused then on the kinds of information that explained the unmarked status of "dogs" as male and of "cats" as female. That discussion showed what it was about the relevance of dogs and cats to households that allowed them to usefully represent men and women in some kinds of conversations concerning domestic and familial roles. In the presentation of the theory we turned to the domains of writing implements (pens and pencils) and reading matter (books, journals, magazines, etc.) to see how contrast sets worked, to explore the nature of form and function, to see how these were distinguished from one another, and to see how each was used in extension.

The first of our separate illustrative examples was that of drinking vessels. In that example we saw a reasonably complete application of the theory to a moderately complex but prosaic domain—a domain, incidentally, that represented no universal or innate entities. We saw how the treatment of cultural objects could vary across languages, even while the process of semantic extension remained constant. We saw also how the process of classification and the process of semantic extension depended on an interplay of the attributes of the objects being labeled, the recent history of experience with the actual objects and with the referents of the named classes, and the semantic associations of the labels. In this example we saw experimental evidence that clearly showed native speakers to be responding to questions about a named class by reference to the properties of core referents (rather than to noncore referents or to some sort of average). That is, we saw experimental confirmation of the theory's claim that the conceptual linkages of a word pertain to core referents and not, either in part or in whole, to extended ones.

Our second separate illustrative example, that of Blackfeet political factions, illustrated the application of the theory to a domain of categories of people instead of things, and to a domain in which extended referents were constantly shifting their category membership and in which the consequences of identifying people or political positions with the alternative categories were strongly contested. Here, our focus was on the use of the labels by native speakers, and on the ways in which they understood (decoded) reference to a political figure or position by means of one or the other category label in any given context. Our third example, that of Renaissance religious controversy, followed up on the Blackfeet example by showing how the theory worked in a politically charged universe in which even the definitions of the two opposed categories were aggressively contested. It also provided an illustration of how the semantic context in which a given politically and religiously important conceptual opposition arose could imply expectations about the position held by one side in the political/religious dispute which that side had continually to respond to—that is, to defend itself against—even where the expectations represented claims that the side not only had not made but even had gone to some lengths to distance itself from.

Our fourth example was that of the division of domestic labor in a Los Angeles community in which both wives and husbands held jobs. It served to illustrate how, in the context of semantic extensions that had significant implications for who did what work, the relative applicability of alternative, potentially relevant attributes was negotiated. We saw the interplay of cultural default definitions and expectations, of personal desires, and of history in the negotiations by means of which one or another task was finally allocated. Cultural defaults concerned both who was supposed to do a given category of task (in what context) and what attributes (or specific activities or special contexts) made some given task closer to or further from the core of the given category. History included both the negotiating spouses' past personal experience and observations (particularly, but not only, in their families of orientation), and their knowledge of the more general history of relevant practices in their society. We saw how the cultural understandings coded in the semantics entailed a kind of moral force that both spouses felt constrained by—even in situations in which each tried to find other arguments by which he or she could convince his or her spouse to accept a redefinition in terms of some other moral standard.

As a final example, we briefly combined the insights gleaned from our preceding examples in order to see what kind of light the semantic theory might be able to throw on a difficult social/conceptual problem in anthropological theory such as that posed by the definitions of ethnicity and of specific ethnic groups as well as by the functioning of such groups. Questions with contested answers include who is to be seen as a member of such a group, who decides membership criteria, how cross-cutting memberships are to be understood, what the relationship is between social participation and categorical attributes as indicators of membership, what role inheritance and socialization play, and so forth. The semantic theory both suggests an explanation of how we, as native speakers of one or another language, manage to know what we are talking about when we use these ambiguous labels, and suggests how the various characteristics we associate with ethnic groups come together.

The examples have each been chosen and developed to represent specific aspects of the theory. No one example exemplifies the whole theory. The theory is not to be seen, then, as being directly inducible from any single example. Similarly, the whole of the theory cannot be directly tested in any one example; in any given case, some parts of the theory are not relevant, while others, although relevant and logically testable, are too difficult to test with the conceptual and technological resources currently available. The theory consists of a set of propositions and of the implications one can deduce from these propositions. My approach to testing has been to try to evaluate the separate propositions as they or particular narrower versions of them have become clearly enough understood and stated for such testing. Since the theory itself is not yet completely developed or specified, any definitive test remains in the future. My hope is that this presentation will encourage others to develop, refine, and evaluate the propositions presented here, and that out of this process will come a better and fuller understanding than we now have of the semantics of natural language.

Appendix: Piagetian Schemas

This book is not about Piaget, and not about schemas, and so I cannot take the time or space to fully explicate or justify my interpretation and use of Piaget's work and insights. I merely want here to give a minimal outline of what I mean, so that readers will not be tempted to confuse my interpretations (of Piaget's theories or of the schema notion) and usage with other more common interpretations. The best summary explication I am aware of the relevant parts of Piaget's theories is that of Flavell (1963—see, for present purposes, especially chapters 2–7). Other summaries include Piaget and Inhelder 1969 and Furth 1969.

Given the preceding, my reasons for preferring Piaget's approach to schemas (and epistemology) over other (and generally more recent) American cognitive psychology and cognitive science versions include the following.

I. Piaget's theories embrace an integrated epistemology that includes the following elements.
    A. Schemas are understood as functioning entities—knowledge in action.
    B. The theory considers how schemas are formed, adapt to their (changing) environments (through assimilation and accommodation), grow, move to equilibrium states, and use old equilibrium states to reach out to new materials (producing new disequilibria, from which in turn the move to equilibrium starts again). The theory shows how in this process of development some schemas become hierarchically embedded in other schemas.
    C. The theory notes the cumulative effects of different kinds of knowing—represented by the famous stages: sensory-motor, concrete operational, formal operational.
        1. Note that the famous stages are, in an important sense, epiphenomenal—they only represent a cumulation of successive dependencies. Learning to talk about doing something is a skill that represents an overlay on our prior knowledge of the doing itself. That is, we have to learn to do something (sensory-motor knowledge) before we can learn to talk knowingly about doing it (concrete operational knowledge), and we have to be able talk knowingly about a class of actions as specific instances before we can abstract out key properties of the class of actions (formal operational knowledge). This is another way of saying that the famous Piagetian Stages simply follow from the way in which knowledge accumulates and builds on prior knowledge. See Flavell 1963:chaps. 2–7 for a good overview of what I am referring to.
    D. Another issue, but related, is what might, after Bateson, be called "metalearning."

237

1. The more we know directly (in our experience) about related things or learning processes, the easier it is for us to leap from (less) experience to (faster) knowledge. We get clearer ideas of what to look for and how to look at it.

2. The Piagetian frame does seem to allow such metalearning. As we have increasing experience with learning to talk about things we do, it becomes easier for us to make each next such transition and, as we have such experience, we experience a kind of metalearning that makes it easier for us to work from verbal descriptions (concrete operational models) given to us by others quickly back to our own behavioral understanding (sensory-motor knowledge). A similar metalearning can take place regarding working back from formal operational models to concrete operational knowledge.

II. The Piagetian perspective raises some interesting questions regarding third-party or indirect learning—that is, learning from what someone else tell us versus only from what we do ourselves. It suggests that we cannot directly learn from such passive experience, but it does allow us to use such observed experience as a guide to our own attempts at gaining relevant experience, as a kind of facilitator that helps us to know what experience to seek and what to look for in that experience.

III. The Piagetian approach tightly integrates knowledge and action. Schemas are not pure knowledge structures but structures in which the acquisition of knowledge always depends on action and in which knowledge is always constituted with respect to relevant action.

IV. Piaget's work embraces a naturalistic experimental method. Piagetian experimental designs are logically tight, but are unlike those of American cognitive psychology in some useful ways.

   A. American psychology tries (or usually tries) to create in a lab a situation in which all elements of normal reality and/or experience that are deemed irrelevant to the issue being examined have been removed. This means that the subjects are isolated from any of the situational context that they normally use in making their everyday analogs of the operations that are being explored in the experiment—which makes the experimental findings harder to generalize to normal life situations outside the laboratory framework than would be the case for more naturalistic laboratory settings. This approach to experimental design also makes the experiments particularly dependent on the presupposition of what is relevant and irrelevant that is built into the basic design—leading to the risk of the kind of experimental design artifacts that I suggest (in chapter 6) for the experiments reported on by Miller (1956).

   B. Piagetian psychology tries to set up reasonably naturalistic (and familiar) situations, while still holding exogenous variables constant. This means that subjects have normal and familiar contextual information available to them; and it means that people (such as myself) from outside the discipline of psychology who want to try to apply the insights have a more straightforward task. And, incidentally, the Piagetian tradition thereby forestalls some of the kinds of complaints that people involved in the situated-knowledge type of approach tend to make about more traditional American psychological approaches to learning and knowledge.

However, there are some missing elements in the Piagetian approach (for my purposes) for which we will have to turn elsewhere. Nevertheless, these elements, contrary to what is sometimes claimed, are not in any sense contradictory to the basic Piagetian epistemology.

    V.   Society and collective knowledge.

        A. Piaget does not attend directly to social aspects of knowledge, including the division of intellectual labor—that is, to the social distribution, social construction, or social transmission of knowledge.[1] But, since, by my lights, society is constructed of interacting individuals, there exists no separate social psychology, but only the application of individual psychology to situations in which people are interacting reciprocally and are tuning their actions/thoughts to what each other does.

        B. In the present volume we are not concerned with individual knowledge and action per se, but only insofar as that individual knowledge and action is applied socially to produce social entities with Durkheimian "emergent properties" (such as the system of language), and only insofar as that individual knowledge is consistently patterned so as to produce Durkheimian "collective representations" (such as the shared content of language). These social issues are not ones to which Piagetian theory has particularly been addressed, but a few simple observations will enable us to see how it applies to them. To obtain a social system of individuals that exhibits emergent properties, we need only understand that the environment to which the schemas in question (schemas of individual people) are adapting includes not just regularities encountered in the world of things, but also regularities experienced in the behavior (and behavioral responses) of other people (see Kronenfeld and Kaus 1994 for a simple simulation that illustrates the point). To obtain collective representations, we need only understand that for some salient socially patterned behavior (such as language), individuals within a given community learning the behavior will all be exposed to essentially similar conditions (as they are with the regularities of the physical world Piaget investigates), and those individuals will have to conform their relevant behavior to fairly close interactive standards. In this situation, they will each form internal representations of the "collective behavior" that they experience and these different internal representations will be very similar from one person to the next.

        C. There do arise a set of inferences that one can make about knowledge/action systems shaped by such interaction that one could not make directly from a consideration of the separate individuals in isolation (e.g., Durkheim's "emergent properties" and "collective representations"). In my thoughts about these social effects I turn to the insights of Durkheim and of Saussure.

    VI. Culture. Piaget does not himself attend to cultural differences, nor make any significant attempt to evaluate his theories cross-culturally. Instead, he seems to rigidly control for cultural effects by situating all of his work within a very homogeneous community. He does not, as I understand it, intend that his particular findings (such as the age at which a child acquires some particular form of conservation) to apply cross-culturally (in different material contexts and in different learning contexts). He does intend that the basic cognitive processes of schema formation, adaptation, and so forth should generally apply. Since his theory is a constructivist one that depends intimately on the organism's active interaction with its environment, I presume that, by it, one would expect (significant) cultural differences (in material or social milieu) to produce differences in what is known and in the timing, context, and linking of learning different kinds of knowledge.

VII. Innate knowledge (1). Piaget does not much emphasize the role of innate or hard-wired knowledge. He does allow that there has to be some, but frames his theory so as to minimize its dependence on such innate knowledge.

    A. His reason—as I infer it, in part, from his discussion of Chomsky's views of innate capabilities (Piaget 1970:12,88–91,141–142;1973:57,69n. 16)—seems to be, in part, his acute awareness of the phylogenetic implications of any claims about hard-wired innate capabilities. That is, any such capability has to have been evolved through the normal processes of biological evolution (genetic recombination, mutation, and selection) in the time period after the animals that have it (humans, in the present case) split off from their nearest relatives who lack it (usually, by such claims as those of Chomsky—and, presumably, Atran [for example, 1990:ix–x]—this means since the time humans and chimpanzees split apart). That is just not enough time to have produced anything terribly new that is terribly complex. The argument is not that "complex mental organs" are in any sense impossible, but only that their complexity relates directly to their phylogenetic depth—and, thus, for human capabilities, to the form in which they are cast.

       Genetic (or hard-wired) modifications or refinements of prior hard-wired capabilities would seem possible. Similarly, one would expect that an interplay of genetic capabilities and the right learning situations could lead not only to the refinement or modification of given biological dispositions, but could also enable such dispositions to be raised to consciousness and brought into the sign systems of language.

    B. In a more general sense, Piaget intended that his epistemological systems ("genetic epistemology") should apply to natural knowledge systems in general, not just to cognitive learning in the human child. Thus, he had no intrinsic opposition to the idea of genetically coded knowledge or to the idea that the evolutionary process would continue to tune such knowledge—but he was acutely aware of the time frame in which such "learning" took place.

    C. I presume, also, that, not knowing what would in the future turn out to be innate, he felt it would be safer to maximize what his learning/knowledge system could handle (and thereby run the risk of later being found redundant in some areas) than to minimize its capabilities (and thereby run the risk of what could turn out to be significant omissions).

VIII. Innate knowledge (2). I am aware that since the time of Piaget's relevant work on the child's earliest learning, other scientists have gained new knowledge about the child's innate capabilities involving, for instance, facial recognition and attending to faces, especially in the context of mother-child interaction. For the reasons outlined above, such findings, while addressing and correcting various specific claims of his, in no way undermine the usefulness I see in the Piagetian approach to epistemology and in the Piagetian model of the schema. In particular, he was clear that there had to be certain innate bases from which relevant schemas then developed; in the absence of specific knowledge, he just kept his assumptions about these as simple as possible. It is also worth noting that the innate capabilities that have been found do not appear to exhibit the kinds of phylogenetic discontinuities that so troubled him in Chomsky's claims regarding innate capabilities.

I will now briefly turn to some other issues that relate to the Piagetian conceptualization I have just offered.

Contrary to the the dynamic knowledge-producing-action conceptualization of schemas that I have taken from Piaget, schemas as conceptualized by many of the cultural models people (for example, Quinn and Holland 1987:25, Holland and Skinner 1987:85, Quinn 1987:179) seem to be more like large Frakean frames (cf. Frake 1964) or similar but somewhat more complex templates for action. References to Rumelhart (1980) regarding what might be called "generic concepts" "stored in memory" (Strauss 1992b; cf. D'Andrade 1987:112–113) contribute to this sense (also see Casson 1983). These schemas do not themselves directly generate any action— either within themselves via reasoning, learning, adapting, or changing, or in the outside world by responding to events or producing behavior (though some versions do provide goals and motivation that can lead to behavior). These relatively generic schemas are more fixed and abstract than are those I am thinking in terms of. In part, this seems to be because they are seen as entities pertaining to groups or cultures rather than to individuals, where individuals are recognized as the initiators of action.

D'Andrade (1987:112–113, and see 1992b:230) raises the issue of the sharing of cognitive systems. The question of what exactly is shared in socially distributed cognitive systems, and of how it is shared and how the various individual versions are kept coordinated, is an important one. The issue has both qualitative and quantitative aspects: What precisely is shared—pieces of structure, or input-output matches, or something else? How much of it has to be shared for what cultural purposes?

The relationship of language to thought and/or language to culture comes up here. My own view, consistent with that of Piaget, accepts the primacy of thought over language, and sees language as a tool that is used to talk about (or store chunks of) thought. In various places in this volume, the language and thought issue comes up, and I offer various reasons for my rejection of the opposed view, which would see language as primary over thought, and which might then see thought as internalized language, or as some other kind of derivative of language. I have explicitly addressed the issue in other publications (see, particularly, Kronenfeld 1975 and 1991).

I want to conclude this appendix by pointing out that it has been included in this volume primarily to give the reader some sense of what I mean by my textual references to schemas. At the same time, the argument of the book does not depend on this particular kind of schema, or even on schema-based knowledge structures. Since my schema discussions are mostly hypothetical at this point, I am not claiming that my forms have been shown to be implementable in the concrete cases, or that they have been shown to be superior to those with which I am contrasting them. The argument of the book does, though, clearly depend on the existence of some sort of rich and flexible knowledge and reasoning system people can make use of when they assess the applicability of signs to referents, and it does depend on such a system's being fairly tightly shared—at least in those areas where effective communication is observed and where such effectiveness implies the necessity of such sharing.

As a secondary goal, I am trying to use this appendix as a way of highlighting issues about our socially structured knowledge structures which seem important in the context of my semantics work—and I am, of course, suggesting the direction in which I think answers will lie.

Note

1. However, Piaget, in his book on structuralism, does make clear his awareness of the social and cognitive nature of the Saussurean sign and his appreciation of the value and importance of this attribute of Saussure's approach to the sign (Piaget 1970:115n.8).

Bibliography

Anderson, Elaine S. 1974. Cups and Glasses: Learning That Boundaries Are Vague. *Journal of Child Language* 2:79–103.

Anderson, Eugene N. 1987. Why Is Humoral Medicine so Popular? *Social Science and Medicine* 25:331–337.

Ardener, Edwin. 1971. Introductory Essay. In *Social Anthropology and Language*, E. Ardener, ed. ASA Monograph 10. London: Tavistock, pp. ix–cii.

Atkins, John. 1974. GRAFIK: A Multipurpose Kinship Metalanguage. In *Genealogical Mathematics*, Paul A. Ballonoff, ed. Paris & The Hague: Mouton, pp.27–51.

Atran, Scott. 1985. The Nature of Folkbotanical Life-forms. *American Anthropologist* 87: 298–315.

———1990. *Cognitive Foundations of Natural History: Towards an Anthropology of Science.* Cambridge: Cambridge University Press.

———1993. Whither 'Ethnoscience'? In Boyer 1993, pp. 48–70.

Attneave, Fred. 1971. Multistability in Perception. *Scientific American* 225(6):62–71.

Bartlett, Frederic C. 1932. *Remembering: A Study in Experimental and Social Psychology.* London: Cambridge University Press.

Basso, Keith H. 1967. Semantic Aspects of Linguistic Acculturation. *American Anthropologist* 67:471–477.

Berlin, O. Brent. 1972. Speculations on the Growth of Ethnobotanical Nomenclature. *Language in Society* 1:51–86.

———1976. The Concept of Rank in Ethnobiological Classification: Some Evidence from Aguaruna Folk Botany. *American Ethnologist* 3:381–399.

Berlin, O. Brent, and Paul Kay. 1969. *Basic Color Terms.* Berkeley: University of California Press.

Black, Mary, and Duane Metzger. 1965. Ethnographic Description and the Study of Law. *American Anthropologist* 67 (no. 6, part 2):141–165. Reprinted in Stephen A. Tyler, ed., *Cognitive Anthropology.* New York: Holt, Rinehart and Winston, pp. 137–165.

Bourdieu, Pierre. 1977. *Outline of a Theory of Practice.* Cambridge: Cambridge University Press.

Boyer, Pascal, ed. 1993. *Cognitive Aspects of Religious Symbolism.* Cambridge: Cambridge University Press.

Brown, Cecil H., and Stanley R. Witkowski. 1981. Figurative Language in a Universalist Perspective. *American Ethnologist* 8:596–615.

Brown, Roger, and Eric H. Lenneberg. 1954. A Study in Language and Cognition. *Journal of Abnormal and Social Psychology* 49:454–462.

Bruner, Jerome S., Jacqueline J. Goodnow, and George A. Austin. 1956. *A Study of Thinking* (with an appendix on language by Roger W. Brown). New York: John Wiley.

Buchowski, Michal, David B. Kronenfeld, Will Peterman, and Lynn L. Thomas. 1994. Language, *Nineteen Eighty-Four*, and 1989. *Language in Society* 23:555–578.

Burling, Robbins. 1964. Cognition and Componential Analysis: God's Truth or Hocus-Pocus? *American Anthropologist* 66:20–28. Reprinted in *Cognitive Anthropology*, Stephen A. Tyler, ed. New York: Holt, Rinehart and Winston, pp. 419–428.

Casson, Ronald W. 1983. Schemata in Cognitive Anthropology. *Annual Reviews in Anthropology* 12:429–62.

Chomsky, Noam. 1964. Current Issues in Linguistic Theory. In *The Structure of Language: Readings in the Philosophy of Language*, Jerry A. Fodor and Jerrold J. Katz, eds. Englewood Cliffs, N.J.: Prentice-Hall, pp. 50–118.

———1965. *Aspects of the Theory of Syntax* .Cambridge: MIT Press.

Colby, Benjamin N., James W. Fernandez, and David B. Kronenfeld. 1981. Toward a Convergence of Cognitive and Symbolic Anthropology. *American Ethnologist* 85:422–450.

Coleman, Linda, and Paul Kay. 1981. Prototype Semantics. *Language* 57:26–44.

Conklin, Harold C. 1955. Hanunóo Color Categories. *Southwestern Journal of Anthropology* 11:339–344.

———1962. Lexicographical treatment of folk taxonomies. In *Problems in Lexicography*, Fred W. Householder and Sol Saporta, eds. Indiana University Research Center in Anthropology, Folklore and Linguistics, publication no. 21, pp.119–141.

———1964. Ethnogenealogical Method. In *Explorations in Cultural Anthropology*, Ward H. Goodenough, ed. New York: McGraw-Hill, pp. 25–55.

D'Andrade, Roy G. 1965. Trait psychology and componential analysis. *American Anthropologist* 67(no. 5, part 2):215–228.

———1985. Character terms and cultural models. In *New Directions in Cognitive Anthropology*, Janet W. D. Dougherty, ed. Urbana: University of Illinois Press, pp. 321–343.

———1987. A Folk Model of the Mind. In Holland and Quinn 1987, pp. 112–148.

———1992a. Schemas and Motivation. In D'Andrade and Strauss 1992, pp. 23–44.

———1992b. Afterword. In D'Andrade and Strauss 1992, pp. 225–232.

D'Andrade, Roy, and Claudia Strauss, eds. 1992. *Human Motives and Cultural Models*. Cambridge: Cambridge University Press.

Deregowski, Jan B. 1972. Pictorial Perception and Culture. *Scientific American* 227(5):82–88.

Dougherty, Janet W. D. and Charles M. Keller. 1982. Taskonomy: A Practical Approach to Knowledge Structures. *American Ethnologist* 9:763–774.

Durkheim, Emile. 1938. *The Rules of the Sociological Method*. Glencoe, Ill.: Free Press.

Eco, Umberto. 1990. After Secret Knowledge. *Times Literary Supplement*, June 22–28, pp. 666, 678. Some Paranoid Readings. *TLS*, June 22–28, pp. 694, 706.

Fillmore, Charles. 1975. An Alternative to Checklist Theories of Meaning. In *Proceedings of the First Annual Meeting of the Berkeley Linguistics Society*, C. Cogen, H. Thompson, G. Thurgood, K. Whistler, and J. Wright, eds. Berkeley: University of California Press, pp. 123–131.

———1977. Topics in Lexical Semantics. In *Current Issues in Linguistic Theory*, Roger W. Cole, ed. Bloomington: Indiana University Press, pp. 76–138.

———1982. Towards a Descriptive Framework for Spatial Deixis. In *Speech, Place, and Action*, Robert J. Jarvella and Wolfgang Klein, eds. New York: John Wiley, pp.31–59.

Flavell, John. 1963. *The Developmental Psychology of Jean Piaget*. New York: Van Nostrand.

Frake, Charles O. 1961. The Diagnosis of Disease among the Subanun of Mindanao. *American Anthropologist* 63:11–32.

———1962. The Ethnographic Study of Cognitive Systems. In *Anthropology and Human Behavior*, Thomas Gladwin and William C. Sturtevant, eds. Washington, D.C.: The Anthropological Society of Washington, pp. 72–85. Reprinted in *Cognitive Anthropology*, Stephen A. Tyler, ed. New York: Holt, Rinehart and Winston, pp. 28–41.

————1964. Notes on Queries in Ethnography. *American Anthropologist* 66:132–145. Reprinted in *Cognitive Anthropology*, Stephen A. Tyler, ed. New York: Holt, Rinehart and Winston, pp. 123–137.

Franzel, Steven C. 1984. Modeling Farmers' Decisions in Farming System Research Exercise: The Adoption of an Improved Maize Variety in Kirinyaga District, Kenya. *Human Organization* 43:199–207.

Friedrich, Paul. 1966. Proto–Indo-European Kinship. *Ethnology* 5:1–36.

————1970. *Proto–Indo-European Trees*. Chicago: University of Chicago Press.

Furth, Hans. 1969. *Piaget and Knowledge*. Chicago: Phoenix (University of Chicago Press).

Gerber, Eleanor, and Michael Chatfield. 1971. A Pre-test Study of the Development of Children's Understanding of Kinship. University of California at San Diego: unpublished ms.

Gladwin, Christina H. 1976. A View of Plan Puebla: An Application of Hierarchical Decision Models. *American Journal of Agricultural Economics* 58:881–887.

————1980. A Theory of Real-life Choice: Applications to Agricultural Decisions. In *Agricultural Decision Making*, Peggy F. Barlett, ed. New York: Academic Press, pp. 45–85.

Gladwin, Hugh. 1974. Semantics, Schemata and Kinship. Revised version of paper presented at Mathematical Social Science Board conference on Formal Semantic Analysis of Kinship, University of California at Riverside, December 1972.

Gladwin, Hugh, and Michael Murtaugh. 1980. The Attentive–Pre-Attentive Distinction in Agriculture Decision Making. In *Agriculture Decision Making*, Peggy F. Barlett, ed. New York: Academic Press, pp. 115–136.

————1984. Test of a Hierarchical Model of Auto Choice on Data from the National Transportation Survey. *Human Organization* 43:217–226.

Gleason, Henry. 1961. *An Introduction to Descriptive Linguistics*, rev. ed. New York: Holt, Rinehart and Winston.

Gombrich, Ernst H. 1960. *Art and Illusion: A Study in the Psychology of Pictorial Representation*. Princeton: Princeton University Press.

Goodenough, Ward H. 1956. Componential Analysis and the Study of Meaning. *Language* 32:195–216.

Goody, Jack. 1986. *The Logic of Writing and the Organization of Society*. Cambridge: Cambridge University Press.

————1987. *The Interface between the Written and the Oral*. Cambridge: Cambridge University Press.

Greenberg, Joseph H. 1966. *Language Universals with Special Reference to Feature Hierarchies*. The Hague: Mouton (Janua Linguarum no. 59).

————1968. *Anthropological Linguistics: An Introduction*. New York: Random House.

————1970. Is Language Like a Chess Game? Distinguished Lecture, American Anthropological Association, 69th Annual Meeting, San Diego. In *Bulletin of the American Anthropological Association* 4:53–67.

————1978. Diachrony, Synchrony and Language Universals. In *Universals of Human Language*, Joseph H. Greenberg, ed. Stanford: Stanford University Press, pp. 61–72.

Greeno, James G., and Joyce L. Moore. 1993. Situativity and Symbols: Response to Vera and Simon. *Cognitive Science* 17:49–59.

Halliday, Michael A. K. 1985. *An Introduction to Functional Grammar*. London: Edward Arnold.

Holland, Dorothy. 1992. How Cultural Systems Become Desire: A Case Study of American Romance. In D'Andrade and Strauss 1992, pp. 61–89.

Holland, Dorothy, and Naomi Quinn, eds. 1987. *Cultural Models in Language and Thought*. Cambridge: Cambridge University Press.

Holland, Dorothy, and Debra Skinner. 1987. Prestige and Intimacy: The Cultural Models Behind Americans' Talk about Gender Types. In Holland and Quinn 1987, pp. 78–111.

Hunn, Eugene. 1976. Toward a Perceptual Model of Folk Biological Classification. *American Ethnologist* 3:508–524.

———1982. The Utilitarian Factor in Folk Biological Classification. *American Anthropologist* 84:830–847.

———1987. Science and Common Sense: A Reply to Atran. *American Anthropologist* 89:146–149.

Hutchins, Edwin. 1980. *Culture and Inference: A Trobriand Case Study*. Cambridge, Mass.: Harvard University Press.

Hymes, Dell. 1964. Discussion of Burling's Paper. *American Anthropologist* 66:116–119. Reprinted in *Cognitive Anthropology*, Stephen A. Tyler, ed., New York: Holt, Rinehart and Winston, pp. 428–431.

Jakobson, Roman. 1939. Signe Zéro. In *Mélanges de linguistique offerts à Charles Bally*. Geneva: Georg et cie., s.a. Reprinted in Jakobson 1971:211–219.

———1952. Pattern in Linguistics. Statement made at the International Symposium on Anthropology (New York, June 1952) and published in *An Appraisal of Anthropology Today*, Sol Tax et al., eds. (Chicago: University of Chicago Press, 1953), pp. 310–314. Reprinted in Jakobson 1971, pp. 223–228.

———1959. Boas' View of Grammatical Meaning. In *The Anthropology of Franz Boas*, Walter R. Goldschmidt, ed. American Anthropological Association Memoir no. 89, pp. 139–145. Reprinted in Jakobson 1971, pp. 489–496.

———1971. *Selected Writings: Word and Language*. The Hague: Mouton.

Jakobson, Roman, and Morris Halle. 1956. *Fundamentals of Langauge* (Janua Linguarum: Series Minor 1). The Hague: Mouton.

Jakobson, Roman, C. Gunnar M. Fant, and Morris Halle. 1951. *Preliminaries to Speech Analysis*. Cambridge, Mass.: MIT Press.

Kahneman, Daniel, Paul Slovic, and Amos Tversky, eds. 1982. *Judgment Under Uncertainty: Heuristics and Biases*. Cambridge: Cambridge University Press.

Katz, Jerrold, and Jerry A. Fodor. 1964. The Structure of a Semantic Theory. In *The Structure of Language: Readings in the Philosophy of Language*, J. Fodor and J. Katz, eds. Englewood Cliffs: Prentice-Hall, pp. 50–118.

Kay, Paul. 1966. Comments on Colby. From comment on "Ethnographic Semantics: A Preliminary Survey," by Benjamin N. Colby. *Current Anthropology* 7:20–23.

———1978. Tahitian Words for Race and Class. *Publications de la Société des Océanistes* 39:81–91.

———1987. Linguistic Competence and Folk Theories: Two English Hedges. In Holland and Quinn 1987, pp. 67–77.

Kay, Paul, Brent Berlin, and William Merrifield. 1991. Biocultural Implications of Systems of Color Naming. *Journal of Linguistic Anthropology* 1:12–25.

Kay, Paul, and Chad McDaniel. 1978. The Linguistic Significance of the Meanings of Basic Color Terms. *Language* 54:610–646.

Keen, Ian. 1985. Definitions of Kin. *Journal of Anthropological Research* 41:64–90.

Keesing, Roger. 1987. Models, "Folk" and "Cultural": Paradigms Regained? In Holland and Quinn 1987, pp. 369–393.

Keller, Janet Dixon, and F. K. Lehman (U Chit Hlaing). 1991. Complex Concepts. *Cognitive Science* 15:271–291.

———1993. Computational Complexity in the Cognitive Modelling of Cosmological Ideas. In Boyer 1993, pp. 74–92.

Kempton, Willett. 1978. Category Grading and Taxonomic Relations: A Mug Is a Sort of Cup. *American Ethnologist* 5:44–65.

————1981. *The Folk Classification of Ceramics: A Study of Cognitive Prototypes*. New York: Academic Press.

Koffka, Kurt. 1935. *Principles of Gestalt Psychology*. New York: Harcourt, Brace & World (Harbinger).

Köhler, Wolfgang. 1947. *Gestalt Psychology*. New York: Liveright.

Kronenfeld, David B. 1970. The Relationship between Kinship Categories and Behavior among the Fanti (Ph.D. diss. Stanford University). Ann Arbor: University of Michigan.

————1973. Fanti Kinship: The Structure of Terminology and Behavior. *American Anthropologist* 75:1577–1595.

————1974. Sibling Typology: Beyond Nerlove and Romney. *American Ethnologist* 1:489–506.

————1975. Kroeber vs. Radcliffe-Brown on Kinship Behavior: The Fanti Test Case. *Man* 10:257–284.

————1976. Computer Analysis of Skewed Kinship Terminologies. *Language* 53:891–918.

————1979. Innate Language? *Language Sciences* 1:209–239.

————1980a. A Formal Analysis of Fanti Kinship Terminology. *Anthropos* 75:586–608.

————1980b. Particularistic or Universalistic Analyses of Fanti Kin-terminology: The Alternative Goals of Terminological Analysis. *Man* 15:151–169.

————1985. Numerical Taxonomy: Old Techniques and New Assumptions. *Current Anthropology* 26:21–41.

————1989. Morgan vs. Dorsey on the Omaha Cross/Parallel Contrasts: Theoretical Implications. *L'Homme* 29:76–106.

————1991. Fanti Kinship; Language, Inheritance, and Kin Groups. *Anthropos* 86:19–31.

————n.d. The Explanation of Kin Terminologies: Morgan, Trautmann and Barnes, and the Iroquois-type Cross/Parallel Distinction. Prepared for the Maison Suger Conference on Dravidian Kinship (Paris, 3–5 June 1993), convened by Maurice Godelier and Thomas Trautmann.

Kronenfeld, David B., James D. Armstrong, and Stan Wilmoth. 1985. Exploring the Internal Structure of Linguistic Categories: An Extensionist Semantic View. In *Directions in Cognitive Anthropology*, Janet W. D. Doughtery, ed. Champaign, Ill.: University of Illinois Press, pp. 91–110.

Kronenfeld, David B., and Henry Decker. 1979. Structuralism. *Annual Review of Anthropology, 8:503–541*.

Kronenfeld, David B., and Hugh Gladwin. n. d. Alternative terminological models in kinship.

Kronenfeld, David B., and Andrea Kaus. 1994. Starlings and Other Critters: Simulating Society. *Journal of Quantitative Anthropology* 4:143–174.

Kronenfeld, Judy Z. 1983. Probing the Relation Between Poetry and Ideology: Herbert's "The Windows." *John Donne Journal: Studies in the Age of Donne*, vol. 2 (no. 1), 55–80.

————1989. Post-Saussurean Semantics, Reformation Religious Controversy, and Contemporary Critical Disagreement. In Peggy A. Knapp, ed., *Assays: Critical Approaches to Medieval and Renaissance Literature*, vol. 5. Pittsburgh: Carnegie-Mellon, pp. 135–165.

————n.d. King Lear *and "The Naked Truth": An Inquiry into the Role of History and Language in Criticism.*

Kroeber, Alfred L. 1909. Classificatory Systems of Relationship. *Journal of the Royal Anthropological Institute* 39:77–84.

Kuhn, Thomas. 1962. *The Structure of Scientific Revolutions*. Chicago, University of Chicago Press.

Labov, William. 1973. The Boundaries of Words and Their Meanings. In *New Ways of Analyzing Variation in English*, Charles-James Bailey and Roger W. Shuy, eds. Washington, D.C.: Georgetown University Press, pp. 340–373.

Lake, Peter. 1989. Anti-Popery: The Structure of a Prejudice. In *Conflict in Early Stuart England: Studies in Religion and Politics, 1603–1642*, Richard Cust and Ann Hughes, eds. London and New York: Longman.

Lakoff, George. 1984. Classifiers as a Reflection of Mind: A Cognitive Model Approach to Prototype Theory. Berkeley Cognitive Science Report no. 19. Berkeley: University of California Institute of Human Learning.

———1987. *Women, Fire, and Dangerous Things: What Categories Reveal about the Mind.* Chicago: University of Chicago Press.

Lakoff, George, and Zoltán Kövecses. 1987. The Cognitive Model of Anger Inherent in American English. In Holland and Quinn 1987, pp. 195–221.

Langacker, Ronald W. 1987. *Foundations of Cognitive Grammar, Volume 1: Theoretical Prerequisites.* Stanford: Stanford University Press.

Lashley, Karl. 1951. The Problem of Serial Order in Psychology. In *Cerebral Mechanisms in Behavior*, Lloyd A. Jeffress, ed. New York: Wiley, pp. 112–136.

Leach, Edmund. 1973. *Claude Lévi-Strauss.* New York: Viking. Reprinted 1976, New York: Penguin. Citations refer to the Penguin edition.

———1976. *Culture and Communication: The Logic by which Symbols Are Connected; An Introduction to the Use of Structuralist Analysis in Social Anthropology.* Cambridge: Cambridge University Press.

Lenneberg, Eric H., and John M. Roberts. 1956. The Language of Experience: A Study in Methodology. *International Journal of American Linguistics* memoir no. 13.

Lévi-Strauss, Claude. 1963. *Totemism.* Rodney Needham, trans. Boston: Beacon Press.

———1969. *The Raw and the Cooked: Introduction to a Science of Mythology.* vol. 1. J. Weightman, D. Weightman, trans. New York: Harper & Row.

Lounsbury, Floyd G. 1956. A Semantic Analysis of the Pawnee Kinship Usage. *Language* 32(1):158–194.

———1964a. The Structural Analysis of Kinship Semantics. *Proceedings of the Ninth International Congress of Linguists.* The Hague: Mouton, pp. 1073–1093. Reprinted in *Cognitive Anthropology*, Stephen A. Tyler, ed. New York: Holt, Rinehart and Winston, pp. 193–212.

———1964b. A Formal Account of the Crow- and Omaha-Type Kinship Terminologies. In *Explorations in Cultural Anthropology*, Ward H. Goodenough, ed. New York: McGraw Hill, pp. 351–393.

———1965. Another View of Trobriand Kinship Categories. *American Anthropologist* 67 (no. 5, part 2):142–186.

———1969. Language and Culture. In *Language and Philosophy*, Sidney Hook, ed. New York: New York University Press, pp. 3–29.

Lutz, Catherine. 1987. Goals, Events, and Understanding in Ifaluk Emotion Theory. In Holland and Quinn 1987, pp. 290-312.

———1992. Motivated Models. In D'Andrade and Strauss 1992, pp. 181–196.

Lyons, John. 1970. *Noam Chomsky.* New York: Viking.

MacLaury, Robert E. 1992. From Brightness to Hue: An Exploratory Model of Color-Category Evolution. *Current Anthropology 33:137–187.*

Meillet, Antoine. 1904–05. Comment les mots changent de sens. *Année Sociologique* 9:1–38.

———1916. Review of *Cours de linguistique Générale*, by Ferdinand de Saussure. *Bulletin de la Société Linguistique de Paris* 64:32–36.

Metzger, Duane, and Gerald E. Williams. 1963. Tenejapa Medicine: The Curer. *Southwestern Journal of Anthropology* 19:216–234.

———1966. Some Procedures and Results in the Study of Native Categories: Tzeltal "Firewood." *American Anthropologist* 68:389–407.

Miller, George A. 1956. The Magical Number Seven, Plus or Minus Two: Some Limits of Our Capacity for Processing Information. *Psychological Review* 63:81–97.

———1965. Introduction. In Zipf 1965, pp. v–x.

———1978. Practical and Lexical Knowledge. In Rosch and Lloyd 1978, pp. 305–319.

Morgan, Lewis Henry. 1871. *Systems of Consanguinity and Affinity of the Human Family.* Smithsonian Contributions to Knowledge, no. 218. Washington, D.C.: Smithsonian Institution.

Mukhopadhyay, Carol C. 1980. *The Sexual Division of Labor in the Family: A Decision-Making Analysis.* Ph.D Dissertation, University of California, Riverside, xv, 358 pp. Ann Arbor: University Microfilms.

———1984. Testing a Decision Process Model of the Sexual Division of Labor in the Family. *Human Organization* 43:227–242.

Neisser, Ulrich. 1976. *Cognition and Reality.* San Francisco: W. H. Freeman.

Nerlove, Sara B., and A. Kimball Romney. 1967. Sibling Terminology and Cross-sex Behavior. *American Anthropologist* 69:179–187.

Newell, Alan, and Herbert A. Simon. 1972. *Human Problem Solving.* Englewood Cliffs, N.J.:Prentice-Hall.

Norman, Donald A. 1993. Cognition in the Head and in the World: An Introduction to the Special Issue on Situated Cognition. *Cognitive Science* 17:1–6.

Ohnuki-Tierney, Emiko. 1981. Phases in Human Perception/Conception/Symbolization Processes: Cognitive Anthropology and Symbolic Classification. *American Ethnologist* 8:451–467.

Piaget, Jean. 1970. *Structuralism.* Chaninah Maschler, ed. and trans. London: Routledge & Kegan Paul.

———1973. *Main Trends in Interdisciplinary Research.* New York: Harper Torchbooks.

Piaget, Jean, and Barbel Inhelder. 1969. The Psychology of the Child. Helen Weaver, trans. New York: Basic Books.

Piercy, Marge. 1976. *Woman on the Edge of Time.* New York: Knopf.

Plattner, Stuart. 1984. Economic Decision Making of Marketplace Merchants: An Ethnographic Model. *Human Organization* 43:265–276.

Quinn, Naomi. 1971. Simplifying Procedures in Natural Decision Making. Paper presented at the MSSB Advanced Research Seminar in Natural Decision Making Behavior, Palo Alto, California, December 13–17.

———1975. Decision Models of Social Structure. *American Ethnologist* 2:19–46.

———1976. A Natural System Used in Mfantse Litigation Settlement. *American Ethnologist* 3:331–352.

———1982. "Commitment" in American Marriage: A Cultural Analysis. *American Ethnologist* 9:775–798.

———1987. Convergent Evidence for a Cultural Model of American Marriage. In Holland and Quinn 1987, pp. 173–192.

———1992. The Motivational Force of Self-Understanding: Evidence from Wives' Inner Conflicts. In D'Andrade and Strauss 1992, pp. 90–126.

Quinn, Naomi, and Dorothy Holland. 1987. Culture and Cognition. In Holland and Quinn 1987, pp. 3–40.

Radcliffe-Brown, Alfred R. 1940. On Social Structure. *Journal of the Royal Anthropological Institute* 70. Reprinted in Alfred R. Radcliffe-Brown, *Structure and Function in Primitive Society* (1952). Glencoe, Ill.: Free Press.

———1941. The Study of Kinship Systems. *Journal of the Royal Anthropological Institute* 71:1–18. Reprinted in Alfred R. Radcliffe-Brown, *Structure and Function in Primitive Society* (1952). Glencoe, Ill.: Free Press.

Randall, Robert A. 1976. How Tall Is a Taxonomic Tree? Some Evidence for Dwarfism. *American Ethnologist* 3:543–553.

———1985. Steps toward an Ethnosemantics of Verbs: Complex Fishing Technique Scripts and the "Unsaid" in Listener Identification. In *Directions in Cognitive Anthropology*, Janet W. D. Dougherty, ed. Champaign, Ill.: University of Illinois Press, pp. 249–268.

Ratliff, Floyd. 1975. On the Psychophysical Bases of Universal Color Terms. *Proceedings of the American Philosophical Society* 120:311–30.

Romney, A. Kimball. 1965. Kalmuk Mongol and the Classification of Lineal Kinship Terminologies. *American Anthropologist* 67 (no. 5, part 2):127–141.

Romney, A. Kimball, and Roy G. D'Andrade. 1964. Cognitive Aspects of English Kinship. *American Anthropologist* 67 (no. 5, part 2):146–170.

Rosch, Eleanor H. 1973. On the Internal Structure of Perceptual and Semantic Categories. In *Cognitive Development and the Acquisition of Language*, T. M. Moore, ed. New York: Academic Press, pp. 111–144.

———1978. Principles of Categorization. In Rosch and Lloyd1978, pp. 28–48.

Rosch, Eleanor H., and Barbara B. Lloyd, eds. 1978. *Cognition and Categorization*. Hillsdale, N. J.: Lawrence Erlbaum Associates.

Rosch, Eleanor H., and Carolyn B. Mervis. 1975. Family Resemblances: Studies in the Internal Structure of Categories. *Cognitive Psychology* 7:573–605.

Rosch, Eleanor H., Carolyn B. Mervis, Wayne D. Gran, David M. Johnson, and Penny Boyes-Braem. 1976. Basic Objects in Natural Categories. *Cognitive Psychology* 8:382–439.

Rose, Michael D., and A. Kimball Romney. 1979. Cognitive Pluralism or Individual Differences: A Comparison of Alternative Models of American English Kin Terms. *American Ethnologist* 6:752–762.

Rumelhart, David E. 1980. Schemata: The Building Blocks of Cognition. In *Theoretical Issues in Reading Comprehension: Perspectives from Cognitive Psychology, Linguistics, Artificial Intelligence, and Education*, Rand J. Spiro, Bertram C. Bruce, and William F. Brewer, eds. Hillsdale, N.J.: Lawrence Erlbaum Associates, pp. 33–58.

Rumelhart, David E., James L. McClelland, and the PDP Research Group. 1986. *Parallel Distributed Processing: Explorations in the Microstructure of Cognition*, vol. I: Foundations, and vol. II: Psychological and Biological Models. Cambridge, Mass.: MIT Press.

Saussure, Ferdinand de. 1916. *Cours de linguistique générale*.

———cf. *Course in General Linguistics*, ed. Charles Bally and Albert Sechehaye in collaboration with Albert Reidlinger. Trans. from the French by Wade Baskin. New York: Philosophical Library (1959).

———cf. *Cours de linguistique générale*. Publie par Charles Bally et Albert Sechehaye, avec la collaboration de Albert Riedlinger. Édition critique preparée par Tullio de Mauro. Paris: Payot (1973).

Schallert, Diane. 1982. The Significance of Knowledge: A Synthesis of Research Related to Schema Theory. In *Reading Expository Material*, Wayne Otto and Sandra White, eds. New York: Academic Press, pp. 13–48.

Schank, Roger C., and R. P. Abelson. 1977. *Scripts, Plans, Goals, and Understanding*. Hillsdale, N.J.: Lawrence Erlbaum Associates.

Shaw, Harry. 1976. *Concise Dictionary of Literary Terms.* New York: McGraw-Hill.

Shweder, Richard A. 1992. Ghost Busters in Anthropology. In D'Andrade and Strauss 1992, pp. 45–57.

Strauss, Claudia. 1992a. Models and Motives. In D'Andrade and Strauss 1992, pp. 1–20.

———1992b. What Makes Tony Run? Schemas as Motives Reconsidered. In D'Andrade and Strauss 1992, pp. 191–224.

Trubetzkoy, Nikolai S. 1969. *Principles of Phonology*. Berkeley: University of California Press. Trans. from *Grundzüge der Phonologie* (Göttingen: Vandenhoeck & Ruprecht, 1958; 3d ed., 1962; originally published in Prague, 1939).

Uexkull, Jakob von. 1957. A Stroll through the World of Animals and Men. In *Instinctive Behavior*, Claire H. Schiller, ed. and trans. New York: International Universities Press, pp. 5–80.

Vera, Alonso H., and Herbert A. Simon. 1993. Situated Action: A Symbolic Interpretation. *Cognitive Science* 17:7–48.

Vike, Halvard. 1991. *Political Discourse in a Norwegian Industrial Community*. Mag. art. thesis, Institutt og museum for antropologi, Universitetet i Oslo (University of Oslo), Oslo, Norway.

Wallace, Anthony F. C. 1965. The Problem of the Psychological Validity of Componential Analyses. *American Anthropologist* 67 (no. 5, pt. 2): 229–248.

Wallace, Anthony F. C., and J. Atkins. 1960. The Meaning of Kinship terms. *American Anthropologist* 62:57–80.

Wexler, Kenneth N. 1970. Embedding Structures for Semantics. Unpublished paper, University of California, Irvine (mimeographed).

Wexler, Kenneth N., and A. Kimball Romney. 1972. Individual Variations in Cognitive Structures. In *Multidimensional Scaling: Theory and Applications in the Behavioral Sciences*, vol II, Roger N. Shepard, A. Kimball Romney, and Sara Nerlove, eds. New York: Seminar Press, pp. 73–92.

Wierzbicka, Anna. 1992. *Semantics, Culture, and Cognition: Universal Human Concepts in Culture-Specific Configurations*. New York: Oxford University Press.

Wilmoth, Stan. 1987. The Development of Blackfeet Politics and Multiethnic Categories: 1934–84. Ph.D. dissertation, University of California, Riverside, vii, 571 pp. Ann Arbor: University Microfilms.

Wittgenstein, Ludwig. 1953. *Philosophical Investigations*. G.E.M. Anscombe, trans. Oxford: Basil Blackwell.

Young, James C. 1980. A Model of Illness Treatment Decisions in a Tarascan Town. *American Ethnologist* 7:106–131.

———1981. *Medical Choice in a Mexican Town*. New Brunswick, N.J.: Rutgers University Press.

Zipf, Paul. 1935. *The Psycho-Biology of Language: An Introduction to Dynamic Philology*. Boston: Houghton Mifflin. Reprinted as Zipf 1965.

———1949. *Human Behavior and the Principle of Least Effort: An Introduction to Human Ecology*. Boston: Addison-Wesley. Reprinted (1965) in facsimile edition by Hafner Publishing Co. (New York and London).

———1965. *The Psycho-Biology of Language: An Introduction to Dynamic Philology*, with an introduction by George A. Miller. Cambridge, Mass.: MIT Press.

Index

Abelson, R. P. 23, 24, 27, 28, 250
Absolute vs. relative features 87
Absolute vs. relative reference point; *See* reference point 97
Absolute universal 110
Accidental attributes or features of a category 183, 211, 218, 234
activity, activity attributes, and activity zones. *See* Sexual division of domestic labor
Allocation of domestic tasks and responsibilities. *See* Sexual division of domestic labor
Alternative semantic analyses 59, 68
American cognitive psychology 238
American Descriptive Linguistics 31, 37, 42, 47–49
Analytic criterion 73
Andersen, Elaine S. 228, 243
Anderson, Eugene N. 143, 243
Arbitrariness of signifier/signified relationship (i.e., of signs) 36, 39, 167
Arbitrariness, partial, of the relationship of signifiers and signifieds to the external world 36
Ardener, Edwin 243
Armstrong, James D. 192, 197, 201, 247
Artifacts of experimental designs. *See* Experimental artifacts vs. robust conclusions about the world
Atkins, John 55, 56, 58, 59, 61, 64, 66, 68, 69, 129, 243, 250
Atran, Scott 13–16, 18, 21, 22, 26, 27, 30, 41, 109, 142, 143, 240, 243
Attneave, Fred 193, 243
Attributes 49, 53, 114, 174, 234
central to functional basis of sign 234
re contrast relations 119, 120, 211
core meanings of, role in negotiations 220
distinctive or key defining. *See* distinctive features 147
essential vs. basic vs. accidental 211
re filled out core referents 211

foregrounding or backgrounding of 49, 50, 114
form vs. function 202, 203
non-defining, derivation from core 173
of referent 235
syntagmatic and paradigmatic contextual effects on use 174
when taken serially 119
Auden, W. H. 210
Austin, George A. 23, 59, 73, 75, 77, 79, 80, 82, 87, 114, 121, 124, 136, 142, 243
Average (vs. prototypic) referents 21

Bartlett, Frederic C. 194, 243
Basic color terms 104, 145, 151–154, 234
order of their emergence 153, 168
interlanguage stability of core color term referents, and variation in number of terms 152–154
Basic features of category defined and illustrated 218
Basic (relatively context free) terms in a domain, number and usefulness of 168
Basso, Keith H. 13, 145, 159, 169, 184, 243
Bateson, Gregory 26, 27, 237
Behavioral patterning compared with terminological patterning 168
Berlin, O. Brent 16, 21, 54, 79, 104, 106, 107, 109, 112, 132, 145, 147, 151–154, 157–159, 166–168, 172, 178, 185, 234, 235, 243, 246
Berlin and Kay research design—applicability to artifactual and culturally specific domains 166
Binary vs. multinary oppositions 39, 49, 61, 130, 142
Binomial expression 108, 109, 113
Biological predispositions. *See* innate capabilities and dispositions
Biological systematics 47
Black, Mary 38, 49, 53, 243
Blackfeet political factions and language 204–209, 224, 225, 235

252

82, 87, 88, 106, 135, 138, 140, 143, 148, 149, 158, 159, 161–164, 167–169, 172, 179, 189, 192, 197, 223, 228, 239, 241, 243, 244, 246, 247
Kronenfeld, J. Z. 210, 247

Lab situation, re situational context—building in natural context vs. abstracting it out. *See* Experimental artifacts
Labov, William 228, 247
Lake, Peter 214, 247
Lakoff, George 13, 15, 21, 22, 29, 247
Langacker, Ronald W. 22, 42, 190, 248
Language 8, 14, 15, 17, 31, 32, 47, 227. *See also langue*
  binomial and trinomial segregates 113
  immunity from conscious or political manipulation 33
  learning 40, 132, 138–141
    role of natural selection—shaping us to it and it to us 40
  as a medium with shaping properties re cognition 17, 41, 151
  as part of our natural world 25
  as a synchronic system 192
  as a tool 40, 100, 143
    for communication 40
    flexible 150
  as a "transparent" medium 25, 29
Language change 8, 32, 175
  effects of mass media and of writing on 33
  role of *parole* (speech) 192
Language/culture relationship 47, 48, 100, 241
Language drift (one-to-many nature of) 175, 187
Language/thought relationship 15, 26, 150, 241
  empirical findings 199, 201
  idealized views
    limited isomorphism between referents and words 198
    neo-Harrisian, language and thought unconnected 197
    pragmatic, language reflects perceived reality 197
    Whorfian, language determines perception 197
  re values 15
langue 18, 31, 32, 42, 63, 135, 139, 161, 163, 165, 175, 191, 228. *See also* Language

as a collective passive mental representation 8, 32, 87, 143, 232
individual internal representations of 25, 32, 33
as induced, individually, from regularities experienced in speech 8, 32
as socially shared and constructed 32, 41
subconscious nature of 33
as a system of signs 35
as a "system of values" 67
shaping role of feedback 234
variant forms within a speech community 175
langue and *langue*-like codes. *See* Collective representations
langue and *parole*, links between 192
Lashley, Karl 141, 189, 247
Leach, Edmund 130, 168, 247
Learning 238
Lehman, F. K. (U Chit Hlaing) 21, 26, 193, 194, 246
Lenneberg, Eric. H. 151, 243, 247
Lévi-Strauss, Claude 61, 67, 70, 130, 247
Lévi-Straussian structuralism 54
Lexeme 33, 48
Linguistic community or language community. *See* Speech community
Linguistic tracking of cultural facts, rate of 102
Linguistics 32, 37, 42, 65
Linnaeus, C. 49
Literal vs. figurative meaning 193
Lloyd, Barbara 249
Long-term memory 121, 131, 137, 142
Lounsburian equivalence rules 155, 156, 158, 178
Lounsbury, Floyd G. 52, 53, 59, 65, 69, 70, 73, 79, 106, 128, 145, 147–149, 151, 152, 154, 155, 157–159, 168, 169, 172, 183, 234, 235, 248
Loyalty. *See* Ethnic groups; Ethnicity
Lutz, Catherine 15, 19, 248
Lyons, John 42, 248

MacLaury, Robert E. 16, 168, 178, 248
Man vs. woman, re marking 101–104
  nurses and doctors 101
Marked vs. unmarked member of an opposition 90
Marking 41, 82, 89, 101, 110, 191
  contextual specificity 101